To

_____

By

_____

On

_____

_____

Books by Gary Thomas

Authentic Faith

Devotions for a Sacred Marriage

Devotions for Sacred Parenting

The Glorious Pursuit

Holy Available

Pure Pleasure

Sacred Influence

Sacred Marriage

Sacred Parenting

Sacred Pathways

Seeking the Face of God

SACRED
MARRIAGE

GIFT EDITION

GARY THOMAS

ZONDERVAN

Sacred Marriage Gift Edition
Copyright 2011 by Gary L. Thomas

Sacred Marriage
Copyright © 2000 by Gary L. Thomas

Devotions for a Sacred Marriage
Copyright © 2005 by Gary L. Thomas

This title is also available as a Zondervan ebook.
Visit www.zondervan.com/ebooks.

Requests for information should be addressed to:

Zondervan, 3900 *Sparks Dr. SE, Grand Rapids, Michigan 49546*

ISBN 978-0-310-33294-7

Published in association with Yates & Yates, www.yates2.com.

Cover design: Michelle Lenger
Cover photography: Joshua Rainey Photography, Veer
Interior design: Beth Shagene

First printing February 2011 / Printed in the United States of America

*This gift edition is dedicated
to the memory of Bill Ehli,
father of my wife, Lisa.
He has given me a gift I can never repay.*

Contents

Devotions for a Sacred Marriage

Introduction

Dear Readers,

My wife and I experience great joy whenever we read and hear the testimonies of those who have read the book you now hold in your hands. The perspective that perhaps God created marriage to make us holy even more than to make us happy has apparently been used by God to restore many homes, reenergize flagging commitments, and open up couples' eyes to the marvelous work God is doing in their souls.

Marriage is filled with remarkable joys, even occasional ecstasies, but it can often lead us through times of tremendous pain. Lisa and I count it an honor that, by means of this book, we can walk through part of this journey with you. We are delighted that Zondervan has decided to make available this beautiful gift edition, which contains not only *Sacred Marriage* but *Devotions for a Sacred Marriage* as well.

Thank you for joining us on this journey of exploring how God uses our marriages to glorify his name and transform us into the image of his Son.

May God bless you as you seek to serve him by becoming the man or woman he created you to be; and may God continue to make your marriage a truly sacred, soul-shaping union that reflects Christ's love for the church.

The peace of Christ,
Gary Thomas

SACRED MARRIAGE

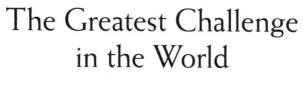

The Greatest Challenge
in the World

A Call to Holiness
More Than Happiness

By all means marry. If you get a good wife, you'll become happy.
If you get a bad one, you'll become a philosopher.
SOCRATES

Like everything which is not the involuntary result
of fleeting emotion but the creation of time and will,
any marriage, happy or unhappy, is infinitely
more interesting than any romance, however passionate.
W. H. AUDEN

I'M GOING TO CUT HIM OPEN.

Historians aren't sure who the first physician was who followed through on this thought, but the practice revolutionized medicine. The willingness to cut into a corpse, peel back the skin, pull a scalp off a skull, cut through the bone, and actually remove, examine, and chart the organs that lay within was a crucial first step in finding out how the human body really works.

For thousands of years physicians had speculated on what went on inside a human body, but there was a reluctance and even an abhorrence to actually dissect a cadaver. Some men refrained out of religious conviction; others just couldn't get over the eeriness of cutting away a human rib cage. While an occasional brave soul ventured inside a dead body, it wasn't until the Renaissance period (roughly the fourteenth to the sixteenth century) that European doctors routinely started to cut people open.

And when they did, former misconceptions collapsed. In the sixteenth century, Andreas Vesalius was granted a ready supply of criminals' corpses, allowing him to definitively contradict assumptions about the human anatomy that had been unquestioned for a thousand years or more. Vesalius's anatomical charts became invaluable, but he couldn't have drawn the charts unless he was first willing to make the cut.

I want to do a similar thing in this book—with a spiritual twist. We're going to cut open numerous marriages, dissect them, find out what's really going on, and then explore how we can gain spiritual meaning, depth, and growth from the challenges that lie within. We're not after simple answers—three steps to more intimate communication, six steps to a more exciting love life—because this isn't a book that seeks to tell you how to have a happier marriage. This is a book that looks at how we can use the challenges, joys, struggles, and celebrations of marriage to draw closer to God and to grow in Christian character.

We're after what a great Christian writer, Francis de Sales, wrote about in the seventeenth century. Because de Sales was a gifted spiritual director, people often corresponded with him about their spiritual concerns. One woman wrote in great distress, torn because she very much wanted to get married while a friend was encouraging her to remain single, insisting that it would be "more holy" for her to care for her father, and then devote herself as a celibate to God after her father died.

De Sales put the troubled young woman at ease, telling her that, far from being a compromise, in one sense, marriage might be the toughest ministry she could ever undertake. "The state of marriage is one that requires more virtue and constancy than any other," he wrote. "It is a perpetual exercise of mortification.... From this thyme plant, in spite of the bitter nature of its juice, you may be able to draw and make the honey of a holy life."[1]

Notice that de Sales talks about the occasionally "bitter nature" of marriage's "juice." To spiritually benefit from marriage, we have to be honest. We have to look at our disappointments, own up to our ugly attitudes, and confront our selfishness. We also have to rid ourselves of the notion that the difficulties of marriage can be overcome if we simply pray harder or learn a few simple principles. Most of us have discovered that these "simple steps" work only on a superficial level. Why is this? Because there's a deeper question that needs to be addressed beyond how we can "improve" our marriage: What if God didn't design marriage to be "easier"? What if God had an end in mind that went beyond our happiness, our comfort, and our desire to be infatuated and happy as if the world were a perfect place?

What if God designed marriage to make us holy more than to make us happy? What if, as de Sales hints, we are to accept the "bitter juice" because out of it we may learn to draw the resources we need with which to make "the honey of a holy life"?

Romanticism's Ruse

If this sounds like a radically different view of marriage, it's important to remember that the very concept of "romantic love," which is so celebrated in movies, songs, and cheap paperbacks, was virtually unknown to the ancients. There were exceptions — one need merely read the Song of Songs, for instance — but taken as a whole, the concept that marriage should involve passion and fulfillment and excitement is a relatively recent development on the scale of human history, making its popular entry toward the end of the eleventh century.[2]

C. S. Lewis — whose marriage to an ailing woman was seen as somewhat "odd" by many of his contemporaries — explained that such a monumental shift in cultural thought as the development of romantic love is "very rare — there are perhaps three or four on record

—but I believe that they occur, and that this [romantic love] is one of them."[3]

This is *not* to suggest that romance itself or the desire for more romance is necessarily bad; good marriages work hard to preserve a sense of romance. But the idea that a marriage can survive on romance alone, or that romantic *feelings* are more important than any other consideration when choosing a spouse, has wrecked many a marital ship.

Romanticism received a major boost by means of the eighteenth-century Romantic poets—Wordsworth, Coleridge, and Blake—followed by their successors in literature, Byron, Shelley, and Keats. These poets passionately argued that it was a crime against oneself to marry for any reason other than "love" (which was defined largely by feeling and emotion), and the lives of many of them were parodies of irresponsibility and tragedy.

One of the writers who embraced this romantic notion with fervor was the sensuous novelist D. H. Lawrence, whose motto was "with *should* and *ought* I shall have nothing to do!" Lawrence fell in love with Frieda Weekley, a married woman, and sought to woo Frieda away from her husband, as his "love" demanded he do. As part of his less-than-noble designs, Lawrence sent Frieda a note, proclaiming that she was the most wonderful woman in all of England.

Being married with three children and having already suffered a couple of affairs, Mrs. Weekley saw through Lawrence's emotion and coolly replied that it was obvious to her he had not met many Englishwomen.[4]

Earlier in this century, Katherine Anne Porter bemoaned how "romantic love crept into the marriage bed, very stealthily, by centuries, bringing its absurd notions about love as eternal springtime and marriage as a personal adventure meant to provide personal happiness." The reality of the human condition is such that, according to Porter (and I agree), we must "salvage our fragments of happiness" out of life's inevitable sufferings.

In her startling and insightful essay on marriage written in the 1940s (titled, interestingly enough, "The Necessary Enemy"), Porter carefully explores the heights and depths of marriage, making the following observations about a young bride:

> This very contemporary young woman finds herself facing the oldest and ugliest dilemma of marriage. She is dismayed, horrified, full of guilt and forebodings because she is finding out little by little that she is capable of hating her husband, whom she loves faithfully. She can hate him at times as fiercely and mysteriously, indeed in terribly much the same way, as often she hated her parents, her brothers and sisters, whom she loves, when she was a child. . . .
>
> She thought she had outgrown all this, but here it was again, an element in her own nature she could not control, or feared she could not. She would have to hide from her husband, if she could, the same spot in her feelings she had hidden from her parents, and for the same no doubt disreputable, selfish reason: She wants to keep his love.
>
> Above all, she wants him to be absolutely confident that she loves him, for that is the real truth, no matter how unreasonable it sounds, and no matter how her own feelings betray them both at times. She depends recklessly on his love.

With only a romantic view of marriage to fall back on, Porter warns, a young woman may lose her "peace of mind. She is afraid her marriage is going to fail because … at times she feels a painful hostility toward her husband, and cannot admit its reality because such an admission would damage in her own eyes her view of what love should be."[5]

Romantic love has no elasticity to it. It can never be stretched; it simply shatters. Mature love, the kind demanded of a good marriage, *must* stretch, as the sinful human condition is such that all of us bear conflicting emotions. "Her hatred is real as her love is real," Porter explains of the young wife. This is the reality of the human heart, the inevitability of two sinful people pledging to live together, with all their faults, for the rest of their lives.

A wedding calls us to our highest and best — in fact, to almost impossible — ideals. It's the way we *want* to live. But marriage reminds us of the daily reality of living as sinful human beings in a radically broken world. We aspire after love but far too often descend into hate.

Any mature, spiritually sensitive view of marriage must be built on the foundation of mature love rather than romanticism. But this immediately casts us into a countercultural pursuit.

In his classic work *The Screwtape Letters,* C. S. Lewis satirically ridicules our culture's obsession with romanticism. The demon Screwtape gloats, "Humans who have not the gift of [sexual abstinence] can be deterred from seeking marriage as a solution because they do not find themselves 'in love,' and, thanks to us, the idea of marrying with any other motive seems to them low and cynical. Yes, they think that. They regard the intention of loyalty to a partnership for mutual help, for the preservation of chastity, and for the transmission of life, as something lower than a storm of emotion."[6]

I think most of us who have been married for any substantial length of time realize that the romantic roller coaster of courtship eventually evens out to the terrain of a Midwest interstate — long, flat stretches with an occasional overpass. When this happens, couples respond in different ways. Many will break up their relationship and try to recreate the passionate romance with someone else. Other couples will descend into a sort of marital guerrilla warfare, a passive-aggressive power play as each partner blames the other for personal dissatisfaction or lack of excitement. Some couples decide to simply "get along." Still others may opt to pursue a deeper meaning, a spiritual truth hidden in the enforced intimacy of the marital situation.

We can run from the challenges of marriage — as doctors did from the human body, refusing to cut open the cadavers and really look at what was going on — or we can admit that every marriage presents these challenges and asks us to address them head-on. If we find that the same kinds of challenges face every marriage, we might assume that God designed a purpose in this challenge that transcends something as illusory as happiness.

This book looks for that purpose and meaning — how can we discover in the challenges of marriage the opportunities to learn more about God, grow in our understanding of him, and learn to love him more?

Numerous married couples have opened up their lives for us in this book, so I suppose it's only fair that I should allow my own marriage to be dissected first.

An Unexpected Engagement

Lisa and I often wonder what would have happened if she had said "yes."

During a free afternoon at a college campus-ministry retreat when we were still dating, I asked Lisa to join a group of us for a round of Frisbee golf.

"No," Lisa said. "I think I'll go for a walk instead."

She had recently returned from a summerlong missions trip to Mexico, and this retreat was supposed to be a time when Lisa and I could get reconnected. We had known each other since junior high and had been dating for about a year, and we were getting "serious." Unknown to Lisa, I had asked my best friend, Rob Takemura, to begin praying about whether I should ask Lisa to marry me. And unknown to me, Lisa and her mother had spent a Saturday afternoon the week before looking at wedding dresses, "just in case" Lisa should ever need one.

I was somewhat frustrated that Lisa wasn't being cooperative, so I said, "Fine, I won't play Frisbee golf either."

"You can," Lisa said. "I don't mind walking alone."

"No, I'll go with you," I said. Neither of us realized it at the time, but this turn of events would change both of our lives.

We walked along the river, set inside a stunning valley on the outskirts of Glacier National Park, and talked for about forty-five minutes. Suddenly, I stopped skimming rocks, and virtually out of nowhere I said to Lisa, "I want to marry you."

Lisa's mouth dropped open.

"Is that a proposal?" she asked, astonished.

I shook my head yes, just as astonished as she was. Lisa came up and hugged me.

"Is that an acceptance?" I asked, and Lisa nodded in the affirmative.

"Whew," she said after a brief moment. "Imagine if I had agreed to play Frisbee."

We laughed about it, and then experienced one of the most intense times emotionally I've ever known. There was a strange, almost mystical commingling of souls. Something was going on inside us, around us, and through us that superseded any physical connection. It was somehow deeper, more meaningful, and more amazing than anything we had ever experienced.

Over the next nine months, we made plans, as any engaged couple does. We talked about missions, family, seminary, serving God—you name it. It was an intense time, and we often prayed, "Lord, wherever you want to take us, however you want to use us, we're all yours."

We never slept together until our wedding night, so the honeymoon was a rather intoxicating experience, but once the honeymoon was over, reality immediately set in like a dense Seattle fog.

Because I was planning to save up money for seminary, we spent our first few months living in a very tiny home, offered to us rent-free by a family friend. I left for work two days after we got back, and Lisa was stranded in a small community, out in the middle of nowhere, and she began to cry.

It was a sunny day, so she called me at work and asked if I could come home early so we could drive to a lake. I thought she was crazy. "I can't just leave work because the weather's nice!" I protested. "Besides, I just started!"

"Well what's the use of getting married if I see you less now than when we were engaged?" she complained.

What's the use, indeed?

Fast-forward ten years. We had three small children, two of them in diapers. I was working for a Christian ministry, and we were still "just making it" financially, ensconced in a town house in northern Virginia. We were about to enter our Friday-night ritual—laundry and a video from Blockbuster.

"What do you want to watch?" I asked Lisa as I gathered my keys and headed out the door.

"Oh, how about a romantic comedy?" Lisa answered.

I cringed. The last three videos we had watched together had been romantic comedies. If I had to watch another impossibly beautiful couple meet under extremely improbable circumstances, fall in love, get in a fight, and then spend sixty minutes falling back in love again, I thought I'd die.

I sighed, turned around, and looked at Lisa. "I'm sorry," I said. "I just can't do it. I have to see at least one building blow up and one car crash. If I can find something that has a little romance to add to that, I'll see what I can do."

I took three steps out the door, then thought to myself, "When did, 'Please, God, change the world through us' suddenly become, 'Should we watch Arnold Schwarzenegger or Julia Roberts?' " I didn't remember any fork in the road or any flashing neon signs that pointed in that direction, but somehow, somewhere, it had happened.

I remembered the intensity of the night on which we had become engaged; the joyful exploration of our honeymoon; filling out a preliminary application for a mission organization; bringing our first child home—but now, ten years later, we had "evolved" into spending Friday nights watching other people fall in love according to the machinations of a Hollywood script.

That night I didn't have any answers, but taking an honest look at my situation definitely shook me awake. What was this thing called marriage? How had I ended up here? Was there no more purpose to it than this?

"It Is Good for a Man Not to Marry"

I became a Christian at a very young age. In truth, I can scarcely remember a moment when God was not an active and conscious presence in my life. Because of this, I felt drawn to Jesus early on.

I was drawn to more than Jesus, however. I also remember being drawn to girls. I had a pretty big crush on a dark-haired girl *in kindergarten!* The first time I actually held hands with a girl was in fifth grade. Tina and I rolled around the skating rink, both of us blushing as the Carpenters' melodious harmonies described us well: "I'm On Top of the World." It sure felt like it!

As I grew older, both of these movements — toward Jesus and toward females — sometimes created an uneasy tension. The man I most admired, the one person on whom I wanted to model my life and to whom I wanted to express my commitment, was a *single* man.

As far back as I can remember, I was fully aware of the long-standing tradition of celibacy — monks and nuns who lived out their dedication to God by pledging to abstain from marriage and sex. Part of me wished I could embrace this; I wanted to be "sold out" for Christ, and in college I struggled with the apostle Paul's words, "It is good for a man not to marry" (1 Corinthians 7:1).[7]

In fact, there is much in Christian history that has unofficially (and at times blatantly) considered married believers to be "second-class Christians" who compromised their integrity or who were too weak to contain their sexual urges. Augustine thought he was being charitable when he wrote, referring to the intent to procreate, "Marital intercourse makes something good out of the evil of lust."[8] While Scripture is reliable and even infallible, Christian history isn't, and unfounded prejudices do exist.

There's no question that the "first pope," Peter, was married. (Jesus couldn't very well have healed Peter's mother-in-law if Peter didn't have a wife!) But there is also evidence in Scripture (1 Timothy 5:9 – 12) that during the first century young widows were already taking vows of celibacy. By A.D. 110, celibates could take vows that mirrored marital vows. This became a little more institutionalized so that by the third century, lifelong vows of celibacy were not uncommon. By the fourth century, such vows were commemorated by a full liturgical celebration.[9]

Although Christianity was born out of Judaism, a religion in which marriage was considered a religious duty (one rabbi suggested that a man who does not marry is not fully a man[10]), it wasn't long until married believers were scarcely an afterthought during centuries of writing on "spiritual theology" (studying how Christian believers grow in their faith, learn to pray, and draw closer to God). Most of the Christian classics were written *by* monks and nuns *for* monks and nuns. The married could at best feebly try to simulate a single pursuit of God; the thought of pursuing God *through* marriage wasn't really given serious consideration; instead, the emphasis was largely on pursuing God *in spite* of marriage.

I carried some of this baggage into my own relationship, but early on, my eyes were opened to a different reality. I remember my brother asking me a few questions about what marriage was like. I thought for a moment and said, "If you want to be free to serve Jesus, there's no question — stay single. Marriage takes a lot of time. But if you want to become more like Jesus, I can't imagine any better thing to do than to get married. Being married forces you to face some character issues you'd never have to face otherwise."

Jesus, of course, was celibate his entire life, so it's somewhat ironic to suggest that marriage is the preferred route to becoming more like him. But Jesus *did* live in a family, and, as Betsy Ricucci points out, that's *all* he had done at the time the Father proclaimed, "This is my Son, whom I love; with him I am well pleased" (Matthew 3:17). "What had Jesus done to receive such praise? Nothing but live in his own home, honoring his parents and serving his father's carpentry business. Apparently that was enough to please God."[11]

Family life is clearly not a cop-out; and after you've been married for a while, you realize that the emphasis on celibacy is slightly overblown. All other things considered, the sexual aspect takes up just a fraction of a married couple's time. I was the first of my group of friends to get married, and I remember one of them asking me if it was still okay to just "drop in" unannounced.

"Oh, you better call first," I said gravely, capturing his attention. "Married couples walk around naked all day long, you know."

For a second, I almost had him!

The real transforming work of marriage is the twenty-four-hours-a-day, seven-days-a-week commitment. This is the crucible that grinds and shapes us into the character of Jesus Christ. Instead of getting up at 3:00 A.M. to begin prayer in a monastery, the question becomes, "Who will wake up when the baby's diaper needs changing?"

Marriage calls us to an entirely new and selfless life. This insight occurred to me some years ago when Lisa and the kids were traveling while I had to stay home and work. For the first time ever, it seemed, I had a free Saturday. For as long as I could remember, I had awakened each weekend and talked over with Lisa what the family would do; I almost didn't know how to ask the question—what do I want to do? Yet that was the question I had asked myself as a single man virtually every Saturday before I was married.

Any situation that calls me to confront my selfishness has enormous spiritual value, and I slowly began to understand that the real purpose of marriage may not be happiness as much as it is holiness. Not that God has anything *against* happiness, or that happiness and holiness are by nature mutually exclusive, but looking at marriage through the lens of holiness began to put it into an entirely new perspective for me.

"But Since There Is So Much Immorality . . ."

I find it fascinating that just after Paul said, "It is good for a man not to marry," he follows it up with these words: "But since there is so much immorality, each man should have his own wife, and each woman her own husband" (1 Corinthians 7:2).

I would do violence to the Greek biblical text to suggest that this passage is referring to anything other than sexual relations — the New International Version tidies it up a bit, but even a cursory exegesis reveals that, clearly, sex is intended. Even so, I suggest that we can elaborate the principle to reveal truth beyond sexual relations. Since there is so much immorality within us — not just lust, but selfishness, anger, control-mongering, and even hatred — we should enter into a close relationship with one other person so we can work on those issues in the light of what our marriage relationship will reveal to us about our behavior and our attitudes.

I found there was a tremendous amount of immaturity within me that my marriage directly confronted. The key was that I had to change my view of marriage. If the purpose of marriage was simply to enjoy an infatuation and make me "happy," then I'd have to get a "new" marriage every two or three years. But if I really wanted to see God transform me from the inside out, I'd need to concentrate on changing *myself* rather than on changing my *spouse*. In fact, you might even say, the more difficult my spouse proved to be, the more opportunity I'd have to grow. Just as physical exercise needs to be somewhat strenuous, so "relational exercise" may need to be a bit vigorous to truly stress-test the heart.

I didn't decide to focus on changing myself so that I could have a tension-free marriage or so that I'd be happier or even more content in my marriage. Instead, I adopted the attitude that marriage is one of many life situations that help me to draw my sense of meaning, purpose, and fulfillment *from God*. Lisa can't make me happy, not in an ultimate sense. Certainly we have some great times together, and she has been a wonderful wife, exceeding my dreams — but these great times are sprinkled with (and sometimes seem to get buried in) the demands, challenges, and expectations of paying the bills on time, disciplining children, earning a living, and keeping a house clean.

I guess what I'm after is a quieter fulfillment, a deeper sense of meaning, a fuller understanding of the purpose behind this intense, one-on-one, lifelong relationship. As a man who believes his primary meaning comes from his relationship with God, I want to explore how marriage can draw me closer to God.

There's another reason to stress this: Marriage, for all of us, is temporary in the light of eternity. The truth is, my and Lisa's relationship with God will outlive our marriage. Most likely the time will come when either Lisa or I precede the other into eternity. The remaining spouse will be left alone, no longer married—perhaps even eventually remarried to someone else.

For the Christian, marriage is a penultimate rather than an ultimate reality. Because of this, both of us can find even more meaning by pursuing God together and by recognizing that he is the one who alone can fill the spiritual ache in our souls. We can work at making our home life more pleasant and peaceable; we can explore ways to keep sex fresh and fun; we can make superficial changes that will preserve at least the appearance of respect and politeness. But what both of us crave more than anything else is to be intimately close to the God who made us. If *that* relationship is right, we won't make such severe demands on our marriage, asking each other, expecting each other, to compensate for spiritual emptiness.

Unfortunately, as a fallible human being I can't possibly appreciate Lisa the way God appreciates her. I can't even begin to understand her the way she longs to be understood. I'd get bored with myself if I was married to me, so it only makes sense that Lisa might occasionally be bored—or at least grow weary—of living with me. But God delights in both of us. God appreciates our quirks and understands our hearts' good intentions even when they might be masked by incredibly stupid behavior.

One thing is sure: Lisa can't look to me to be God for her. And even when I try to love her like only God can love her, I fail every time and on every count. I give it my best, but I fall short every day.

Looking for Love in All the Wrong Places

We need to remind ourselves of the ridiculousness of looking for something from other humans that only God can provide. Our close friends have a son named Nolan. When he was just four years old, he saw me carrying some rather large boxes and asked me, in all sincerity, "Gary, are you strongest, or is God strongest?"

His dad laughed a little *too* hard at that one. And of course we adults think it's absurd to compare our physical strength with God's. But how many of us "adults" have then turned around and asked, perhaps unconsciously, "Are you going to fulfill me, or will God fulfill me?" For some reason, *that* question doesn't sound as absurd to us as the one about physical strength, but it should!

I believe that much of the dissatisfaction we experience in marriage comes from expecting too much from it. I have a rather outdated computer—a 486—so I know there are some things I simply can't do with it; there's just not enough memory or processing power to run certain programs or combine certain tasks. It's not that I have a *bad* computer; it's just that I can't reasonably expect more from it than it has the power to give.

In the same way, some of us ask too much of marriage. We want to get the largest portion of our life's fulfillment from our relationship with our spouse. That's asking too much. Yes, without a doubt there should be moments of happiness, meaning, and a general sense of fulfillment. But my wife can't be God, and I was created with a spirit that craves God. Anything less than God, and I'll feel an ache.

This is a book that looks and points *beyond* marriage. Spiritual growth is the main theme; marriage is simply the context. Just as celibates use abstinence and religious hermits use isolation, so we can use marriage for the same purpose—to grow in our service, obedience, character, pursuit, and love of God.

You've probably already realized that there was a purpose for your marriage that went beyond happiness. You might not have chosen the word "holiness" to express it, but you understood there was a transcendent truth beyond the superficial romance depicted in popular culture. We're going to explore that purpose. We're going to cut open many marriages, find out where the commitment rubs, explore where the poisoned attitudes hide, search out where we are forced to confront our weakness and sin, and learn how to grow through the process.

The ultimate purpose of this book is not to make you love your spouse more—although I think that will happen along the way. It's to equip you to love your God more and to help you reflect the character of his Son more precisely. At the very least, you'll have a new appreciation for the person with whom you have embarked on this journey.

Finding God in Marriage

Marital Analogies Teach Us
Truths About God

*[Marriage] is the merciless revealer,
the great white searchlight turned
on the darkest places of human nature.*
KATHERINE ANNE PORTER

EVERY YEAR NINE OF MY COLLEGE BUDDIES GET TOGETHER FOR A weekend retreat. Several years ago one of my friends pulled me aside and mentioned that he was considering returning home that night; he and his wife were hoping to conceive another child, and the time was right, by his wife's calculations.

"Do it," I urged him. "You can be back by breakfast."

"I don't know ...," he hesitated.

"Do it," I said more strongly, and another friend weighed in with his support.

Later he assented and went home. That night a child was conceived.

I look at that child now and smile, wondering if he'll ever know how close he came to not being (and how much he owes me!). There are few more dizzying realities of life than cooperating with God to produce another human being. If my friend and his wife had waited another month, perhaps they would have had a girl, or a shorter boy, or a boy with darker hair. It's amazing.

This aspect of the marital experience—cooperating with God to bring children into being—should be particularly meaningful for Christians (and a key reason why having difficulty conceiving can be so painful to so many couples). The picture of God as Creator is central to his authority, identity, and purpose. In fact, the Bible is framed around the fact that God is Creator. The first thing we learn about God in the book of Genesis is that he created the heavens and the earth (see Genesis 1:1); the last image of the New Testament shows God creating a new heaven and a new earth. When God says, "I am making everything new!" (Revelation 21:5), the word "making" is in the present tense—it's an ongoing process. God walks into eternity creating.

This is just one of several analogies that connect various aspects of marriage with our understanding of God. A giant thread runs throughout Scripture comparing God's relationship to his people with the human institution of marriage. In this chapter, we're going to explore how these various analogies use the experience of marriage to teach us valuable truths about the nature of God. Through the experience of being married, we can come to know God in new ways.

Divine Romance

Hosea leads us into a startling reality—God views his people as a husband views his wife: " 'In that day,' declares the LORD, 'you will call me "my husband"; you will no longer call me "my master." ... I will betroth you to me forever' " (Hosea 2:16, 19a). Think about the difference between "husband" and "master"—and all that these images conjure up in your mind. God wants us to relate to him with an obedience fueled by love and intimacy, not by self-motivated fear, and with a loyalty to a divine-human relationship, not a blind adherence to "principles." A husband harbors a passion toward his wife that is absent in a master toward his slave.

How do you view God—as master, or as husband?

Isaiah uses marital imagery to stress how God rejoices in his people: "As a bridegroom rejoices over his bride, so will your God rejoice over you." (Isaiah 62:5b) We live in a world where many people are simply too busy or too preoccupied to notice us. But God *delights* in us. We make his supernatural heart skip a beat.

At times, Jesus himself employed this marital imagery, referring to himself as the "bridegroom" (Matthew 9:15) and to the kingdom of heaven as a "wedding banquet" (Matthew 22:1 – 14). This picture is carried over into the culmination of earthly history, as the book of Revelation talks about "the wedding of the Lamb" in which "his bride has made herself ready" (Revelation 19:7).

The breakdown of *spiritual* fidelity is often depicted with marital analogies as well. Jeremiah compares idolatry with adultery: "I gave faithless Israel her certificate of divorce and sent her away because of all her adulteries" (Jeremiah 3:8). Jesus picked up on this same imagery, referring to an "adulterous" generation (Mark 8:38). In context, Jesus is not attacking human sexual foibles; he is agonizing over a spiritually unfaithful nation that is violating its divine marriage to God.

Throughout Christian history, teachers have explored the similarities between the marital union and the various mysteries of faith that also involve a union: Besides the Trinity there is the joining of divinity and humanity in the person of Jesus Christ; the Eucharist, in which the bread and the wine are joined to signify the body and blood of Christ; Christ's union with his church; and other similar analogies.

Ruminating on these analogies is not merely amusing wordplay. For Christians seeking to gain spiritual insight from their marriage, these analogies provide the necessary ingredients for serious, contemplative reflection. The reason God became flesh was so that we might know him; correspondingly, God did not create marriage just to give us a pleasant means of repopulating the world and providing a steady societal institution for the benefit of humanity. He planted marriage among humans as yet another signpost pointing to his own eternal, spiritual existence.

As humans with finite minds, we need the power of symbolism in order to gain understanding. By means of the simple relationship of a man and a woman, the symbol of marriage can call up virtually infinite meaning. This will happen only when we use our marriage to *explore* God. If we are consumed with highlighting where our spouses are falling short, we will miss the divine mysteries of marriage and the lessons it has to teach us.

In the next section we're going to accent one particular analogy to showcase how these life-pictures can bring together our marriage and our faith as well as teach us about the purpose of marriage. While future chapters may seem more "practical," it's important that we briefly explore the doctrine behind Christian marriage, and what makes the marriages of believers different from the marriages of unbelievers. This difference is showcased in the preeminent marital analogy of Christ and his church.

Reconciliation

There's an old rabbinical story about how the spot was chosen for God's holy temple. Two brothers worked a common field and a common mill. Each night they divided whatever grain they had produced and each took his portion home.

One brother was single and one was married with a large family. The single brother decided that his married brother, with all those kids, certainly needed more grain than he did, so at night he secretly crept over to his brother's granary and gave him an extra portion. The married brother realized that his single brother didn't have any children to care for him in his old age. Concerned about his brother's future, he got up each night and secretly deposited some grain in his single brother's granary.

One night they met halfway between the two granaries, and each brother realized what the other was doing. They embraced, and as the story goes, God witnessed what happened and said, "This is a holy place—a place of love—and it is here that my temple shall be built."

The holy place is that spot where God is made known to his people, "the place where human beings discover each other in love."[1]

Marriage can be that holy place, the site of a relationship that proclaims God's love to this world, but Christian thinkers haven't always elected to look at marriage this way. For all their ambivalence about whether marriage is an inferior state, the early church fathers at least recognized that the analogy of reconciliation is the highest aim of marriage, pointing as a sign to the union of Christ with his church. Paul explores this theme in his letter to the Ephesians (5:22–33).

One of these early thinkers, Augustine (A.D. 354–430), suggested that there are three benefits of marriage: offspring, faith (fidelity), and sacrament. Of the three benefits, he clearly points to the latter (sacrament) as the greatest. This is because it is possible to be married without either offspring or faith, but it is not possible to be (still) married without indissolubility, which is what a sacrament points toward. As long as a couple is married, they continue to display—however imperfectly—the ongoing commitment between Christ and his church. Thus, simply "sticking it out" becomes vitally important.

Centuries after Augustine, Anglican Reformers responded to these three blessings with three "causes." An early (1549) prayer book suggests that marriage is for procreation, a remedy against sexual sin, and mutual comfort.[2] This last element unfortunately replaced the sacramental aspect of marriage (namely, showcasing Christ and his church) with something much more pedestrian (namely, relational comfort).

Knowing *why* we are married and should stay married is crucial. This will lead us into a discussion brilliantly argued by Maryland pastor C.J. Mahaney in an audiotape series on marriage titled *According to Plan*. The key question is this: Will we approach marriage from a God-centered view or a man-centered view?[3] In a man-centered view, we will maintain our marriage as long as our earthly comforts, desires, and expectations are met. In a God-centered view, we preserve our marriage because it brings glory to God and points a sinful world to a reconciling Creator.

More than seeing marriage as a mutual comfort, we must see it as a word picture of the most important news humans have ever received — that there is a divine relationship between God and his people. Paul explicitly makes this analogy in his letter to the Ephesians. You've probably read these words (or heard these words quoted) dozens, if not hundreds, of times: "Husbands, love your wives, just as Christ loved the church and gave himself up for her to make her holy, cleansing her by the washing with water through the word, and to present her to himself as a radiant church, without stain or wrinkle or any other blemish, but holy and blameless" (Ephesians 5:25–27).

Though theologically I am on the "side" of the Protestants, I must declare to my medieval Anglican brothers that I believe it is unfortunate and sad when something so profound as living out an analogy of Christ and his church is reduced to experiencing this relationship as merely something that will help us avoid sexual sin, keep the world populated, and provide a cure for loneliness.

In fact, both the Old and New Testaments use marriage as a central analogy — the union between God and Israel (Old Testament) and the union between Christ and his church (the New Testament). Understanding the depth of these analogies is crucial, as they will help us determine the very foundation on which a truly Christian marriage is based. If I believe the primary purpose of marriage is to model God's love for his church, I will enter this relationship and maintain it with an entirely new motivation, one hinted at by Paul in his second letter to the Corinthians: "So we make it our goal to please him" (2 Corinthians 5:9).

What Makes God Happy?

Paul answers a lot of questions for us when he says, "We make it our goal to please him." Ask ten people on the street what their goal in life is, and you'll get an amazing variety of answers.

For the Christian, Paul couldn't be clearer — his "consuming ambition, the motive force behind all he does,"[4] is *to please God*. But

Paul doesn't just say pleasing God is *his* "consuming ambition," he assumes it will be *ours* as well: "*We* make it our goal to please him."

When something is the motive force behind all we do, it becomes the driving force for every decision we make. And Paul is crystal clear: The first question we should ask ourselves when doing anything is, "Will this be pleasing to Jesus Christ?"

The first purpose in marriage — beyond happiness, sexual expression, the bearing of children, companionship, mutual care and provision, or anything else — is to please God. The challenge, of course, is that it is utterly *selfless* living; rather than asking, "What will make me happy?" we are told that we must ask, "What will make God happy?" And just in case we don't grasp it immediately, Paul underscores it a few verses later: "Those who live should no longer live for themselves but for him who died for them and was raised again" (2 Corinthians 5:15).

I have no other choice as a Christian. I owe it to Jesus Christ to live for him, to make him my consuming passion and the driving force in my life. To do this, I have to die to my own desires daily. I have to crucify the urge that measures every action and decision around what is best for me. Paul is eloquent regarding this fact: "We always carry around in our body the death of Jesus, so that the life of Jesus may also be revealed in our body" (2 Corinthians 4:10).

Just as Jesus went to the cross, so I must go to the cross, always considering myself as carrying around "the death of Jesus" so that his new life — his motivations, his purposes, his favor — might dominate in everything I do.

This reality calls me to look at my spouse through Christian eyes: "So from now on we regard no one from a worldly point of view ..." (2 Corinthians 5:16a). The reason is clear: "If anyone is in Christ, he is a new creation; the old has gone, the new has come!" (5:17). Part of this new identity is a new ministry, one that is given to *every Christian*, as it is inherent in the person of Jesus Christ: "All this is from God, who reconciled us to himself through Christ and gave us the ministry of reconciliation" (5:18).

Think about this. The very nature of Christ's work was a reconciling work, bringing us together again with God. Our response is to become reconcilers ourselves. C. K. Barrett defines reconciliation as "to end a relation of enmity, and to substitute for it one of peace and goodwill."[5]

Clearly Paul is talking about carrying the message of salvation. But we cannot discuss with any integrity the ending of "a relation of enmity" and the dawning of "peace and goodwill" if our marriages are marked by divorce, fighting, and animosity. Everything I am to say and do in my life is to be supportive of this gospel ministry of reconciliation, and that commitment begins by displaying reconciliation in my personal relationships, especially in my marriage.

If my marriage contradicts my message, I have sabotaged the goal of my life: to be pleasing to Christ and to faithfully fulfill the ministry of reconciliation, proclaiming to the world the good news that we can be reconciled to God through Jesus Christ. If my "driving force" is as Paul says it should be, I will work to construct a marriage that enhances this ministry of reconciliation—a marriage that, in fact, incarnates this truth by putting flesh on it, building a relationship that models forgiveness, selfless love, and sacrifice.

The last picture I want to give the world is that I have decided to stop loving someone and that I refuse to serve this person anymore, or that I have failed to fulfill a promise I made many years before. Yet this is precisely the message many Christians are proclaiming through their actions. According to pollster George Barna, self-described "born-again" Christians have a higher rate of divorce than nonbelievers (twenty-seven percent to twenty-three percent). Those who adopt the label "fundamentalist Christian" have the highest divorce rate of all (thirty percent).[6] We can't carry a message well if we don't live it first.

How can I tell my children that God's promise of reconciliation is secure when they see that my own promise doesn't mean a thing? They *may* get over it, but in that case I will have presented a roadblock rather than a stepping-stone to the gospel.

What most divorces mean is that at least one party, and possibly both, have ceased to put the gospel first in their lives. They no longer live by Paul's guiding principle, "I make it my goal to please him," because the Bible is clear in its teaching. God says, "I hate divorce" (Malachi 2:16). If the goal of the couple was to please God, they wouldn't seek a divorce.

I know there are exceptions. Paul allows divorce when the other spouse isn't a believer and abandons the believer; Jesus considers marital unfaithfulness as possible grounds for divorce. Certainly, exceptions are to be assumed—at least in the realm of separation—if one's kids are in danger by continuing to live with a particular parent; but most of the cases of divorce among Christians do not involve such situations. They are far more likely to involve two Christians who have distorted their priorities in life.

One of the reasons I am determined to keep my marriage together is not because doing so will make me happier (although I believe it will); not because I want my kids to have a secure home (although I do desire that); not because it would tear me up to see my wife have to "start over" (although it would). The first reason I keep my marriage together is because it is my Christian duty. If my life is based on proclaiming God's message to the world, I don't want to do anything that would challenge that message. And how can I proclaim reconciliation when I seek dissolution?

This analogy of reconciliation does more than merely provide the purpose for our marriage. It also helps us live out this purpose, even when "lightning strikes."

When Lightning Strikes

There is something mesmerizing to me about standing beneath a tree that is seven hundred years old. "What was happening here when this tree first started growing?" my daughter asked me as we hiked the western slope of the North Cascades in the state of Washington.

"Not much," I laughed, stunned by the realization that this tree was nearly two hundred years old when Martin Luther was born.

One of the reasons the trees on the western slope of the Cascades survive so long is quite simple: The Washington forests are so wet that lightning strikes cause relatively few fires. Whereas the traditional forest, if left alone, might face a lightning-initiated fire every fifty or sixty years, in this part of the Cascades it would be about once every two hundred years. Lightning strikes still come, but they're not as devastating, so trees have had a much longer time to take root and grow.

I think that's a good picture of a marriage that is based on the ministry of reconciliation. Strong Christian marriages will still be struck by lightning — sexual temptation, communication problems, frustrations, unrealized expectations — but if the marriages are heavily watered with an unwavering commitment to please God above everything else, the conditions won't be ripe for a devastating fire to follow the lightning strike.

If I'm married only for happiness, and my happiness wanes for whatever reason, one little spark will burn the entire forest of my relationship. But if my aim is to proclaim and model God's ministry of reconciliation, my endurance will be fireproof.

Practicing the spiritual discipline of marriage means that I put my relationship with God first. Just sticking it out is a victory in and of itself and creates a certain glory. The only real claim to fame in a forest full of trees is being seven hundred years old. As far as pure aesthetics go, you couldn't even see the very top of this particular tree in the Washington forest. From where we stood, it was just a straight and enormously wide trunk, covered with spiderwebs. We were walking in a forest filled with trees, but the National Parks Service put a sign in front of this tree for one reason, and for one reason only: It had survived for seven centuries. It had simply gone the distance, and in so doing it commanded attention.

In a society where relationships are discarded with a frightening regularity, Christians can command attention simply by staying married. And when asked why, we can offer the platform of God's message of reconciliation, followed by an invitation: "Would you like to hear more about that good news of reconciliation?"

In this sense, our marriages can be platforms for evangelism. They can draw people into a truth that points beyond this world into the next. Just by sticking it out in our marriages, we can build a monument to the principle and the practice of reconciliation.

Years ago Paul Simon wrote a best-selling song proclaiming "Fifty Ways to Leave Your Lover." A Christian needs just one reason to stay with his or her "lover": the analogy of Christ and his church.

3

Learning to Love
How Marriage Teaches Us to Love

Marriage requires a radical commitment to love our
spouses as they are, while longing for them to become what
they are not yet. Every marriage moves either toward enhancing
one another's glory or toward degrading each other.
DAN ALLENDER AND TREMPER LONGMAN III

If you treat a man as he is, he will stay as he is.
But if you treat him as if he were what he ought to be and could be,
he will become the bigger and better man.
JOHANN WOLFGANG VON GOETHE

IF YOU WERE A MALE BELIEVER AROUND THE TIME OF MOSES AND Joshua, your job was to fight. As the Israelites entered the Promised Land, they were sometimes chastised for their cowardice and lethargy and their refusal to go into battle: "How long will you wait before you begin to take possession of the land that the Lord, the God of your fathers, has given you?" (Joshua 18:3).

"Go into battle," for a long time, was the rallying cry from God.

Jesus came with a new challenge — a far more difficult one. Someone once asked him what the greatest commandment was, and Jesus replied that there were two (see Matthew 22:34–40). It wasn't enough to love God with all your heart, soul, mind, and strength. If you really wanted to please God, Jesus said, you must love others.

Marriage can be the gym in which our capacity to experience

and express God's love is strengthened and further developed. To get there, we have to realize that human love and divine love aren't two separate oceans but rather one body of water with many tributaries. We show our love for God in part by loving our spouses well.

We can never love somebody "too much." Our problem is that typically we love God too little. The answer is not to dim our love for any human in particular; it's to expand our heart's response to our Divine Joy.

Marriage creates a climate where this love is put to the greatest test. The problem is that love must be *acquired*. Katherine Anne Porter writes, "Love must be learned, and learned again and again; there is no end to it. Hate needs no instruction, but waits only to be provoked."[1]

Love is not a natural response that gushes out of us unbidden. Infatuation sometimes does that — at the beginning of a relationship at least — but hate is always ready to naturally spring forth, like the "Old Faithful" geyser at Yellowstone National Park. Christian love, on the other hand, must be chased after, aspired to, and practiced.

The popular culture completely misunderstands this principle. One of the cruelest *and* most self-condemning remarks I've ever heard is the one that men often use when they leave their wives for another woman: "The truth is, I've never loved you." This is meant to be an attack on the wife — saying in effect, "The truth is, I've never found you *lovable*." But put in a Christian context, it's a confession of the man's utter failure to be a Christian. If he hasn't loved his wife, it is not his wife's fault, but *his*. Jesus calls us to love even the unlovable — even our enemies! — so a man who says "I've never loved you" is a man who is saying essentially this: "I've never acted like a Christian."

When we love well, we please God. This shouldn't be hard to figure out. The best way for someone to get into my good graces is to be kind to my children. All Christians are God's children; by loving others, we bring enormous pleasure to our heavenly Father.

I'm a regular user of public libraries. Anyone who frequents these institutions eventually encounters the street people who come in on cold days. One day I was walking toward the computer terminals when the smell of one such individual became almost overpowering. Out of the corner of my eye, I saw a man hunched over a table, his tattered clothes and unkempt hair marking his lack of any permanent address.

There are men and women who have dedicated their lives to reaching people such as these. Most cities have a "gospel mission" that take in people off the street. Sometimes people tell me how much God has "used" me in their lives, but I shake my head when I think of the street missions. It's easy to be "used" when you get to sit in front of a computer in your home and do something you enjoy. It's hardly sacrificial when I'm given well-furnished rooms in hotels and carted across the country in an airplane.

But Christian love is displayed in loving the most difficult ones to love. Bestselling author Philip Yancey writes, "Through the ages, Christian saints have chosen the most unDarwinian objects for their love."[2] This is in response to Jesus' call that when we hold a banquet, we shouldn't invite our friends because they might invite us back and thus repay us for our hospitality. Instead, Jesus said, invite the lame, the paralyzed, the poor, the blind — those who can't pay you back (see Luke 14).

That's what's so difficult about Jesus' call to love others. On one level, it's easy to love God, because God doesn't smell. God doesn't have bad breath. God doesn't reward kindness with evil. God doesn't make berating comments. Loving God is *easy,* in this sense. But Jesus really let us have it when he attached our love for God with our love for other people.

In the marriage context, we have absolutely no excuse. God lets us *choose* whom we're going to love. Because we get the choice and *then* find it difficult to carry out the love in practice, what grounds do we have to ever stop loving? God doesn't command us to get married; he offers it to us as an opportunity. Once we enter the marriage relationship, we cannot love God without loving our spouse as well.

Divorce represents our inability to hold to Jesus' command. It's giving up on what Jesus calls us to do. If I can't love my wife, how can I love the homeless man in the library? How can I love the drug addict or the alcoholic? Yes, this spouse might be difficult to love at times, but that's what marriage is for — *to teach us how to love.*

Allow your marriage relationship to stretch your love and to enlarge your capacity for love — to teach you to be a Christian. Use marriage as a practice court, where you learn to accept another person and serve him or her. And please don't limit this "love" to "spiritual" things like praying, preaching, and exhorting. Part of the experience of love is delighting each other in very "earthy" ways. This, too, is a biblical truth, as we'll see in the next section.

Holy Happiness

Although young men in Israel were called to serve God by fighting in wars, God did make one exception. It's buried in the book of Deuteronomy: "If a man has recently married, he must not be sent to war or have any other duty laid on him. For one year he is to be free to stay at home and bring happiness to the wife he has married" (Deuteronomy 24:5).

In all my seminarian theology, I left little room for the thought that God would want me to devote myself to making my wife happy. My wife was there to join me as I evangelized, studied Scripture, taught younger believers, did "the work of the ministry." The thought that God wants me to serve him by concentrating on making my wife happy was extraordinary. Can it mean, then, that if my wife is unhappy, I'm failing God?

Although verse 5 of Deuteronomy 24 addresses just the first year of marriage, it's reasonable to assume that every spouse should spend some time thinking about how to make their spouse happy — and celebrating the profound reality that making their spouse happy pleases God. On a very practical level, a husband who plots how to make his wife laugh every now and then is serving God. A wife who plans an unforgettable sexual experience for her husband is serving

God. A husband who makes sacrifices so his wife can get the recreational time she needs is loving God.

When Jesus said, "Love the Lord your God ... love your neighbor," he opened up the vistas of love and removed the walls that encase us. He made divine love and "religion" much bigger than we realize.

This is a prophetic word to today's society. There are legions of books published every year that teach us how to care for ourselves. As our society becomes increasingly fractured, there is a virtual obsession with looking out for ourselves, standing up for ourselves, and bettering ourselves. This emphasis on meeting our own needs can become ridiculous. You need only consider the book I once saw advertised that was titled, *Sex for One: The Joy of Self-Loving*.

While our society has become expert in self-care, we seemingly have lost the art of caring for others. *Sacrifice* has taken on such negative connotations that people fear being a "codependent" more than they fear being perceived as selfish.

And yet Scripture says in effect, "Make your wife happy. Sacrifice yourself *daily*. You'll find your life only when you first lose it."

A campus pastor named Brady Bobbink decided to take Scripture's admonitions about love seriously. Brady married relatively late in life. He had become well known as a speaker on discipleship and single living, and he was in high demand, with plenty of opportunities to "serve God" through his gift of teaching.

When Brady asked Shirley to become his wife, life changed dramatically. Shirley had two children from a previous marriage, and it wasn't long before Shirley and Brady began to pray about having a child of their own.

"What would it mean for me to love my wife in this situation?" Brady asked himself. In prayer, Brady made a pledge. If Shirley had another baby, for the first year he wouldn't accept any outside speaking engagements other than the ones his current position required him to take. Shirley subsequently became pregnant and gave birth to their first boy, Micah.

Months later, Brady received a lucrative opportunity to speak in Singapore. Brady is a student of history and loves to travel. The chance to go to the Far East was a once-in-a-lifetime opportunity, plus it would give him the chance to teach Christians from another culture.

He excitedly told Shirley about this great opportunity, then remembered his pledge midway through his conversation, and said out loud, "I can't go."

Shirley tried to release Brady from his pledge. "Honey, I'll be fine," she said.

It would have been easy for Brady to play religious games here. "I certainly could have justified it on a noble idea," he admitted, "preaching to another culture, but if that had really been my passion, I would have moved there and taken my wife and kids with me."

Some might think Brady was passing up an opportunity to please God by taking his gospel message to another nation, but Brady realized he could please God by loving his wife in a season in which she needed extra help and attention. To stay home and care for his wife in her need was every bit as much "Christian service" as leaving his hometown to go preach the gospel when he was single.

"To fail to love my wife and kids rightly in the name of loving other people rightly is a sham," Brady insists.

John Barger: Learning to Love

Dr. John Barger gave an extraordinary address to a gathering of men on December 12, 1987. The address included his testimony of how he had walked the road from being a domineering husband to a serving one. The crux of the message, however, wasn't just that husbands can do better. We all know that. What inspired me so much about his words was Dr. Barger's message that by learning to love his wife, he got a better grip on how he could love his God.

I want to share some of Dr. Barger's story with you. It begins with his confession of the way in which many men view women:

It's easy to scorn women, and most men do. We see women as physically weak, easy to intimidate, bound to the menial tasks of motherhood, emotional, illogical, and often petty. Or we see them as temptresses; in desire we idolize them and parade them across the pages of magazines, yet we scorn and hate them for their commanding sexual power over us. Male scorn for women affects every aspect of our lives: our relations with our mothers, our girlfriends, our secretaries, our wives, our children, the church, and even God himself.

I do not speak here merely of *your* scorn of women; I speak of *mine* as well. My relatives grew up on the streets during the Depression, learning early the fury and scorn that characterize so many people in dire circumstances: drinking heavily and seeing women alternately as sex objects or servants.... As a result, I swaggered through marriage for many years, ruling my wife Susan and my seven children with an iron hand while citing Scripture as justification for my privileges and authority. After all, Scripture explicitly commands wives to obey their husbands.

Years of dominating my wife and children left them habitually resentful and fearful of me, yet unwilling to challenge me because of the fury it might provoke.... I alienated Susan and the children, and lost their love. Home was not a pleasant place to be—for them or for me. By 1983, Susan would have left me if it weren't for the children, and even that bond was losing its force.

Then a number of dramatic events occurred, which wrought a profound change in my moral, psychological, and spiritual life.[3]

The first of these "dramatic events" was when Dr. Barger watched his wife endure a difficult delivery. Susan's placenta tore loose, and she started hemorrhaging. The baby was stillborn. Dr. Barger describes further what happened:

At two in the morning in a stark, bright hospital delivery room, I held in my left hand my tiny lifeless son, and stared in disbelief at his death.... I had the power to make [my family's] lives worse by raging against my baby's death and my wife's lack of love, or to make their lives better by learning to love them properly. *I had to choose.* And it was a clear choice, presented in an instant as I stared at my tiny, helpless, stillborn infant cradled in my hand. In that critical instant, with God's grace, I chose the arduous, undramatic, discouraging path of trying to be good.

I don't have time ... to tell you of all the afflictions we endured in the next four years: sick children, my mother's sudden death, my losing my job as a teacher, three more miscarriages, and finally a secret sorrow that pierced both of us to the very core of our beings.

In the midst of these many afflictions, I found that the only way I could learn to love, and to cease being a cause of pain, was to suffer, endure, and strive every minute to repudiate my anger, my resentment, my scorn, my jealousy, my lust, my pride, and my dozens of other vices.

I began holding my tongue.

I started admitting my faults and apologizing for them.

I quit defending myself when I was judged too harshly — for the important thing was not to be right (or to be well-thought-of) but to love.

As I had made myself the center of my attention for too many years already, I said little about my own labors and sorrows; I sought to know Susan's, and to help her to bear them.

And, frankly, once I started listening to Susan — once I began really hearing her and drawing her out — I was startled at how many and how deep were her wounds and her sorrows. . . . Most were not sorrows unique to Susan. They were the sorrows that all feel: sorrows that arise from the particular physiology of women and from their vocation as mothers, which gives them heavy duties and responsibilities while leaving them almost totally dependent on men for their material well-being and their spiritual support; sorrows that arise from loving their husbands and children intensely, but not being able to keep harm from those they love; sorrows that arise from the fact that in our society even the most chaste of women are regularly threatened by the lustful stares, remarks, and advances of men; and sorrows that arise because our society in general still considers women stupid, flighty, and superficial, and still places very little value on women and shows very little respect for them. . . .

Women . . . suffer these wounds far more often and with a greater intensity than most of us men ever realize. And unless we ask them, women generally do not speak to us of these sorrows — perhaps because we men so often dismiss their troubles as insignificant or write off women themselves as simply weak and whiny. . . .

Can men . . . withdraw the sword of sorrow that pierces every woman's heart? I don't think so. Their problems are generally not the kind that have a solution, but rather form the very fabric of their daily existence. . . .

One of my friends, when confronted at the end of his long workday with his wife's complaints about the noise, the troubles, and the unending housework, snapped back at her in exasperation: "Well, do you want me to stay home and do the housework while you go off to the office?" You understand his point: He couldn't solve her problems. What did she want him to do?

I'll tell you: She wanted him to listen, to understand, and to sympathize. She wanted him to let her know that despite her problems, her exhaustion, her dishevelment, he loved her — to let her know that it caused him sorrow that she was suffering and that if it were possible, he would change it for her.

Dr. Barger's earnest efforts at renewing his love for his wife and reaching a new plane of understanding worked. It took three years of "patience, listening, and growing in Susan's trust," spending "literally hundreds of hours talking," but eventually Susan's anger dissipated, overcoming her cynicism, which in turn "softened her and gentled her."

Living in a renewed marriage, life became unusually sweet. John and Susan believed they were "on the verge of a long and happy marriage," when tragedy struck again.

Susan was diagnosed with terminal cancer.

An eight-month battle ensued, and Dr. Barger was challenged to express his new love in very concrete ways. Caring for a seriously ill person is extremely difficult work, but John welcomed it as an opportunity "to show her how much I really loved her."

Even though Susan was given the best care, the cancer won out, and Susan died. She breathed her last breath surrounded by her family and dearest friends, and holding the hand of her beloved husband.

Dr. Barger looked back on their lives together with bittersweet feelings. The hurt was encased in their renewal — now that they had become best friends, now that he had learned the deeper meaning found in truly loving rather than in dominating, he had to say goodbye. But the sweetness was in remembering an unusual love, knowing that he had experienced something that most of us yearn for but don't find — true, soul-deep companionship.

In his contemplations, Dr. Barger discussed how this experience with his wife reflected on his relationship with God:

> Consider the virtues I have recommended as necessary to a deep relation with your wife: patience, listening, humility, service, and faithful, tender love. I hope it is not heretical for me to claim that in his dealings with us, God acts in many ways like a woman.
>
> Women are capable of and sometimes commit magnificent acts that manifest incredible power and awaken in us men a profound awe, if not fear and trembling. Yet when they love, they love quietly; they speak, as it were, in whispers, and we have to listen carefully, attentively, to hear their words of love and to know them.
>
> Isn't God also this way?
>
> Doesn't he intervene in most of our lives in whispers, which we miss if we fail to recollect ourselves and pay careful attention — if we do not constantly strive to hear those whispers of divine

love? The virtues necessary in truly loving a woman and having that love returned—the virtues of listening, patience, humility, service, and faithful love—are the very virtues necessary for us to love God and to feel his love returned. As we cannot lord it over women if we are to know them and grow intimate with them, so we cannot lord it over God if we are to know him and grow intimate with him.

We cannot successfully demand the love of a woman or the love of God. We have to wait. And just as a woman's heart is melted when she encounters in us weakness accompanied by our humble admission of it, so God's heart is melted and he is most tender and gracious to us when he encounters in us weakness accompanied by our humble admission of it.

While this story targets males, I suspect the same principle is true for women. That terrifyingly difficult man to love just may be your gateway to learning how to love God. This is a biblical truth. The beloved disciple John lays it out bluntly: "If anyone says, 'I love God,' yet hates his brother, he is a liar. For anyone who does not love his brother, whom he has seen, cannot love God, whom he has not seen. And he has given us this command: Whoever loves God must also love his brother" (1 John 4:20–21).

This man or this woman seems so different from you, I know. That's why it seems so difficult to love him or her. When you think on one level, she thinks on another. When you're certain this perspective matters most, he brings in another angle entirely. And you ask yourself, "How can I possibly love someone who is so different from me?"

And yet consider, if you can ask this question with integrity, try asking yourself this one: How could you possibly love God? He is spirit, and you are encased in flesh and bones. He is eternal, and you are trapped in time. He is all holy, perfect, sinless, and you—like me —are steeped in sin.

It is far less of a leap for a man to love a woman or for a woman to love a man than it is for either of us to love God.

But I think it's more than that. I think marriage is designed to call us out of ourselves and learn to love the "different." Put together in the closest situation imaginable—living side by side, sleeping in the same room, even, on occasion, sharing our bodies with each other—we are forced to respect and appreciate someone who is so radically different.

We need to be called out of ourselves because, in truth, we are incomplete. God made us to find our fulfillment in him—the Totally Other. Marriage shows us that we are not all there is; it calls us to give way to another, but also to find joy, happiness, and even ecstasy in another.

There are no lessons to be learned when a husband dominates his wife. There are no inspiring examples to emulate when a wife manipulates a husband. But love unlocks the spiritual secrets of the universe. Love blows open eternity and showers its raindrops on us.

Christianity involves believing certain things, to be sure, but its herald, its hallmark, its glory is not in merely ascribing to certain intellectual truths. The beauty of Christianity is in learning to love, and few life situations test that so radically as does a marriage.

Yes, it is difficult to love your spouse. But if you truly want to love God, look right now at the ring on your left hand, commit yourself to exploring anew what that ring represents, and love passionately, crazily, enduringly the fleshly person who put it there.

It just may be one of the most spiritual things you can do.

4

Holy Honor

Marriage Teaches Us to Respect Others

We are all in the gutter, but some of us are looking at the stars.
OSCAR WILDE

We must never be naïve enough to think of marriage as a safe harbor from the Fall....
The deepest struggles of life will occur in the most primary relationship affected by the Fall: marriage.
DAN ALLENDER AND TREMPER LONGMAN III

I WORK ALL DAY," BRIAN LAMENTED TO ME, "COME HOME, HELP FIX dinner, play with the kids, clean up the dishes, put the kids to bed, and bang! it's 9:30 and I'm dead-tired."

"What's your wife doing all this time?" I asked.

"She's on the Internet, spending all her time in one of those chat groups."

"Seriously?"

"Oh, yeah. She spends hours every day 'talking' to people on the computer. She 'talks' to them more than to me or the kids. It's disgusting."

Just a couple hours later, Brian was changing a diaper on his newborn when Cheryl began launching into how Brian was ruining their marriage by running up debt, never playing with the kids, failing to take spiritual leadership, and never helping around the house.

My wife was startled. She had known Brian since high school and had always thought of him as the type of father who would be very involved with his kids and rather frugal in financial matters.

It was stunning to hear two such wildly divergent accounts of the same marriage. Throughout the rest of the day, Brian and Cheryl were caustic in their comments; they had become adversaries, not allies, and a general pall pervaded the air around them.

"Yeah, Gary, *get him*," Cheryl said, as I played a hand of cards that put Brian's point total in jeopardy. This wasn't the good-natured ribbing of genuine affection; it was malicious glee at an enemy's fall.

As I reflected on this day, I remembered something I had once read. Francis de Sales, the seventeenth-century author of the classic, *An Introduction to a Devout Life*, wrote something in a letter that is simple, but powerful: "Have contempt for contempt."

Both Brian and Cheryl were so full of their contempt for each other that they spent all their time ruminating on each other's failures. Clearly one (and more likely, both) were either lying about the situation at home or had a seriously skewed perception of what was really going on in their marriage.

This chapter deals with the discipline of showing respect, particularly to your spouse. The sad truth is that comparatively few Christians think of giving respect as a command or a spiritual discipline. We are obsessed with *being* respected, but rarely consider our own obligation to respect others.

Scripture has much to say in this regard. We are commanded to respect our parents (Leviticus19:3); the elderly (Leviticus 19:32); God (Malachi 1:6); our spouse (Ephesians 5:33; 1 Peter 3:7); and, in fact, *everyone*: "Show proper respect to everyone," urges Peter, the devoted disciple of Jesus (1 Peter 2:17).

All of us have a visceral desire to be respected. When this desire isn't met, we are tempted to lapse into a self-defeating response. Rather than work to build our own life so that respect is granted to us, we work to tear down our spouse in a desperate attempt to convince ourselves that their lack of respect is meaningless. Spiritually, this becomes a vicious and debilitating cycle that is extremely difficult to break.

God has a solution that, if we adopt it, will revolutionize our relationships. While many people fight to *receive* respect, Christian marriage calls us to focus our efforts on *giving* respect. We are called to honor someone even when we know only too well their deepest character flaws. We are called to stretch ourselves, to find out *how* we can learn to respect this person with whom we've become so familiar. And in this exploration, we are urged to "have contempt for contempt."

The Explored River

I have some vivid memories of the first week of our marriage. One such memory is that of looking through our medicine cabinet and picking up this metal thing that looked like scissors with an attached jaw. "What in the world is this?" I asked.

"That's to curl my eyelashes," my wife answered—a practice you don't see as much anymore, but it was fairly common in the early eighties.

"You really do that?" I asked.

"Of course I do," she said.

I was stunned. Nobody had ever told me this. It had never occurred to me that straight eyelashes were a sign of lax hygiene.

"So what do you women say when you walk through the mall," I asked, " 'Oh, look at that woman; she forgot to curl her eyelashes —and she's out in public'?"

"Don't be silly," my wife said, yanking the eyelash curler from my hand.

Young marriage can be full of such revelations. You think that everybody keeps the garbage under the left side of the kitchen sink —until you find out that your wife's family kept it on the porch.

"But it doesn't go there!" you protest.

"Why *not?*" your new wife asks.

"Because my mom never put it there!"

It took me years to accept the fact that Lisa likes to keep certain medicines in the spice cabinet. If you ask me, there is something inherently wrong with storing Pepto-Bismol next to the vanilla flavoring and the salt. But that's how her family did it.

After time, however, these interesting little mysteries become all too familiar—and that's when contempt can begin to seep in.

Mark Twain tells the sobering tale about deeply exploring the Mississippi River he loved so very much. After virtually memorizing the river's bends, twists, and turns, and navigating its waters with rapt admiration, he was chagrined to wake up one day and find that the river had lost much of its poetry. The mystery of that mighty waterway had been replaced with a boring predictability. He had literally loved his love out of that river.

Every marriage goes through this stage. An enrapturing love quiets down to a predictable routine. The mystery is replaced with an almost comical familiarity—the wife knows exactly how the husband will sit on the couch, the husband knows exactly how his wife will answer the phone.

The wife of a couple we know decided to get her husband some golf clubs for his birthday. She went to a store and told the owner, "Here's the money for a set of clubs. My husband and I will come in here tomorrow night. He'll look over these clubs, then walk over to talk to me about it, then go back to the clubs and touch the ones he decides are the best option. At that point, I want you to walk up to him and say, 'Your wife already paid for these yesterday. Happy Birthday.'"

The clerk was surprised and a little suspicious, but he agreed to the plan.

The next day, our friend took her husband to a restaurant next door to the golf shop. After dinner, the husband (as predicted) pointed to the shop and said, "You mind if we just stop in there?"

"Not at all," the wife said.

The husband walked through the shop and settled on two sets of clubs. He then walked back to his wife and conferred with her about them, then returned to the clubs and touched the set he thought would be best. The owner came up and went through his spiel.

When love becomes this familiar, is it possible to "love our love" out of a person?

It's said that the great nineteenth-century poets, Robert Browning and Elizabeth Barrett Browning (who penned the often-quoted — and much-parodied — "How do I love thee? Let me count the ways . . ."), never actually saw each other entirely naked. Their sustained passion is legendary — was it because of this physical mystery that their passion was so long and so intensely maintained?

As our partners and their weaknesses become more familiar to us, respect often becomes harder to give. But this failure to show respect is a sign of spiritual immaturity more than an inevitable pathway of marriage. Consider Paul as he wrote to the Corinthians. Even though he was addressing a church full of quarrelers (1 Corinthians 1:11), unlearned and simple people (1:26), "worldly" infants (3:1 – 3), arrogant egocentrics (4:18), a man sleeping with his father's wife (5:1), greedy men suing fellow believers (6:1), and childish thinkers (14:20), he still honors them by saying, "I always thank God for you . . ." (1:4). He knew them well enough to be familiar with all their faults, yet he continued to be thankful for them. Why? The key is found in the second half of verse 4: "I always thank God for you *because of his grace given to you in Christ Jesus*" (italics added).

As C.J. Mahaney so eloquently explains it, we can be thankful for our fellow sinners when we spend more time looking for "evidences of grace" than we do finding fault. If my wife is more aware of where she falls short in my eyes than she is of how I am witnessing evidences of God's grace in her journey of progressive sanctification, then I am a legalistic husband, akin to a Pharisee. Giving respect is an obligation, not a favor; it is an act of maturity, birthed in a profound understanding of God's good grace.

Challenging Our Prejudices

I walked in the door one night and Lisa immediately handed me the phone. "Gail is freaking out," she said, "and James needs to talk to you."

I took the phone and found that Gail and James were, indeed, going through a difficult time.

"Gail says that I'm repressing her," James said, somewhat sarcastically. "She thinks I don't respect her and that I belittle her."

"Really?" I said.

"Yeah. And now she wants me to go see her counselor, but I don't feel right about that."

"Why not?" I asked.

"Well, Gail's counselor is a woman, and I'm just not sure that, well, you know, that I would trust her."

"Let me get this straight," I replied. "Gail doesn't think you respect her as a woman. You don't think that's true, but you don't want to go to this counselor because she's a woman and you're not sure you trust her?"

There was a long silence.

I knew this challenge would come up eventually. The first time I saw Gail, I knew why James had chosen her. James was raised a "man's man," and he was looking for a "man's woman." We talked, in fact, about the women he had dated. I didn't see any women who could have challenged him, who would push him, threaten him, or compete with him in any way. I saw women who had probably been browbeaten by their fathers and so were perfectly content to go along with a husband who wanted a pretty, thin, and preferably blond wife attached to his right arm who knew how to smile, talk, laugh, make love, and take care of babies.

Gail wanted a real relationship. She had outgrown being just an adornment, and James was facing a crisis. It wasn't, however, a crisis —as James initially thought—of Gail "freaking out." It was a crisis of James being forced to confront his prejudicial attitudes toward women in general and toward Gail in particular.

Jesus purposely confronted similar attitudes that lay hidden within the disciples. He blatantly broke with rabbinical tradition to speak with the woman at the well (see John 4). Not only was it unheard of for a rabbi to be alone with a woman, but to discuss theology was virtually unthinkable. One rabbi, when it was suggested to him that women be taught the Law for particular circumstances, replied, "If any man gives his daughter a knowledge of the Law it is as though he taught her lechery."[1]

That's why, when referring to the disciples' reaction upon finding Jesus talking to the woman at the well (John 4:27), the word "surprised," or "marveled," is used to translate the Greek word *thaumazo,* which carries the sense of incredulity: "How could this be happening?" "Am I really seeing what I think I'm seeing?"

No doubt, much of the disciples' wonderment arose from their exposure to their blatantly anti-woman culture. Women in Palestine at the time of Jesus were subject to numerous rejections. They weren't counted among those who would make up the minimum number of ten required for a service to take place in a synagogue; their witness had no validity in law courts; they weren't considered fit for education (the Talmud says, "The words of the Torah will be destroyed in the fire sooner than be taught to women"); and they were often segregated from the rest of society and shut up in their houses. The disparagement of women is seen in a boldly derogatory prayer often uttered by ancient Jewish men: "Praised be God that he has not created me a Gentile; praised be God that he has not created me a woman; praised be God that he has not created me an ignorant person."

In bold moves and with courageous words, Jesus challenged and confronted these attitudes about women, lifting women up and including them in his inner circle of confidantes and supporters (see Luke 8:1 – 3). He valued women, and he wanted them to be around him — yet there was never even a whisper or hint of scandal, because Jesus acted with genuine love and purity.

It wasn't until my friend James was married that he was able to confront the misogynistic views he held about women. He had to hear his own wife say, "You don't respect me because I'm a woman," and he had to be snared by his own words, "She's a woman, and I'm just not sure that I trust her," before he could see his sinful attitude.

The Difference

Many of the marital problems we face are not problems between individual couples—Jim and Susan, Mark and Diane, or Rob and Jill. They are the problems between men, generally, and women, generally. They are problems that arise because we are either too lazy or too selfish to get to know our spouse well enough to understand how different from us they really are.

I had to learn this the hard way. I'll spare you all the gory details, but getting to Raleigh, North Carolina, from Bellingham, Washington, this particular time involved five hours of driving, four airports, three rental car reservations, two very tired travelers, and one absolutely crazy taxi driver who acted just like a character out of a Seinfeld episode.

I was traveling with my oldest daughter, who was ten years old at the time, planning to drop her off at a friend's house in northern Virginia while I traveled south to Raleigh. Due to a canceled flight, I dropped Allison off after 11:00 P.M., then drove until about 1:00 A.M., when weariness forced me to stop.

I got up rather early the next morning and completed the drive into Raleigh, where I was scheduled to address a rather large crowd that evening. Before the meeting, I had to complete a phone interview, send some galleys to a publisher by overnight mail, and return a couple phone calls—all this while trying to squeeze in some time to go over my speech.

Just an hour or so before I had to be in the hotel ballroom, I checked in with my wife. After just a few sentences, she was in tears, something about a computer program not working right, and would we have to spend money to buy a new computer? I was doing my best to get spiritually prepped for the talk; following such an exhausting trip, I felt I needed some focused time to be prepared, and I resented Lisa's tears, particularly at that very moment. I remember thinking, "Can't she just be a little stronger when I'm on the road? I don't need this."

I tried to pray through my frustration, but I remained rather agitated. "Great!" I thought. "What a disposition to have just before I face all those people!" I tried not to blame my wife for making me like this, but I was having less than one hundred percent success.

"A guy who travels just needs someone who's stronger at home," I kept saying to myself, then repented, then found myself repeating the statement with even more vigor.

Two weeks later I read a remarkable personal-experience piece in *The Washington Post Magazine*. Liza Mundy wrote about participating in an editorial meeting, and then being horrified when she found herself starting to cry. She was hot, bothered, and tired — nothing extraordinary, but it all combined to make her want to cry. She writes, "Suddenly the heat had moved to my face and tears were springing to my eyes and I was blinking and blinking, hoping to drive them back. Only of course that was futile, because, as a friend later put it so beautifully, at this point in a crying-in-the-office experience, 'You're no longer crying because of what they're saying. You're crying because you're crying.' "

Then, a paragraph or so later, Mundy wrote something that astonished me. " 'Pay no attention to these tears; they are meaningless. I'm thinking quite clearly; this conversation isn't upsetting me nearly as much as it seems. I'm just fatigued and a little bit stressed and feeling hot!' was what I wanted to say. Because I knew, like most women perhaps, that sometimes tears are no more significant than sweating."

As a man, I equate tears with weakness, with near devastation. For me to cry in an office would require a major tragedy to precipitate it. And that's when I understood that perhaps tears mean something entirely different for me than they do for Lisa. I see tears and think she's falling apart. She experiences tears and thinks she's merely sweating.

If for some reason Lisa and I split up and I married someone else I thought was "stronger" emotionally, I might very well find myself in the same situation. Something that bothered me about Lisa may actually be true about most women. It was a man-woman thing, not a Gary-Lisa thing.

Months later I watched as Lisa fought back tears on a Good Friday. Our youngest daughter, Kelsey, had put a shirt in the laundry with glitter on it, so it hadn't come clean and she wouldn't be able to wear it to church, as planned. Lisa's eyes grew wide — I've seen this so many times in fourteen years — and she started blinking so she wouldn't cry.

I'm standing in the doorway. *What a thing to cry about,* I thought. *Glitter on a shirt? Big deal!*

And then I applied the discipline of respect: "Gary, stop it! Tears mean something different to her. Don't judge your wife."

I kept my mouth shut, her tears quickly subsided, and we went to church without a big fuss.

Notice the process here: I had to learn to better understand Lisa before I could truly respect her, and I had to respect her before I could fully love her. This is a tremendously spiritually therapeutic process, an emptying of my self so I can grow more in my love for others.

Charles Williams refers to "a mutual invasion, breaking down both selves, so that both can be transformed by the love both receive."[2] I needed to be "broken down" so that I could be transformed.

An attitude of judgment doesn't break me; it puffs me up. It fills me with arrogance. When I learn to give respect, I become transformed in the process.

Spiritual Equality

As moral entities, men and women are equal before God. This truth doesn't mean that they are synonymous, or that their roles will be or should be the same. But it does mean, as Scripture teaches, that *both* male and female are made in the image of God. This is the teaching of Genesis 1:27, and it is a teaching also affirmed by Paul in the New Testament when he wrote to the Galatians that there is "neither … male nor female" in Christ Jesus (Galatians 3:28).

The fact that my wife is made in the image of God calls me to a far more noble response than simply refraining from being condescending to her. Certainly, it is wildly inappropriate for me to look down on Lisa because she's a woman, but not acting with disdain toward her is a far cry from what her creation in the image of God really calls me to do, namely, to honor her.

My family once went through the National Gallery of Art, looking at some original Rembrandts, and one of my very tactile children reached out to touch the painting. My wife let loose with a harsh whisper and grabbed our child's hand before it could even reach the canvas. "This is a *Rembrandt!*" she hissed under the guard's glare. "You *can't* touch these!"

My wife was created by God himself! How dare I dishonor her? In fact, shouldn't it even give me pause before I reach out to touch her? She is the Creator's daughter, after all!

The difficulty with honoring our spouse is that it calls us to adopt attitudes and actions that go far beyond merely saying that we won't dishonor him or her. As Betsy and Gary Ricucci point out, "Honor isn't passive, it's active. We honor our wives by demonstrating our esteem and respect: complimenting them in public; affirming their gifts, abilities, and accomplishments; and declaring our appreciation for all they do. Honor not expressed is not honor."[3]

The biggest challenge for me in upholding my spiritual obligation to honor my wife is that I get busy and sidetracked. I don't mean to dishonor her; I just absentmindedly neglect to actively honor her.

The Maryland pastor I cited earlier, C.J. Mahaney, has learned to honor his wife almost instinctually. His sister tells of a time when C.J. and his wife were holding their first baby. Many parents are familiar with the "idolatry of the firstborn," but C.J. demonstrated his maturity when someone came up to him and said, "I bet she's the apple of your eye." C.J. immediately pointed to his wife and said, "No—*she* is the apple of my eye."[4]

The reason that giving respect to my wife is a spiritual discipline as much as it is a marital one is simple: I've found that the more I honor my wife in particular, the more I honor other women in general. The reverse is true as well. The glib statement "Oh, that's just women for you" betrays a serious spiritual disease. "*Just* women" are made in the image of God. Such a comment comes dangerously close to maligning the Creator who made women *just the way they are.*

Giving respect to others brings light and life into our lives. It leads us in the end to respect the God who created all of us and shapes us as he sees fit. It is an essential discipline, and marriage provides daily opportunities for us to grow in this area.

Let's look at some practical ways in which we can begin to build contempt for contempt in our relationships.

Building Contempt for Contempt

Adopt a Holy Double Standard

Sadly I spent the first few years of my marriage adding up the pluses and minuses of my and my wife's various personality traits. The problem was simple: I was spending too much time on my pluses and her minuses. Then I read a passage written by John Owen, one of the greatest Puritan scholars ever: "The person who understands the evil in his own heart is the only person who is useful, fruitful, and solid in his beliefs and obedience. Others only delude themselves and thus upset families, churches, and all other relationships. In their self-pride and judgment of others, they show great inconsistency."[5]

I realized that I was being deluded by my sense of self-righteousness. Instead of focusing on what Lisa could improve, I should have been on my knees, begging God to change *me.* This thought was magnified one morning when I awoke and started praying through Scripture. All of a sudden, a question startled me: "Does Lisa feel like she's married to Jesus?"

I almost laughed out loud, until I was shaken by another thought. I am told over and over in Scripture that my duty as a Christian is to become more and more like Jesus Christ. Over time, my wife *should* start to feel like there's at least a family resemblance. I realized how pitifully short I had fallen in my task of improving myself for my wife's sake.

"But wait!" the selfish me wanted to cry out. "What about *her?*" I began thinking about how my wife could improve and how that would undoubtedly help our marriage immeasurably, but then I remembered a passage written by William Law, the great eighteenth-century Anglican writer:

> No one is of the Spirit of Christ but he that has the utmost compassion for sinners. Nor is there any greater sign of your own perfection than you find yourself all love and compassion toward them that are very weak and defective. And on the other hand, you have never less reason to be pleased with yourself than when you find yourself most angry and offended at the behavior of others. All sin is certainly to be hated and abhorred where it is, but then we must set ourselves against sin as we do against sickness and diseases, by showing ourselves tender and compassionate to the sick and diseased.[6]

These were hard words to take in. Essentially, Law is telling me that when my respect slips into contempt, it's because *I'm* weak, not because my wife is failing. If I were really mature, I would have the same compassion for her weaknesses as Christ does. Respect is a spiritual discipline, an obligation that I owe my wife.

Fortunately, a change in my life helped me see things from a different perspective.

Gain a New Understanding

My wife and I entered a new journey in our marriage when I became self-employed. To save on overhead, we decided that I would work out of our home. The only problem was that, at the time, we lived in a town house.

With three children.

In other words, I'd really be working out of our *bedroom*.

When other married couples found out what we were doing, they were frequently amazed. "And you still *like* each other?" they'd ask.

In fact, working at home did wonders for our marriage. For the first time, I could see for myself what it was like to spend an entire day being Lisa. Oh, I used to see that every weekend, but what makes her life difficult isn't an occasional forty-eight-hour stretch — it's the cumulative, never-ending, day-in-and-day-out responsibility of raising and teaching kids in a homeschool environment, while also cleaning the house, planning meals, and preparing for her own Bible study. And then, when your husband comes home, you're supposed to have enough energy left over to act like a wife.

On the other hand, my wife saw what it was like for me to sit in front of a computer all day long. Some days I was tired. Other days I was sick. Sometimes the weather outside was beautiful, but always I stayed in my chair and worked. I made the phone calls I didn't want to make but that I needed to make. She saw my determination and discipline. And she had a front-row seat from which to witness the pressure of meeting deadlines or of accepting assignments I knew would be tough but for which there was no doubt we needed the money they would generate.

Over time, we developed a profound appreciation for what the other person was doing. Both of us now understand in a much clearer way the challenges facing each of us and why it can sometimes be so hard to act like the perfect husband or wife. We're not married in a carefree Garden of Eden. We're married in the midst of many responsibilities that compete for our energy. This new understanding has ushered in a stronger empathy for each other in our weaknesses and peculiarities.

You don't have to work out of your own home to experience this empathy. Instead of focusing your energy on resentment over how sparsely your spouse understands you, expend your efforts to understand him or her. As a spiritual exercise, find out what your spouse's day is really like. Ask her. Ask him. Draw them out—what is the most difficult part of your day? When do you feel like just giving up? Are parts of your day monotonous? Is there something you constantly fear? Take time to do an inventory of your spouse's difficulties rather than of your spouse's shortcomings.

Cultivate Gratitude

Thanksgiving is a privilege—it creates a positive focus in my life—but it is also an obligation: "Give thanks to the LORD, for he is good" (Psalm 136:1). "Give thanks in all circumstances" (1 Thessalonians 5:18). Remember how Paul gave thanks for the Corinthians (see 1 Corinthians 1:4).

When I am thankful for my spouse, the control that the familiarity of contempt has on me is broken. I look for new things to be thankful for. I try not to take the routine things she does for granted. I never eat at somebody's house without thanking them for providing a meal; why should I not give my wife the same thanks I'd give someone else?

There are few things that lift my spirits more than simply hearing my wife or children say, "Thanks for working so hard to provide for us." Those nine words can lift a hundred pounds of pressure off my back.

Contempt is conceived with expectations. Respect is conceived with expressions of gratitude. We can choose which one we will obsess over—expectations, or thanksgivings. That choice will result in a birth—and the child will be named either contempt, or respect.

Remember the Effects of the Fall

We need to understand how profoundly broken this world is. Sin has radically scarred our existence. As a result of the Fall, I will labor with difficulty and angst (Genesis 3:17–19). Lisa will mother our children and enter relationships with mixed motives and frustrated aims (Genesis 3:16).

Even an unusually good marriage is unable to completely erase the effects of sin's curse on individuals and on society. Dan Allender and Tremper Longman write, "We must never be naïve enough to think of marriage as a safe harbor from the Fall....The deepest struggles of life will occur in the most primary relationship affected by the Fall: marriage."[7]

The problem is that even though we can't go back to the idyllic existence prior to the Fall, we were created with an understanding of what the pre-Fall days were like — in other words, we know what relationships *should be* like, but we are incapable of making them perfectly in tune with that ideal: "Our souls are wired for what we will never enjoy until Eden is restored in the new heaven and earth. We are built with a distant memory of Eden."[8]

This calls me to extend gentleness and tolerance toward my wife. I want her to become all that Jesus calls her to become, and I hope with all my heart that I will be a positive factor in her pursuit of that aim (and vice versa). But she will never fully get there this side of heaven, so I must love and accept her in the reality of our lives in a sin-stained world.

Accepting the fallenness of this world — with its bitter disappointments, physical limitations, and myriad demands — helps me to understand how difficult life is for Lisa, which helps me in turn to have contempt for contempt.

In the days when I still worked outside the home, I remember occasions when Lisa and I would preplan a romantic evening. Flush with morning's zest, we'd plan a "hot" night. Romance would fly. For a few brief moments, we would make the earth melt away and enjoy the blessed fruits of conjugal intimacy.

Then I'd go to work, throughout the day occasionally thinking about what marital pleasures awaited me in just a few hours. When I came home, however, I not infrequently was met at the door by a wife who wanted nothing more than a solitary bath and an early start on a good night's sleep.

"But if you still want to, you know, I can go along with it," she might say.

"That's not fair!" I used to think. "I don't want just a willing wife. I want an eager one!"

But now I see the process — the kitchen floor that has enough cereal on it to feed a family of mice for three winters; the pressure of getting the homeschooling lessons done, while lunches need to be made and clothes need to be washed and ballet and soccer practice need to be accounted for; and ...

And I realized it was nothing personal, but sometimes wives just get tired. That's just the way it works in a fallen world. Lisa didn't want to get tired. But she's made of flesh and blood — and what else could I expect?

In many of my seminars, I stress this over and over again: Husbands, you are married to a fallen woman in a broken world. Wives, you are married to a sinful man in a sinful world. It is guaranteed that your spouse will sin against you, disappoint you, and have physical limitations that will frustrate and sadden you. He may come home with the best of intentions and still lose his temper. She may have all of the desire but none of the energy.

This is a fallen world. Let me repeat this: You will never find a spouse who is not affected in some way by the reality of the Fall. If you can't respect *this* spouse because she is prone to certain weaknesses, you will never be able to respect *any* spouse.

Looking Out for Each Other

Several years ago, returning from a trip, I stepped inside the front door and felt like I had walked every one of the four hundred miles I had just driven. I had spoken six times in four days, and had driven through four different states to get where I needed to go. I pulled into the driveway thinking, "I'm so tired. All I really want to do is watch a football game." And as I walked into the door, Lisa was thinking, "Good, he's finally home! I've had the kids to myself all weekend and they're driving me crazy."

This is the stuff that five-star marriage fights are made of. These are the situations that feel like they are specifically cooked up in hell.

And then, to my astonishment, I discovered that Lisa and I had matured. I tried to play with the kids as best I could. I had brought them some flavored popcorn, and we talked at the kitchen table as they ate—yet I noticed Lisa was being incredibly sensitive to how tired I must be.

"You've got to be exhausted," she said. "Let me take care of the kids tonight."

But hearing her say that made me *want* to take care of the kids. I realized that even though she had a valid reason to pass the nighttime duties on to me, she was being hard on herself and easy on me; and that made *me* want to be hard on myself and easy on *her*.

We don't always act this way, by any means, but it's wonderful when we do. I think we're led to this approach by the apostle Paul, who confessed that he was "the worst of sinners" (1 Timothy 1:16). I don't think there's a better recipe in all the Bible to help us become better spouses. If we assume that our spouse has the hardest road to travel and that we miss the mark most frequently—and then act accordingly—we'll find a mix that's just about right.

Contempt is born when we fixate on our spouse's weaknesses. Every spouse has these sore points. If you want to find them, without a doubt you will. If you want to obsess about them, they'll grow—but *you* won't!

Jesus provides a remedy that is stunning in its simplicity yet foreboding in its difficulty. He tells us to take the plank out of our own eye before we try to remove the speck from our neighbor's eye (see Matthew 7:3–5).

If you're thinking "but my spouse is the one who has the plank," allow me to let you in on a secret: *You're exactly the type of person Jesus is talking to.* You're the one he wanted to challenge with these words.

Jesus isn't helping us resolve legal matters here; he's urging us to adopt humble spirits. He wants us to cast off the contempt—to have contempt for the contempt—and learn the spiritual secret of respect.

Consider the type of people Jesus loved in the days he walked on earth—Judas (the betrayer); the woman at the well (a sexual libertine); Zacchaeus (the conniving financial cheat); and many others like them. In spite of the fact that Jesus was without sin and these people were very much steeped in sin, Jesus still honored them. He washed Judas's feet; he spent time talking respectfully to the woman at the well; he went to Zacchaeus's house for dinner. Jesus, the only perfect human being to live on this earth, moved toward sinful people; he asks us to do the same, beginning with the one closest to us—our spouse.

Build contempt for contempt. Give honor to those who deserve it —beginning with your spouse.

5

The Soul's Embrace
Good Marriage Can Foster Good Prayer

A magnificent marriage begins not with knowing
one another but with knowing God.
GARY AND BETSY RICUCCI

JUST A FEW MONTHS AFTER WE WERE MARRIED, AS A FAVOR TO SOME friends, Lisa and I agreed to swap beds with another couple.

They had a waterbed and wanted to move into an upper apartment where waterbeds weren't allowed. Because we lived in a basement apartment, the weight of the waterbed didn't matter, and Lisa and I decided to give our friends a break.

It was an act of charity we soon lived to regret.

Most difficult for me was the fact that throughout all my years of singleness, I enjoyed sleeping alone. Somewhat to my dismay, I learned that Lisa is a "cuddler." It took me months to learn how to sleep with someone touching me.

With the waterbed, it got even worse. When one of us moved, it was like trying to sleep on top of a tsunami. I hated it. To make matters more complicated, Lisa has a tendency to drift toward my side of the bed, pushing me over further and further. One night I awoke with my cheek mashed against the wooden frame of the bed.

"This is ridiculous," I thought, so I got out of bed and went over to the other side, slipping in next to Lisa so that I'd have three-fourths of the bed free. You can guess what happened. I awoke early the next morning with my face smashed against the *other* side.

"This bed has *got* to go," I insisted.

Just as difficult for me as learning to sleep as a married man was learning to pray as a married man. Overnight everything had changed. My usual rituals and spiritual habits just didn't seem to "fit" my life anymore. I had to find new ones.

The Importance of Marriage to Prayer

I took my prayer life seriously, with good reason. The words of Jesus and his disciples, not to mention two thousand years of Christian tradition, bear witness to the same reality—prayer is essential to the Christian life. There is no faith without prayer. To be a strong Christian, we must be strong pray-ers. There is no other way.

Paul urges us to pray *continually* (1 Thessalonians 5:17). This puts prayer on a far higher plane than mere intercession. It marks prayer as the heart of our devotion, the constant awareness of God's presence, our consistent submission to his will, and our frequent expressions of adoration and praise.

John Henry Newman, a nineteenth-century English scholar and churchman, wrote, "Prayer is to the spiritual life what the beating of the pulse and the drawing of the breath are to the life of the body."[1] Martin Luther insisted, "As it is the business of tailors to make clothes and of cobblers to mend shoes, so it is the business of Christians to pray."

J. C. Ryle observed, "Prayer is the very life-breath of true Christianity." A modern writer, Terry Glaspey, sums it up well when he writes, "Prayer is a work to which we must commit ourselves if we are to make sense of our lives in the light of eternity."

I like that last phrase—prayer is how we make sense of our lives in the light of eternity. Prayer helps us to regain the proper priorities, discern biblical wisdom, and make right judgments. Without prayer, Glaspey might say, we live as temporal people with temporal values. Prayer pushes eternity back into our lives, making God ever more relevant to the way we live our lives.

The Christian who fails to pray will fail to grow as she should and will be trapped in a perpetual spiritual adolescence. J. C. Ryle again:

> What is the reason that some believers are so much brighter and holier than others? I believe the difference, in nineteen cases out of twenty, arises from different habits about private prayer. I believe that those who are not eminently holy pray *little,* and those who are eminently holy pray *much.*

When you understand the centrality of prayer in Christian spirituality, few verses are more astounding than 1 Peter 3:7: "Husbands, in the same way be considerate as you live with your wives, and treat them with respect as the weaker partner and as heirs with you of the gracious gift of life, so that nothing will hinder your prayers."

When Peter says that men must be considerate of their wives and treat them with respect *so that nothing will hinder their prayers,* he's directly connecting our attitude toward our wives with *the* fundamental Christian discipline.

If prayer is the essence of spirituality, and if a wrong attitude in marriage destroys that activity, it behooves men in particular to pay careful attention here.

I soon discovered that I was not alone in finding it more difficult to pray as a married man. Martin Luther confessed to the same dilemma. And verse 7 of 1 Peter 3 explains why. The rules changed when I got married. A condition was placed on my prayer life, and that condition is tied directly to how I view and treat my wife.

I will never again be able to approach prayer "as if" I were a single man. God sees me, in one sense, through my wife. This means that if I want to grow as a married pray-er, I can't make believe that I'm a celibate monk. I can't simply parrot the practices of medieval scholars who addressed single men and women in their pursuit of God.

In fact, much Christian teaching has gotten it exactly backwards. We're told that if we want to have a stronger marriage, we should improve our prayer lives. But Peter tells us that *we should improve our marriages so that we can improve our prayer lives.* Instead of prayer being the "tool" that will refine my marriage, Peter tells me that marriage is the tool that will refine my prayers!

A man might be able to preach a sterling sermon, write inspiring books, and quote the Bible front to back. But if he hasn't learned how to be a servant to his wife, to respect her, and to be considerate of her, then his spirituality is still infantile. His prayer life — the lifeblood of his soul — will be a sham.

Empty Accomplishments

The evangelical world tends to value "accomplishers," people who get things done. The danger of this is that spouses often pay the biggest price for some of these accomplishments, and "true" spirituality can easily suffer as a result.

Bill McCartney became famous almost overnight in Christian circles during the early nineties. He was a highly successful college football coach *and* he was running the hottest ministry of the decade, namely, Promise Keepers. Yet during this time, his wife was lonely and hurting. She relates that she was in "an emotional deep-freeze," her depression becoming so great that she lost eighty pounds.[2] McCartney was too preoccupied with his football team and — ironically enough — with the Promise Keepers' ministry to take notice.

As McCartney's star rose, his wife Lyndi said something truly gripping. "I just felt like I was getting smaller and smaller and smaller." In his book, *Sold Out,* McCartney reflects, "It may sound unbelievable, but while Promise Keepers was spiritually inspiring to my core, my hard-charging approach to the ministry was distracting me from being, in the truest sense, a promise keeper to my own family."

To McCartney's credit, once he realized what was happening, he took the drastic step of retiring from coaching football — an incredible sacrifice that his wife took to heart — and the McCartneys were able to put their marriage back together.

Making someone else feel smaller so that we can feel larger is antithetical to the Christian faith, a complete rejection of the Christian virtues of humility, sacrifice, and service. So often Jesus left the crowd to minister to the individual, while we rationalize leaving the individual—particularly our spouse—to curry favor with the crowd.

Godliness is *selflessness,* and when a man and woman marry, they are pledging to stop viewing themselves as individuals and start viewing themselves as a unit, as a couple. In marriage, I am no longer free to pursue whatever I want; I am no longer a single man. I am part of a team, and my ambitions, dreams, and energies need to take that into account.

This reining in of my ambition is so very valuable spiritually. The truth is, God's kingdom can move forward without a single one of us. Our perceptions of indispensability are usually based more on our arrogance than on our desire to be faithful. Faithful participation in God's kingdom invites and encourages others as we serve; it doesn't diminish them. Biblical truth finds its basis in community and in serving the community—and this community starts with the marital relationship. If a man or woman is unrelentingly ambitious, willing to ignore or to sacrifice a spouse as they pursue their own agenda, they will almost undoubtedly be unrelentingly ambitious toward others as well, bringing them on board to serve *their* purposes, not to engage them in mutual kingdom service.

If, for instance, a man views his wife solely as someone to cook for him, provide him with sexual satisfaction, and keep a quiet home while he alone serves God, he will also browbeat others to "fall in line" regardless of whether that specific role is suited for them. If a woman essentially abandons her family to ambitiously "serve" God, she will likely display the same lack of compassion and empathy for others as she does for her own family who feel her absence keenly. I've seen these personalities. Whether in men or women, there develops an underlying ruthlessness, a demanding spirit, and a stark self-absorption that permeates every task and relationship as the person seeks to manipulate others into joining their own orbit rather than seeking to launch people into God's. There is a veneer of religiosity, but a polluted, foul-smelling spirit reveals itself as soon as you get underneath the surface.

We have valued the wrong activities when we look only at a person's outward accomplishments. *Our relationships—especially our marriages—are an integral part of our ministry.* If we truly want to provide a genuine witness to the world and serve God's kingdom with integrity, we would do well to take Ron Sider's words to heart: "Think of the impact if the first thing radical feminists thought of when the conversation turned to evangelical men was that they had the best reputation for keeping their marriage vows and serving their wives in the costly fashion of Jesus at the cross."[3]

I was terrified when I first realized what 1 Peter 3:7 was saying. Now that I was married, my prayer life would have to pass a different test. Iron-will discipline was no longer enough. If I wanted to enjoy unimpeded prayers, I'd have to be considerate of Lisa. I'd have to respect her, cherish her, and honor her.

As I've grown older, I've learned to treasure a genuine spiritual authenticity that is marked in large part by a person's *relationships* more than by his or her so-called "accomplishments." There's a pastor at my church, Jim Murphy, who used to be a plumber before he was asked to join the pastoral staff. Though he has taken courses on occasion at a seminary, he doesn't have an advanced degree. He's a thoughtful man with a passionate heart for missions. For over a decade, he has faithfully filled his position as an associate pastor. Because there are other pastors in administrative positions, Jim isn't even "number two" in the hierarchy of what is a relatively large church (about 1,500 members). In short, he wouldn't make anyone's almanac of "distinguished national Christian leaders."

But he may be one of the most godly men I know. I was particularly moved when I heard Jim's wife say, "Jim is a saint. He really is." Jim wasn't present when Peggy said this. And though Peggy may not even remember saying it, with these seven words she preached one of the most challenging sermons I've ever heard. I'm still trying to live up to Jim's example. Would my wife say, "Gary is a saint. He really is"? Could she?

I don't think so.[4]

So, men, ask yourself a question: "Do I respect my wife?" If prayer has been a problem area for you, this could be the first place to look for some answers to why you've been having difficulties. And then follow this thought with another question you can ask your wife: "Am I considerate of you?" Allow her, even encourage her, to be honest. Let her tell you what it feels like when her son hears you say, "That's just like a woman for you!" and then notices a sharper tone in her son's voice the next time he speaks to her. Allow her to open up about how she feels during her monthly cycle when she wants to slow down a little, maybe sleep a little more, and be pampered, but the man she is married to is concerned only with whether dinner will be served on time. If you want to be really bold, ask her how considerate you are when you're making love.

If you want to grow toward God, you must build a stronger prayer life. If you're married, to attain a stronger prayer life you must learn to respect your spouse and be considerate.

Sex and Prayer

There is yet another biblical passage in which marriage and prayer are linked. This one deals specifically with sex. Speaking to husbands and wives, Paul challenges, or at least questions, the ascetic practice of abstaining from sexual relations within marriage. (Where you place the commas and emphasis in this sentence is crucial for a right exegesis—I'm following the interpretation offered in the commentary on 1 Corinthians written by Dr. Gordon Fee.)[5] Paul sees this abstention as dangerous, and he very practically suggests, "Do not deprive each other, unless perhaps by mutual consent and for a time, so that you may devote yourselves to prayer" (1 Corinthians 7:5).

In the past this verse was often understood as implying that *sex* can distract us from prayer. Another possible reading is that *abstinence within marriage* can distract us from prayer. How so?

A married man or woman facing keen sexual frustration might find it difficult to pray simply because his or her thoughts are failing to focus on the eternal. In a healthy individual, sexual desire can be satiated; sleeping with your spouse can leave your heart, mind, and soul free, for a time, to vigorously pursue God in prayer without distraction. In essence, Paul is suggesting, "Use marriage the way God intended it. Meet your sexual needs by making love to your spouse. Then your mind and soul will be more open to prayer."

Paul is a practical pastor. He recognizes that the sex drive is a biological reality. By engaging in sexual relations within a permanent, lifelong relationship, a major temptation and distraction is removed, and our souls are placed at rest. This is especially important for contemplative prayer, a type of prayer in which the mind must be unusually free of distractions.

While it might sound bizarre, Paul is telling Christian husbands and wives that they can serve their partner and at the same time create the climate for an enriching prayer life by serving each other sexually. Our evangelical culture in particular might have difficulty embracing this explanation. I've certainly never read a book on prayer that included the step, "If you're married, have sex on a regular basis," but it seems clear that this is what Paul intends here!

What this means to me is that God views my life as a seamless garment. I'm not divided into "holy Gary" and "secular Gary." There's no "Gary the husband" versus "Gary the Christian." It's not a compromise for me to desire to grow in prayer *and* to express my sexuality.

God made me—and he made you—a complete human being. I can give myself unabashedly and enthusiastically to my wife and still give myself unreservedly to God. I can express sexual desires in a marital context, and I can still be passionate about prayer. The two go together. Even stronger than that, the two *complement* each other.

Not only are my sexual desires and my spiritual needs not competitive, they are mutually supportive.

Prayer and Dissension

I've discovered that there is another aspect of marriage that greatly affects my prayer life, one that can at times be extremely irritating: unresolved disputes. While Jesus doesn't specifically address marriage in the context in which he makes the following statement, clearly, his counsel fits the marriage relationship. Jesus said, "If you are offering your gift at the altar and there remember that your brother has something against you, leave your gift there in front of the altar. First go and be reconciled to your brother; then come and offer your gift." (Matthew 5:23–24).

Here is a picture of someone approaching God in prayer. As she kneels, she remembers that things aren't right between her and somebody else. Before she continues praying, her energies should be directed — as far as it depends on her (see Romans 12:18) — on reconciling with that other person — who could, of course, be her spouse. God hates dissension (see Proverbs 6:19) and treasures unity (see Psalm 133:1).

Marriage can force us to become stronger people, because if we want to maintain a strong prayer life as married partners, we must learn how to forgive. We must become expert reconcilers. Friction will inevitably develop. Anger will surely heat up on occasion. So we must learn to deal with conflict as mature Christians — or risk blowing off our prayer life in the process.

Marriage virtually forces us into the intense act of reconciliation. It's easy to get along with people if you never get close to them. I could undoubtedly allow a certain immaturity to remain in my life as a single man, choosing not to deal with my selfishness and judgmental spirit; I have, in fact, done that on a number of occasions in the past. While I'm not proud of this, I can think of one or two people with whom it has been very difficult for me to get along. I've chosen to handle this by not going deeper in a relationship with them. I'm not obligated to be in a relationship with everybody, so there's nothing inherently wrong with simply "sidestepping" people who really raise your blood pressure.

That option is obliterated in marriage. My wife and I live together every day. We are going to disagree about some things, and I am unquestionably obligated to maintain my intimacy with her. When we face unrealized expectations, disappoint each other, or even maliciously wound each other, will we allow dissension—which God hates—to predominate, or will we do the necessary relational work to press ahead to unity?

If you want an unimpeded prayer life, you must see the question that concludes the last paragraph as a rhetorical one. Jesus makes it absolutely clear that you must choose unity if you want to maintain a vital prayer relationship with God. Dissension is a major prayer-killer. Looked at from this perspective, the institution of marriage is designed to force us to become reconcilers. That's the only way we'll survive spiritually.

In this, ironically, marriage points us *away* from our spouse and toward God. What do I mean by this? Listen to the wisdom of James, one of the pillars of the New Testament church:

> What causes fights and quarrels among you? Don't they come from your desires that battle within you? You want something but don't get it.... You quarrel and fight. You do not have, because you do not ask God (James 4:1–2).

Many marital disputes result precisely from this: "You want something but don't get it." James says we don't get it because we're looking *in the wrong place.* Instead of placing demands on your spouse, look to God to have your needs met. That way you can approach your spouse in a spirit of servanthood.

Those of us who have been married for a while tend to forget the "single ruse." By that I mean the tendency on the part of some (certainly not all) single young people to think that what they really need is to find "the one." Once their life mate is found, they assume, everything else will fall into place. Their loneliness, their insecurity, their worries about their own significance—all this and more will somehow mystically melt away in the fire of marital passion.

And, for a very short season, this might appear to be the case. Infatuation can be an intoxicating drug that temporarily covers up any number of inner weaknesses.

But marriage is a spotlight showing us that our search for another human being to "complete" us is misguided. When disillusionment breaks through, we have one of two choices: Dump our spouse and become infatuated with somebody new, or seek to understand the message behind the disillusionment—that we should seek our significance, meaning, and purpose in our Creator rather than in another human being.

Approached in the right way, marriage can cause us to reevaluate our dependency on other humans for our spiritual nourishment, and direct us to nurture our relationship with God instead. No human being can love us the way we long to be loved; it is just not possible for another human to reach and alleviate the spiritual ache that God has placed in all of us.

Marriage does us a very great favor in exposing this truth, but it presents a corresponding danger—getting entangled in dissension. For the sake of prayer, it is essential that we live in unity. For the sake of unity, our passions and desires must be God-directed.

Expanding Prayer

"Where are you going, Dad?"

My son, then quite young, watched me intently as I laced up my boots.

"To the battlefield."

"It's kind of wet," he said, looking outside. "Why you goin' there?"

I sighed. We lived in a town house at the time, with our three small children. "I just pray a little better out there," I said, and he nodded.

Marriage—and having kids—forced me to expand my prayer life. If I insisted on a quiet moment to close my eyes, bow my head, and have an uninterrupted hour, I'd have to wake up at 4:00 A.M. Our oldest daughter is like her mother—a night owl. She often falls asleep long after I do. Our son is wired like me—he likes to wake up before the sun shines in his window. Without a large house, there isn't much privacy at any time of the day.

But in many ways this has been a blessing. It is unfortunate that I used to view prayer only as a quiet, perhaps even cerebral, activity. The reduction of prayer to an "every head bowed, every eye closed" exercise limits the power and scope of how we relate to God. Marriage can blow the lids off these boxes.

In his book *Prayer and Modern Man,* Jacques Ellul relates how true prayer "largely overflows the confines of the spoken language." He adds that the words used in the Old Testament to designate prayer are "action verbs," words like "to caress," or "to prostrate oneself."[6]

If we connect our marital experience to our Christian faith, we can learn the power of prayer in new ways. By physically experiencing what it means to gently and lovingly caress my wife, perhaps I'll be able to understand new dimensions of prayer. How might God like to be touched and caressed? Can my verbal praises be like a hand lovingly stroking a cheek?

It took a long time for me to even be able to consider this. Sex is so mysterious when you're young, and often—at least it was for me—synonymous with guilt. And even within marriage, sometimes it's hard for me to imagine, "God is a part of this?!" You might very well be tempted to occasionally shout "hallelujah" during a sexual encounter, but I'm not sure God is always the object of such a declaration!

But let's explore this. The Old Testament verb "to prostrate oneself" gives us room for reflection. While we must never lapse into worshiping the created, there are those intense moments in which the unity of marriage and even the ecstasy of physical union lead you to stand in awe before another, wanting to fully offer yourself, without reservation. When a wife says to her husband, "Take me, I'm yours," she demonstrates a trust that whatever the husband does will be done out of love and with genuine concern and care. It is a remarkable testimony to self-giving and to the joy of intimacy.

This is the love experienced by two of history's most famous lovers, Abelard and Heloise, even though they entered their love with less than chaste affection. Abelard was a twelfth-century theologian and philosopher. As a teacher, he had taken a vow of chastity, which was severely tested when he became smitten with one of his pupils, Heloise. Because physical love was forbidden and marriage was out of the question, Abelard resisted for a time, but eventually fell. Heloise bore him a child, and the two were secretly married. When Heloise's uncle found out what had happened, he had Abelard castrated. Abelard took this assault as rightful punishment and became a monk; Heloise became a nun.

Heloise's passionate, "prostrating" devotion to Abelard is seen in the first letter she wrote to him: "God knows, I have ever sought in thee only thyself, desiring simply thee and not what was thine."[7]

Heloise's love was so intense that she saw Abelard as her sun, with herself as merely the moon that could reflect Abelard's light. This perspective led her to virtually debase herself lest she challenge the glory of her beloved: "And if the name of wife seemed holier or more potent," she confessed, "the word mistress was always sweeter to me, or even — be not angry! — concubine or harlot; for the more I lowered myself before thee, the more I hoped to gain thy favor, and the lest I should hurt the glory of thy renown."

This desire to diminish, almost debase, yourself for another, simply to lose yourself in their presence and favor, carries this Old Testament sense of prostrating devotion. As one who has spent many hours reading the Christian classics, it is remarkable to me how closely this sense mirrors the humble declarations often uttered by God's saints as they wrote out their prayers. This was the holy debasement that fueled many of the ascetic practices of earlier Christians — sitting on a tall pole for decades, living in cramped cages, cultivating leeches on their bodies—in an effort to express their commitment, love, and adoration toward God. However misguided we might find their actions, their motivation was to physically express a spiritual truth: "God is all, we are nothing. And to show God how much he is all and how much we are nothing, we will live this way."

I'm not suggesting we go back to these physical practices, but there is a humble spirit behind these acts that we would do well to consider in this arrogant age. I wonder if it isn't possible for the marriage relationship to reawaken this humility within us. If we experience a shadow of this surrender before a sinful human being during a sexual encounter, can we not learn to offer ourselves equally unreservedly to a perfectly loving and absolutely benevolent God?

Abelard would later write—quite appropriately, for our discussion—that God "is not to be loved as Abelard loved Heloise, but as Heloise loved Abelard," adding that God is to be loved "for his own perfection, even to the point of eventual renunciation of the beatitude [happiness or blessings] he has promised us."

We often love God for what that love brings us, but Heloise learned to love Abelard solely for who he was. That forbidden love brought her nothing but pain, but she would rather have shame and pain with Abelard than peace and happiness without him.

Can we say the same about our love for God?

This inner orientation of prostrating prayer invokes absolute renunciation of all that God offers us for the sake of enjoying God himself. If you have ever experienced even the shadow of this prostration in your marriage, you can gain new insights in prayer. It can teach us to "lose ourselves in prayer" with God.

What I'm suggesting is that we connect our marriages with our faith in such a way that our experience in each feeds the other. The next time you caress your spouse, think about how that caress might open up new avenues for your prayer life. The next time you are virtually overcome by passion for your spouse, consider how you can offer yourself with equal abandon to your God. Don't be afraid to use all aspects of marriage—even sexual expression—to expand your prayer life.

So then, we see how in many different ways marriage feeds into and builds our prayer lives. By learning to respect others, meeting each others' sexual needs, overcoming dissension, and using the analogies of marriage to foster more creative prayer, we can build and maintain active, growing, and meaningful prayer lives.

6

The Cleansing
of Marriage

How Marriage Exposes Our Sin

*Marriage is the greatest test in the world ... but now I
welcome the test instead of dreading it. It is much more
than a test of sweetness of temper, as people sometimes think;
it is a test of the whole character and affects every action.*

T. S. ELIOT

*Marriage is the operation by which a woman's vanity and
a man's egotism are extracted without anesthetic.*

HELEN ROWLAND

*One of the best wedding gifts God gave you was a
full-length mirror called your spouse. Had there been
a card attached, it would have said, "Here's to helping
you discover what you're really like!"*

GARY AND BETSY RICUCCI

ADMITTEDLY, IT WASN'T YOUR TYPICAL DATE. A FORMER HIGH SCHOOL girlfriend was visiting me at college—she was attending Moody Bible Institute at the time—so we decided to spend a Saturday visiting a monastery in British Columbia.

We were greeted cordially and warmly by a priest. Over his shoulder, I noticed an extremely young monk—barely out of his teens, if that—approach us. He saw the young woman I was with and immediately dropped his eyes, passing us with his head bowed.

I was passionate about God in college, and I knew this man must be passionate too, given the path he had chosen. Yet his simple act of averting his eyes spoke so loudly about the different ways we were pursuing the Almighty. I spent the entire day in the company of a female companion, while this young monk couldn't allow an inadvertent glance to become a five-second look. The experience certainly gave me pause, enough so that I can still picture his young face, the angle of his bowed head, the quick shuffle of his feet as he walked away.

As someone who has great respect and love for Christian tradition, I can't deny that, historically, Christian spirituality has been infatuated with celibacy. "After all," many teachers have said, "Jesus Christ himself was celibate—what other argument do we need?" There has been an undeniable prejudice that to become *truly* holy, to earnestly pursue sanctity, one must embrace the single life.

At times, this thought has wounded thoughtful Christians. Mary Anne McPherson Oliver confesses, "It finally dawned on me that for thirty-odd years I had lived in one intimate partnership, a fact of tremendous significance to my being and to my spiritual life, yet the *couple* in tradition was virtually nonexistent as a theologically and spiritually significant unit.... I finally came to the simple realization that spirituality as written and taught is basically celibate and/or monastic, and I am not."[1]

The three of us who met that day at the monastery were all in pursuit of holiness, but all of us would take a radically different path. The young man continued living as a celibate monk. I became a married full-time writer and teacher, living in the United States. My former girlfriend married and then became a missionary to Egypt. Marriage didn't eclipse my concern for holiness (at Regent College, my master's thesis was on the doctrine of sanctification), but did it involve a compromise?

Here's the crux—the young man in the monastery *entered* celibacy consciously as a path toward holiness. Is it possible to enter marriage consciously as a path toward holiness? If so, how?

The Sanctification of Marriage

Although many early church leaders viewed most sexual activity (except for that intended solely for procreation) as suspect at best and mortally sinful at worst, they didn't (interestingly enough) necessarily consider celibacy a more difficult life than marriage. In fact, some of the ancients realized that the marital life could be even *tougher* than the celibate life.

Centuries ago, Pseudo-Athanasius quoted a female teacher named Syncletica as saying, "Therefore we will not seduce ourselves with the thought that people who are in the world are carefree. For perhaps in comparison they toil much more than we do. In general for women the hatred in the world is great; for they bear children difficultly [sic] and in danger, and they endure nourishing babies with milk, and they are ill with them when their children are ill; and they survive these things, without having a result for their labor."[2]

Ambrose had similar thoughts. "Let us compare ... the advantages of married women with that which awaits virgins.... She marries and weeps. How many vows does she make with tears? She conceives, and her fruitfulness brings her trouble before offspring.... Why speak of the troubles of nursing, training, and marrying? These are the miseries of those who are fortunate. A mother has heirs, but it increases her sorrows."[3]

One night during the earlier years of our marriage, I woke up and was astonished at my wife's endurance. We had two children at the time. It was a stressful season for me, and my wife had gone out of her way to schedule a very romantic evening to ease my mind. Later that night, however, our children became ill. One of them was still nursing, and the other insisted on being cared for by Lisa.

Lisa was exhausted. She had been up late with me, and now she was suffering a hungry nursing baby's desperate sucks for breast milk that wasn't there. When the baby was put down, Lisa had to hold a feverishly hot toddler in her lap, stroking her hair, putting a damp cloth on her forehead.

93

I saw my wife giving virtually every inch of her body in selfless service, and the thought hit me, "She's a saint!" That night, being a celibate nun would have sounded like a dream vacation to Lisa. How could anyone suggest that she had compromised her growth in holiness by entering a life situation that called for such heroic selflessness?

In fact, if celibacy (emotional or situational) is entered into selfishly, it can destroy us every bit as much as unbridled sensuality. C. S. Lewis writes the following about our heart:

> If you want to make sure of keeping it intact, you must give your heart to no one, not even to an animal. Wrap it carefully round with hobbies and little luxuries; avoid all entanglements; lock it up safe in the casket or coffin of your selfishness. But in that casket — safe, dark, motionless, airless — it will change. It will not be broken; it will become unbreakable, impenetrable, irredeemable.[4]

It probably will not be a productive conversation to argue either celibacy or marriage as the preferred pathway to holiness. Christians have walked both paths successfully. The important thing is to view the challenges of our particular life situation as a platform for growth. An athlete who truly wants to improve his performance doesn't look for the easiest workout; he looks for the one that will challenge him the most. Marriage certainly has its challenges, but when these are faced head-on, our marriage can nurture our devotional lives in enriching ways. One of the ways is by unmasking our sin and our hurtful attitudes and thus leading us into the spirit of humility.

Unveiled Faces

Paul writes in Ephesians 5:25, "Husbands, love your wives, just as Christ also loved the church." He goes on to say that Christ gave himself up for the church that he might "make her holy" and "cleanse" her, so that the church would be "without stain or wrinkle or any other blemish" (Ephesians 5:27).

Loving something and purifying something go hand in hand. A husband who truly loves his wife will want to see her grow in purity. A wife who truly loves her husband will want to see him grow in godliness. Both will put growth in godliness above affluence, public opinion, or personal ease.

What marriage has done for me is hold up a mirror to my sin. It forces me to face myself honestly and consider my character flaws, selfishness, and anti-Christian attitudes, encouraging me to be sanctified and cleansed and to grow in godliness.

Kathleen and Thomas Hart write, "Sometimes what is hard to take in the first years of marriage is not what we find out about our partner, but what we find out about ourselves. As one young woman who had been married about a year said, 'I always thought of myself as a patient and forgiving person. Then I began to wonder if that was just because I had never before gotten close to anyone. In marriage, when John and I began ... dealing with differences, I saw how small and unforgiving I could be. I discovered a hardness in me I had never experienced before.' "[5]

I experienced this same phenomenon. In ninth grade I was voted "most polite kid" for the annual yearbook. I have always thought of myself as reasonably patient and charitable—that is, until I got married and discovered how passionately annoyed I can become at pulling out empty ice cube trays.

When I grew up, my family lived by a simple rule: If you take out an ice cube, you refill the tray before you put it back in. Now I'll pull out a tray and find nothing more than half an ice cube—which I call an ice *chip*.

It was amazing how much such a small detail irritated me. I asked Lisa, "How much do you love me?"

"More than all the world," she professed.

"I don't need you to love me that much," I said. "I just want you to love me for seven seconds."

"What on earth are you talking about?" she asked.

"Well, I timed how long it takes to fill an ice cube tray and discovered it's just seven sec—"

"Oh Gary, are we back to that again?"

It finally dawned on me one day that if it takes Lisa just seven seconds to fill an ice cube tray, *that's all it takes me as well.* Was I really so selfish that I was willing to let seven seconds' worth of inconvenience become a serious issue in my marriage? Was my capacity to show charity really that limited?

Indeed it was.

Being so close to someone—which marriage necessitates—may be the greatest spiritual challenge in the world. There is no "resting," because I am under virtual twenty-four-hour surveillance. Not that Lisa makes it seem like that—it's just that I'm aware of it. Every movie I rent is rented with the understanding that I will watch it with Lisa next to me. Every hour I take off for recreation is an hour that Lisa will know about. Where I eat at lunch (and what), how I'm doing on a particular diet—my appetites and lusts and desires are all in full view of Lisa.

This presupposes, of course, that I'm willing to be confronted with my sin—that I'm willing to ask Lisa, "Where do you see unholiness in my life? I want to know about it. I want to change it."

This takes tremendous courage—courage I am the first to admit I often lack. It means I'm willing to hear what displeases Lisa about me, as well as to refuse to become paralyzed by the fear that she will love me less or leave me because the sin in me is being exposed.

I don't naturally gravitate toward the honesty and openness that leads to change. My natural sin-bent is to hide and erect a glittering image. Dan Allender and Tremper Longman describe the dichotomy in forceful words: "Man was meant to be a bold creative artist who plunges into the unformed mystery of life and shapes it to a greater vision of beauty. At the Fall he became a cowardly, violent protector of nothing more than himself. Intimacy and openness were replaced by hiding and hatred."[6]

Marriage, they add, is "the relationship where depravity is best exposed and where our dignity is best lived out."[7] Just go back in time to the days of Adam and Eve. The first marriage was the context for the first sin. And the first obvious result of the Fall was a breakdown in marital intimacy. Neither Adam nor Eve welcomed the fact that their weaknesses were now as obvious as a little girl's first attempt at makeup. All of a sudden they felt kind of funny about being naked. And they started blaming each other.

Do you hide from your spouse? Or do you utilize the spotlight of marriage to grow in grace? Some of us need this spotlight to understand how truly sinful we are.

Howard Hendricks told about a time he had just completed a sermon and an eager young man came up to him and called him a "great man."

On the drive home, Hendricks turned to his wife and said, "*A great man.* How many great men do you know?"

"One fewer than you think," she answered.

I have frequently stated that I think God often gives wives to influential men in part to keep their husband's feet on the ground. When someone receives constant adulation, it is invaluable to have another person come alongside who will see through to the real you.

Blaise Pascal wrote, "We have not sufficiently plumbed the wretchedness of man in general, nor our own in particular, when we are still surprised at the weakness and corruption of man."[8] Being in a marriage relationship forces me to realize where I fall short; it encourages me to "plumb" both the wretchedness of man in general and myself in particular.

As a spiritual exercise, few things are more profitable than this kind of examination. François Fénelon, an eighteenth-century Christian mystic, wrote that "all the saints are convinced that sincere humility is the foundation of all virtues,"[9] an opinion shared by the great Anglican writer, William Law: "[Humility] is so essential to the right state of our souls that there is no pretending to a reasonable or pious life without it. We may as well think to see without eyes or live without breath as to live in the spirit of religion without the spirit of humility."[10]

And what is humility? In part, Fénelon tells us, it is "a certain honesty, and childlike willingness to acknowledge our faults, to recover from them, and to submit to the advice of experienced people; these will be solid useful virtues, adapted to your sanctification."[11]

I believe it *is* possible to enter marriage with a view to being cleansed spiritually, if, that is, we do so with a willingness to embrace marriage as a spiritual discipline. To do this, we must not enter marriage predominantly to be fulfilled, emotionally satisfied, or romantically charged, but rather to become more like Jesus Christ. We must embrace the reality of having our flaws exposed to our partner, and thereby having them exposed to us as well. Sin never seems quite as shocking when it is known only to us; when we see how it looks or sounds to another, it is magnified ten times over. The celibate can "hide" frustration by removing herself from the situation, but the married man or woman has no true refuge. It is hard to hide when you share the same bed.

The Dating Dance

I have a theory: Behind virtually every case of marital dissatisfaction lies unrepented sin. Couples don't fall out of love so much as they fall out of repentance. Sin, wrong attitudes, and personal failures that are not dealt with slowly erode the relationship, assaulting and eventually erasing the once lofty promises made in the throes of an earlier (and less polluted) passion.

All of us enter marriage with sinful attitudes. When these attitudes surface, the temptation will be to hide them or even run to another relationship where the attitudes won't be so well known. But Christian marriage presumes a certain degree of self-disclosure. When I gave my hand in marriage, I committed to allow myself to be known by Lisa—and that means she'll see me as I am—with my faults, my prejudices, my fears, and my weaknesses.

This reality can be terrifying to contemplate. Dating is largely a dance in which you always try to put the best face forward — hardly a good preparation for the inevitable self-disclosure implied in marriage. In fact, I wouldn't be surprised if many marriages end in divorce largely because one or both partners are running from their own revealed weaknesses as much as they are running from something they can't tolerate in their spouse.

May I suggest an alternative to running? Use the revelation of your sin as a means to grow in the foundational Christian virtue of humility, leading you to confession and renouncement. Then go the next step and adopt the positive virtue that corresponds to the sin you are renouncing. If you've used women in the past, practice serving your wife. If you've been quick to ridicule your husband, practice giving him encouragement and praise.

View marriage as an entryway into sanctification — as a relationship that will reveal your sinful behaviors and attitudes and give you the opportunity to address them before the Lord. But here's the challenge: Don't give in to the temptation to resent your partner as your own weaknesses are revealed. Correspondingly, give them the freedom and acceptance they need in order to face their own weaknesses as well. In this way, we can use marriage as a leg up, a piercing spiritual mirror, designed for our sanctification and growth in holiness.

Receiving Another's Sin

This manner of viewing marriage points to another important principle — not just having *my* sin exposed, but reflecting on how I treat my wife when *her* sin is exposed. Do I use this knowledge to crush her, humiliate her, or gain power over her, or do I use it to gently and lovingly lead her into imitating the character of Jesus Christ?

Possessing the knowledge of someone's sin is a powerful and dangerous thing. On several occasions, men have pulled me aside and shared their frustration with their difficulty in forgiving their wives for having an affair. Their natural tendency is to throw the affair back in their wives' faces. It's a vicious grasp for power. As soon as their wives point out something that needs to be changed in their lives, their natural inclination is to say: "Oh, does this mean you're going to run back to Jim if I don't change?" Or: "Well, I might lose my temper but at least I know how to control myself sexually!"

The men usually hate saying these words as much as the wives hate hearing them. They are cruel and vindictive comments, but sometimes we are cruel and vindictive husbands.

"Do you ever tell your wife how much you hate it when you say these things?" I asked one man.

"Yeah, but she still hates hearing them, even though she knows I hate saying them."

In order for this discipline to work, we will have to link it with the discipline of forgiveness (discussed in chapter 9). This discipline of having our own sin exposed and being a spotlight for our spouse is a difficult one to master. It takes tremendous courage, and it takes what will seem (particularly to men) like an almost melodramatic gentleness. The marital relationship shouldn't be a "grilling" experience but rather a nurturing one—encouraging one another on the pathway of sanctification: "Therefore encourage one another and build each other up" (1 Thessalonians 5:11).

Let's look at a real-life example of how having the sin revealed in our lives can help us grow by demonstrating our true motivations.

The Sin Behind Dissatisfaction

Greg looked at his wife, Sharon, (not their real names) and tried not to show what he was really feeling. They were celebrating their eighth anniversary with a dinner, and Greg was, well, bored. An avid computer geek, Greg felt chagrined that he would much rather be talking about computers with a colleague than trying to find something to say to his wife.

Sharon's choice for the dinner setting was a funky antique store/ restaurant. Greg collects old metal advertisement signs, and he had to fight the urge to get up and go browsing in the antique shop. This was his wedding anniversary, he reminded himself; he should want to share it with his wife, and not wander off alone seeking his own satisfaction.

But Greg believed his wife's world had shrunken to an almost unbearable degree. She had little to say beyond giving a tedious, play-by-play account of the day's events. "And then, right after I mopped the floor, I went up to take a shower and guess what? Rebecca dropped her entire bowl of applesauce and didn't clean it up. Peter walked right through the mess and started making applesauce footprints all over the house! *And I had just cleaned the floors!*"

Greg nodded, struggling mightily against his internal thoughts. He felt bad because he knew his wife wanted something he wasn't sure he could give her — she wanted someone to be interested in these domestic challenges, and frankly, keeping floors clean wasn't all that interesting to Greg. Greg has a fertile mind — he loves figuring out computer glitches ("It's like a digital crossword puzzle," he explains), and his wife's seemingly endless anecdotes of messes and hassles put him to sleep.

"But Greg," I suggested a few days later, "this is how you *serve* your wife — by listening to her world. Do you think Jesus' mind was excited by washing the disciples' feet and listening to their foolish arguments over and over again? Besides, these *are* your kids. Of course Sharon's going to think you're interested in what happens to them throughout the day."

Greg reluctantly nodded his head. "I guess. But . . ." His pause told me we were about to get to the crux of the matter. "Well, there's this woman I work with. We're able to talk code — something Sharon has absolutely no interest in — and when we figure out problems together, there's nothing else like it. I feel so close to her."

There was another long pause. "Sharon and I have nothing in common anymore."

Right then and there the selfish lie was exposed. "Nothing in common?" I asked. "What about Peter and Rebecca?"

"Well, maybe the children."

"And having conceived them together, and caring for them together—including cleaning up after them—counts less in your book than connecting a bunch of numbers in order to write computer code with this other woman? Is that what you're saying? Do your children mean so little to you that you find them less engaging than creating a new program that will be obsolete in eighteen months?"

"Ouch," Greg said, blowing out a long breath. "I guess I hadn't thought of it that way."

Greg wanted to "rewrite" his reality so that his thoughts wouldn't sound as evil as they really were. The truth is, he *did* value writing computer code over spending time with his family—but instead of admitting and reevaluating that attitude, he blamed everything on his wife: "Sharon's boring," "Sharon doesn't understand me," "We've grown apart." These accusations were much more comfortable for him than admitting, "I am selfish, and I am having serious priority problems—even to the point of mentally risking an affair."

If we approach it in the right manner and are willing to look honestly at our deepest motivations, marriage can be like a photograph. Looking at pictures isn't always pleasant. I remember once when we looked at some photographs we had just picked up at the store, and I realized for the first time how much weight I had put on. "Whoa—where did that chin come from?" The natural inclination is to blame the camera angle, but the truth is, those fifteen pounds were showing from every angle!

The same thing happens with our sin in marriage. We resent the revealed truth, and we are tempted to take it out on our spouse—the camera, so to speak.

In my book *The Glorious Pursuit,* I reflect on a truth that I believe applies here. A mature Christian finds his or her fulfillment in living faithfully before God—that is, in *being* a mature person, not in being *around* a particular person. Much of our marital dissatisfaction stems in actuality from self-hatred. We don't like what we've done or become; we've let selfish and sinful attitudes poison our thoughts and lead us into shameful behaviors, and suddenly all we want is *out*.

The mature response, however, is not to leave; it's to change —*ourselves*.

Whenever marital dissatisfaction rears its head in my marriage—as it does in virtually every marriage—I simply check my focus. The times that I am happiest and most fulfilled in my marriage are the times when I am intent on drawing meaning and fulfillment from becoming a better husband rather than from demanding a "better" wife.

If you're a Christian, the reality is that, biblically speaking, you can't swap your spouse for someone else. But you can change yourself. And that change can bring the fulfillment that you mistakenly believe is found only by changing partners. In one sense, it's comical: Yes, we need a changed partner, but the partner that needs to change is *not* our spouse, it's *us!*

I don't know why this works. I don't know how you can be unsatisfied maritally, and then offer yourself to God to bring about change in your life and suddenly find yourself more than satisfied with the same spouse. I don't know *why* this works, only that it *does* work. It takes time, and by time I mean maybe years. But if your heart is driven by the desire to draw near to Jesus, you find joy by becoming like Jesus. You'll *never* find that joy by doing something that offends Jesus—such as instigating a divorce or an affair.

In the nineteenth century, Marie d'Agoult left her children to follow after the most famous pianist of her day, Hungarian composer and virtuoso Franz Liszt. After the ardor of her infatuation cooled and the reality of missing her children set in, Marie is said to have made this observation: "When one has smashed everything around oneself, one has also smashed oneself."

Sin will lead to self-destruction if we allow it to. The same sin that confronts two different men can lead one to a greater understanding, and therefore to greater maturity and growth, at the same time that it leads another man into a cycle of denial, deception, and spiritual destruction.

The choice is ours. Sin is a reality in this fallen world. It's how we respond to it that will determine whether our marriages become a casualty statistic or a crown of success.

7

Sacred History

Building the Spiritual Discipline of Perseverance

*It is very hard to be entirely faithful, even to things,
ideas, above all, persons one loves. There is no
such thing as perfect faithfulness any more than there is
perfect love or perfect beauty. But it is fun trying.*
KATHERINE ANNE PORTER

*May the Lord direct your hearts into
God's love and Christ's perseverance.*
2 THESSALONIANS 3:5

MARTI ENTERED MARRIAGE WITH AN ENORMOUS BURDEN — A PRE-
viously failed relationship (not marital) that had included sexual
activity and a gut-wrenching breakup. As a result, she struggled
with feelings of insecurity, even after she and her husband were married. She just couldn't get over the perception that "conflict leads to
breakup, and breakup leads to intense pain."

After several years of marriage, Marti and her husband started
fighting over financial problems. Weeks of vigorous discussion (and
occasional bouts of yelling) ensued, but no conclusions were drawn.
The dispute became so acute that the marital relationship started
showing the strain. There was little joy — just angst and frustration.

Marti subconsciously slipped back into feelings that were born
out of her earlier failed relationship. Because she still hurt over the

dissolution of that bond, she experienced acute anxiety over whether her marriage could survive this challenge. In her past, unresolved issues meant an inevitable breakup, so she secretly began mourning a relationship that had not yet died.

Then one night, after yet another vigorous and ultimately unresolved discussion, Marti's husband did something so wonderfully prophetic and profound that Marti will never forget it as long as she lives. You could see the joy of her husband's tender care reflected in her eyes as she told the story:

"He wrapped his arms around me and said, 'Marti, you need to know that no matter what we decide or don't decide, I'm never going to quit on this marriage. Even if we have to live with this tension for the rest of our lives, *I will never leave you.*' "

Marti burst into tears as she shared this story. Even though there was nearly constant contention in her marriage, she didn't want this relationship to end, and now her husband had promised that it wouldn't.

Marti and her husband embraced the sacredness of their history together; they both found great meaning in the simple fact that the marriage would survive. Suddenly, the original problem seemed less immense and monumental. At any rate, it was less significant than the overall fact that their history together was secure.

We proclaim the prophetic grace of marriage when we understand the sacredness of building a history together. German philosopher Friedrich Nietzsche suggested that marriage is a "long conversation," urging us, therefore, to marry a friend. If this is true, it is but a shadow of another conversation that has preceded our own.

The God of Abraham

A well-known theologian was once asked to give the best piece of evidence for the existence of God. Without hesitating, he said, "The Jew."

Throughout a tumultuous history, the Jewish people have sometimes hung by the slenderest of threads as yet another tyrant or enemy sought their extinction. Yet for centuries, they have survived. Theirs is a dramatic and affectionate history.

There is a theological reality embedded in this history. The God of the Old Testament is unique in that he attached himself to a people. For thousands of years, loyal adherents worshiped the god of the hills, the god of the valley, or the god of the sea, but the idea that there was a God of Abraham, Isaac, and Jacob—a God of people—this was something new!

Even more stunning was the direct line of this relationship—from Adam and Eve to Abraham and Sarah, from Abraham and Sarah to David and Bathsheba, from David and Bathsheba to Mary and Joseph. There was a sacredness to this history. Meaning was derived from the fact that God had been with the fathers, grandfathers, great-grandfathers, and their fathers and grandfathers before them.

This relationship between God and his people was anything but easy. There were periods of great joy and celebration (witness the love affair of God and his people when Solomon dedicated the temple); seasons of frustration and anger (when God allowed foreign tyrants to conquer); times of infidelity and apostasy (when Israel chased after other gods); and excruciating seasons of silence (including a four-hundred-year stretch between the Old and New Testaments).

Now take these examples and break them down, thinking of them in a smaller context. There were times of great joy and celebration, frustration and anger, infidelity and apostasy, and excruciating seasons of silence. Sound like any relationship you know? Your own marriage, for example?

Viewed through this lens, the marriage relationship allows us to experientially identify with God and his relationship with Israel. Has your marriage had periods of great joy and celebration? God can relate to and rejoice with you. Have you perhaps experienced the heartbreaking betrayal of unfaithfulness? Or the frustration of mournful silence? If so, you are not alone, and you have been given the raw materials with which to build a more intimate relationship with God.

One characteristic holds the history of God and Israel together —*perseverance*. When Israel turned her back on God, God didn't turn his back on Israel. He may have stepped back for a time, but the overall commitment remained concrete and steadfast.

I particularly relate to the four hundred years of silence between the Old and New Testaments. So often it isn't that our marriages are either good or bad—they just are. We get tired of the routine and the sameness, and our souls occasionally grow numb toward each other.

Kathleen and Thomas Hart depict it this way: "Marriage is a long walk two people take together. Sometimes the terrain is very interesting, sometimes rather dull. At times the walk is arduous, for both persons or for one. Sometimes the conversation is lively; at other times, there is not much to say. The travelers do not know exactly where they are going, nor when they will arrive."[1]

Adding to this sometimes numbing effect of "sameness" is the fact that this walk is longer for us than it was for our ancestors. In previous centuries, many marriages were cut short because women frequently died during childbirth. Thomas Cranmer, the famous archbishop of Canterbury from 1533–1553, lost his wife in the first year of his marriage. Jeremy Taylor (1613–1667), an English bishop and writer *(The Rule and Exercises of Holy Living* and *The Rule and Exercises of Holy Dying)* lost his wife after less than thirteen years of marriage. John Calvin's wife didn't make it to their tenth wedding anniversary, and John Donne's wife, Anne, died just sixteen years after they were married.[2]

Men didn't live as long as they do today either. As recently as 1870, a woman couldn't count on her husband still being alive when their youngest child left home. In 1911, the average length of marriage was twenty-eight years; by 1967, it had risen to forty-two years.

Today you can virtually define marriage by using the language of perseverance—the maintenance of a long-term relationship. With medical advances and increasing life expectancy, you now have to pass your sixtieth or even seventieth wedding anniversary before you merit mention on Paul Harvey's newscast.

This relatively new phenomenon of being married for six or seven decades can pay rich dividends for our spiritual life and growth. Marriage helps us to develop the character of God himself as we stick with our spouses through the good times and the bad. Every wedding gives birth to a new history, a new beginning. The spiritual meaning of marriage is found in maintaining that history together.

In fact, some experts suggest it takes from nine to fourteen years for a couple to truly "create and form its being."[3] When I hear of couples who break up after just three or four years, I feel sad because they haven't even begun to experience what being married is really like. It's sort of like climbing halfway up a mountain but never getting to see the sights; you're in the middle of the task, your soul is consumed with the struggle, but it's much too soon to experience the full rewards. Evaluating your marriage so soon is like trying to eat a cake that's half-baked. Becoming one—in the deepest, most intimate sense—takes time. It's a journey that never really ends, but it takes at least the span of a decade for the sense of intimacy to really display itself in the marriage relationship.

The Spiritual Discipline of Perseverance

We live in a nation of quitters. Employees quit their jobs as soon as the going gets tough, employers quit on their employees as soon as profits dip a quarter of a percentage point. People routinely quit on their church and join another congregation at the slightest provocation. The Bible even warns that some will quit on their faith (see 1 Timothy 4:1).

Jesus talks about this temptation to abandon the faith in the parable of the sower—which could more accurately be called the parable of the soils, because that is what the teaching is really about. In Luke 8, Jesus warns that some will hear God's word and believe for a while, "but in the time of testing they fall away" (verse 13). Others hear but have their faith choked by "life's worries, riches and pleasures, and they do not mature" (verse 14). But those commended by Jesus are those who "hear the word, *retain it, and by persevering* produce a crop" (verse 15, italics added).

True Christian spirituality has always emphasized perseverance: "To those *who by persistence* in doing good seek glory, honor and immortality, he will give eternal life. But for those who are self-seeking and who reject the truth and follow evil, there will be wrath and anger" (Romans 2:7–8, italics added).

Righteousness — true holiness — is seen *over time* in our persistence. It is relatively easy to "flirt" with righteousness — being occasionally courteous to other drivers (if you happen to be in a good mood), helping someone in need by opening the door for them (if you have time), throwing a few extra bucks into the offering plate (as long as you won't miss them). But this behavior is in reality superficial righteousness. The righteousness God seeks is a *persistent* righteousness, a commitment to continue making the right decision even when, perhaps hourly, you feel pulled in the opposite direction. Holiness is far more than an *inclination* toward occasional acts of kindness and charity. It is a commitment to persistent surrender before God.

Married men or women who find themselves "falling in love" with someone else will have to continually make a choice to not act inappropriately and to watch their tongue. It will require far more than a one-time decision for them to maintain their integrity; they will have to *persevere* in righteousness.

Because marriage is such a long conversation, it goes through many, many stages. Some of these are more difficult than others. Certainly, the raising of small children presents an enormous challenge to fostering intimacy and having "fun." It's exhausting work. Two researchers, William J. Lederer and Don D. Jackson, note that they "have never observed a generally constant collaborative union between spouses during the period when they are raising children."[4]

Life presents us with some seasons that, quite frankly, must be endured. There are many miraculously fulfilling moments we will experience as we raise our kids; but other aspects of our lives—including solitary time together as a couple—will, of necessity, suffer. This is merely a season, and it is foolish to quit persevering during a time when *any* marriage will have to adapt and reevaluate previous expectations.

What causes us to give up on our marriages? Although Jesus wasn't specifically addressing the marriage relationship in his parable of the soils, he covers many of the sources of our failure to persevere in marriage. Some of us give up when "the time of testing" comes (Luke 8:13). We thought marriage would be easy; when it gets hard, we bail out.

Others give up when they are choked by "life's worries" (Luke 8:14). Marriage counselors tell us that money problems have destroyed more marriages than just about anything else. There is also our selfishness and our sin—both of which are capable of polluting a once-precious affection.

What gives us the power to persist in doing good? Paul hints at the answer in the Romans 2 passage mentioned above. He notes that in our persistence we seek "glory, honor and immortality" (Romans 2:7). These are words that point to an alternate history, to an afterlife (there is, after all, no immortality in this world). Persistence doesn't make sense unless we live with a keen sense of eternity. We'll expand on this thought in the next chapter, but this truth needs to make a brief appearance here as well.

Persons struggling with infatuation for someone who is not their spouse may need to make a decision that in the short run may make them *less* happy and bring them *less* pleasure (though I would argue that the decision will, in many cases, make them *more* fulfilled in the long run). Christian endurance is based on the idea that there is another life, commonly known as heaven, which is eternal and for which this world is a preparation. The coming world is so glorious, weighted with so much honor, that it is worth making sacrifices now to receive glory, honor, and immortality there.

Around which world is your life centered? Your marriage will

111

ultimately reveal the answer to that question. If we have an eternal outlook, preparing for eternity by sticking with a difficult marriage makes much more sense than destroying a family to gain quick and easy relief. Most divorces are marked by the actions of someone running from, at most, a few difficult decades—and for this relief, people are throwing away glory and honor that last for eternity. It's a horrible trade!

The holiness that will be rewarded in heaven is a *persistent* holiness. Read through the entire Bible, and I promise you, you won't find one reference to a "crown in heaven" that goes to the person who had the "happiest" life on earth. That reward just doesn't exist. Nor is there a heavenly ribbon for the Christian who felt the least amount of pain.

The priority of a sacred history is an *eternal* priority. Marriage is a beautiful and effective reminder of this reality. One of the most poetic lines in Scripture, one that I wish every husband and wife would display in a prominent place in their home, is found in verse 5 of 2 Thessalonians 3: "May the Lord direct your hearts into God's love and Christ's perseverance."

That's what I want my heart filled with: *God's love* and *Christ's perseverance.* There's the Bible's best recipe for holiness and a "successful" life here on earth. Oh that my heart could be directed into more and more of God's love! Oh that I could learn the patient perseverance of Christ himself!

The alternative is explained in chapter 2 of Paul's letter to the Romans. Instead of heavenly rewards, some will receive "wrath and anger." And who are they? "Those who are self-seeking and who reject the truth and follow evil" (Romans 2:8). What is more self-seeking than to ignore what is best for your children—an intact, peaceable home—and to dump a marriage because you're tired of your spouse, even though doing so may seriously diminish your ministry of reconciliation discussed in chapter 2?

I wish men in particular would realize the dangers inherent in divorce, at least from the perspective of a woman. My eyes were opened to this in an entirely new way one day as I saw the peril of ever breaking the marital history.

An Uncertain Future

One of the great dangers of breaking a marriage history is that we can't know the future. Let me explain with a true story.

My selfishness was seen at its most despicable level the day I was picked up at the airport by a woman from the group that had invited me to speak. I was directed to sit in the back of her van with her son, but as soon as the door opened, I cringed. The van was filthy. I was wearing slacks and a sports coat; I had to speak later in the day, so I was particularly wary about sitting in that seat, as I was fairly certain I would have some type of food clinging to my backside when I climbed out.

Not wanting to offend the woman, I tried my best to inconspicuously flick off as much of the food and dirt as possible before I sat down, but her son behind me wasn't making my job easy, urging me to quickly find a seat.

Terrible, selfish thoughts ran through my head — "How could she let her van get like this when she knew she would be picking me up?"

Within hours, I found out that this woman was divorced — and thus living as a single mom. "That helps to explain the dirty van," I thought. "She has her hands full."

Then, as we got to know each other even better, she shared that she was in the middle of rounds of chemotherapy. The drugs made her so sick that she could work just one day a week — as a waitress, in fact. The next six days were spent gathering sufficient strength to go back to the restaurant and eke out another hundred dollars. She was earning next to nothing, trying to parent three kids by herself, and enduring chemotherapy — yet she had sacrificed her time and energy and money (gas certainly isn't free!) to "taxi" me around town, volunteering her time for a good cause.

She was an absolute hero, and I was furious with myself. I had silently begrudged a dirty seat, absorbed by my own potential embarrassment at walking into a new place with food hanging from my clothes—something that was utterly insignificant compared to the real-life challenges this woman was facing.

After I repented and started thinking like a servant instead of a prima donna, I then turned my thoughts toward her husband. How could a professing Christian man allow a woman with whom he had conceived three children go through this ordeal alone? I felt so sorry for this woman; my heart bled for her. My next phone call to my wife was filled with the account of this sad story. "What kind of man," I sputtered, "wouldn't immediately rush to the aid of someone in this situation when he had already pledged before a church full of people to be with her 'in sickness and in health?' How hard does a heart have to be to not be moved by the suffering of someone you once loved?"

When this husband divorced this woman, he couldn't have anticipated that she would get cancer, of course, but that's why we build a *sacred* history—none of us can accurately see into the future. This woman set aside her career and hadn't built up any particular vocational skills as she raised this man's three children. She made herself vulnerable for his benefit. And after that—after he had built his career and she was still saddled with tremendous responsibility for the rearing of three children—he broke their history together and left her nearly destitute.

When you divorce your spouse, you have no idea what the future holds for him or her. The situation can, and often does, lead to chaos, because odds are that at least one spouse will need care in the not-too-distant future. Certainly such neglect qualifies as the "self-seeking" that Paul says naturally results in God's "wrath and anger."

Also subject to this anger are those who "reject the truth." Clearly, Paul is talking about the truth of salvation here, but there's also another truth to be inferred from this passage—the truth of God's will and his laws.

Most of us know that God hates divorce because Scripture says it explicitly: " 'I hate divorce,' says the LORD God of Israel" (Malachi 2:16). Jesus elaborated on this perspective on divorce, telling his disciples that "anyone who divorces his wife, except for marital unfaithfulness, causes her to become an adulteress, and anyone who marries the divorced woman commits adultery" (Matthew 5:32). The only reason God made provision for divorce in the Old Testament, Jesus added elsewhere, was because he was dealing with hard hearts (see Matthew 19:8 – 9).

This, my friends, is *truth.* To reject it, Paul warns in Romans 2, is to risk God's wrath and anger. I'm still amazed at Christian men who can leave their wives and children nearly destitute financially, so that they can pursue a new relationship—all the while trying to maintain the illusion that Jesus Christ is still Lord of their life.

A good friend of mine called up a college buddy recently, and his wife said, "I'm sorry, but Greg's not here."

"Where is he?" Mike asked, casually.

"He *left.*"

There was a tone in her voice that defined the "he left" as traumatic and final.

The college buddy has three small children. Mike said he wanted to shake his friend and say, "Do you have *any* idea how evil you're acting?"

But our culture doesn't look at separation as evil, does it? It's "romantic." It's "courageous." It's "for the best, in the long run."

Building a sacred history together teaches us to be *persistent in doing good,* even when we want to do something else. This commitment to perseverance teaches us the basic Christian discipline of self-denial. As part of this, we must reject "self-seeking" behavior and instead think about the future, a future that points beyond this world to the next. If you don't believe in heaven, divorce can make a lot of sense. Once heaven becomes part of the equation, the cost of divorce— God's wrath and anger, jeopardizing the future with a selfish attitude —becomes much too high.

SACRED MARRIAGE

The Ideal

We have reached high to make a strong point. Divorce, by definition, is a failure—of love, forgiveness, and patience, or (at the very least) it is the result of poor judgment in choosing a difficult partner in the first place. But we are all failures at some point. Jesus' words are frequently severe; according to Matthew 5:28, I and virtually every other man alive must be considered an adulterer. One lustful look and *Boom!* we've fallen. One angry exclamation, "You fool!" and, according to Jesus, I'm in danger of being thrown into the fire of hell (see Matthew 5:22).

Jesus makes a number of harsh, seemingly unrelenting statements pertaining to how we should live, and there isn't a man or woman alive who hasn't broken some of those commands. But look at the life of Jesus, and you see tremendous mercy. The adulterous woman isn't condemned—she's simply told not to continue in her sin (see John 8:11). Jesus once said that if we put our hand to the plow and look back, we're not fit for the kingdom of God (see Luke 9:62), but he willingly and lovingly took Peter back after Peter had disowned him three times (see Mark 14:66–72).

If you're reading this after you've gone through a divorce, you serve no one—least of all God—by becoming fixated on something you can't now undo. That's what forgiveness and grace are for—a fresh start, a new beginning.

I have affirmed a high ideal in part to encourage people mired in a difficult marriage to hang in there. At the risk of emptying what we've just said, however, we need to be honest. It is going too far to equate leaving your spouse with leaving your faith. There are certainly severe spiritual repercussions every time you break an oath, and one thing that makes divorce even more perilous spiritually is that the marriage vow is an oath that is broken over time. Rather than being a sin of passion—something you do but immediately regret—divorce is a considered decision, with plenty of opportunities

116

to reconsider and reject it. This makes it, at best, a very dangerous choice spiritually.

But sometimes divorce can even be the right choice. Matthew records an exception for infidelity (see Matthew 19:9); Paul articulates an exception for being married to an unbeliever who refuses to remain in the marriage (see 1 Corinthians 7:15).

Anyone who has been married for any length of time should be able to understand how truly difficult marriage can be, and how, even among Christians, tensions can rise so high and hurt can be so deeply embedded that reconciliation would take more energy than either partner could ever imagine possessing in ten lifetimes. In many cases, God can and will provide the energy; in some cases, people are just not willing to receive it.

Before a divorce is final, I'm usually going to encourage someone to hang in there, to push on through the pain, and to try to grow in it and through it. Happiness may well be beyond them, but spiritual maturity isn't—and I value character far above any emotional disposition. With heaven as a future hope, spiritual growth as a present reality, and, in many cases, children for whom our sacrifice is necessary, an intact marriage is an ideal worth fighting for. But that doesn't mean we should treat those whose marriages have crumbled as second-class Christians. Jesus spoke of high ideals and absolutes —but he loved real people with acceptance and grace.

And, of course, sometimes divorce is foisted on a partner unilaterally. Such was the case with a woman I know by the name of Leslie. Many Christians encouraged Leslie to give up, to stop holding on, and to start dating even before her divorce was final. If Leslie had been concerned only for her own emotional health and happiness, she might have quickly taken their advice. But today, even after traveling such an arduous road as divorce, Leslie has grown closer to the Lord by respecting and cherishing her sacred history with her ex-husband. It is not a happy history, but it is a history that has paid generous spiritual dividends—and that's the beauty of doing things God's way.

Even when we're sinned against, we can grow through the experience by the grace of God.

Broken History: Leslie

"Leslie, I'm leaving you."

Leslie backpedaled in disbelief. She never thought she would hear those words. As a young girl growing up she imagined a white wedding dress, a happy couple, a home full of children. Her fantasies had not left room for the devastating chill these words carried, spoken by a man to whom she'd entrusted her life, her body, her deepest secrets and intimacies. And now he was telling her that he couldn't stand to be around her anymore.

At the time both Leslie and Tim were committed Christians. Although they had lived together before their wedding, they had recommitted their lives to the Lord before they got married, and immediately they began growing in their faith. They attended a Bible study and regularly prayed together. In the early years of their relationship, people often commented, "Y'all have such a good marriage," and the couple would humbly respond, "It's the Lord's doing, not ours."

The first cracks appeared about six years into their marriage when Tim confessed to a one-night stand. He told Leslie he was deeply sorry and was willing to seek counseling. After a lot of tears, they were able to put the affair behind them.

Leslie had to work through some issues of trust, but the good times returned. Five years passed, Tim was being trained as a church elder, and Leslie was working full time directing a Christian ministry. They were enduring the pain of infertility but had passed through the angst to begin the process of adoption. In fact, they had passed the first home study and now were preparing for a second. Soon, Leslie hoped, she would be a mother.

And then Leslie felt Tim slipping away. The fears seemed irrational at first — just a premonition, nothing more — but the corroborating evidence grew. The distance became acute when Leslie traveled with Tim to a national convention. She felt crushed and humiliated when Tim left her alone for long periods of time and then treated her rudely when they finally did get together. Leslie became "hysterically upset," something for which she is now ashamed, causing Tim to withdraw even further.

At home, Leslie confided to a prayer partner, "If I didn't know Tim better, I'd think he was getting ready to leave me."

"That's ridiculous," her prayer partner assured her.

Tim was gone on business for a total of three weeks and scheduled to return on a Saturday afternoon. Leslie was anxious for him to be home on time. She wanted them to be ready for the second adoption home study that was scheduled for early Monday morning.

Tim didn't return home on Saturday afternoon (or evening), as expected. Leslie put the dinner dishes away and went to bed, expecting Tim to join her later that night. She woke up, wondering if Tim would be lying beside her — but he still hadn't made it home. Leslie went to church that Sunday morning, convinced that she would see Tim's car in the garage when she got back, but the garage was empty.

Her heart was beginning to sink, and then, later that evening, Leslie heard a noise coming from the garage. She opened the door and saw Tim putting his golf clubs in the trunk of the car.

"What's going on, Tim?" she asked. He had been gone for three weeks. Surely he wasn't preparing to go play golf in the morning.

And then the words came — those four soul-numbing words that blasted Leslie's world apart: "Leslie, I'm leaving you."

"*What?*"

"I'm leaving you."

Leslie almost collapsed on the spot. "You can't leave me," she lamented.

"I am. I don't love you anymore. I haven't loved you for a long time."

Leslie felt hysteria taking over again, and she began to panic emotionally. "I forced myself to remain calm," she remembers, "because I knew becoming hysterical wouldn't make him stay. Besides, I didn't want him to remember me in a hysterical fit."

Then Leslie looked at Tim's hand and felt her heart stop. Tim wasn't wearing his wedding ring.

"You're not wearing your wedding ring. Does that mean you're going to start dating?"

"Yes."

Slam! His immediate, calm, almost casual reply took her breath away.

"Do you know who?" The fear started rising. Did she really want to hear this?

"Yes — but I'm not leaving you for anyone in particular. You and I just aren't right for each other. I've been living a lie all these years, and I'm tired of it."

"Tim, please, won't you stay the night? Just one night?"

"I can't."

Leslie began to feel herself losing control. She didn't become hysterical, but the tears took over and she lost her composure. She held on until Tim drove away, *then* she became hysterical.

The sobs that came up from within her were deep and pervasive. Finally, Leslie knelt down on a chair to pray, but there was still too much agony inside her. She simply couldn't pray on her own. Instead she stood up, stumbled to the phone, and dialed some close friends. "Tim just left me," she whispered through her tears. "Can you come over?"

Leslie and her friends wept and prayed, prayed and wept, and wept and prayed some more. After hours of spiritual struggle, Leslie finally felt a release and some semblance of peace.

"Would you like me to spend the night?" one of her friends asked.

"No, I'll be okay," Leslie said. She's thankful now that at the time she didn't realize what really lay ahead.

Telling the News

Because Leslie directed a Christian ministry, she knew she would have to tell her staff what had happened. They were very supportive and rallied around Leslie, but their response was surprisingly difficult for her to take.

"It was hard for me to receive," Leslie confesses. "The Lord really dealt with my pride. I was always the one who had to give and give, but God wanted me to enter a period of weakness."

As Leslie prayed throughout the week following Tim's departure, she sensed that God was asking her to tell her story to the church and ask for prayer. Leslie couldn't imagine doing this; she thought she had to put on a strong face because she led a ministry. "God," she argued, "they'll think I haven't been a good wife so how can I possibly be adequate to run the ministry center? If I'm incapable of keeping a husband, how can I keep a ministry going?"

During the church service that Sunday morning the worship leader did something that has never been done before or since that day: He asked the congregation to share prayer requests or praises. Leslie gulped, sighed, and stood up. Every eye in the church was fixed on her. She swallowed hard, then said, "I need the church to know that Tim left me last week...."

A big, horrible gasp followed, but Leslie continued. "Tim and I really need your prayers for our marriage to be healed."

Being the weak one was devastating for Leslie, but it "blew the windows open" in her church with respect to other marriages that were reeling. For that Leslie was thankful, even as she waited for her own marriage to be healed.

False Hope

What helped Leslie make it through the first few months of her separation was her confident expectation that Tim would come back. She was optimistic that once she was able to understand why Tim left and what she had done wrong, she could "fix" everything and her marriage would be okay. But it wasn't okay, and it wasn't going to be okay. Tim was actively dating and showing little interest in reconciliation.

Bitterness became a frequent seducer, but Leslie fought it off, in part because God had begun to reveal some of her own failings — the self-righteousness with which she had treated her husband and the way she expected so much of herself and of him, for starters.

For the first time, Leslie was able to see the chains of perfectionism that had bound her for so many years. She remembered how, before Tim left her, she had bristled inside when her pastor pointed a finger her way and said she was a sinner. "Where do you see sin in my life? Just tell me so I can get rid of it."

"I saw that there was no grace and no mercy in my Christian life," Leslie admits. Months went by, and then years — and then finally the day that Tim told Leslie he was marrying someone else.

Shared Sufferings

Sometimes depression would creep up on Leslie, bringing a good dose of fear with it, especially as Tim's wedding day drew near. But then — there's no other way for Leslie to describe it — the Lord would take her face in his hands and say, "Leslie, look at *me.* Look at me."

As the marital breakup began to appear permanent, Leslie began to grieve anew. She berated herself at times, blaming herself, thinking that if she had only done something differently, Tim wouldn't have left.

"That's not true," she sensed God telling her. "*I* loved him perfectly, and he's left me too."

Leslie wept at that thought, and she began to feel a new kinship with the Lord. Somehow she was *sharing* in his sufferings. They were going through this *together.*

Well-meaning Christian friends eventually started asking Leslie if she was dating yet. Leslie did her best to mask her shock and respond with grace. She still wore her wedding ring, and while some Christians felt that she should "just let go," the ring was a sign of a covenant Leslie had made not just with Tim, but with God. Even though Tim had walked out of the relationship, the Lord was still there — so two out of the three parties were hanging in there.

"The wedding ring didn't represent my love for Tim anymore," Leslie says. "That old love was dead. But it represented my commitment before the Lord — the One before whom I said, 'till death do us part.'"

Right up until the day Tim remarried in 1998, Leslie wore her wedding ring and kept praying for a reconciliation. By remaining faithful in the midst of unfaithfulness, her eyes were opened to God's presence in a new way. "The faithlessness of Israel and the faithfulness of God, as well as the faithfulness of Hosea and the faithlessness of Gomer, really spoke to me," Leslie says. "This entire experience has helped me to get to know God better. I've gained a sense of the incredible unconditional love that his covenant represents. The more I sought God's permission to take off my ring and start dating, the more he would talk to me about his covenant promise."

This, in a nutshell, is one of the key messages of this book. Even when something as tragic as betrayal, unfaithfulness, and an unwanted divorce are foisted on us, the experience can be used for spiritual benefit. By remaining true herself and by respecting the sacredness of her history with Tim even though he no longer respected that history, Leslie learned valuable spiritual lessons and drew closer to God in the process.

But Leslie was a pioneer of sorts. Most of her fellow Christians couldn't understand why she wouldn't just "give up." "They could understand why someone would take back a wayward child — the whole bit about the prodigal son," she says. "But with a husband and wife, many Christians just don't see it."

But now Leslie sees God in a whole new light.

The Divine Husband

Leslie now says, "God is the perfect Husband. He has met my needs before I even anticipated them. I'm not just talking about big things either. He has met my small, personal needs in very intimate ways."

Two weeks before Easter 1998 — just months before Tim's wedding — Leslie was asked to speak at a church that was decorated with beautiful Easter lilies. Since the divorce, Leslie has lived on a substandard income. She believes that God wanted her to forgive Tim and not fight to "make him pay" for leaving her, so she lives under extremely tight budget constraints. Buying an Easter lily, she thought, would be a "frivolous expense," but she found herself wistfully praying, "They sure are beautiful, Lord. I would love to have one." It was a silent prayer, and her request was spoken to no one.

The day before Easter, Leslie went into work and saw an Easter lily on her desk. Leslie stopped, stared, and then began to weep. Though the lily was from a friend, Leslie accepted it as a gift from God, who had heard her prayer and now was buying his "wife" a flower for Easter.

"By losing my earthly husband, I've drawn closer to my heavenly one." Leslie says it emphatically: "*He's my Husband,* my Provider, my Sustainer." Though Leslie's relationship with God used to be based on "performance," this season of hurt and pain has taught her how to receive from God.

I spoke with Leslie less than two weeks before Tim's wedding. "God can still restore my marriage," Leslie told me, "but even if he doesn't, he's still God." She paused, looking wistful. Tears welled up from the bottom of her eyes.

"This has been such a rich time for me spiritually, Gary. I wouldn't trade it for anything."

"Think about that for a second, Leslie," I asked her. *"Do you really mean that?"*

"I do — with all my heart. It's been so rich, so profoundly life-changing. Of course, I can't say I'm glad my marriage broke up, but I *am* glad for the fruit it has created."

Leslie has entered a new realm. She has learned the secret that regardless of what others do to us — even if they betray us in the most intimate sense — God can use that occasion to draw us closer into his heart. And then, God can use it to draw others to him as well.

As a special blessing, two years after Tim left Leslie, Leslie's father called her on the phone. "I've watched what you've gone through," he said. "I've seen how you've reacted, and I want what you have."

This was a profoundly moving conversation for Leslie, for, like Tim, her father had been unfaithful to his wife (Leslie's mother), leaving Leslie to grow up with the pain of a broken home. But all the anguish began to melt away as Leslie went through the "Romans Road" with her father in a hotel room, and her father knelt down and prayed to receive Jesus Christ as his Lord and Savior at the age of sixty-two.

There is an exalted truth in this conversion experience. What really happened was that by remaining faithful to an unfaithful husband, Leslie demonstrated the truth of a God who remains faithful to an unfaithful people. Her father had heard the gospel many times, but it wasn't until he saw it displayed in Leslie's life that he wanted it for himself.

Leslie is even able to smile now. "How can I not thank God?" she asks me. "Quite honestly, I'm more than willing to pray, 'God, you can have my marriage if it means the salvation of my family.' Tim's a believer, I know that, so he's going to heaven. If his leaving me can lead others to God, I'm willing to endure that."

Just one final note before we leave Leslie's story: Not long ago, a man called Leslie for help. His wife had left him. He was gravitating toward bitterness and anger, but Leslie pointed him in a different direction.

"This season in your life can be so productive spiritually if you use it to allow God to break you, shape you, and remake you," she told him. "We're always looking at what our spouses have done wrong, but God wants to deal with our own heart first."

Tell the Story

If we are serious about pursuing spiritual growth through marriage, we must convince ourselves to refrain from asking the spiritually dangerous question: "Did I marry the 'right' person?" Once we have exchanged our vows, little can be gained spiritually from ruminating on this question.

A far better alternative to questioning one's choice is to learn how to live with one's choice. A character in the Anne Tyler novel *A Patchwork Planet* comes to realize this too late. The book's thirty-year-old narrator has gone through a divorce and now works at an occupation that has him relating almost exclusively with elderly people. As he observes their long-standing marriages, he comes to a profound understanding:

> I was beginning to suspect that it made no difference whether they'd married the right person. Finally, you're just with who you're with. You've signed on with her, put in half a century with her, grown to know her as well as you know yourself or even better, and she's *become* the right person. Or the only person, might be more to the point. I wish someone had told me that earlier. I'd have hung on then; I swear I would. I never would have driven Natalie to leave me.[5]

Half the battle is just keeping our "story" alive.

In the late 1950s, Ruth Bell Graham published a children's book titled *Our Christmas Story*. Her husband, Billy Graham, wrote the following in the foreword:

> When it was suggested that Ruth tell the Christmas story for children everywhere, we were delighted. But we had to warn the publisher that "our" Christmas story would be different from the

traditional manger scene that spells Christmas for many people. Of course, the manger scene is an important part of Christmas in our home — the joyous and beloved climax to the story. But it is only a part of the story. For Christmas does not begin in the stable of Bethlehem. It does not begin in the Gospel of Luke, but in the Book of Genesis.

This is only right; Christmas Eve and Christmas morning are merely the climaxes to a long-running story set in motion centuries before. It's a fascinating tale, one that God follows with all the passion of a husband, the hurt of a betrayed friend, the frustration of a wise parent, and the perspective of an aggrieved Lord and King. It would not be fair to judge that history at any one point, for it is the history of God and his people Israel — his bride and his spouse — taken together over the long run, that tells the complete story.

Learning to cherish my sacred history with Lisa has been one of the most spiritually meaningful practices in my life. We have an unusual story, going back to the state of being, for two weeks, "junior high sweethearts." We have created a history together that is enriching, meaningful, and laden with passion. Yes, we have had to travel through a few valleys to get to where we are. Yes, there were moments when the history seemed threatened, but if the journey had its difficulties, the sights along the way and our destination have been worth it.

Popular author Jerry Jenkins encourages us to revel in our own marital story. He writes:

> Tell your [marital] story. Tell it to your kids, your friends, your brothers and sisters, but especially to each other. The more your story is implanted in your brain, the more it serves as a hedge against the myriad forces that seek to destroy your marriage. Make your story so familiar that it becomes part of the fabric of your being. It should become a legend that is shared through the generations as you grow a family tree that defies all odds and boasts marriage after marriage of stability, strength, and longevity.[6]

Don't abort your history with the spouse whom God has called you to love. Don't cheapen the experience of walking hand in hand with the God who can identify with every relational struggle you face.

"May the Lord direct your hearts into God's love and Christ's perseverance."

Sacred Struggle
Embracing Difficulty
in Order to Build Character

Ven you're a married man, Samivel, you'll understand
a good many things as you don't understand now,
but vether it's worthwhile, goin' through so much,
to learn so little, as the charity-boy said ven he got
to the end of the alphabet, is a matter o' taste
CHARLES DICKENS

One was never married, and that's his hell;
another is, and that's his plague.
ROBERT BURTON, ENGLISH CLERGYMAN

They dream in courtship, but in wedlock wake.
ALEXANDER POPE

Because marriage, more than any other relationship,
reflects God's involvement with us and
bears more potential to draw our hearts to heaven,
it can more readily give us a taste of hell.
DAN ALLENDER AND TREMPER LONGMAN III

THERE ARE FEW NATURAL WONDERS MORE STARTLING IN THEIR beauty than Mount Everest, the highest spot on earth. Geologists believe that the Himalayas were created by the Indian continent crashing into Eurasia. "Crashing" is a writer's hyperbole; actually, the two continents collide with a movement of about ten centimeters per year. But slow and steady does the job. As India keeps moving inward, compressing and lifting southern Eurasia, a spectacular natural treasure continues to be created.

If there were no collision between India and Eurasia, there would be no Himalayas. Without the wrenching force of continental shifting, the world would be a poorer place aesthetically.

In the same way, the "collisions" of marriage can create relationships of beauty. Beauty is often birthed in struggle. These points of impact may not be "fun"—in fact, they can make us feel like we're being ripped apart—but the process can make us stronger, build our character, and deepen our faith.

The great spiritual writer and director François Fénelon wrote, "The more we fear to suffer, the more we need to do so." Suffering is part of the Christian life, modeled by Jesus Christ himself, who suffered immeasurably in his service to God. Dietrich Bonhoeffer wrote that if we do not have something of the ascetic in us, we will find it hard to follow God.

And yet most of those who leave marriage and break its sacred history do so precisely because it's tough. Few people leave a marriage because it's too easy! This tendency to avoid difficulty is a grave spiritual failing that can and often does keep us in Christian infancy. The great spiritual writers warned that this life *is* difficult and that we should use the difficulty to be built up in our character.

William Law, an eighteenth-century Anglican writer, asks, "How many saints has adversity sent to Heaven? And how many poor sinners has prosperity plunged into everlasting misery?" John Climacus, who wrote *the* Eastern classic on the Christian faith in the fifth century, mocks our demand to have it easy and to shun struggle: "I would not consider any spirituality worthwhile that wants to walk in sweetness and ease and run from the imitation of Christ."

Jesus promised us that *everyone* will be seasoned with fire, and every sacrifice will be seasoned with salt (see Mark 9:49, NEW KING JAMES VERSION). The desire for ease, comfort, and stress-free living is an indirect desire to remain an "unseasoned," immature Christian. Struggle makes us stronger; it builds us up and deepens our faith.

But this result is achieved only when we face the struggle head-on, not when we run from it. Gary and Betsy Ricucci point out, "Our Lord has sovereignly ordained that our refining process take place as we go *through* difficulties, not around them. The Bible is filled with examples of those who overcame as they passed *through* the desert, the Red Sea, the fiery furnace and ultimately the cross. God doesn't protect Christians from their problems—he helps them walk victoriously *through* their problems."[1]

If your marriage is tough, get down on your knees and thank God that he has given you an opportunity for unparalleled spiritual growth. You have the prime potential to excel in Christian character and obedience.

Appreciating Struggle

As a cross-country runner, my most satisfying victories were those that took every ounce of strength I possessed. Races that I won easily, though less painful, were ultimately less satisfying. I remember one race run against a smaller school. I went out hard, but not too hard, and lost their lead runner within the first mile. I then slowed up and allowed our number-two runner to catch up, and we ambled through the rest of the race together. I was even talking to my friend as we raced over the familiar trails.

It was a pleasant race, but I wasn't proud of my performance. I hadn't even been tested, so there was little to be proud about.

But there was another race, this one involving six different high schools. The weather was hot for Washington state, and I went out at a bruising pace and nearly ran myself into the hospital. There were about a dozen times in that three-mile race when I had to make a conscious decision not to quit as yet another runner pushed up to challenge for the lead.

When I finally collapsed across the finish line, I was almost too tired to be elated over the win. I developed a very high fever that night and was sick for three days, but even in the pain of that recovery I knew I had given it my all, and there was a certain awe in that knowledge. It wasn't fun, by any means, but it was very *meaningful.*

Struggling successfully and profitably brings a deeper joy than even trouble-free living. I once flipped through a magazine spread of a well-known celebrity, photographed in his bathrobe and slippers, walking out of an opulent house with a stunning view, and yet this image carried no attraction for me. In truth, it made me somewhat sick. The lifestyle this photograph was depicting—free of responsibility or labor, coddling in abundance—might be nice for a week or two every year, but as a way of life it seemed offensive and uninviting.

God created us in such a way that we need to struggle to stay alive. Challenge is what keeps us seasoned. But to be profitable, our struggle must have *purpose,* and it must be *productive.* Two people who do nothing but fight in their marriage and make each other miserable are not engaging in a helpful spiritual exercise. It's only when we put struggle within the Christian context of character development and self-sacrifice that it becomes profitable.

Jesus portrayed struggle as the entry point into the Christian life, stressing that it would be a *daily* reality of our faith: "If anyone would come after me, he must deny himself and take up his cross *daily* and follow me" (Luke 9:23, italics added). To many Western Christians, this verse might sound melodramatic When I look at my life honestly, I have to admit that in many ways I have it unusually easy. I am not ridiculed or persecuted for my faith—in fact, as a Christian writer and speaker, my faith has the peripheral and favorable effect of supporting my family.

This relative ease of life as a Christian is a benefit experienced by very few generations before us. Medicine has become so advanced that many of us can live virtually pain-free lives. We have machines to wash our clothes and do the dishes, and cars that move us at 70 MPH from one place to the next. I can wake up in Seattle and have dinner in New York that same evening.

We have it so easy that we can begin to be lulled to sleep, thinking that life *should* be easy or that it will *always* be easy. Once it gets a little difficult, we tend to become consumed with trying to make our lives comfortable again. But by doing so we miss a great spiritual opportunity.

As Lisa and I read about many of the assaults on Mount Everest, we learned that mountain climbers will often step back from a particularly difficult overhang or stretch and discuss how to surmount it. Much of the fun in the sport is encountering the challenges and figuring out a way to get around them. If mountain climbing were easy, it would lose a great deal of its appeal.

Our relationships can be looked at the same way. Instead of immediately thinking about how we can take a helicopter to the top, we might take a climber's approach and think, "This is really tough. This is a challenge, no doubt about it. How do I keep loving this person in the face of this challenge?"

Thomas à Kempis noted that "the more the flesh is wasted by affliction, so much the more is the spirit strengthened by inward grace. And sometimes he is so comforted with desire of tribulation and adversity, for the love of conformity to the cross of Christ, that he would not wish to be without grief or tribulation."

Ask yourself this question: Would I rather live a life of ease and comfort and remain immature in Christ, or am I willing to be seasoned with suffering if by doing so I am conformed to the image of Christ?

It is unrealistic to assume that the initial pledge of marital fidelity will be an "easy" one to keep. Otto Piper points out that "there is always an element of mistrust implied in the marriage contract."[2] The reason we promise to love each other "till death do us part" is precisely because our society knows that such a promise will be sorely tried—otherwise, the promise wouldn't be necessary! We don't make public promises that we will regularly nourish our bodies with food or buy ourselves adequate clothing.

Everyone who enters the marriage relationship will come to a point where the marriage starts to "rub" somewhat adversely. It is *for these times* that the promise is made. Anticipating struggle, God has ordained a remedy, holding us to our word of commitment.

In this struggle we become nobler people. One of the great challenges we encounter as we encourage Christians to grow is that we are obsessed with raising children who need to be taught their manners, while we assume that our own characters are fully developed. They're not. There are numerous areas in which both you and I can continue to grow. Nobility, sacrifice, and unselfishness are just a few.

Sweet Suffering

Without degenerating into becoming a masochist, the mature Christian recognizes and appreciates the sweet side of suffering. Teresa of Avila wrote, "Lord, how you afflict your lovers! But everything is small in comparison to what you give them afterward." This is the same reality experienced by John Climacus, who centuries before Teresa wrote, "If individuals resolutely submit to the carrying of the cross, if they decidedly want to find and endure trial in all things for God, they will discover in all of them great relief and sweetness."

This teaching simply mirrors Paul's words in 2 Corinthians 4:17: "For our light and momentary troubles are achieving for us an eternal glory that far outweighs them all."

Because we have hope for eternity, we do not become nearsighted, demanding short-term ease that would short-circuit long-term gain. Our demands for comfort and ease show us what we truly value. It is the definitive demonstration of whether we are living for God's kingdom and service or for our own comfort and reputation.

A heavyweight boxing champion who dodges all serious contenders to consistently fight marshmallows is derided and ridiculed—and rightly so. Christians who dodge all serious struggle and consciously seek to put themselves in whatever situations and relationships are easiest are doing the same thing—they are coasting, and eventually that coasting will define them and—even worse—shape them.

If there is one thing young engaged couples need to hear, it's that *a good marriage is not something you find, it's something you work for.* It takes struggle. You must crucify your selfishness. You must at times confront, and at other times confess. The practice of forgiveness is essential.

This is undeniably hard work! But eventually it pays off. Eventually, it creates a relationship of beauty, trust, and mutual support.

It helps when we view our struggles in light of what they provide for us spiritually rather than in light of what they take from us emotionally. Working through disagreements is taxing. There are a million things I'd rather do than put in the time and effort to leap over a relational hurdle. If I'm in my marriage for emotional stability, I probably won't last long. But if I think it can reap spiritual benefits, I'll have plenty of reason to not just *be* married, but *act* married.

Otto Piper challenges us, "If marriage ... is a disillusioning experience for many people, the reason is to be found in the passivity of their faith. People dislike the fact that the blessings of God may only be found and enjoyed when they are persistently sought (Matthew 7:7; Luke 11:9). Marriage is, therefore, both a gift and a task to be accomplished."[3]

Don't run from the struggles of marriage. Embrace them. Grow in them. Draw nearer to God because of them. Through them you will reflect more of the spirit of Jesus Christ. And thank God that he has placed you in a situation where your spirit can be perfected.

Let's take a close look at two individuals who struggled mightily in their marriages—but who became outstandingly influential people as a result.

The Great Emancipator[4]

One could conclude that Abraham Lincoln was an unusual man of principle simply by the way he approached courtship, not to mention the way he approached marriage.

In 1836, Lincoln agreed to marry a woman whom he had not seen for three years — risky at best, treacherous at worst — and Abe had plenty of time to regret his promise. When he was finally brought face-to-face with his prospective bride, Lincoln's heart sank. "She did not look as my imagination had pictured her," he wrote.

Indeed not. "I knew she was oversize," he admitted, "but she now appeared a fair match for Falstaff." When he looked at her face, to his horror he found "I could not for my life avoid thinking of my mother." This was due in part to two features: the woman's "lack of teeth" and Lincoln's treelike assessment of her age — "nothing could have commenced at the size of infancy, and reached her present bulk in less than thirty-five or forty years."

"In short," he summarized, "I was not at all pleased with her."

But then Lincoln did something that shocks modern sensibilities. Because he had given his word, he was determined to marry her. He went through the process of courting, and then dropped to one knee and requested this woman's hand in matrimony.

A hilarious scene followed. The woman ended up rejecting *him*. At first Lincoln thought she was just being polite, so he went through the accepted rites of pressing her to reconsider, until he realized that she had no inclination or intention of ever becoming his wife.

Lincoln concluded, "Others have been made fools of by the girls; but this can never be with truth said of me. I most emphatically, in this instance, made a fool of myself."

You'd think Lincoln might have been more careful when choosing his next fiancée, but Mary Todd was hardly the type of woman with whom one could enjoy a quiet evening. She was, in fact, a woman of intense impulses and tremendous temper, though this, ironically enough, was some of her attraction for the future president. Lincoln called her the "first aggressively brilliant, feminine creature" who had crossed his path.

Shortly after the wedding, Mary became discontented with their house, telling Lincoln that "everybody who was quality" in their society lived in a two-story house. Lincoln tried the ruse that so many husbands have used — assenting to the idea, but not appropriating the funds. Rather than prolong the debate, as many wives of her day would have done, Mary simply waited until Lincoln left town on business for several weeks, then contracted with a carpenter to add another story.

As the years passed, Lincoln learned patience in other ways. Mary's bouts of temper made retaining hired help extremely difficult; Lincoln responded by giving the girls an extra weekly dollar. After one particularly forceful eruption between Mary and a maid, Lincoln quietly patted the girl on the shoulder and said, "Stay with her, Maria. Stay with her."

When a salesman called on the White House and was treated to Mary's fervid verbal assault, he marched right up to the Oval Office — those were different days, to be sure — and proceeded to complain to President Lincoln about how the first lady had treated him. Lincoln listened calmly, then stood and gently said, "You can endure for fifteen minutes what I have endured for fifteen years."

Lincoln suffered numerous indignities at the hand of his wife, from Mary's publicly throwing coffee in his face to her profligate spending. In those days, presidents were not quite as well off as they are today, but Mary went on bizarre spending binges, during one stretch buying hundreds of pairs of gloves.

When the Lincolns lost Willie — Mary's favorite son — the ensuing grief began to crack Mrs. Lincoln's fragile psyche. It became more and more difficult for her to control her hysterics, and at times Lincoln himself did not help matters much. Once he even led his wife to a window, pointed to a lunatic asylum, and said, "Mother, do you see that large white building on the hill yonder? Try and control your grief, or it will drive you mad and we may have to send you there."

It was in the aftermath of this tremendous grief (losing his son) and distraction (watching his wife fall apart) that Lincoln was called on to give the speech that would mark him for posterity. Lincoln's political life was as precarious at this point as was his home life. As the Civil War dragged on, Abe's political favor crashed. When told that the president would address the crowd at Gettysburg — gathering to commemorate the fallen soldiers—a fellow politician scoffed, "Let the dead bury the dead."

Shortly before Lincoln left for Gettysburg, his son Tad became ill, and this once again intensified Mary's hysterics, as she was newly reminded of the son she had lost less than two years earlier. With all the distractions at home, Lincoln was able merely to scribble out a few notes as he left for Pennsylvania.

In this highly emotional moment, Lincoln could be forgiven for delivering his words with less-than-powerful rhetoric. One reporter described Lincoln's delivery as "a sharp, unmusical treble voice." The applause was scattered and restrained, so much so that Lincoln believed he had failed miserably. He leaned over and told a friend, "It is a flat failure and the people are disappointed."

But the words were true and genuine, and they were moving and powerful—and as the newspapers recorded them without Lincoln's understandable gloom coloring them, the nation was inspired as never before. The Gettysburg Address is one of the most famous speeches ever delivered on American soil, and those words would eventually be carved in stone, accompanying Lincoln into posterity. It may be a cliché to say this, but it's still true: He shone brightest when his personal life was darkest.

The connection one can make between Lincoln's marriage and his mission is not difficult. It is easy to see how a man who might quit on a difficult marriage would not have the character to hold together a crumbling nation. Lincoln was virtually obsessed with saving the Union; what better training ground than the difficult marriage that required such tenacity from him?

It's important to see that not only did Lincoln's difficult marriage not deter him from achieving greatness, one might argue that it actually helped prepare him for greatness. Lincoln's character was tested and refined on a daily basis so that when the true test came, he was able to stand strong.

Had Lincoln been obsessed with happiness, he wouldn't have mustered the strength to put up with Mary or to hold the nation together. He sensed a call to destiny, something that would in his mind supersede personal comfort, and his obedience to that destiny made world history.

In virtually any poll on the presidents, Lincoln comes out near the top. Some historians have suggested that he may well have been our most successful president ever. Interestingly enough, a 1982 poll of historians put Mary Todd Lincoln at the absolute bottom of first ladies.

This story exposes the lie behind the thinking of the pastor who declares, "I really could have done something if I hadn't married this woman," or the wife who says to herself, "Just think what I might be if I weren't bound to such a loser." One of our greatest presidents was, without question, married to one of the most difficult first ladies.

It's fitting that Abraham Lincoln should be known as the "great emancipator." Once, when traveling through a throng of slave refugees, Mary asked her husband how many of the little children were named Abraham Lincoln. The president responded—truthfully, not boastfully—"Let's see. This is April 1863. I should say that of all those babies under two years of age perhaps two-thirds have been named for me."

"Emancipator" means deliverer from bondage and oppression. Perhaps Lincoln's example can deliver us from the oppression of an empty pursuit of happiness. Perhaps he can set us free from the notion that a difficult marriage will hold us back rather than prepare us for our life's work; maybe he can yet cut us loose from the chains that bind us to the seeking of tension-free lives over the building of lives of meaning and character.

The Great Aviator[5]

Imagine being a young, Ivy League-educated woman in the 1920s; you love books and harbor dreams of becoming a writer or a poet. Your father is a United States ambassador and your family is well-respected and well-off. You have been raised to esteem refinement, good manners, and "superior breeding."

And through your father's door walks a man who is larger than life. Yet he is everything you have been taught not to respect — an adventurer rather than a scholar, a man who tinkers with engines rather than with words. He is from humble origins, but his transatlantic flight from New York to Paris has given him a fame almost unparalleled in the history of this country.

Thus begins the account of Anne Morrow Lindbergh's marriage.

While I was writing a biography of a famous race-car driver, the publisher sent me a catalogue that lists celebrity addresses; it includes everybody from Albert, the crown prince of Monaco, to Tiger Woods and Renée Zellweger (an up-and-coming actress). The type is small, in two columns, fitting about 140–150 names per page. The catalogue runs *seventy-one* pages. Do the math, and you'll realize just how many "celebrities" there are today.

It was a different era earlier in this century, particularly before World War II. Charles Lindbergh's successful flight across the Atlantic put him in a class all by himself. His fame was virtually unparalleled. Today you couldn't really pick a "favorite" celebrity; the list of who's in and who's out changes with every year-end issue of *People* magazine.

But Lindbergh was undoubtedly, for a time, the most famous and popular man in America — perhaps in the world. Imagine having Wall Street close down for a parade in *your* honor — a parade that drew 4.5 million people! Lindy's popularity reached such heights that women would check into hotel rooms he had just left so that they could bathe in his bathtub and sleep in his bed. Lindbergh found he couldn't even send his shirts to the laundry — they never came back. And Lindy had a particularly difficult time balancing his checkbook, because most people refused to cash his checks. They opted instead to keep them as souvenirs.

When Anne Morrow met Charles Lindbergh, she was prepared to thoroughly dislike the famous aviator. A Smith-educated, well-bred, bookish sort of woman, Anne wasn't about to be swept off her feet by what she called "all this public-hero stuff." She wrote in her diary, "I certainly was not going to worship 'Lindy' (that odious *name,* anyway)." Her teacher derided Lindbergh, saying Charles was "really no more than a mechanic ... had it not been for the lone eagle flight, he would now be in charge of a gasoline station on the outskirts of St. Louis."

In spite of Anne's initial resolve not to be swept off her feet by this great adventurer, much to her own consternation she did find herself smitten after she met him. Somehow the man who bore that "odious" name suddenly became "keen, intelligent, burning, thinking on all lines." Anne feverishly poured words into her journal that were more reminiscent of a lovesick adolescent than an aspiring poet: "The intensity of life, burning like a bright fire in his eyes. Life focused in him—when he in turn focuses his life, power, force on *anything,* amazing things happen."

Because of Lindy's fame, dating presented several problems. As soon as he was seen with a young woman, newspapers ran photographs and started speculating about an engagement. Early on, Lindy warned Anne, "Don't worry about *my* publicity. It's coming to me anyway. I've got to take it, but I don't want it to be embarrassing for you."

Anne learned to play along. When she wrote to her sisters, she used the code name "Robert Boyd" in place of Charles Lindbergh, lest her letters be intercepted and leaked to the press.

Being an early aviator—in the days before tabloids hired helicopters—had its advantages. Sometimes Lindy would fly Anne to a deserted field on Long Island, giving them the opportunity to talk quietly and privately. As Anne got to know Charles better, she had ambivalent feelings. In one sense, he overwhelmed her, but in another sense she recognized how very different they were. The two of them, adventurer and poet, seemed like an utter and complete mismatch. She poured out her thoughts in a letter to her sister: "As you can see, I am completely turned upside down, completely overwhelmed, completely upset. He is the biggest, most absorbing person I've ever met, and doesn't seem to touch my life anywhere, really."

"Don't Wish Me Happiness"

When the engagement was settled on, Anne knew that life with Lindy wouldn't be easy. The quiet country house, the life of relative ease and luxury and privacy that she had envisioned, wouldn't be possible with Lindy. She wrote in a letter to a friend, "Corliss, if you write me and wish me conventional happiness I will *never* forgive you. Don't wish me happiness—I don't expect to be happy, but it's gotten beyond that, somehow. Wish me courage and strength and a sense of humor—I will need them all."

Anne's joy at her wedding was tempered in part by the ridiculous lengths to which she and her new husband had to go in order to escape the public eye. To slip out of the wedding, Anne lay down in a borrowed car, passing the usual crowd of reporters that gathered at her parents' gate. She and Lindy then changed cars, drove to Long Island, and rowed out to a boat that had been left anchored for them in the water.

The effort paid off. The newlyweds enjoyed two unusually quiet days until they were recognized while refueling. They were pursued and hounded for the rest of their honeymoon.

While everyone raved about how "lucky" Anne was to capture the world's most eligible bachelor—a perception she chafed against, as it assumed that Lindy wasn't lucky to have *her*—the private young woman struggled to get used to her sudden notoriety.

"It is difficult to believe or even to remember how little privacy we had; how hard we struggled to be alone together," she reminisced many years later. "In Mexico City, reporters waited for us at the Embassy gates, their cars and cameras set to follow us. At [my parents'] weekend house ... enterprising photographers climbed up onto nearby roofs and miradors to photograph us in our garden. Disguised, we sneaked out of back doors, went to friends' houses, changed cars, and fled into the wild country of Mexico, which was then considered dangerous because of bandits. We went flying. Here at least we were not followed. After passing through the barrage of cameras at the flying field we could take off and leave the crowds behind, landing for a picnic on the plains—alone at last."

This flight from photographers and journalists came at a cost. As Anne herself points out, "total isolation is not normal life any more than total public exposure. Like criminals or illicit lovers, we avoided being seen in the world together and had to forgo the everyday pleasures of walking along streets, shopping, sightseeing, eating out at restaurants, or taking part in public events. Even social occasions at the Embassy or in my parents' home in Englewood, NJ, were not free from intrusion. Servants were offered bribes, letters were stolen, telegrams often leaked out, reporters talked to unsuspecting guests or friends and printed distorted anecdotes about our private life, or, if they ran short of material, they simply invented stories."

Although Anne was a very insightful person with literary ambitions, early on in her relationship with Charles that part of her life had to be curtailed. Charles warned her to "never say anything you wouldn't want shouted from the housetops, and never write anything you would mind seeing on the front page of a newspaper."

Anne reflects: "I was convinced I must protect him and myself from intrusion into our private life, but what a sacrifice to make never to speak or write deeply or honestly! I, to whom an experience was not finished until it was written or shared in conversation. I who had said in college that the most exciting thing in life was communication . . . The result was dampening for my kind of inner life. I stopped writing in my diary completely for three years and since even letters were unsafe, I tried to write cautiously or in family language and jokes."

Try to imagine what it must have been like to live in the midst of such intense public curiosity. Even in the Lindberghs' most intimate moments, they had to be guarded: "Of course, once we were married I could talk freely to my husband, but only in the privacy of a plane, a wilderness, or a bedroom. And even in a hotel room, I must be sure that the windows and the transom to the hall were closed to eavesdroppers."

The "dream life" that all the papers wrote about so exuberantly had its dark side. Anne laments, "We had no private life—only public life.... We had no home; we lived in hotels, planes, or other people's homes. We traveled constantly."

This is not the life that someone "born to letters" envisions. It is not the environment or existence that a quiet, reflective poet would choose. Anne felt keenly the breakneck pace. In a cry for sympathy, she lamented to her mother, "We can never catch life unawares. It is always looking at us."

Set Free with Sorrow

In 1932, the fame took a cruel and malicious turn. The Lindberghs' eighteen-month-old child, Charles Lindbergh Jr., was taken from his crib in the Lindberghs' New Jersey home. The kidnappers left a note on the windowsill demanding a ransom in exchange for his safe return. Negotiations lasted for six weeks, after which a ransom was paid, but the child wasn't returned. Four excruciating weeks later —ten weeks in all—the ordeal came to a tragic end when the little child's dead body was found discarded in the woods, just a few miles from the Lindberghs' home.

As a father of three children, I can't imagine a more difficult experience to live through than the loss of a child. A kidnapping—the uncertainty, the waiting, and then finding the body—must have been devastating. It is one thing for fame to steal your poetry or your hopes for a quiet life. It is another thing altogether when fame steals and destroys your firstborn child.

Because the boy had been abandoned in the woods, animals had gotten to him; it took awhile for authorities to positively identify the body. Adding severe insult to cruel injury, some photographers broke into the morgue and published photos of Anne's partially decomposed son for all to see.

This was a parent's worst nightmare, compounded fifty times. Yet, ironically enough, it was this tragedy that released Anne to write again. She had allowed the absurdity of fame to put a part of her inner core to sleep, but something in the magnitude of this tragedy brought new life, like green grass poking up in the aftermath of a devastating forest fire.

"There were other values, I was beginning to learn, more important than discretion or even privacy," Anne writes. "As I discovered the following spring, in the abyss of tragedy, I needed to return to a deeper resource. I had to write honestly. So one can say perhaps that sorrow also played its part in setting me free."

Think about this line: "Sorrow also played its part in setting me free." So often today sorrow is something that is to be avoided at all costs. Sorrow is the enemy, the persecutor, the fearful emotion. If there is sorrow in our marriage, we must leave our marriage, for how could anyone suggest that I remain in an unhappy marriage? While few of us would (or even should) have the courage to willingly choose sorrow, when we find ourselves in it, if we quieted our souls down —if we learned to float in it rather than thrash about like a drowning emotional victim—we might find, as Anne did, that it can be used to set us free.

Anne isn't sentimental about this, just honest and vulnerable: "What I am saying is not simply the old Puritan truism that 'suffering teaches.' I do not believe that sheer suffering teaches. If suffering alone taught, all the world would be wise, since everyone suffers. To suffering must be added mourning, understanding, patience, love, openness, and the willingness to remain vulnerable."

Anne is right, of course. A difficult marriage, in and of itself, may not cause us to grow. We have to apply ourselves to understanding, love, and patience—we must commit ourselves to a pursuit of virtue —within that difficult marriage. We can't control how our spouse will act or how the world will act, but we can control how we will act and how we will respond.

This perspective puts us in the driver's seat. No longer tossed about as a "victim of sorrow," we become the architects of a new character. It is either this—or giving up control and allowing the toxic eruption of bitterness to pollute our souls.

It may sound antiquated to talk about the pursuit of "virtue" in today's world, but this is only because we don't fully understand what virtue truly represents. At its root, virtue means "strength." It's related to a word that more directly addresses this meaning: "*vir*ile." Virtue is strength—power to do what is right; power to make the right choice; power to overcome the weakness of sin, bad choices, victimhood, and self-pity.

Years later, as Anne Lindbergh reflected on the kidnapping, she remarked that she found comfort in two teachings—one Christian, and one Buddhist. "Undoubtedly," she wrote, "the long road of suffering, insight, healing, or rebirth, is best illustrated in the Christian religion by the suffering, death, and resurrection of Christ."

The other story concerns a mother who approached Buddha after losing her child. Legend has it that Buddha told her that all she needed for healing was a single mustard seed from a household that had never known sorrow. You can probably guess the ending. The mother traveled from door to door, house to house, threshold to threshold, and was never able to find a family without sorrow. She never received the mustard seed she was looking for, but she did receive understanding, truth, wisdom—and perspective.

The same conclusion could be made about marriage. Every marriage has sorrows. Every marriage has trials. There isn't a shared bedroom in this country where tension doesn't occasionally or perhaps frequently lift its snarling head. Many a pillow has been a solemn receptacle for soul-felt tears, cried late at night or even all throughout the day. We don't get to choose which sorrows or trials we are called to bear, only that we must endure them.

Liberating Force

Although Charles Lindbergh was famous, and by most accounts a gracious man, there were aspects of his character that brought tremendous grief to Anne. Charles's stoicism was such that he saw crying as a weakness. Accordingly, he insisted that if Anne had to cry, she do it alone, in her room. He made one exception; after the baby was found dead, he let Anne weep without rebuke.

Later in their marriage, Charles's fame spoiled into infamy. Lindbergh made half a dozen trips to Germany and vehemently opposed American entry into World War II. Soon thereafter he was sneered at as vehemently as he had been cheered.

"Imagine," his sister-in-law wrote, "in just fifteen years he had gone from Jesus to Judas."

He was also a controlling and somewhat eccentric man. One of his daughters told a biographer, "There were only two ways of doing things—Father's way and the wrong way." When Anne told Charles she wanted a new stove, he insisted that she wait until they could discuss the purchase "from personal, economic and military standpoints." Once, as Charles prepared to leave on a trip, he made Anne cancel their children's dental appointments, fearing that war might break out with the Soviets (which could lead the enemy to poison the water supply).

These are admittedly somewhat petty concerns, but the fame, the tragedy, the way Anne and Charles were so radically different from each other—all these created enormous and serious tension. Had Anne focused on these difficulties and let herself obsess over them, she could easily have turned bitter and withdrawn and found herself with a shrunken life. Instead of becoming an alcoholic or turning to food for comfort or taking things out on her children and ruining them, Anne chose to apply virtue to suffering and thereby enlarge her life significantly.

Out of this difficult marital situation, Anne became a woman of tremendous accomplishment—the first United States woman, in fact, to get a glider pilot's license. In spite of her preference for books and for conversation over against adventure, Anne learned to use the radio and became remarkably proficient at using Morse Code.

When their second son Jon was young, Anne and Charles went on a North Atlantic survey flight that covered four continents and lasted just two weeks shy of six months. Anne's work as copilot and radio operator for the survey was recognized by the National Geographic Society, which in 1934 awarded her the Hubbard Gold Medal for distinction in exploration, research, and discovery. She was the first woman ever to receive this award.

As life slowed down, Anne was finally able to put more effort into writing. She wrote numerous books — including many bestsellers — in the 1950s and 1960s. Eugene Peterson includes Anne's *Gift From the Sea* in his selective list of books that are "spiritually formative in the Christian life," calling it "a penetrating account of a homemaker/mother/wife who goes to the seashore for a few days and finds metaphors among the seashells that connect the presence of God and the meaning of the soul in the traffic of her everyday housewife world."[6]

Her difficult marriage didn't confine her — it released her. Anne recounts, "As a married woman, I had my husband at my side and developed a new confidence. I always feel like standing up straight when he is behind me."

This is what a good, difficult marriage does. Marriage can never remove the trials — in fact it almost always creates new ones. But even difficult marriages to difficult men can give women the strength to become the people God created them to be. (So it is for men married to difficult women as well.)

In one of her journals Anne reflects on this: "To be deeply in love is, of course, a great liberating force and the most common experience that frees — or seems to free — young people.... The sheer fact of finding myself in love was unbelievable and changed my world, my feelings about life and myself. I was given confidence, strength, and almost a new character. The man I was to marry believed in me and what I could do, and consequently I found I could do more than I realized, even in that mysterious outer world [flying] that fascinated me but seemed so unattainable. He opened the door to 'real life' and although it frightened me, it also beckoned. I had to go."

If someone had sat Anne down before she agreed to Lindy's marriage proposal and told her what the fame would *really* be like, and how *difficult* it would be for a bookish woman to become an adventurer's copilot (Lindy was insistent that his wife become a true partner), and how much pain notoriety would bring when their child was kidnapped—would she still have said yes?

Perhaps. We can never know for sure, but I suspect from the strength displayed in Anne's writings that she would have consented. In a collection of letters and journal writings titled *Hour of Gold, Hour of Lead,* Anne talks about how "the hour of lead"—difficult, burdening times—can be "transmuted" into an "hour of gold."

"A decade later," she wrote, "when our tragedy was behind us, buried and overlaid with new life, I wrote a poem which described this transmutation as I had experienced it. It was one of those poems that shoot up whole, a spear of insight, from some deep unconscious level."

Second Sowing

For whom
The milk ungiven in the breast
When the child is gone?
For whom the love locked up in the heart
That is left alone?
That golden yield
Split sod once, overflowed an August field,
Threshed out in pain upon September's floor,
Now hoarded high in barns, a sterile store.
Break down the bolted door;
Rip open, spread and pour
The grain upon the barren ground
Wherever crack in clod is found.
There is no harvest for the heart alone;
The seed of love must be
Eternally
Resown.

As long as our pain and wisdom and lessons are "locked up in the heart" or "hoarded high in barns," they remain sterile and unfertile.

To grow in the midst of difficulties, we must "rip open" the bags of grain and seeds and pour them out wherever we see fertile ground. This is the classic death and rebirth theme of Christianity, in which "the seed of love must be eternally resown." It is the essence of a spiritually meaningful marriage.

Mere Troubles

Some of you might be thinking, "My marriage situation is much worse than most. You don't understand *my* difficulties." We have to accept something here if we are going to avoid missing the message: We often can't choose which trials we face.

When we moved back to Washington state from Virginia, I had to renew my driver's license, which involved taking a vision test. I was asked to look into a machine and read the letters. I knew I must have made a mistake when the woman said, "Please start by reading the letters in the left column."

I read them again.

"That's the middle column," she stated.

I looked back in the machine. "You mean there are three columns?" I asked.

"Is something wrong with you?" she asked.

There were so many ways in which I could answer that question that I just remained silent. In fact, I suffer from keratoconus in my left eye, which severely curtails my sight and virtually obliterates my peripheral vision. I wasn't even aware that there was a third column.

Some people have asked me if this bothers me, but just about everyone I know has some physical malady—a bad back, severe allergies, migraine headaches, arthritis. We don't get to pick and choose which part of our body goes out of whack, but most of us will face the degeneration of something as we grow older.

I think we need the same attitude with our marriage. All of us experience certain things about our spouses that may be difficult for us to accept. I've known men who were married to alcoholics and women who were married to demanding tyrants who showed little appreciation or respect.

But here's where it gets difficult for most of us—where it causes us to lose the lessons learned through Lincoln and Lindbergh. Some might say, "Being famous doesn't sound so bad," and they wish they could exchange their troubles for Anne's. Others might think, "I wouldn't mind being married to such a contentious woman if I could be the president of the United States!"

For those of us who live relatively "anonymous" lives; for those couples who silently grieve over their own personal and private trials; for those who seem lost in a difficult marriage but don't particularly view their "mission" in life as meaningful—maybe they work in a factory and are wondering just what their mission in life actually *is*—trials seem to take on an added weight. In cases like these our trials don't appear to us as a teacher, but more like a taskmaster, a tyrant, a brutal burden.

In the previous chapter, we touched briefly on the importance of an eternal perspective. Eternity helps us to maintain a sacred history. It also helps us to endure struggle. Remember Paul's words in Romans 2:7–8: "To those who by persistence in doing good seek glory, honor and immortality, he will give eternal life. But for those who are self-seeking and who reject the truth and follow evil, there will be wrath and anger."

If we live without an eternal perspective, earthly trials become larger than life. Without the hope of heaven or the sense of the importance of a growing character and refinement, there is nothing to prepare for, nothing to look forward to; it is like practicing and practicing, but never getting to actually play a game. Life gets boring, tedious, and tiresome.

If we are seeking glory, honor, and immortality before God, daily and quiet persistence, faithfulness, and obedience is the road to get there. Anonymous sufferings are actually the best kind, Jesus tells us—otherwise, others might recognize us and compliment us and that, alone, will be our reward (see Matthew 6:16–18).

Christianity doesn't make much sense without the reality of heaven. The great classical writers never let go of this heavenly hope; eternity undergirded virtually every word they uttered. Paul himself said that if we have hope only for this life, "we are to be pitied more than all men" (1 Corinthians 15:19).

If we take our faith seriously and make our way through a difficult marriage in pursuit of witnessing God's reconciling love for a sinful world, then a difficult marriage becomes part of our exercise to prepare us for heaven. Of course, the editors of *People* magazine won't care two hoots about our pursuit; the refinement of our character won't make it into the pages of *Sports Illustrated* or *Vanity Fair*—but heaven will notice, God will notice, and eventually the promise of Jesus will come true: "The last will be first" (Matthew 20:16).

I feel sorry for Christians who try to live obedient lives without keeping heaven firmly in their sights. Meditating on the afterlife is one of the best spiritual exercises I know of. Personally, it strengthens me like few other spiritual disciplines do. "I can endure this," I say to myself, "because it will not always be this way."

Cynics will say I'm falling into Marx's trap. Marx, you'll recall, called religion "an opiate" for the people. Yet Marx had it exactly backwards, at least as far as his words pertain to Christianity. Opium deadens the senses; Christianity makes them come alive. Our faith can infuse a deadened or crippled marriage with meaning, purpose, and—in what we so graciously receive from God—fulfillment. Christianity doesn't leave us in an apathetic stupor—it raises us and our relationships from the dead! It pours zest and strength and purpose into an otherwise wasted life.

God never promises to remove all our trials this side of heaven—quite the contrary!—but he does promise that there is meaning in each one. Our character is being perfected, our faith is being built, our "heavenly reward" is being increased.

There's a scene from *Star Wars* that I'm somewhat ashamed to admit still tears me up inside. After Luke Skywalker, Princess Leia, and Hans Solo save the rebel forces, they are honored as they enter a great hall. They walk down a long aisle, with everybody standing at attention, and then they climb some high steps, until the leader of the rebel forces honors them in front of everybody.

The reason I think this hits me so hard is that it shadows a heavenly truth I yearn for. Jesus never told us to erase our ambition. Jesus never said to shun all thought of rewards. He told us to turn from *earthly* ambition and to shun *earthly* rewards. He said in effect, "Put yourself last here on earth, and in heaven you'll be first." That's a trade, not a complete denial! That thirst for glory you feel in your heart is part of what makes you human—Jesus just wants us to focus it on heaven, looking for our rewards there.

Now to believe this isn't to suggest that we just "hang on" until heaven comes. I've found that obedience to God creates quiet fulfillment in the present. There is a spiritual satisfaction that comes even in the midst of our trials. It is a demeanor that may not be as "showy" as gleeful happiness, but it is much less subject to moods and makes for much more permanent a disposition.

A difficult marriage does not pronounce a death sentence on a meaningful life. It presents several challenges, to be sure, but it also provides wonderful opportunities for spiritual growth. Look at your marriage through this lens—What am I learning? How is this causing me to grow? What is this doing for me from an eternal perspective?—and see if it doesn't lighten the load, at least somewhat. More important, contrast how your marriage draws you closer to God and shapes you in the character of Jesus Christ with how closely it draws you to the elusive state of carefree happiness. Look at your situation through the lens of eternity, the lens employed by the apostle Paul:

> Now if we are children, then we are heirs—heirs of God and co-heirs with Christ, if indeed we share in his sufferings in order that we may also share in his glory. I consider that our present sufferings are not worth comparing with the glory that will be revealed in us (Romans 8:17–18).

9

Falling Forward
Marriage Teaches Us to Forgive

*The couple is unlike the individual in that it must act
for its own preservation in a much more deliberate way
than the individual. Individuals might contemplate suicide,
but rarely forget to eat, whereas couples often forget
to nourish their relationship.*
MARY ANNE MCPHERSON OLIVER

*Love is a heart that moves.... Love moves away
from the self and toward the other.*
DAN ALLENDER AND TREMPER LONGMAN III

*Merely being faithful to your spouse is quite a testimony
in this society. But as you go beyond that to communicate love
for your spouse in a consistent, creative, and uninhibited way,
the world can't help but notice. God will be honored.*
GARY AND BETSY RICUCCI

*When a girl marries,
she exchanges the attentions of all the other men
of her acquaintance for the inattention of just one.*
HELEN ROWLAND

A TRUE STORY:

A businessman moved over slightly as a young man crowded
into the airplane seat next to him. They both fastened their seat

belts and the businessman good-naturedly inquired as to whether the young man was traveling on business or pleasure.

"Pleasure," the young man replied. "I'm on my honeymoon."

"Your honeymoon?" the businessman asked, mystified. "Where's your wife?"

"Oh, she's a few rows back. The plane was full, so we couldn't get seats together."

The plane hadn't started rolling yet, so the businessman said, "I'd be happy to change seats with her so that the two of you can be together."

"That's okay," the young man replied. "I've been talking to her all week."[1]

Keep in mind that one researcher found that the average married couple actively communicates on the average just twenty-seven minutes a week, and that they exchange the most words on their third date and the year before a divorce.[2]

One of the great spiritual challenges for any Christian is to become less self-absorbed. We are born intensely self-focused. The discipline of Christian marriage calls us into the Christian reality of sharing and enjoying fellowship in a uniquely intimate way. Maintaining an interest in and empathy for someone else is by no means an easy discipline to maintain — but it is a vital one. It is a skill that must be learned.

Many years ago, I and a few close friends celebrated our high school graduation by hiking on Mount Rainier. Before I attempted to jump a fast-moving creek, one of my friends advised me, "Just make sure you fall forward." The advice was well heeded. Even if I didn't make the jump, as long as I kept my momentum going forward, I wouldn't be swept into the stream.

The advice has stayed with me down through the years, as I believe that Christian marriage is also about learning to fall forward. Obstacles arise, anger flares up, and weariness dulls our feelings and our senses. When this happens the spiritually immature respond by pulling back, becoming more distant from their spouse, or even seeking to start over with somebody "more exciting." Yet maturity is reached by continuing to move forward past the pain and apathy. "Falls are inevitable. We can't control that, but we *can* control the direction in which we fall—toward or away from our spouse.

In Hollywood language, romance is expressed as a passive activity. Usually couples will say they have "fallen" in love. Or they may talk about being "swept off their feet." Adulterous couples sometimes even say, "We couldn't help ourselves; it just happened!" This passivity is as foreign to Christian love as the moon is to the earth. Christian love is an aggressive movement and an active commitment. In reality we *choose* where to place our affections.

Donald Harvey writes, "Intimate *relationships,* as opposed to intimate experiences, are the result of planning. They are built. The sense of union that comes with genuine spiritual closeness will not just happen. If it is present, it is because of definite intent and follow-through on your part. You choose to invest, and do. It's not left to mere chance."[3]

It took years for me to understand I have a Christian obligation to continually move *toward* my wife. I thought that as long as I didn't attack my wife or say cruel things to her, I was a "nice" husband, but the opposite of biblical love isn't hate, it's apathy. To stop moving toward our spouse is to stop loving him or her. It's holding back from the very purpose of marriage.

The Male Masquerade

At the risk of offending some readers, I think it's necessary to point out that this is one area of spirituality that may be more difficult, generally, for men than for women. First, men tend to be less communicative, perhaps not realizing the message of disinterest this sends. It's one thing to *think* warm thoughts about your spouse; it's quite another to *express* them. Many men don't realize the damage they do simply by remaining silent.

Secondly, men tend to view independence as a sign of strength, maturity, and "manhood." Interdependence is more than a long word —for men it is often a bitter pill to swallow, a sign, even, of weakness.

While this sense of independence may be culturally celebrated, it is not a biblical truth. It needs to be critiqued using the framework of the nature of God. While it is true we must be willing and unafraid to stand alone, if need be (consider Jesus on the cross), it is even more true that the movement of God is a movement toward people, even sinful people. The reason Jesus stood alone was so that others could be brought near to God. In essence, he stood alone in order to gather his children to himself. His solitary act was a radical statement of the importance of community. If we desire to be remade in God's image, we will be molded in such a way that we move toward others.

In fact, for most men, the flight from others is an act of cowardice, not courage. A man can't handle a maturing relationship with a woman his age, so he divorces his wife and marries someone the age of his daughter in a futile attempt to preserve his "power." Another man is unwilling to face the fact that his wife is not his "mother," but a partner who expects to receive as well as to give, so he sulks and gives his wife the silent treatment, rather than own up to his own sense of neediness. Still other men may be unwilling to enter the "give-and-take" required of a complementary relationship, so they ignore their wives and throw themselves into their work—where they are always in charge and where their subordinates must bend to their will.

These are not profiles in courage; they are monuments of male shame.

When God calls me to continually move toward my wife, he is calling me to shape myself into his very image.

Ebbing Emotions

One of the things that makes "falling forward" so difficult is the reality of conflicting emotions. Madeleine L'Engle wrote a simple poem that captures this marvelously.[4] Her words are directed toward God, but I think they apply just as well to anyone with whom we have a relationship of love:

> Dear God,
> I hate you.
> Love, Madeleine.

Have you ever experienced this frustrating reality of being disgusted with someone while at the same time knowing that you love them dearly? L'Engle is honest about her frustration with God, yet the last two words make all the difference — even though she is exasperated with her Creator, she is pledged to move toward him. "Love, Madeleine" becomes the denominator that defines every numerator. No matter what the exasperation is about, no matter how intense the frustration, Madeleine's relationship with God is marked by that foundational love.

That's how it should be with our marriages. Even in the moments of anger, betrayal, exasperation, and hurt, we are called to pursue this person, to embrace them, and to grow toward them, to let our love redefine our feelings of disinterest, frustration, and even hate.

The Blood of Marriage

This call to "fall forward" puts the focus on initiating intimacy. We cheapen marriage if we reduce it to nothing more than a negative "I agree to never have sex with anyone else." Marriage points to a gift of self that goes well beyond sexual fidelity. Mary Anne Oliver calls it an "interpenetration of being." I like that phrase. Getting married is agreeing to grow together, into each other, to virtually commingle our souls so that we share a unique and rare bond. When we stop doing that, we have committed fraud against our partner; we made a commitment that we're not willing to live up to.

This "interpenetration" can be a wonderful — and even fun — experience. Lisa and I have been married for almost fifteen years now. About three years ago, we began saying the same things in some uncanny ways. During one of our son's soccer games, I went up to a friend and said, "If they gave near misses half a point, we'd be killing them."

Jill's eyes grew wide. "Did you just hear Lisa say that?"

"No."

"Lisa just told me the exact same thing, just ten seconds ago."

This has started to happen with enough regularity that sometimes it feels almost creepy. Many married couples have experienced this same phenomenon. Our thinking and our turn of phrases have literally been so shaped by each other's presence that we have begun to resemble one person.

Such an "interpenetration of being" points to a reality that goes far beyond sexual exclusivity. Marriage is defined by a positive virtue. It presumes the *gift* of self. Kathleen and Thomas Hart write, "One can do many external deeds of love and still hold back the really precious gift, the inner self. This gift can be given only through communication."[5]

Communication is thus the blood of marriage that carries vital oxygen into the heart of our romance. At first, communication can seem glorious. In the rush of infatuation, the person standing before us seems virtually infinite in his or her mystery, beauty, insight, and ability to create the feeling of pure pleasure in us. Just a few months or perhaps years later, it is amazing how finite and earthy this "angel" has become.

Part of this is simply the humbleness of the human condition. G. K. Chesterton once remarked that if there is anything more ridiculous about humans other than the fact that they have two legs, it is that they sometimes make an opening in their faces and then put portions of the outer world into that opening (describing, of course, that process we call *eating*). No matter how lovely a young woman, no matter how smooth a young man, eventually the human flaws will appear. Funny noises and smells come out of all of us. It's the discovery of these banal realities that often causes us to "pull back," as if the other person has tricked us.

Along with verbal communication comes physical communication—the act of touching. This includes sexual expression, but also nonsexual touch. As a rule, I can't stand having someone touch my face, but my wife can't get enough of having her own face touched. It took me years to understand just how important it is for Lisa that I routinely stroke her cheek. She wants to be touched—especially when she knows that the touch is not done for the purpose of leading to something else.

And while men may need to be reminded of the importance of frequent nonsexual touching, many wives have learned that if a woman is not pursuing her husband sexually, just about every other movement toward her husband may go unnoticed. Jill Renich writes, "A wife may demonstrate her love in innumerable other ways, but it is often negated by her rejection or lack of enjoyment of sex. You may be a great housekeeper, a gourmet cook, a wonderful mother to your husband's children, but if you turn him down consistently in the bedroom oftentimes those things will be negated. To a man sex is the most meaningful declaration of love and self-worth."[6]

There's a classic scene in an old Woody Allen movie. A husband and wife are separately questioned by a marriage counselor, and the viewer is privy to their differing responses. The counselor first asks the wife, "How often do you and your husband have sex?"

The wife responds, "Almost always. Three times a week."

The counselor is then shown asking the husband, "How often do you and your wife have sex?"

The husband responds, "Almost never. Three times a week."

For the most part, this is a male-female thing, but occasionally, the roles are reversed and it's the wife who laments the relative infrequency of sexual relations. The other stereotype, of course, is the wife's desire to have conversation and the husband's preference for silence. This issue is one where both sides can grow toward each other in selflessness, regardless of whether they find themselves in the traditionally feminine or masculine roles.

Interpenetration of souls is a *duty* incumbent on every husband and wife. Some of us naturally gravitate toward the desire for sex, and some toward verbal communication. We have a duty to meet our spouse in their need. Correspondingly, we also have a Christian duty to not demand too much of our spouse. The wife can recognize that her husband may be able to tolerate just so much conversation; the husband will need to accept the idea that daily sexual relations may be less than enticing to most wives.

This commitment toward interpenetration teaches us to surrender our own demands at the same time that we strive to meet our spouse's demands. Ideally, if both spouses do this, the end result will be a marvelous and happy compromise. Usually, however, it's not nearly this easy, and one spouse begins to give far more than the other. This is the ground on which marital breakdown often begins.

But what if that "giving" spouse found motivation other than through his or her own desires? What if they viewed meeting the other partner's demands as part of their own spiritual formation? Instead of saying, "Why should I talk to her or be affectionate when she never wants to have sex?" a husband might say, "Regardless of how often we make love together, out of a desire to please God and grow spiritually and internally, I'm going to make myself available for long conversations with my wife."

Typically, marriage books will describe such a scene, and then say, "and when the husband does that, he'll find that his wife suddenly has a new desire to join him in bed!" But this is grossly overstating the case. I'm not suggesting that the husband should meet his wife's needs in order that his own needs can be better met. I'm suggesting that he do it as a spiritual exercise. The harder it is, the more he'll profit from it. If his wife immediately repays him in a physical way, he might go to sleep with a smile on his face, but, perhaps, with less spiritual training.

A mature husband and wife can grow leaps and bounds spiritually as they learn to compromise and move toward the other. But it is often the case that one spouse doesn't care about spiritual growth; they may be fully consumed with their own desires and sense of need. While such a situation may result in a less satisfying and less happy marriage, it can still provide the context for Christian growth. A Christian is never dependent on the response of others to grow spiritually. It's our own heart's decisions that matter.

Talking and touching are thus two of the most important ways we give ourselves to each other. The refusal to give the gift of self can sometimes be malicious. At other times, this "withholding" may not be done consciously. We just wake up one day and realize that we have made no effort to keep moving toward our spouse physically, emotionally, and spiritually. Most of us, in fact, probably never approached the relationship of marriage with the thought that "apathy" is the antithesis of Christian love. As long as we're not mean, vindictive, or cruel, we may think we're fulfilling our Christian duty.

But we're not.

The truth is, I owe my wife this "gift of self." When I refuse to fall forward and begin withholding myself, I am saying in effect, "I will no longer be married to you on a spiritual level."

The Discipline of Fellowship

The spiritual discipline embedded in learning to fall forward can be described as the "discipline of fellowship." In addition to the more general nature of pursuit, this discipline is further nurtured through three spiritual practices: learning not to run from conflict, learning how to compromise, and learning to accept others. These practices will serve us well both in the church and in the home.

Not Running from Conflict

I've seen churches fight about the stupidest things, and I've seen long-term ministry partners get into the most awful rows—and tear a church apart in the process. The spiritual discipline of fellowship is not easy. Sinful people wound each other, imperfect people see reality differently, and egocentric people have a difficult time perceiving somebody else's perspective.

The problem is, *all of us* are sinful, imperfect, and egocentric!

Marriage provides the small experimental laboratory whereby we can learn to engage in spiritual fellowship. Everything that happens broadly in social contexts has a mirror in marriage—disagreements, wounding words, conflict of interest, and competing dreams.

When disagreements arise, the natural tendency is to flee. Rather than work through the misunderstanding (or sin), we typically take a much more economical path—we search for another church, another job, another neighborhood, another friend, another spouse.

Marriage challenges this "flight" tendency. It encases us with a rock-hard, given-to-God promise that insists we work through the problem to arrive at some sort of resolution.

Mature adults realize that *every* relationship involves conflict, confession, and forgiveness. Unless you truly enjoy hanging around a sycophant, the absence of conflict demonstrates that either the relationship isn't important enough to fight over or that both individuals are too insecure to risk disagreement.

Conflict provides an avenue for spiritual growth. To resolve conflict, by definition we must become *more* engaged, not less. Just when we want to "tell the other person off," we are forced to be quiet and listen to their complaint. Just when we are most eager to make ourselves understood, we must strive to understand. Just when we seek to air our grievances, we must labor to comprehend another's hurt. Just when we want to point out the fallacies and abusive behavior of someone else, we must ruthlessly evaluate our own offensive attitudes and behaviors.

It's this self-emptying act of understanding that explains how successfully negotiated conflict creates an even stronger bond in the end. "Make-up sex" has become a cliché, but there's a truth buried in there somewhere. When conflict arises and is overcome, the couple has *had* to move toward each other. They've "fallen forward," sought resolution, and in the process built an urgent hunger for each other.

Glossing over disagreements and sinful attitudes and behaviors isn't fellowship; it's polite pretending. True fellowship insists that we fall forward.

Learning to successfully negotiate conflict will have a direct influence on our relationship with God, for the time will come when we feel we have a bone to pick with him too. One of the most famous "fights" in the Bible involved God and Jacob. The two combatants wrestled all night long, and the encounter so transformed Jacob that his name was changed to Israel ("he struggles with God"). Near the end of the confrontation, Jacob insisted that God "bless" him (see Genesis 32:26). God eventually granted Jacob's request, and then built an entire nation out of the descendants of this conniving, deceitful man.

Sometimes we too will find ourselves wrestling with God. "How could you take this child away from me?" "How could you allow Jim to lose his job, just when we need it most?" "How come you stay up there all silent and aloof?"

It is not a mark of Christian maturity to pretend that we are not bothered by our heavenly Father's silence. A healthy spirituality will call us to fall forward with God no less than with our spouse. This "falling forward" is certainly a more appropriate response than simply "writing God off" and kicking him out of our lives at the first sign that he is doing something or allowing something that we don't understand.

Like Jacob, "wrestling" with God may very well result in an unforeseen blessing. We may also—as did Jacob—receive a "lifelong limp," but any interaction with God will prove beneficial, provided the movement is always toward him.

Compromise

The second way we practice the spiritual discipline of fellowship within marriage is by learning to compromise. Sadly the word "compromise" is seen as such a dirty word by many in our society, but virtually every relationship, if it is to continue and grow, must embody compromise in some shape or form. As the Whiteheads so poignantly stress, far from being a cop-out, compromise can be a way of saying, "I love you." It's proof that we're willing to give ground for no other reason than that we value the ongoing relationship more than we do asserting our rights, preferences, or wishes. Compromise is the cement of fellowship.

Many congregations have had to tackle how to serve the younger members' desire for "contemporary worship" without losing the "traditional worship" of the older members. Some churches have opted to go with two services; others have tried to combine liturgy and informality. Some have sold off the organ, others have built a bigger organ but occasionally leave it silent while somebody plays a guitar. Churches everywhere are learning the art of compromise.

In the same way, couples must learn to compromise over the mundane (where do we celebrate the Christmas holiday?) and the profound (how many children should we have?). For such compromise to work, there must be numerous "mini-funerals." We must choose to die to ourselves, to give ground, and, conversely, not to gloat when ground is given to us.

Acceptance and Loyalty

A third discipline of fellowship is learning to accept real people. So often, new members will attend a church and rave about the pastor's teaching, the worship leader's ability to cultivate the presence of God, and the friendliness of the other church members. And then, a year or two later, when they've heard the pastor's best stories, grown bored with the worship leader's favorite songs, and are expected to invite others to come for lunch rather than be invited themselves, it's amazing how what was once "the best church in the world" is now "a dead and dying body."

This too mirrors what often happens in a marriage. The man

whom the wife once thought of as confident is now seen as arrogant. The wife who attracted her husband with her "quiet and gentle spirit" is now seen as a weak woman unworthy of respect.

Marriage based on romanticism embraces an idealized lie (infatuation) and then divorces the reality once it presents itself. Marriage based on life in Jesus Christ invites us to divorce the lie (an idealized view of our spouse) and embrace reality (two sinful people struggling to maintain a lifelong commitment). As the Whiteheads observe, "The challenge is not to keep on loving the person we thought we were marrying, but to love the person we did marry!"[7]

The discipline of fellowship requires us to learn the art of loyalty. Just because the church down the street has called a younger and more exciting pastor doesn't mean we should blow off years of commitment and relationships at a prior church and go to hear the new "star." Just because a younger woman or a more sensitive man appears on the scene doesn't mean we renege on the life commitment we have made.

It's all about falling forward. You meet someone you find very exciting and attractive, but you choose to put strict limits on the relationship and instead redouble your efforts to declare your commitment to your spouse. You feel hurt and wounded by your partner's selfishness, but instead of sulking and responding with the silent treatment, you take the initiative to express your feelings in a gentle and respectful way.

Ironically, falling forward also leads in the end to greater marital satisfaction. Although the purpose of this book is to help us use our marriages to draw closer to God, when we do that, we often find that our marriages will improve as well, increasing our own satisfaction. Donald Harvey puts it succinctly: "Couples who place their relationship in a high-priority position have the greatest potential for achieving what they want out of the marriage. Those who do not have a lesser potential. It's as simple as that."[8]

When you entered this relationship of marriage, you committed to keep moving toward your spouse. Any step back, any pause, any retreat, is an act of fraud. Learn to move toward the person God has given to you for the purpose of teaching you how to love.

Fostering Forgiveness

What do we do when our spouse doesn't want us to fall forward—when, in fact, our spouse is pushing us away?

The Bible provides clear guidance. The father let the prodigal son go, but love demanded that the father always be ready with open arms to "fall forward" should the son ever return (see Luke 15:11–32).

Someone else's action can't dictate our response. God sent his Son into a world that hated him. If God had waited for the world to be "worthy" to receive him, his Son would never have come. This truth entails yet another spiritual discipline of fellowship, in fact, one of the most difficult spiritual disciplines of all—the discipline of forgiveness.

The more enterprising among us might attempt to use our spouse's sin as an excuse to pull back, but this is hardly a Christian response, because *all* of us sin against each other. In fact, I believe one of marriage's primary purposes is to teach us how to forgive. This spiritual discipline provides us with the power we need to keep falling forward in the context of a sinful world.

The Call to Grace

A stonemason in Seattle followed a wife's directions and carved a headstone for the woman's husband with the traditional words:

"Rest In Peace."

A few months later, the wife discovered that her husband had been unfaithful, so she returned to the stonemason and asked him to add four more words. The stonemason did as he was told, and the gravestone now reads:

Rest In Peace ...
Till We Meet Again.

There's something about sin in marriage that strikes us at a deeper level than when others sin against us. A sense of betrayal is added to the sin, so that when we're wronged, we may be so offended we want to continue the dispute into the grave.

We get married for all sorts of reasons. "Because it gives us an opportunity to learn how to forgive" probably doesn't top the list of most honeymooners, but the spiritual practice of continually moving toward someone provides an excellent context in which we can practice this vital spiritual discipline. Sin in marriage (on the part of both spouses) is a daily reality, an ongoing struggle that threatens to hold us back. You will never find a spouse who is without sin. The person you decide to marry will eventually hurt you—sometimes even intentionally so, making forgiveness an essential spiritual discipline.

Paul offers some wonderfully helpful words in the book of Romans. He writes that "no one will be declared righteous in [God's] sight by observing the law; rather, through the law we become conscious of sin" (Romans 3:20).

Having read this verse seemingly a hundred times or more, I've been well warned, and you have too: Our spouses will never achieve a "lawful" sinlessness. It just won't happen. We will be sinned against and we will be hurt. When that happens, we will have a choice to make: We can give in to our hurt, resentment, and bitterness, or we can grow as a Christian and learn yet another important lesson on how to forgive.

The law wasn't created by God for two spouses to hold each other up to an impossible standard with which they could then beat each other over the head. A "self-righteous" spouse is an obnoxious spouse, even if, by the letter of the law, they're momentarily "blameless" and in the right. Eventually, that spouse will slip up too.

What then, ultimately, are we called to?

Paul goes on to say that "now a righteousness from God, *apart from law,* has been made known" (Romans 3:21, italics added). It's a righteousness based on the "redemption that came by Christ Jesus" and on "faith" (Romans 3:24, 27).

Marriages invariably break down when a pious partner impales his or her spouse on the law. None of us can live up to the law; all of us will break it. Marriage teaches us—indeed, it practically forces us—to learn to live by extending grace and forgiveness to people who have sinned against us.

If I can learn to forgive and accept my imperfect spouse, I'll be well equipped to offer forgiveness outside my marriage. Forgiveness, I'm convinced, is so unnatural an act that it takes practice to perfect.

Loving the Sinner

It was a cockroach, and the Israeli housewife hated cockroaches. Even worse, the cockroach wouldn't die, so the woman stepped on it, threw it in a toilet, and then sprayed a full can of insecticide on it until finally the cockroach stopped moving.

Satisfied, the wife left the bathroom.

Her husband came home from work later that day. While sitting on the toilet, he threw a cigarette butt into the bowl. The insecticide fumes ignited, and the husband received serious burns in a rather sensitive area of his anatomy.

The wife immediately called the paramedics. They arrived within a matter of minutes, examined the man, and decided that the burns were sufficiently serious to warrant hospital attention, so they put him on a stretcher and carried him down the stairs.

After they found out how the husband had been injured, the paramedics found it difficult to contain their laughter. Their mirth grew the more they tried to stifle it, and they ended up laughing so hard while descending the stairs that they dropped the husband, breaking his pelvis and ribs.[9]

I imagine that this man's forgiveness was sorely tried. But even in the best of circumstances, forgiveness isn't easy. Our natural minds work against it.

One time I spoke at a staff retreat for an Episcopalian church at a Roman Catholic lay order's retreat center. The chapel was very small but very distinguished, and I poked around a little shortly after I arrived. I saw a confessional in the back so I opened the door and was startled to find, of all things, a file cabinet.

Sometimes that's what marriage is like: Our spouse has confessed sins and weaknesses to us, and we've kept every confession in a mental file cabinet, ready to be taken out and used in our defense or in an attack. But true forgiveness is a process, not an event. It is rarely the case that we are able to forgive "one time" and the matter is settled. Far more often, we must relinquish our bitterness a dozen times or more, continually choosing to release the offender from our judgment.

This is why forgiveness is so very hard. In his book *What's So Amazing About Grace?* Philip Yancey writes the following:

> In the heat of an argument my wife [and I] were discussing my shortcomings in a rather spirited way when she said, "I think it's pretty amazing that I forgave you for some of the dastardly things you've done!" … Forgiveness … is no sweet platonic ideal to be dispensed into the world like air-freshener sprayed from a can. Forgiveness is achingly difficult, and long after you've forgiven, the wound — my dastardly deeds — lives on in memory. Forgiveness is an unnatural act, and my wife was protesting its blatant unfairness.10

The Claude Lanzmann-filmed documentary on the Holocaust titled *Shoah* records the gripping moment when a leader of the Warsaw ghetto uprising talks about the bitterness that remains in his heart: "If you could lick my heart," he says, "it would poison you."

A number of marriages are like that. The infighting and personal attacks have become so bitter that the participants have developed poisonous hearts. The tragedy, of course, is that a poisonous heart doesn't just pollute the person who licks it; it is itself an infected organ that pours toxic bile into a person's own life. Forgiveness, in this sense, is an act of self-defense, a tourniquet that stops the fatal bleeding of resentment.

Any life situation that exercises our ability to extend forgiveness is a life situation that can mold us further into the character of Jesus Christ. I know of few life situations that call us to such a regular practice of forgiveness as the relationship of marriage.

Henri Nouwen once defined forgiveness as "love practiced among people who love poorly." This sums it up so well. I love poorly, you love poorly, all of us love poorly—if in fact Jesus is taken as the model of someone who loves well. We can either berate our spouse for being less than perfect, or we can wrestle with and win some victories over our own demons that make offering forgiveness so difficult.

In the practice of this discipline, marriage forces us to embrace that most difficult of Christian clichés: "Hate the sin and love the sinner." This is a staggering thing to do, as every self-righteous fiber within us pushes us to transform repulsion toward sin into repulsion toward the sinner—and therefore repulsion toward our spouse. Philip Yancey encourages us to move in the direction of loving the sinner by thinking what it must have been like for Jesus. Because Jesus was morally perfect, imagine what platform Jesus had to be disgusted! And yet no one loved sinners with the depth that Jesus did.

C. S. Lewis confessed that he too struggled with how to truly love the sinner while hating the sin. One day it suddenly became clear:

> It occurred to me that there was one man to whom I had been doing this all my life—namely myself. However much I might dislike my own cowardice or conceit or greed, I went on loving myself. There had never been the slightest difficulty about it. In fact the very reason why I hated the things was that I loved the man. Just because I loved myself, I was sorry to find that I was the sort of man who did those things.11

We extend this charity to ourselves, so the question begs to be asked: Why do we not extend this same charity to our spouse? Melissa did, and it changed her life.

The Ultimate Betrayal

Melissa thought of her marriage as a "deeply committed" one "with a real sense of partnership. It was a secure place, a place of healing and growth. I loved my marriage."

In 1997, after nearly twenty-five years of marriage, this "secure place" was rocked. Her husband Bryant, a pastor, began withdrawing, losing himself in computer chat rooms. He was urged by an associate to take some time off. Bryant agreed to two months, then announced that he needed a full year for a "retooling" and that he would not be returning to pastoral duties at the church. His district pastor, however, urged Bryant to reconsider. He did—and resumed his position.

Shortly thereafter, for the first time in her marriage, Melissa began to wonder whether her husband had always been faithful. She began experiencing gynecological problems and then was diagnosed with a low strain of a sexually transmitted disease. As the director of a crisis pregnancy center, Melissa was well versed in STDs and their consequences. Bryant looked his wife in the eyes and insisted that there was no way he could have given her the STD.

Melissa watched Bryant slowly implode. He became hypercritical and depressed. He kept going back to sit at the computer. He went to a counselor to try to find help, but in October Melissa caught him back on the computer and asked, "Do you have a significant relationship with someone on-line that makes you unwilling to give up the chat rooms?"

Bryant donned a sheepish look—"like a boy caught stealing cookies," Melissa remembers—and sighed.

"Yes," he finally answered. "And we have had some phone contact."

Bryant went back to his counselor at Melissa's insistence. The counselor persisted in working on Bryant's deception, so when

Melissa confronted Bryant once again, he was more willing to be honest. "Am I foolish to believe I have an STD all by myself?" she asked. There was nothing but silence.

That was the most awful period of silence that Melissa had ever known. And in that silence — as Bryant himself would say in a moment — Melissa had her answer. It was October 16, 1997, a date she will never forget.

At first, Melissa went numb. She retreated into her living room, grabbed her Bible, and started reading from the book of Hosea. "God knows about betrayal and unfaithfulness," she said to herself. "I need to know how this works."

Bryant followed her, but Melissa wasn't ready yet to tackle this as a couple. She had a few things to work through individually first. All she could say to him at that point was, "Others have survived this. It's my desire to survive this also."

The numbness remained for several days until Saturday, when Melissa remembered to her horror that Bryant's family would be coming in for a special celebration on Sunday to honor Bryant's mother's birthday.

Bryant was still the pastor and Melissa was still on the worship team, so a very broken husband and wife showed up for church that Sunday morning with a heavy spirit. Melissa's resolution to "keep going" was almost obliterated shortly after the warm-up session for worship had begun, for she discovered that Bryant had chosen worship songs that focused on "intense, personal songs of love."

"It was killing me, practicing those songs," Melissa remembers. "I ran off into a side room and sat there thinking, 'I can't do this.'"

Melissa gathered herself together and stepped outside the practice room — and the first thing she saw was that about a third of those in attendance were related to Bryant. One of those people was her unsaved brother-in-law, who was dying of cancer.

There followed an intense moment of personal pain, which was curiously mixed with a deep empathy for her dying relative. This created a spiritual breakthrough for Melissa, and she found herself praying, "Lord, you must be orchestrating something here that is bigger than my pain. I know these songs aren't about me. They're about you and the lost."

Surrounded by her husband's family, Melissa helped lead worship and then listened to Bryant preach. Her resolve was rewarded when her ailing brother-in-law made a commitment to receive Jesus Christ as his Lord and Savior.

"I'll never forget how profound that was to me," Melissa remembers. "Though my pain was devastating, it wasn't bigger than God."

Shaken out of her stupor, Melissa knew she had to begin to forgive. "I remember looking at Bryant and saying, 'I know I have to forgive you. I'm going to.' But I was not flooded with a great sense of forgiveness. I was confronted with the truth of *having* to forgive. Forgiveness was something I could walk into."

She shared her struggle with a pastor, who assured her that forgiveness doesn't imply or confer trust and it doesn't remove the pain. Melissa learned that giving forgiveness was vital to her spiritual survival and growth. "The Lord taught me that it's a matter of obedience. If I'm going to keep my heart open to God through this whole awful process, I'm going to have to be obedient."

Notice that Melissa's first focus was vertical. She was willing to forgive her husband *because that's what she had to do in order to stay right with God.* The marriage was secondary at this point. Melissa was more concerned with doing what was right spiritually than with anything else.

Because bits and pieces of Bryant's story leaked out over time, forgiveness became a constant discipline in Melissa's life. There was always something new to digest and try to understand. She fought against bitterness — she loved being a pastor's wife and she loved being a part of their church, and she knew that Bryant's actions had taken away from her something very precious.

Several months later, Bryant finally came completely clean. He laid out everything he had done. Many hurtful things were disclosed, including the fact that he had had another affair and thought he might still be "in love" with this woman.

Biblically, Melissa knew she was well within her "rights" to kick Bryant out of her life and start over, but she never seriously considered that option. "Forgiveness was the harder option, definitely, but I never felt in my heart that [divorce] was the right thing to do."

This is the key, I believe, to Melissa's spiritual maturity and growth through this awful ordeal. She told me, *"I've always lived my life by conviction and the harder road is not something I'm afraid to take."*

It was precisely on the hard road of suffering that Melissa started growing, learning lessons, and drawing closer to her God. She would never choose to go through this kind of trial again, but by adopting the right spirit and being willing to forgive, she experienced growth in ways she never could have otherwise.

"I've learned that even when we're in great pain, we're not excused from considering others and from carrying out our call to witness to God's faithfulness."

Though Melissa was feeling numb, she learned selflessness by focusing on her concern for her children, the welfare of the church, and even Bryant's soul. Rather than lashing out in anger at him, she was more broken over the spiritual consequences of his actions than over how those actions offended and affected her.

Frankly, this amazes me! Listening to Melissa talk, I feel like I'm hearing a saint-in-training. And I am!

It was a tough, tough time of testing, but choosing forgiveness kept bitterness and anger at bay. It saved her marriage in the end, brought Bryant around, and moved Melissa many steps closer to more fully modeling the person of Jesus Christ. Why? I think back to what Melissa said: *"The harder road is not something I'm afraid to take."*

God's nature is to forgive. God's character is such that he died a brutal death for the sake of the very people who abused him. Such forgiveness doesn't come naturally to any of us. It must be learned, and often learned again, even though the process can be excruciatingly painful, hurtful, and horrendous. If we refuse to take the "harder road" because it's more difficult, we'll never mature.

I asked Melissa the hard questions. If my wife had been unfaithful, I think the most difficult thing of all would be renewing our physical intimacy. How could you forget what your spouse had done?

But by traveling the road of forgiveness, Melissa testifies that she and Bryant have entered a "honeymoon" phase of marriage—two-and-a-half decades past their wedding! Bryant's unfaithfulness was a terrible experience, and the hurt it caused was real and constant. Melissa would surely never choose to go through it again. But adopting the right attitude of forgiveness helped her apply what Francis de Sales told a troubled young woman looking for advice about marriage (see chapter 1): "The state of marriage is one that requires more virtue and constancy than any other. It is a perpetual exercise of mortification.... From this thyme plant, in spite of the bitter nature of its juice, you may be able to draw and make the honey of a holy life."

Melissa was given a bitter juice. She offered that juice to God, who made spiritual honey in her life.

I've seen people do the opposite. During one conference I spoke at, a woman who was very open about her own struggle with eating disorders confessed to her inability to forgive her husband for his past use of pornography. Her husband had been gracious, forgiving, and gentle as she had gained over a hundred pounds after they were married, but she had little empathy for any man who used photographs of naked women in the same way that she used food. Her understandable hurt but unfortunate bitterness kept her from seeing the similarities between their two struggles. She was so full of her own conflict, she couldn't have any empathy for somebody facing a different conflict.

The key to the discipline of fellowship is understanding this fundamental reality: All of us face struggles, and each one of us is currently facing a struggle that we're having less than one hundred percent success overcoming. If we're married, the fact is we're also married to someone who is failing in some way.

We can respond to this "bitter juice" by becoming bitter people, or we can use it as a spiritual discipline and transform its exercise into the honey of a holy life. In this fallen world, struggles, sin, and unfaithfulness are a given. The only question is whether our response to these struggles, sin, and unfaithfulness will draw us closer to God —or whether it will estrange us from ourselves, our Creator, and each other.

Will we fall forward, or will we fall away?

Make Me a Servant

Marriage Can Build in Us a Servant's Heart

*How great, then, is the constraint in marriage, which
subjects even the stronger to the other; for by mutual constraint
each is bound to serve. Nor if one wishes to refrain can he
withdraw his neck from the yoke, for he is subject to the
[sexual desires] of the other.... You see how plainly
the servitude of marriage is defined.*

AMBROSE

THE ESSENCE OF CHRISTIANITY IS FOUND IN PHILIPPIANS 2. THERE
Paul urges us to do nothing (it's these absolutist words that can make
Scripture so troubling) "out of selfish ambition or vain conceit, but in
humility consider others better than yourselves. Each of you should
look not only to your own interests, but also to the interests of others"
(Philippians 2:3–4).

Paul escalates this teaching by calling us to emulate Christ Jesus,
who, though he was "in very nature God, . . . made himself nothing, taking the very nature of a servant" (Philippians 2:6–7).

To be a Christian is to be a self-volunteering servant. It is not
sufficient to merely voice our assent to a few choice doctrines. We
are called to act in such a way that we put others above ourselves.
We are expressly forbidden from exalting ourselves for the sole purpose of furthering our own comfort or fame. Otto Piper nails the
marriage relationship's potential to create a servant heart in us when

he describes marriage as "a reciprocal willingness of two persons to assume responsibility for each other."[1]

It's precisely this servant call that makes marriage so beneficial spiritually—and so difficult personally. When I asked my wife to marry me, I was just twenty-two years old. My decision was based almost entirely on what I thought she would bring to the marriage. She looked good; we had fun together; she loved the Lord. And my suspicion is that her thoughts were running in the same direction: Can this guy support me? Do I find him attractive? Would he be a good father?

These aren't bad questions to ask, but once the ceremony is over, if we want to enter a truly Christian marriage, we have to turn 180 degrees and ask ourselves, "How can I serve my mate?"

For much of the past century this was a question that most Christian men didn't take all that seriously. It was assumed that the wife would unilaterally serve her husband in virtually all matters. Even though our culture is now challenging this view, a few men are still so abhorred by the thought of serving their wives that they have decided to go outside the United States to find what amounts to a slave-bride.

A company called Cherry Blossoms feeds off the poverty of the Philippines (annual per-capita income in 1997 was $1,160) to offer "matchmaking" services between older American males and young (sometimes extremely young) Filipino women. The men pay to receive a catalogue titled *Island Blossoms,* which has photographs and brief personal sketches of available women. They then pay Cherry Blossoms another fee for the women's addresses.

The men offer the women a way out of the highly populated and muddy squatters' towns that are populated by houses as small as walk-in closets. But this "salvation" comes at a price. One man sent a two-page, single-spaced contract to a prospective bride that read, in part:

Your primary function in life is to serve me.... Your secondary function is to be a model mother ... but never to the extent that it will conflict with proper attention to me.... You will rise approximately at 6:00 A.M. After going to the bathroom, brushing your teeth, combing your hair, cleaning your face with alcohol or Seabreeze, you will wake the children.... Each day there will be absolute order in the house by the time that I arrive.... You will clean your face no less than three times a day.... You will immediately reply VERBALLY when I speak to you.... When we make love, I expect that you do so at any and all times and with enthusiasm.[2]

Another man seemed determined to find the most desperate bride so that she would be extremely agreeable sexually once she got into the States. In a letter to one interested young woman, he wrote: "There are two young ladies ... who have written that they would do ANYTHING for me ... if only I gave them a chance to be my permanent partner and, of course, the opportunity to come to the United States with me. Tell me, Vilma, how do you feel about that?... Would you do anything I ask?" He then mentions a particular sexual activity and writes, "My preference is [for a] partner [who] would be willing, able, and skillful enough to perform that activity for me, at any time."

This attitude is so offensive to the spirit of Christianity and Christian marriage, it borders on being nothing but lifetime prostitution. Because the man has the money, he wants to buy the woman's services—for a lifetime, instead of for a night, but buy them nonetheless. Sex is something he expects to receive, not something he plans to give. Perhaps it's not so surprising that one young "Cherry Blossom" bride complained that on her wedding night, "it felt like rape."

While some elements of the feminist movement have led to atrocious moral positions—legalized and largely unregulated abortion, for one example; the absurd disregard of sex roles, for another—the challenge that women are not to be treated by their husbands as unilateral servants was—dare I say it?—a prophetic one. Unfortunately, rather than hearing the call to both men and women to serve each other, all too frequently women are hearing the call to become as self-serving and self-absorbed as men.

Gary and Betsy Ricucci challenge this view:

> Contrary to popular opinion, woman was not created for her own fulfillment. (That goes for the men, too!) She was created to be a helper and a nurturer. Now that is not an easy assignment to accept. We tend to bristle and think, *There must be something more significant than that!* What homemaker hasn't found herself asking, after the fiftieth load of laundry in a week or when facing yet another sink full of dirty dishes, "Is there anything significant about what I'm doing here?" Yet in God's eyes, nothing is more significant than servanthood. The path to genuine greatness lies in serving.
>
> Grasping for power or recognition is natural. Servanthood is supernatural. So many women are missing out on the supernatural today because they are caught up in the "search for significance." Ironically, the more they search for it, the less satisfied they feel. Why? Significance is found in giving your life away, not in selfishly trying to find personal happiness.[3]

A Man's Love: The Sacrifice Behind Service

Although many speak of the sterility of modern seminaries, I had a completely different experience at Regent College (in Vancouver, British Columbia). The faculty there challenged me in many ways, including the way in which I treated my wife.

I remember the semester when I worked as a teacher's assistant for Dr. Gordon Fee. He and his wife invited a few students and their wives over for dessert. Lisa was pregnant with our first child—and showing it. Listening to Dr. Fee's lectures, I had learned a great deal about how to preach a moving sermon. Reading Dr. Fee's writings, I had had the book of 1 Corinthians opened up to me in new ways. But I was about to learn something about being a husband.

Lisa walked in the door, and Dr. Fee immediately jumped up. "Here," he said, "you need the softest chair."

His words were seasoned with sincerity and genuine concern. My wife was surprised at the attention, but she took the chair and sat down. I sat beside her. Dr. Fee, I noticed to my embarrassment, was still standing.

"Now," he said, "can I get you a pillow for your back?"

"No, I'm fine," Lisa said.

"How about a glass of water? Do you need something to drink?"

"That would be great," my wife answered.

Dr. Fee marched into the kitchen. He came back with a full glass. "Is the heat all right?" he asked. "Are you too cold, too hot? Do you need to raise your feet?"

Lisa was almost blushing by this time, and I was greatly humbled. I had never served my wife in the way that my seminary professor was now doing. Just seeing his empathy, his dedication to making another person comfortable, and his willingness to put himself entirely at my wife's disposal was an eye-opener, to be sure. I saw the heart of a servant and realized I had a long way to go in order to grow into maturity as a husband.

It was one thing to be shown up by a seminary professor. I was even more chagrined when I found my growth as a husband exceeded by that of a professional football player.

Four-time All-Pro NFL linebacker Chris Spielman had played football for twenty-six of his thirty-three years. He is the type of guy who relishes the game, even going to rather absurd lengths to get ready for a contest. On one occasion, he slept in the nude with the air-conditioning blasting so that he could be fully prepared for the brutally cold winter chill that envelops Buffalo's Rich Stadium.

He met his wife Stefanie in 1983 when he was just seventeen years old. They were married six years later in 1989. Stefanie is beautiful — she worked as a model before she became a full-time mother — and the two embarked on a rich marriage. Spielman played for many years with the Detroit Lions, and then signed with the Buffalo Bills in 1996.

The year 1997 came with a fistful of trials. In July, just as preseason camp was getting started, a doctor spoke the words that married couples fear most: breast cancer. Stefanie, the beautiful model, opted for a mastectomy, to be followed by six weeks of chemotherapy, a time period during which she would lose all her hair.

The Spielmans have two small children (both were under five years old at the time) and Chris knew that the chemo treatments would pretty much drain his wife's energy. He had a decision to make. "It was my test," Chris told *People* magazine.[4] "It was my defining moment."

In a show of solidarity, Chris shaved his head. Even more important, he quit football—not forever, but for a year—until Stefanie was back on her feet.

"[Stefanie] always supported me one hundred percent," Chris explains. "I had to offer it back."

This was a sacrifice that Stefanie didn't want Chris to make. "I never cried about the cancer or how it hurt," she confessed. "I cried because of what it was doing to Chris."

Now, instead of watching game film and meeting with the coaches, Chris wakes up early to feed the kids (he's learned that his oldest hates to have any of the food on her plate touch any other food), and then he gets Stefanie up an hour or so later, after he has her breakfast ready. He then does the laundry, takes the kids to their gymnastics lessons, and makes sure Stefanie gets her medication.

I have no idea whether or not Chris is a Christian, but clearly he has learned the meaning of sacrificial giving to his wife. Somehow he's learned to live out what Paul urges men to strive toward in Ephesians 5:25. Paul tells husbands that they should love their wives, as Christ loved the church, and he explains—quite explicitly—*how* Christ loved the church: by *giving up his life for her.*

Chris told *GQ* magazine, "For ten years our entire lives had been about me. My career came first, always. Stefanie made every sacrifice in the world to support me unconditionally.... What kind of husband would I be if I didn't drop everything for Stefanie when she got sick? Did I want her *sister* to have to hold her hand while she suffered, because I wasn't there? Did I want Stefanie's *mother* to have to sit with her in the hospital while they were shooting needles into her and filling her up with those awful chemicals, or did I want to be there myself?... This is my family. This is my responsibility. This is my home. This is my duty."[5]

In his audiotape series *According to Plan*, C.J. Mahaney pleads with men to recover this sense of sacrifice. He points out that sacrifice isn't sacrifice unless it costs us something, and then he leaves a challenging question hanging in the air: "Gentlemen, what are we doing each day for our wives that involves sacrifice? What are you doing each day for your wife *that is costing you something?*"[6]

In his trademark style, Mahaney keeps laying down the grace-generated conviction. "Will I take advantage of my wife's godliness," he asks, "or will I seek to emulate the One who laid down his life for me?"

To make this teaching practical, C.J. explains how sacrifice for him is being willing to "talk details" with his wife in the evening. "When the day is over, I don't want to relive it," he confesses, "which is my selfish perspective.... [This silence] doesn't meet my wife's needs, doesn't create intimacy."

My friend Dr. Kevin Leman likes to point out that he has yet to meet a man who, after a long day at work, thinks to himself, "What I really need right now is a long, forty-five-minute talk with my wife." But that's precisely why a man's willingness to engage in such conversation is so beneficial to him spiritually—it costs him something. It teaches him to sacrifice.

In 1998, I was asked to give an evangelistic talk at a university on "Jesus: Liberator of Women or Sexist?" The most scandalous thing I said in the mind of one student was when I talked about "mutual submission." Some of the students were so inundated with "take care of yourself, do your own thing, look out for number one" that the thought of submitting to anybody was as radical as anything they had ever heard. "Sacrifice" and "relationship" simply did not belong in the same sentence as far as they were concerned. Paul's words are nothing short of radical in today's culture.

Marriage creates a situation in which our desire to be served and coddled can be replaced with a more noble desire to serve others —even to sacrifice for others. This is a call for both husbands and wives. The beauty of marriage is that it confronts our selfishness and demands our service twenty-four hours a day. When we're most tired, most worn down, and feeling more sorry for ourselves than we ever have before, we have the opportunity to confront feelings of self-pity by getting up and serving our mate.

The Mark of Christian Marriage

It is precisely this notion of sacrifice and service that will help us reclaim spirituality for married couples. Dietrich Bonhoeffer wrote that "Christian marriage is marked by discipline and self-denial.... Christianity does not therefore depreciate marriage, it sanctifies it."[7]

This is an area where traditional Christian spirituality has been weak. For centuries, Christian spirituality was virtually synonymous with "celibate spirituality," something that Mary Anne McPherson Oliver refers to as "inadequate and in some cases even pernicious, particularly for couples." Oliver proceeds to define celibate spirituality as "all the religious lifestyles which fully exclude sexual relating, and in which the primary responsibility is to the self and the primary relational ideal one of flexible, unattached availability."[8]

While Oliver's remarks might seem a bit harsh—many monks and nuns lived generous and gracious lives, reaching out to others with genuine concern and compassion—doesn't such a self-centered focus, laid out so starkly, strike you as antithetical to the others-centered teaching of Jesus Christ? It is laudable when someone decides to give himself or herself unreservedly to the Lord, but is it any less laudable when a man or woman decides to give himself or herself not just to the Lord, but to another human being as a lifelong co-servant, agreeing with that other person to raise and serve children who will in turn grow to love and serve the Lord and others as well?

The reason this thought may not have been obvious to so many for so long is that the vast majority of people do not enter marriage with a view to becoming a servant. The marriage relationship is often seen as a selfish one because our motivations for marrying often *are* selfish. But my desire is to reclaim marriage as one of the most selfless states a Christian can enter.

To fully sanctify the marital relationship, we must live it together as Jesus lived his life—embracing the discipline of sacrifice and service *as a daily practice*. In the same way that Jesus gave his body for us, we are to lay down our energy, our bodies, and our lives for others.

Kathleen and Thomas Hart refer to the "paschal mystery" of marriage—the process of dying and rising as a pattern of life for married people. Each day we must die to our own desires and rise as a servant. Each day we are called to identify with the suffering Christ on the cross, and then be empowered by the resurrected Christ. We die to our expectations, our demands, and our fears. We rise to compromise, service, and courage.

In this sense, a true Christian marriage proposal is an *offer*, not a request. Rather than saying in effect, "Will you do this for me?" when we invite another to enter the marriage relationship, the real question should be, "Will you accept what I want to give?"

If marriage is daily approached from this perspective, there can be no issue of disillusionment on the part of either partner, as both will become consumed with how well they are carrying out their duty of serving their spouse.

The "Worthy"

The important thing to remember is that service is a spiritual discipline we owe to God, and it can only be lived out as it is applied to others. I learned long ago that God has called me to serve him through people, regardless of whether those people are "worthy" of being served. For years I worked with a ministry that reached out to women facing crisis pregnancies. One of the challenges — in some people's minds at least — was that these women were merely reaping what they had sown, so why should we help them?

To be sure, many people are in desperate straits because of sinful choices and actions. But John examines it from another angle: "If anyone has material possessions and sees his brother in need but has no pity on him, how can the love of God be in him?" (1 John 3:17). For John, there's no mention of a *sinless* brother or sister in need. His teaching is far more blunt — their *need* defines our obligation. It's a matter of God's love, not human evaluation or judgment.

I reach out to people because God has loved me and has asked me to love others in return, not because the people I am loving are "worthy" of love or because they'll thank me for it in the end. It's not for me to make judgments about their "worthiness." I don't know how I could do that anyway. It's for me to love God by loving others.

God is always worthy of being obeyed and served, so when I act out of obedience to him, the person who receives my service doesn't have to be deserving — they're benefiting from what I owe *God*. Yes, this truth is hard to apply in marriage, where demands and expectations are so plentiful, but I try to remind myself of this fact: God is always worthy of being obeyed, and God calls me to serve my spouse — so regardless of how she treats me at any particular moment, I am called to respond as a servant.

Jesus' example has challenged me greatly in this regard. *None* of the disciples deserved to have their feet washed at the Last Supper — all of them would abandon him within a few hours — yet Jesus went ahead and did it anyway (see John 13:1 – 17). In fact, Jesus even washed the feet of Judas, *who was just hours away from betraying him.*

God doesn't tell us to love only those who deserve it or to serve only those who serve us back. If you are in a one-sided marriage where you feel like you're giving and giving and never receiving, my heart goes out to you. You can partially redeem such a situation by becoming more God-oriented. Remind yourself that you are also in a situation where you can grow spiritually by leaps and bounds. If the heart of Christianity is service, any situation that shapes the spirit of a servant in you is worthwhile—even a lopsided marriage.

But we need more than mere grudging acceptance of a difficult truth. Part of Christian service is performing it with a beautiful spirit.

The Spirit of Service

One of the challenges of Christian virtue is living out the teaching of the Scriptures that stress the inner reality behind the external action. Jesus said we might do the right thing (give money, for instance) for the wrong reason (to show off), in which case we lose our reward (see Matthew 6:1–4). Without a doubt our service can be subject to wrong motivations.

It's certainly possible that a spouse might render service in an attempt to exert her or his own superiority: "Strong personalities are tempted to assume one-sidedly the whole responsibility for their marriage. Rather than ask the partner to perform certain services they want to do everything themselves. . . . While it looks like sacrificial love, this is in fact a passion to dominate the other person."[9]

"Service" includes allowing your spouse to give—if, of course, they are willing to give. In other words, service isn't just washing somebody else's feet; at times it's letting *your own* feet be washed.

Another aspect of true service is that it's performed willingly. A begrudging, complaining service is not a Christian one. I have a habit that I'm sure would be very frustrating to ninety-five percent of the wives who are reading this—I like to watch movies in the same way I like to read books. Instead of watching a two-hour movie in one chunk, I'll often stretch it out over two or three nights. I'll watch the first half hour to get familiar with the characters, the second forty-five minutes to get a handle on what the conflict is going to be, and the final thirty minutes or so to watch the resolution. This gives me time to think about the movie as well as to get in bed early, because I like to start work early.

I had rented a movie one weekend and started to watch it at this pace—a bit on Saturday, and then a second chunk on Sunday evening. It was getting late in the evening (for me, at least!), so I mentioned that I thought I'd go to bed and finish the movie on Monday.

"I'm almost done with the laundry," Lisa said. "Stay and watch just a little bit more with me."

I agreed, and so I watched for about another fifteen minutes. Lisa still hadn't completed her task.

"I'm going to go to bed," I said again. "You can keep watching it; I'll just rewind it. If I stay up any longer, I'm going to resent you in the morning."

Technically, if I had wanted to "serve" Lisa, I would have stayed up, I guess, until she was done. But I also know my limits, and if my service starts to become stained with resentment, I'm not serving God in it. True Christian service is freely given.

I've learned to guard not just my servant's actions, but my servant's *spirit*. If I serve Lisa with little puffs of exasperation, grunting every time I lift a finger on her behalf, I'm exhibiting a proud, false-martyr's spirit, not the attitude of Jesus Christ.

I go back to imagining the scene that day as Jesus washed Judas's feet. Do you think Jesus was especially rough as he scrubbed Judas's toes? Do you think he maybe gave Judas's ankle a little twist, just enough to let him know that he knew what was about to happen?

I don't think so.

This principle of marriage as a freely given arena of service leaves room for the understanding that each partner in the marriage will have different roles and different avenues of service. Over fifteen years of marriage, Lisa and I have settled into certain habits like an old pair of jeans. When we come back from a trip, Lisa invariably checks the phone messages while I unload the car. Lisa hates filling up the car's gas tank, so before I leave on a trip, I try to make sure it's full. If Lisa knows I'm coming home, she'll nurse that tank until she's riding on nothing more than fumes.

I don't resent this, and Lisa doesn't resent the fact that she's usually folding laundry when she watches a movie while I just sit there like an all-star couch potato.

We're not just after the imitation of Christ's *actions* in our home. We also want to model Christ's *spirit* and *attitude*. There are times to serve—and times to receive service.

The beauty of this commitment is that it makes both Lisa and me God-dependent rather than spouse-dependent. If Lisa is faithfully serving me when I'm in a surly mood and I'm not exactly falling over myself to show my appreciation, she still receives an inner affirmation and sense of fulfillment from God. She has the joy of that inner witness that tells her that her Creator is pleased with her.

To become a servant is to become radically *strong* spiritually. It means you are free from the petty demands and grievances that ruin so many lives and turn so many hearts into bitter cauldrons of disappointment, self-absorption, and self-pity.

There is true joy when true service is offered up with a true heart.

Money, Money, Money

Service entails far more than occasionally helping out with the dishes or giving our spouse "a night off" from watching the kids. The spirit of service will color virtually every aspect of marriage, including how we spend our money and our time. Dan Allender and Tremper Longman speak to this issue so well that I want to quote them at length:

> Money is the medium of power. More often than not, the issue is not money, but power. The battle is not about who is most trustworthy or whose heart most deeply desires to sacrifice for the other but about who controls the most palpable means of setting the family agenda.
>
> Time becomes a commodity of contention as well. Should a wife work, requiring her husband to take care of the kids after he gets home from his job? Is the husband spending too much time with his colleagues and neglecting his wife?

These conflicts over time and money cloud the real issue: Are we willing to sacrifice for the good and the glory of the other? Quarrels over money and time usually reflect a demand to "own" our life rather than to serve the other with our wealth and existence. The typical fight over who ought to pick up the kids usually is about whose time is more valuable, who works the hardest, and who is least appreciated. It is not wrong to alternate chores or divvy up responsibilities, but the hurtful interactions usually reflect drawing battle lines over more petty matters.[10]

The next time you battle it out with your spouse over time or money, pause and remind yourself that your prayers to become more like Jesus Christ are being put to the test. Be willing to honestly ask yourself this question: Am I playing a petty power game, or am I using the sometimes unpleasant realities of life to shape my stubborn nature toward that of a servant?

How do a husband and wife use money and time to serve instead of to dominate or manipulate? By appreciating your spouse, by seeking first to understand him or her, by emptying yourself and not immediately assuming that your task, your time, your perceived need is the most important.

The world got a dramatic picture into the very heart of greed when it watched the National Basketball Association get into a bitter feud in 1998 and 1999 over how to divide two billion dollars of revenue. You would think that dividing two billion dollars would be somewhat of a pleasant exercise, and that the mind-boggling sum (with relatively few people involved) would tend to create good feelings of thankfulness, benevolence, and generosity — but that wasn't the case at all. The whole situation was marked with rancor, judgment, bitter accusations, and personal attacks.

I've seen the same rancor and spite as husband and wife divide up $35,000, $50,000, or $100,000. The amount doesn't matter nearly as much as the spirit behind how the money is used. The fact of the matter is, the process of spending money invokes fundamental motivations, priorities, and expectations.

How can I spend my money in a spirit of service? By remembering that I will be most fulfilled as a Christian when I use everything I have—including my money and time—as a way to serve others, with my spouse getting first priority (after God). This commitment absolutely undercuts petty power games. If I humiliate my wife by pointing out how much more important I am to the family's financial well-being, or if she points out how utterly helpless I am in doing certain domestic chores, we don't just cheapen each other; we cheapen ourselves. We destroy the entire notion of Christian fellowship by denying that every part has its place in the body of Christ (1 Corinthians 12:14–31).

These little acts of sacrifice will not always be rewarded or even noticed by our spouse—that's what can make them all the more difficult over the passage of time. But if we guard our hearts from bitterness and resentment, we will receive affirmation where it counts and where it means the most—from our heavenly Father.

Just as the spirit of service colors the way we spend our money and our time, so it affects the way we relate to our spouse sexually. The marital bed is yet another area where our service skills are put to the test.

Absolute Power Corrupts—or Serves?

Golf legend Gary Player was once asked by a reporter what he would do if he had to choose between his wife Vivienne, to whom he had been married for forty-two years, and his favorite golf club. Without hesitating, Player responded, "I sure would miss her." When he got back to his hotel, Player found his beloved driver on the bed, draped in a provocative negligee.

The nature of sexual desire is such that it bestows tremendous relational power. The only sexual life a Christian spouse can legitimately enjoy is the romantic life a spouse chooses to provide. This makes manipulation and rejection ever-present spectators in the marital bed. Anything denied physically becomes an absolute denial, because there is no other legitimate outlet. (On the other hand, placing an unbearable sexual burden on a spouse in an attempt to meet other, unfulfilled needs can also be a manipulating abuse of power.)

The old adage "power corrupts, and absolute power corrupts absolutely" is particularly true in a microcosmic way in marriage. Few things in human experience match the absolute power of sexual desire in marriage. Sometimes if I'm in a foul mood, the mere knowledge that my wife is "eager" tempts me to be maliciously uninterested. This is a shameful and tyrannical display of power — "I have what you want, and you're not going to get it, so there!" It's a form of Hitlerism within relationship, using power to destroy, condemn, and hate.

A contrasting example of the appropriate use of power is seen most clearly in Jesus' last night on earth. In verse 3 of chapter 13 of his Gospel, John tells us that "Jesus knew that the Father had put all things under his power," but instead of acting like a spiteful tyrant, Jesus got up from the meal and washed his disciples' feet. Instead of using his power to pout, chastise, or gloat, Jesus uses it to serve.

The spiritual beauty of sexuality is seen in service, lovingly meeting the physical desires and needs of our mate. The spiritual meaning of a Christian's sexuality is found in giving. When we have power over another and we use that power responsibly, appropriately, and benevolently, we grow in Christ, we become more like God, and we reflect the fact that we were made to love God by serving others.

Whether sexuality becomes a celebration of service or a point of contention depends largely on one or both partners' selflessness. The sexual relationship thus provides an excellent opportunity for two Christians to experience the testing of their virtue in real-world ways. It is no exaggeration to say that the true nature of our spiritual character may be best demonstrated when we are engaging in sexual relations.

Where sex becomes spiritually debilitating is when it ceases to become reciprocal. One of the problems with adolescent sexual awakening — as well as with a fascination with pornography and the like

—is that it is usually divorced from the concept of giving. It too quickly becomes all about experiencing, receiving, trying to understand the mystery—in a word, about *getting*.

It is so easy, and yet so spiritually fatal, to take a shortcut here. Sex gives us a capacity to give to someone in a startlingly unique and human way. And yet sex is often used to take, to demand, to coerce, to shame, and to harm.

Honestly ask yourself these questions: Is sex something I'm giving to my spouse, or withholding? Is sex something I am demanding, or offering? Is sex something I am using as a tool of manipulation, or as an expression of generous love? If God looked at nothing other than my sexuality, would I be known as a mature Christian or as a near pagan?

There are many books that focus on the technical mastery of sex, and I suppose such books have their place. But the true challenge of sex is in its spiritual mastery. A growing, healthy, giving, and selfless sex life is not easy to maintain. And yet it provides the setting for tremendous spiritual growth.

Devoid of this emphasis on service, sex seems like the antithesis of an ascetic, self-controlled, and disciplined life. But looked at within the context of service, sex leads to the apex of spiritual maturity —being able to walk through something so powerful as the ultimate human pleasure and yet use it to serve rather than to demand, exploit, or abuse. Catholic philosopher Dick Westley observes, "The fact is that sexual activity, when it is truly love-making and the work of the spirit, is the antithesis of self-indulgence. It is the height of asceticism."[11]

Isn't it marvelous that God can use something as earthly and mundane as sexual angst or financial frustration to cause us to mature spiritually? Learning to give sexually instead of take, learning to lessen your own demands and to be more sensitive to your spouse's demands—these small choices will reap big dividends in your spiritual life because they are teaching you to become more selfless. You are imitating Jesus Christ and taking on the nature of a servant, which is your calling as a Christian.

It's wonderful when a husband and wife enjoy rich, fulfilling, and even exciting sexual relations. And there is nothing wrong with having this as one of your goals. But alongside this goal — in fact, *above* this goal — should be the desire to become a better Christian. Use the marriage bed to learn how to serve another and how to deny yourself, and the spiritual benefits will be many.

This same motivation can color all aspects of marital life. Household chores, conversation, time, money — enter these areas of need in your marriage with a desire to grow in the grace of giving. Pray that God might use them to root out your selfishness and to teach you to become gentle, forgiving, gracious, and kind.

Becoming more like Jesus is the essence of Christianity, and none of us can say with any degree of sincerity that we have cornered the market on being a servant. Our marriages provide opportunities every day for us to be pushed further in this direction.

Sexual Saints

Marital Sexuality Can Provide Spiritual Insights and Character Development

*Like all truly mystical things, love is rooted deeply
and rightly in this world and this flesh.*
KATHERINE ANNE PORTER

*Gifts of a loving Creator, our bodies are not barriers
to grace. If we could truly accept this, then we would
know God even in the ambiguous delights of our sexuality.*
EVELYN AND JAMES WHITEHEAD

*We find God in the contact of our bodies,
not just in the longing of our souls.*
EVELYN AND JAMES WHITEHEAD

I WAS IN JUNIOR HIGH, WALKING TOWARD A GROUP OF BUDDIES, when my best friend at the time came out of the circle and stopped me.

"No," he said. "You don't want this."

"What are you talking about?" I asked, hurt that this guy, of all people, would spurn me.

"This isn't for you."

I learned later that my friend was keeping me from a book that was making the rounds at our school. It had something to do with sex — complete with pictures — and the dog-eared corners attested to its being quickly stashed in sock drawers and under mattresses in numerous adolescent-occupied homes.

Most of us are introduced to sex in shameful ways. The viewing of "dirty" books or the experience of sexual abuse at the hands of an older person often usher us prematurely into the world of sexual knowledge. The natural result is that most of us have to overcome some deep-seated anxieties about sex. Many Christians don't see sex as a gift for which to be thankful, but as a guilt-ridden burden to be borne. And naturally, anything so intimately connected with guilt is difficult to view as a ladder to the holy.

Some of this guilt—which psychologist Willard Gaylin calls "the guardian of our goodness"[1]—is justified. When we stray outside God's perfect will, we *should* feel guilty. But guilt is not infallible, nor does it always turn itself off when it is no longer applicable.

In spite of the uncomfortableness with which we approach sexuality, most married Christians know that sexual intimacy can produce moments of sheer transcendence—brief, sunset-like glimpses of eternity. On the underside of ecstasy we catch the shadow of a profound spiritual truth.

Thus we are caught in the perplexity that sex often represents both the best and the worst moments of our lives. While sex may at times create moments that mark our deepest shame, it can also make us feel more alive than ever before.

In this chapter it is my desire to move past the harm and shame brought about by sex experienced outside the protecting walls of virtue, and examine how it is possible for this very fleshly experience to sharpen our spiritual sensitivities. If sex is going to turn us toward God and each other, it is vital that we examine it with Christian understanding. Christian spirituality serves us in at least three ways here: It teaches us the goodness of sex while reminding us that there are things that are more important than sex. It allows us to experience pleasure without making pleasure the idol of our existence. It teaches us that sex can certainly season our lives but also reminds us that sex will never fully nourish our souls.

To begin to view sex in this positive sense, as a mirror of our desire and passion for God, the institution of marriage becomes all-important. If we think about sex *only within the confines of marriage*—thereby sanctifying it as God intended it—the analogy of sex leading us toward God may not seem so far-fetched. To be sure, sex is abused within the marriage relationship as well, so let's take this a step further. Add in the notion—which we discussed earlier—that sex is to be used to serve our spouse, as well as the analogy that our restlessness for the sexual experience mirrors our restlessness for God, and the ability to use our sexuality as a spiritual aid may begin to make more sense.

So, in order to benefit from the insights of this chapter, try to move past the hurt, shame, guilt, and angst that you associate with sex because of what you may have experienced, talked about, or seen depicted outside the marital relationship. Homosexuality, premarital sex, fantasy-laden masturbation, hard-core pornography—none of that constitutes "sex" as we're defining it here. Redefine sex as it was in Eden, as it was when Adam "knew" Eve and began to populate the world. Think of sex only in these terms, and *then* think of how God can reveal himself to you within your marriage through the gift of sexual pleasure.

It might sound shocking, but it's true: God doesn't turn his eyes when a married couple goes to bed. It only stands to reason that we shouldn't turn our eyes from God when we share intimate moments with our spouse.

Ambivalent Ancestors

For centuries, Christian spiritual writers have viewed sexuality as problematic at best. The Christian church has delicately tiptoed around the essentiality of sex, attempting to rein in its power by regulating its tides—sometimes with almost comical effect:

In the second century, Clement of Alexandria allowed unenjoyed and procreative sex only during twelve hours out of the twenty-four (at night), but by the Middle Ages, preposterous as it now seems, the Church forbade it forty days before the important festival of Christmas, forty days before and eight days after the more important festival of Easter, eight days after Pentecost, the eves of feast days, on Sundays in honor of the resurrection, on Wednesdays to call to mind the beginning of Lent, Fridays in memory of the crucifixion, during pregnancy and thirty days after birth (forty if the child is female), during menstruation, and five days before communion!

This all adds up to 252 excluded days, not counting feast days. If there were thirty of those (a guess which may, in fact, be on the conservative side), there would then have been eighty-three remaining days in the year when (provided, of course, that the woman did not happen to be menstruating or pregnant or in the post-natal period, and provided that they intended procreation) couples could with the permission of the Church have indulged in (but not enjoyed) sexual intercourse![2]

All this reminds me of the time my children and I were at the beach. The tide was coming in — and the kids had built a sand castle. For forty-five minutes we fought desperately to save the sand castle from the encroaching sea. We built large barriers around the castle and carried in large pieces of driftwood to serve as a block, but eventually, of course, the sea won and the sand castle was ruined.

Trying to put so many burdensome restrictions (even within marriage) on such a powerful force as sexual expression is ultimately futile. It's like trying to hold back the sea. The desire to regulate marital sex comes, at least in part, from our fear of it. Common sense tells us that sex is necessary for the human race to continue — God's command to Adam that he "be fruitful and increase in number" (Genesis 1:28) was an *explicit commandment* to engage in sexual relations — but religious apprehension makes us think that the "most holy" amongst us will somehow shun its pleasure. This, tragically, would mean that only the *least* holy would actually raise children — which doesn't bode well for the faith of the next generation.

This fear of sex prepared its assault early on, particularly in the interpretation of the obviously erotic Song of Songs. The clear implication of Origen's work (around A.D. 185–254) was that fleshly, intoxicating pleasure had no place in this world. Only "spiritual delights" counted for anything. Dan Allender and Tremper Longman point out, "Origen interpreted the highly sensual Song of Songs in an allegorical, spiritual manner, doing to that book the same thing he did to his body when he took a knife and castrated himself."[3]

A century later, at the famous Council of Nicea (A.D. 325), certain radicals started suggesting that bishops must be celibate. A well-respected ascetic bishop, Paphnutius, opposed this suggestion vigorously, rightly arguing that it *was* "chastity" for a man to "cohabit" with his wife.[4] It was particularly significant that an ascetic bishop pledged to chastity had the wisdom to argue this position, as he clearly had nothing to gain from it. But Paphnutius was certainly the exception, and his opinion was soon buried by the weight of the famed church father Augustine (354–430).

Augustine—who stamped Christian thought like few others—taught that sexual intercourse transmitted original sin, thereby (perhaps unintentionally but surely regrettably) entangling sin and sex for centuries to follow. As a result, the church often had a difficult time reconciling sanctity with a sexually active life. Mary Anne McPherson Oliver points out that very few canonized saints were married and that "none of these few were canonized as models for conjugal virtue."[5]

By the fourth century, Ambrose was calling marriage "honorable," but he tempered the compliment by calling chastity "more honorable." Institutionally there was still this sense in which sexual intercourse was "excused" *provided* it was participated in for the sake of procreation. All other sexual relations within marriage still constituted "venial" sin (excusable, but a black mark nevertheless).

There *were* moments of enlightenment, however. There is evidence that in medieval times, priests would sometimes bless a newlywed couple in their bridal bed. Interestingly enough, the Puritans seemed unusually at ease when it came to embracing sexual pleasure. Richard Baxter wrote that husband and wife should "take delight" in the love and company and conversation of each other. He wrote, "Keep up your conjugal love in a constant heat and vigor." He added that spouses must not suffer their love "to grow luke-warm."[6]

But most gains were short-lived, relatively speaking. An ancient Sarum rite (on which the 1549 Anglican Prayer Book was based) had, since at least A.D. 1125, nuptial rites that included the words, "with my body I thee worship." This was rather bold and provocative for any period in the church, let alone the Middle Ages, so perhaps it is not surprising that these words were stricken from the Anglican Prayer Book in 1786.

Reconciling sex and sanctity has never been fully accomplished up to this very day, though the Second Vatican Council relinquished somewhat the idea of married believers as second-class Christians. In a document titled, "The Call of the Whole Church to Holiness," the Roman Catholic Church "emphasizes that all God's people are called to the fullness of Christian sanctity, and that sanctity is available to all in and through their particular vocations."[7]

Even so, the few canonized saints in the twentieth century who had been in marriage relationships were, as Mary Anne McPherson Oliver observes, routinely martyrs or stigmatics, widows/foundresses of religious orders, and husbands who had left wife and family to become missionaries or hermits. These individuals were extolled *in spite* of being married, not because they exhibited an unusual commitment to holiness within marriage.

Perhaps we can be charitable toward the ancients' (and our own) uneasiness with sex in part because few of us can deny the truth that, in one sense, "sex is a heavy burden that God has laid upon mankind."[8] While it is beyond doubt that the Bible has a favorable and positive view of sex — witness the Song of Songs, for instance — biblical writers are also acutely aware of the snare of sexual sin and our propensity to spoil the good gift God has given us.

This human inclination is precisely why the institution of marriage is so crucial as we seek to navigate the sea of sexual desire. It is the only context in which sexuality becomes spiritually meaningful and helpful.

Laying the Groundwork for Spiritually Meaningful Sex

A Biblical View of Sexuality

As in all things, proper theology even among "lay" Christians is vital if we are to adopt a fully biblical view of sexuality that will allow us to incorporate the experience of physical intimacy into a spiritually meaningful vision of faith. We Christians can learn a thing or two from the Jewish foundations of our faith.

There are theological reasons why the Christian church has had more difficulty dealing with sexual activity than our Jewish ancestors. To the ancient Jew, nothing was more important than the preservation and purity of the family line. As the "chosen people," Jews viewed divorce in the case of barrenness as perfectly acceptable. Practically the worst thing you could do to a spouse was to deny him or her children, because progeny was how the unpolluted, God-chosen race would continue.

Jewish views about sex went beyond procreation. Ancient Jewish women were given three "fundamental rights": food, clothing, and the *onah*—sexual intercourse apart from the duty of procreation. A religion based on bloodlines can ill afford to look down on procreative activity.

The ancient Jewish text *The Holy Letter* (written by Nahmanides in the thirteenth century) sees sex as a mystical experience of meeting with God: "Through the act [of intercourse] they become partners with God in the act of creation. This is the mystery of what the sages said, 'When a man unites with his wife in holiness, the Shekinah is between them in the mystery of man and woman.' "[9] The breadth of this statement is sobering when you consider that this *shekinah* glory is the same presence experienced by Moses when God met with him face-to-face (see Exodus 24:15 – 18).

In contrast to medieval Christian prohibitions, Nahmanides recommends that married couples regularly experience sexual intercourse on the Sabbath in celebration of their faith. The reason he could advocate this was his firm belief that everything God made — including the sexual organs and thus the sense of sexual touch — is good because God has declared it so (Genesis 1:31).

With Christians, however, salvation is not about family blood but spiritual faith. Procreation is no longer the highest end; faith is. Thus if someone avoids a sexual union so that they can foster a deeper faith, they are frequently assumed to have chosen the "higher" way. But just because (in the Christian view) sex no longer services salvation or the propagation of God's kingdom on earth doesn't mean that sex has nothing to teach us in the way of sanctification (or growth in holiness). We can continue to believe that for the purpose of salvation faith takes precedence over procreation while still appreciating the Jewish aspect of seeking the *shekinah* glory in the marital bed.

To use our sexuality as a spiritual discipline — to integrate our faith and flesh, so to speak — it is imperative that we become theologically grounded enough to incorporate into our thinking a Jewish view of sexuality. God made flesh, and when God made flesh, he created some amazing sensations. While the male sexual organ has multiple functions, the female clitoris has just one — sexual pleasure. By design, God created a bodily organ that has no other purpose than to provide women with sexual ecstasy. This wasn't Satan's idea — it was God's. And God called every bit of his creation "very good" (Genesis 1:31).

Betsy Ricucci has approached this issue from a feminine perspective: "Within the context of covenant love and mutual service, no amount of passion is excessive. Scripture says our sexual intimacy should be exhilarating (Proverbs 5:19, *New American Standard Bible*). . . . Believe it or not, we glorify God by cultivating a sexual desire for our husbands and by welcoming their sexual desire for us."[10]

If guilt rather than gratitude casts a shadow over your experience of sex, practice thanking God for what sex involves. For instance, a woman could pray, quite explicitly—but in all holiness—"God, thank you that it feels enticing when my husband caresses my breasts." Couples could even pray together, thanking God for the pleasure surrounding the act of marital consummation. This simple act of thanksgiving can sanctify an act that all-too-many Christians divorce from their spiritual life with God. The reason it feels good is because God designed it so.

Once we evaluate the theological foundations on which we build our view of marital sex, we also need to examine our emotional attitudes. In this case, gratitude must replace guilt.

Gratitude Must Replace Guilt

In his book *Music Through the Eyes of Faith,* Harold Best tells the true story of a young man who became heavily involved in a satanic cult. "This was no offhanded cult," Best writes, "but one of profoundly serious intention." The cult developed a sophisticated and elaborate liturgy focusing on the compositions of Johann Sebastian Bach.

The young man later became a Christian and started attending worship services at a local church. Everything went well until the church organist belted out a piece composed by Bach. The young believer was overcome by fear and dread and fled the sanctuary.

Best writes that Bach's work "represents some of the noblest music for Christian worship. To this young man, however, it was not noble at all, but rather epitomized all that was evil, horrible, and anti-Christian."[11]

Sex is that way for some Christians. Past associations and guilt feelings have created severe spiritual roadblocks. While few would suggest that Bach's compositions are inherently evil, the young man *felt* that they were so because of how Bach's works had been abused in his past experience. In the same way, some Christians try hard not to believe that sex is inherently evil, but because of previous negative experiences, to them it certainly *feels* evil. The effects of these roadblocks can be lessened through a proper biblical understanding of sex, as well as through the practice of confession and repentance. If your history contains abuse, you may want to consider seeking counseling as a way to help you gain a new, and hopefully more favorable, perspective on sex.

Sex cannot pay spiritual dividends if its currency is shrouded in unfounded and illegitimate guilt. Gratitude to God for this amazing experience is essential; otherwise, the powerful feelings associated with sex will lead us to focus on self.

Ironically, the idolatry of sex and obsessive guilt over sex accomplish the same thing—they keep the focus on self, whether it be out of enjoyment or despair. Gratitude, on the other hand, turns our hearts toward God.

It took me awhile to realize how I was inadvertently insulting God by my hesitation to accept the holiness of sex and pleasure. I don't have any problem imagining someone seeking God by enduring the pain of a fast. But what kind of God am I imagining if I can allow pain but not pleasure to reveal God's presence in my life? Instead of being suspicious of pleasure and the physical and spiritual intimacy that comes from being with my wife, I need to adopt an attitude of profound gratefulness and awe.[12]

Once we have reevaluated our theology and our emotional attitudes, we also need to reconsider our expectations—that is, what *type* of intimacy we are seeking.

View Your Spouse as More Than a Lover

The third step to becoming fully prepared to use sexuality as a spiritual discipline is to remember that in Christian marriage, husband and wife are more than lovers. They are brother and sister in Christ.

During my engagement to Lisa, I gave her a poem titled "My Sister, His Bride," in which I talked about how the step we were taking toward marriage was so monumental in this world, but that there already existed an even more significant eternal bond between us that would actually outlive our status as husband and wife: brother and sister in Christ. There is a depth to this spiritual brother/sister relationship that is all too frequently left unexplored.

Otto Piper explains it this way: "The believer who conducts his marriage as in the Lord will seek to make his marriage transcend mere sexuality by emphasizing his fellowship with God. Then the spouse is not only a sexual partner but also and above all a brother or sister in Christ. In this way the instinctive longing inherent in all love becomes real: our earthly lives are transmuted into lives with God."[13]

This means that while physical pleasure is good and acceptable, we mustn't reduce sex to a merely *physical* experience. It is about more — much more — than that. Sex speaks of spiritual realities far more profound than mere pleasure.

When Paul tells us that our bodies are temples of the Holy Spirit (1 Corinthians 6:19), our contemplations on the significance of sex take on an entirely new meaning. What a woman is allowing inside her, what a man is willingly entering — in a Christian marriage, these are *sanctified* bodies; bodies in which God is present through his Holy Spirit; bodies coming together, celebrating, but in a spirit of reverence and holiness.

If Paul tells us that a man is not to join himself to a prostitute because his body is a holy temple — that is, if we are to use such imagery to *avoid* sinning — can a Christian not use the same imagery to be drawn *into* God's presence in a unique way as he joins his body with his wife? Isn't he somehow entering God's temple — knocking on the door of *shekinah* glory — when he joins himself to a fellow believer? And isn't this a tacit encouragement to perhaps even think about God as your body is joined with your spouse?

Otto Piper urges us to view the sex act as a physical picture of a deeper spiritual reality: "We have come together in [God], called by him, creating a family, serving him, he living in both of us, we now expressing, physically, the spiritual truth that he has created—we are no longer two, but one."[14]

This spiritual element of sex is a crucial aid to help men experience deliverance from sexual addictions. When sex is reduced to pleasure alone, no wife can possibly meet a husband's expectations. Pleasure, by nature, is ephemeral. It's fleeting. I read an article written by a Christian who had overcome a serious addiction to pornography, and he made it quite clear that he always needed a *new* magazine. Although he possessed enough naked pictures to wallpaper his house (more than he could possibly look at in the course of a day), he needed the thrill of getting *new* pictures of *new* women.

A wife can't reinvent herself on a daily basis, so a man can't kick a passion for pornography by trying to turn his wife into a centerfold. He must search for, and find, something much different in the marital bed. He can seek the deeper (but oftentimes quieter) fulfillment of spiritually meaningful sex, looking for God and for Christian fellowship behind the pleasure—not running from the pleasure, to be sure, but not making an idol of that pleasure either.

Remember—every hunger that entices us in the flesh is an exploitation of a need that can be better met by God. The only context for godly sex is marital sex. Illicit sex is spiritual junk food—immediately sweet, but something that will poison our spiritual appetite until we crave that which will ultimately destroy us. Illicit sex will do nothing but diminish our sensitivity to holiness, righteousness, and God's presence in our lives.

The deeply physical and fleshly experience of sex can be enjoyed without guilt, but there is an even deeper spiritual fulfillment inherent when a man and woman engage in sexual relations. Don't reduce sex to either a physical or spiritual experience. It is both—profoundly so.

Now that we've examined our theology, our emotional attitudes, and our expectations regarding sex, we must become comfortable with the oftentimes fearful yearning inherent in sexual desire.

Reconciling the Power of Sex

Sex is not a physical need in the same way that food is — you can survive a lifetime without a single orgasm. But it is certainly a physiological *drive*. It is predictable, and it is physical as well as emotional. Most important, this physical desire — which feels like a need — that a man and woman have for each other *is there by God's design. God* put this "need" in us.

How do we approach this sense of need from a Christian perspective? It might help if we see hidden in this analogy the sense of need that represents our longing for God — that we are incomplete without him and need to join ourselves to him anew. Thomas Hart observes that "our fascination with sex is closely related to our fascination with God."[15]

Sex cannot *replace* God. Sex will not suffice as a substitute for God. But a healthy look at sex can provide fruitful meditation on our need and desire for God — the sense of incompleteness followed by the joy and fulfillment made all the sweeter after finally giving ourselves to another.

If there were no great need, the fulfillment would be less sweet. It is only when I am truly hungry that I fully appreciate a good meal. Passion is a fearful thing to some of us. The sense of longing reminds us that we are incomplete by ourselves, but the fact is that God made us incomplete. We need him; we need others.

I remember reading the Song of Songs as a young man with great discomfort, in large part because I was terrified of ever wanting someone as desperately as those two lovers wanted each other. Such wanting, I knew even at a young age, can lead to tremendous pain, disillusionment, and grief.

It is frightening to want God. What if he doesn't show up? It is even scarier to want another human. What if they spurn our advances or use our desire as a weapon against us?

Here is the difficulty: There is no guarantee that our spouse will not use our desire against us. But while this provides a point of possible manipulation, it also provides an avenue of spiritual growth. We can use this sense of need as a way to grow as servants of each other. In a healthy Christian marriage in which both husband and wife lovingly seek to fulfill the sexual desires of each other, both can learn that God will minister to them as well. Just as Jesus uses the example (Matthew 7:9) of an earthly father who will not give his son a stone when he asks for bread — and encourages his followers to likewise trust God to give good gifts — so a man or woman may be able to open up their heart to God when they experience how their spouse is generous in meeting their need for sexual expression.

The truth is, without this physiological drive many couples would slowly drift apart. We are by nature selfish beings who hide from each other. Maintaining a steady pursuit toward and empathy for another human being goes against our sinful, egocentric bent. By creating a physical desire, God is inviting us to participate in the spiritual reality of learning to share, have fellowship with, and enter the life and soul of another human being in a profound way.

The above thoughts are intended to legitimize the use of sexual expression as a tool of spiritual development. It would take an entire book to fully explore this subject, but in the next section we're going to consider a few representative examples of *how* a married couple might use aspects of their physical intimacy to grow spiritually.

Spiritual Development
Through Sexual Expression

Bernard of Clairvaux (1090–1153) taught that carnal or earthly love is actually the first step in human experience that leads us to love God — sort of like in kindergarten, where we learn to get along with others and sit behind a desk before the "real schooling" begins in first grade. He took this one step further when he suggested that, carnal as we are, our love for God in this life will fittingly have a carnal element. Certainly, as you read some of the testimonies of mystics, their unabashed love for God has this near-erotic element.

Instead of running from this element of sexual expression, we can channel it in the proper direction. C. S. Lewis wrote, "Pleasures are shafts of the glory as it strikes our sensibility.... Make every pleasure into a channel of adoration."[16] In this section, we seek to do just this — turn earthly marital pleasures (and challenges) into channels of holy adoration.

Many books provide guidance on a variety of sexual positions and on ways to keep sex fresh. Here, I'd like to look at the spiritual side of sexuality, examining how we can be transformed spiritually through this very physical act. We'll do this by seeking to have our notion of beauty transformed; learning to give what we have; being called out of ourselves; learning to become passionate; and cultivating the art of celebration.

Gaining God's View of Marital Beauty

Marriage takes the raw force of sexuality and connects it with emotional intimacy, companionship, family responsibilities, and permanency of relationship. In so doing, it provides a context that encourages spiritual growth by moving us to value character, virtue, and godliness over against an idealized physical form.

To prepare for a part in a major motion-picture release in which nudity would be prevalent, an internationally famous actress spent up to five hours a day in a gym, working out with a personal trainer. All this would refine the body-enhancing surgery that had taken place earlier in her life. With enough time and money, and a professional hairdresser and makeup team, virtually any woman can "look good."

I won't deny that one of the reasons I was first attracted to Lisa was because I thought she looked good. But what if looking good became Lisa's obsession? Does God think three hours a day in a gym, working feverishly against the realities of nature to preserve an adolescent stomach (with the hips of a mature woman and the breasts of a nursing mother), is a good and profitable use of time?

Jesus' disciple Peter doesn't leave us to guess the answer. He says, quite explicitly, that women shouldn't focus on an external beauty that requires "outward adornment," but instead aspire after a beauty "of your inner self, the unfading beauty of a gentle and quiet spirit, which is of great worth in God's sight" (1 Peter 3:3–4).

Notice that in their pursuit of beauty, wives are directed toward creating a beauty that is of great worth *in God's sight.* Husbands might focus on the wrong things, but Peter still urges wives to direct their lives toward God's view of beauty. This instruction is crucial for a number of reasons.

In C. S. Lewis's *The Screwtape Letters,* the demon Screwtape laments that Wormwood has allowed his man to get victory over sexual temptation. Screwtape's next step is this: "If we can't use his sexuality to make him unchaste we must try to use it for the promotion of a desirable marriage." Keep in mind here that "desirable" is from a *demonic* perspective, meaning "disastrous" from a Christian perspective. Referring to demonic hosts, Screwtape continues:

> It is the business of these great masters to produce in every age a general misdirection of what may be called sexual "taste." This they do by working through the small circle of popular artists, dressmakers, actresses and advertisers who determine the fashionable type. The aim is to guide each sex away from those members of the other with whom spiritually helpful, happy, and fertile marriages are most likely....
>
> As regards to the male taste we have varied a good deal. At one time we have directed it to the statuesque and aristocratic type of beauty, mixing men's vanity with their desires and encouraging the race to breed chiefly from the most arrogant and prodigal women. At another, we have selected an exaggeratedly feminine type, faint and languishing, so that folly and cowardice, and all the general falseness and littleness of mind which go with them, shall be at a premium....
>
> And that is not all. We have engineered a great increase in the license that society allows to the representation of the apparent nude (not the real nude) in art, and its exhibition on the stage or the bathing beach. It is all a fake, of course; the figures in the

popular art are falsely drawn; the real women in bathing suits ... are actually pinched in and propped up to make them appear firmer and more slender ... than nature allows a full-grown woman to be.... As a result we are more and more directing the desires of men to something which does not exist—making the role of the eye in sexuality more and more important and at the same time making its demands more and more impossible. What follows you can easily forecast![17]

The Christian duty of married men is to reverse this propensity and make the "role of the eye in sexuality" *less* important as we embrace the spiritual reality of what is taking place. Sight will always matter to men—that's how God wired us—but we can become mature in what we long to see. *Appetites can be cultivated.* Different cultures enjoy different foods because the inhabitants have eaten such foods all their lives. My kids would wrinkle their noses if my wife dropped rice in front of them for breakfast; in China, children would look askew at a bowl of Cheerios.

The same principle holds true for taste in sexual desirability. Different eras appreciate different shapes in women because of whatever happens to be in fashion. While today's supermodels lean toward waifishness (with adult-sized breasts but adolescent stomachs and thighs), an old Sanskrit word *(gajagamini)* describing the then-ideal of female beauty in ancient India is literally translated "woman who has the gait of an elephant." History has not come up with *the* definitive beauty. The debate has never been resolved. What men and women obsess about, fantasize over, and concentrate on will shape what they desire.

A godly marriage shapes our view of beauty to focus on internal qualities. *The Holy Letter* argues that when a man chooses a woman for her physical beauty alone, "the union is not for the sake of heaven."[18] Beauty is wonderful, but it is not the only or even the highest value when we seek Christian marriage.

A single woman is likely to face strong temptations to become the type of woman a man would want to marry—and that might very well compete with the type of woman who lives a responsible life before God. But single women know that men are attracted to a certain physical shape and so might be inclined to put more effort into changing physically than changing internally by growing in godliness. Marriage can set women free from this vain pursuit; once they are married, they can focus more intensely on the internal beauty that God finds so attractive.

This is not to suggest that either men or women should shun the care of their physical bodies and become unfit. Keeping in good shape is a gift we can give to our spouse. But so is the grace of *acceptance*—particularly on the part of husbands—in recognition that age and (in the case of women) childbearing eventually reshape every individual body. Marriage helps to move men from an obsession over bodies "that do not exist" into a reconsideration of priorities and values.

For instance, marriage calls us to redirect our desires to be focused on *one woman* or *one man in particular* rather than on society's view of attractive women or men in general. We men are married to women whose bodies we know intimately. And out of these bodies, our own children have been born. God gives us each other's bodies as gifts in which to delight. But in receiving our gift, we must not covet another's.

On the day I was married, I began praying, "Lord, help me to define beauty by Lisa's body. Shape my desires so that I am attracted only to her." I knew from the book of Proverbs that I was to take delight in *my wife,* not in women in general. The writer says, "May you rejoice in the wife of your youth. A loving doe, a graceful deer —may her breasts satisfy you always, may you ever be captivated by her love. Why be captivated, my son, by an adulteress? Why embrace the bosom of another man's wife?" (Proverbs 5:18–20).

I cannot fully explain this without embarrassing my wife, so I'm going to speak generally. God has answered my prayer. The physical characteristics that distinguish my wife are the characteristics that I generally find most attractive in other women.

But just as important is a wife who works on internal beauty, who makes the pursuit of sanctification an even greater pursuit than wanting to fit into a size-four dress. This is a beauty that never goes out of style.

Married sexuality helps form us spiritually by shaping the priorities of what we value and hold in high esteem. Many of us don't realize how truly shallow this world and its values really are. A young man or woman can become ridiculously wealthy and incredibly famous—regardless of whether they are a person of character, high morals, or exemplary wisdom—if they're willing to disrobe in the latest Hollywood blockbuster. The net effect is that many people who aren't able to display one particular body type feel *devalued.*

I'm convinced that, with God's Spirit within us, we can become enamored with the things that enamor God. By denying myself errant appetites and by meditating and feeding on the right things— including being "captivated" by my wife's love—I will train myself to desire only what is proper to be desired. This doesn't mean I can't appreciate another person's beauty. It does mean I can appreciate without obsessing. I can see without wanting to enter into a sexually or emotionally inappropriate relationship.

Maturity demands that we adopt this view. Evelyn and James Whitehead put it so simply and powerfully: "When the body is love's only abode, change becomes an enemy."[19] From a Christian perspective, *change is not an enemy, but it is, in fact, the purpose of marriage* —assuming that the change we desire is to become more holy. If my acceptance of my wife is based only on my feelings about her outward appearance rather than on her inner qualities, time will slowly but surely erode my affection.

Those who live only for sexual pleasure and stimulation know only a very limited life—and probably experience a high degree of frustration as time inevitably takes its toll on their aging bodies. Those who find meaning and fulfillment not just in sexuality but in parenting their children, serving God, engaging in a consistent prayer life, and living virtuously have a much broader base from which to enjoy life. A thoughtful and godly marriage will move us in this direction.

Give What You Have

Do you remember the first time you saw your spouse naked? Some good friends of mine tried to "ease into it" on their wedding night. They decided to take a shower together, with the lights out. Unfortunately, the tub began to overflow. It was dark, remember, so they couldn't figure out what was going on with this unfamiliar hotel bathtub drain. Much to their chagrin, they were forced to turn on the lights and start mopping up *in the nude.* Their "twilight transition" turned into a spotlight extravaganza!

It is one thing to stand naked and relatively trim in front of your partner in your early twenties. But what about in your late thirties, forties, or sixties? What about after the wife has given birth to a child (or two or three), and the husband's metabolism has slowed down, depositing "love handles" around his waist?

Continuing to give your body to your spouse even when you believe it constitutes "damaged goods" can be tremendously rewarding spiritually. It engenders humility, service, and an other-centered focus, as well as hammering home a very powerful spiritual principle: Give what you have.

There are many times in which we are called to keep serving God even though we know that the situation is less than ideal. Maybe we want to share the gospel with a neighbor, but we just don't think we're smart enough or that we know the Bible well enough. Or perhaps we hear about a worthwhile charity and wish we could give thousands of dollars, all the while knowing it will be difficult to come up with even a twenty-dollar bill.

Marriage teaches us to give what we have. God has given us one body. He has commanded our spouse to delight in that one body —and that body alone. If we withhold from our spouse our body, it becomes an absolute denial. We may not think it is a perfect body, but it is the only body we have to give.

By no means am I suggesting that it is *easy* to give, but I am saying it is *worthwhile* to give. It is rewarding to say, "I'm willing to give you my best, even if I don't think my best is all that great." That kind of commitment reminds me of Peter, who told the Jerusalem beggar, "Silver or gold I do not have, but what I have I give you. In the name of Jesus Christ of Nazareth, walk" (Acts 3:6).

So many people fail to give God or others anything simply because they can't give everything. Learn to take small steps of obedience toward God — offering what you have, with all its blemishes and limitations — by offering what you have to your spouse.

Calling Us Out of Ourselves

One of the most perplexing problems for me when considering Christian spirituality has been admitting how much we are affected by chemistry. It is sobering to see someone virtually cured from serious disorders through a readjustment of their chemical imbalance.

Scientists have shown that men become more nurturing as they age and as their testosterone level decreases, and older women often become more ambitious as estrogen levels go through adjustments. As hormones play less of a role, the sex differences begin to blur somewhat (but are never entirely eclipsed).

Our sexuality is indelibly connected with bodily urges that are chemical in nature. I can abstain for quite some time, but abstinence changes in nature as time builds. I don't always like the fact that a spiritual struggle has such a physical relief, but it's the way God made me — and you.

There's another way of looking at this, however. Sex may be God's way of calling us to connect with each other. This need for physical expression will sometimes literally force us to work through and resolve emotional and spiritual conflict. This is where a biblical view of divorce and remarriage is essential. Too many Christians enter the process of divorce assuming they can automatically remarry as soon as the divorce papers are finalized. But let's say we were to accept the biblical view (and our civil laws and church leaders were to support this), which would in most cases declare something like this: "You may opt for a divorce, but you cannot ever engage in sex again with anyone else for the rest of your life." Most, if not all, of the men would find or create a way to be reconciled. They would not choose celibacy.

I remember talking frankly to two Christian men once about the ideals of Christian marriage. I cracked them up when I freely confessed, "You bet I've swallowed arguments because I wanted something from my wife later that night." They both admitted, somewhat sheepishly, that they too had done the same thing. I'm not proud of the fact that I'm less willing to stand up for my beliefs when I feel "the urge"—and I particularly don't like the fact that what feels like a physical need directs my spiritual attitudes—but I can learn to use that physical need for spiritual benefit.

Let me put this succinctly: We can learn to use the sex drive to groom our character. Out of a need to be intimate with their wives, husbands may learn to show tenderness and empathy. Wives may use physical intimacy to help capture their husbands' interest emotionally. Emotionally. Idealistically, we would seek opportunities to grow because that's what we're called to do as Christians. Realistically, it doesn't hurt to have such a physical need pushing us in that same direction of growing in character.

Remember, we are *fallen* saints. God has redeemed us, to be sure, but all of us are still mired in sin. Our sanctification will never be perfect this side of heaven. Something as important as preserving marriage—especially in the earlier years when the kids are small and stability is supremely important—can't be left merely to altruistic motives.

The sex drive literally calls us out of ourselves and into another. Provided that the "other" is our spouse, this is a fruitful exercise. It reinforces the "falling forward" concept we talked about in chapter

9. As we are called out of ourselves, we nurture interdependence and fellowship, two very valuable Christian practices.

The Price of Passion

From the record of King David's life and his psalms, it is clear that he was an unusually passionate man. When Nathan the prophet tells the story of a wealthy man who stole a poor man's only lamb, David is incensed. "The man who did this deserves to die!" (2 Samuel 12:5), he rails, not realizing that Nathan is talking about him. And when David writes of his passion for God, he does so with an almost unparalleled fever of emotion — "My soul thirsts for you, my body longs for you, in a dry and weary land where there is no water" (Psalm 63:1).

There is no doubt that David's passion occasionally got him into trouble — the story of Bathsheba is well-known — but nowhere in Scripture are we told to go to the other extreme and choose a passionless existence. In fact, we are told in the book of Revelation that God would rather have us hot or cold, anything but the putrid "lukewarm" (Revelation 3:16).

The German philosopher Martin Heidegger argued that our passions tune us into the world. *Tune us into the world* ... Think about that for a moment. A sexually fulfilled and active wife radiates a certain energy. A man who is sexually satisfied with his wife exudes a sense of well-being. Passion is a very healthy thing.

Just as love expands us, so passion can as well. Passion is not meted out, decreasing every time it is expressed. In fact, the opposite is often the case — the more passionate we become about one thing, the more passionate we tend to become about many other things. A man who is passionate about his wife can be passionate about justice, about God's kingdom, about his own children, about the environment. On the flip side, if he is facing serious sexual problems within his marriage, a feeling of frustration and a certain despondency is liable to settle like a cloud over his work, his faith, and his fellowship. He is likely to become selfishly preoccupied and self-absorbed.

"Stoicism" has never been a Christian philosophy. If truth be told, we serve a passionate God who feels deeply.

Our passions are what make us come alive. The apathetic person is a *pathetic* person. While we often fear our passions because they can carry us into an affair, a fight, or some other destructive behavior, the solution is not living a *less* passionate life but finding the right things to be passionate about.

The history expressed in the Bible and in the two thousand years of Christian experience attest to the fact that Christian spirituality is largely about maintaining our thirst and passion for God and his purposes in this world. Admittedly, at times our passions can lead us astray, but Christian marriage teaches us to manage these passions, like the dam keepers in Washington state. You can hardly drive a hundred miles on the western side of Washington without coming across a dam of some type, so my family is familiar with the process. Sometimes dam managers opt to let the water flow rather freely; other times they hold it down to a trickle.

That's what marriage teaches us to do. Sometimes it is healthy and good to let marital passions run free, even if we fear that we are almost crossing the line over into lust. Some people make the mistake of believing that because they have been burned by their passion and their sexual hunger, the antidote is to completely cut it off. They do to sex what an anorexic does to food: I don't want to overeat and become fat, so I won't eat at all.[20] This isn't a healthy attitude — it's a demented one.

The healthy life is a life of saying yes and no. I travel quite a bit, so there are many times that my wife and I must fast from sexual expression. Couples with young kids, particularly babies, soon learn that they can no longer express themselves sexually whenever they get the inclination. At other seasons, our spouse may be ill or worn-out, and it would be unkind to place sexual expectations on them. In such situations, sexual fasting is appropriate and necessary.

But times of "feasting" are also necessary. In fact, every no we say to sex should be placed in the context of a corresponding yes:

To fast from sexual contact because *eros* is evil is not a Christian discipline but an unholy and unhealthy flight from creation. The no of fasting is fruitful only if we have some deeply valued yeses in our life. The arduous discipline of fasting complements our feasting: we need something to *fast for*. Without some compelling values to pursue and defend, we have no reason to hold back any stirring or impulse.[21]

In other words, abstinence is not a cul-de-sac or dead end; it is a long on-ramp. My denial of sexual expression when I'm apart from my wife is empowered by what the future holds when I get home. I am not truly saying *no*, but rather, *wait*. Rather than being a complete denial, it is a channeling of desire into the proper place. Sexual abstinence for singles (who are not called to celibacy) has this same nature. Teens are urged to *wait* because by doing so their future marital relations will be all the sweeter. Faithfulness seasons the marital bed in many delightful and profound ways.

I don't want to overspiritualize this. We don't always have to think "spiritual" thoughts when we are enjoying conjugal relations. Passions call us to enter fully into life. Passion is at the heart of the Sabbath commandment, which has two sides: Six days you shall work —engage yourself vigorously—and the seventh day you shall rest. Work hard, then rest well. Both are necessary for a meaningful life. At times, sex will have distinctly spiritual overtones; at other times, it will be a celebration of physical pleasure. Both are holy within marriage.

The bottom line is this: Passion and engagement are extremely important. They should be cultivated in marriage and brought to bear on all of life.

Celebration

I tend to be overly serious in my faith, and so I was greatly challenged when I came across an old book written by Elton Trueblood titled *The*

Humor of Christ. Trueblood writes, "Any alleged Christianity which fails to express itself in gaiety, at some point, is clearly spurious."[22] He has plenty of biblical support to back this up. There were at least three major feasts prescribed in the Old Testament—Passover, Weeks, and Tabernacles—as well as many other religious celebrations (see Leviticus 23; Numbers 28, 29). These could be elaborate affairs. The Feast of Tabernacles, for example, involved a seven-day feast in which the Israelites were *commanded* to rejoice and forbidden to mourn.

The fact is, God is worthy of infinite celebration. Jesus said at one point that if the crowds had not broken forth in praise, the very stones would have cried out (see Luke 19:40). God forbid that we would get shown up by a bunch of rocks!

I have to constantly break out of my "serious" rut. That's just my nature. I tend to view celebration as "flighty" or less reverent—but that's a personal prejudice I'm trying to overcome.

Marital sexuality provides a unique context for celebration. Naked in each other's arms, it doesn't matter if you have a portfolio worth a million dollars or if you're struggling with the realities of a negative net worth. You could be lying in a luxurious bed on the top floor of the Waldorf-Astoria Hotel or enjoying a night away from the kids at a Motel 6. You could be delighting in a honeymoon as you celebrate life in your twenties or thirties, or renewing your passion as you celebrate life in your sixties or seventies. Regardless of your station or status in life, you're celebrating a deeply human dance, a transcendent experience created by no less a preeminent mind than that of Almighty God himself.

There is a time to fast. There is a time to "take up our cross daily." There is a time to be "seasoned with fire." But there is also a time to be virtually transported to another world through the intimate sharing and exploration of our spouse's body.

Some of us need to be reminded to celebrate with zeal. Others of us need to be reminded that there is a place for thoughtful sobriety, quiet reverence, and deliberate duty. The marriage relationship makes available to us a full, responsive, and responsible human experience

—assuming responsibility, to be sure, but along with that responsibility relishing the very real and earthy pleasure of sexual activity, an intense celebration that gently reminds us of the heavenly existence that awaits all God's children.

Beyond Touch

It may take some couples many months to be comfortable viewing their sexual intimacy as a form of spiritual expression, faith, and maturity. Unfortunately, while Christians should be leading the way in this regard, adherents of other faiths have preceded us on a popular level. There are numerous books today that seek to integrate Eastern philosophy and Tantric spirituality with sexuality, but in most cases these books use spirituality to heighten physical sensations. We are suggesting precisely the opposite—that the physical sensations can heighten our spiritual sensitivities. The Christian worldview doesn't disparage the physical; it embraces it. But in doing so, it reminds us that there are higher values than physical pleasure—that this world is passing away, and true joy and fulfillment can only be found in a relationship with God and in *holy* fellowship with his children.

To fully embrace marital sexuality and all that God designed it for, couples must bring their Christianity into bed and break down the wall between their physical and spiritual intimacy. Donald Goergan writes, "The dichotomy between sexuality and spirituality and between celibacy and marriage is destructive and inappropriate. Integration lies in seeing how we can be both sexual and spiritual simultaneously and in seeing that choosing one way of life does not imply the inferiority of the other."[23]

Sex is about physical touch, to be sure, but it is about far more than physical touch. It is about what is going on *inside* us. Developing a fulfilling sex life means I concern myself more with bringing generosity and service to bed than with bringing washboard abdomens. It means I see my wife as a holy temple of God, not just as a tantalizing human body. It even means that sex becomes a form of physical prayer—a picture of a heavenly intimacy that rivals the *shekinah* glory of old.

Our God, who is spirit (John 4:24), can be found behind the very physical panting, sweating, and pleasurable entangling of limbs and body parts. He doesn't turn away. He wants us to run into sex, but to do so with his presence, priorities, and virtues marking our pursuit. If we experience sex in this way, we will be transformed in the marriage bed every bit as much as we are transformed on our knees in prayer.

12

Sacred Presence

How Marriage Can Make Us
More Aware of God's Presence

The Christian family is a product of faith.
It offers the matchless opportunity of suffusing
every relationship of daily life with the Spirit of God.
Since the spouses have to live together and are unable
to escape each other, every moment of the day
and every activity in the home form a challenge to live
in common according to the divine purpose.
OTTO PIPER

SINCERITY ISN'T ENOUGH.

I found this out the hard way early on in my marriage. Just weeks after our wedding, Lisa had her twentieth birthday. I was a new husband then, completely uninitiated in the finer arts of marital conversation, so when Lisa said, "Don't worry, my birthday's no big deal," I made a terrible mistake.

I believed her.

What else could I do? My campus pastor had told me, "Go for the godly ones," so I had. Lisa was, indeed, one of the godliest women I had met in college. The only problem was, my college pastor never warned me that godly women can occasionally lie.

Consequently, I didn't put much thought into what I should do for Lisa's birthday. Besides, I was in a new job and feeling slightly ill

225

as well, so I wasn't at all prepared to meet the high expectations of something that "didn't really matter."

The day before Lisa turned twenty, I stepped into a bookstore and bought her three books. Early the next morning, I handed them to her with a smile.

It's a good thing *I* was smiling that day, so at least one of us was. I had to learn that getting Lisa books because *I* like books isn't love — no, that's hope! (I get the two confused sometimes.) Love is choosing something that will affirm Lisa and show her that I know her and appreciate her.

A friend of mine made a similar mistake. Jim once bought Peggy a measuring cup for her birthday. According to Jim, this was the "mother of all measuring cups," a two-cup, super-deluxe model. According to Peggy, it may have been Jim's biggest marital failure ever.

Jim and I both had to learn that when it comes to loving our wives, "sincerity" isn't enough. We need substance.

James, the biblical writer of the book that bears his name, tells us that the same thing is true when it comes to our relationship with God. "Spirituality" has become such a popular word in our culture, but the highest value many people place on "spirituality" these days is sincerity — according to the popular view, it doesn't matter what we believe or even who we believe in, as long as we are sincere about it.

This is, however, *not* biblical truth. James 1:27 puts this to rest with a dozen words that introduce the truth about spirituality: "Religion that God our Father accepts as pure and faultless is this...." If there is a religion that God finds acceptable, then there must be a religion that he finds unacceptable. If there is a way that God wants to be loved, then there must be a way he doesn't want to be loved.

In other words, sincerity alone isn't enough.

This is not the place to give a decisive or exhaustive definition of "Christian spirituality," but one of the most important components of that spirituality concerns its relational aspect. Christian spirituality is not a search for spiritual enlightenment, new experiences, or esoteric wisdom. It is rather rooted in a passionate pursuit of, and response to, a spiritual being—God himself. I like the Whiteheads' definition: "Christian spirituality can be described as our consistent efforts to respond to the delights and demands of God's presence in our life."[1]

The operative word here is *presence*. The great Christian writers of the past stressed the importance of living in constant awareness of God's presence. Those who have advanced in the Christian life have learned to develop almost a mystical memory that keeps them attuned to the fact that God is always with them, always ready to whisper his words of challenge, encouragement, affirmation, and loving rebuke. He is always watching, always caring, always hearing.

One of the ways to describe practicing God's presence as a discipline is *turning*. François Fénelon, one of the great Christian mystics of all time, wrote the following in the seventeenth century:

A general rule for the good use of time is to accustom oneself to live in a continual dependence on the Spirit of God, receiving from moment to moment whatever it pleases him to give us, referring to him at once in the doubts which we necessarily run into, *turning* to him in the weakness into which goodness slips from exhaustion, calling on him and lifting oneself to him, when the heart, swept away by material things, sees itself led imperceptibly off the path and finds itself forgetting and drifting away from God [emphasis added].[2]

Perhaps the classic literary work on this aspect of the Christian life is Brother Lawrence's *Practicing the Presence of God*. Also writing in the seventeenth century, Lawrence, a humble monk, learned to take special delight in God's continual presence, with the result that he felt equally close to God peeling potatoes in the kitchen as kneeling at the altar in prayer.

Brother Lawrence said that we should "establish ourselves in the presence of God by continually talking to him," suggesting that it was a "shameful thing" to allow trivial thoughts to break into this spiritual conversation. He urged us to "feed our souls on lofty thoughts of God, and so find great joy in being with him."

Early on, practicing the presence is largely a discipline; over time, the discipline of practicing God's presence begins to feel more natural. As Brother Lawrence observes, "In the beginning a persistent effort is needed to form the habit of continually talking with God ... but after a little care his love brings us to it without any difficulty."[3]

It was this pursuit of God's presence that sent so many men and women into monasteries and convents. These earnest souls believed that they could best experience the delight of God's presence by engaging in a life free from the encumbrances of earning a living and caring for a family. Although ancient religious orders differed substantially, most often a monk's or nun's life was structured around this remembrance—this constant awareness—of God. The day began and ended with prayer, there were often long periods of enforced silence, and the community itself created an environment that encouraged its citizens to look heavenward.

How can we, as married saints, use the daily rush of activities and the seeming chaos of family life as a reminder of God's presence? To be sure, we have many challenges to overcome, but isn't there a way we can use marriage to *draw* us to God rather than allow it to dull our senses and lead us into a practical atheism, in which we give lip service to God but live as if he simply does not exist? Rather than letting marriage blunt our spiritual sensitivities, can we use it to awaken our souls in new and profound ways?

There is a marvelous picture in the Old Testament that suggests that we can indeed!

Between the Cherubim

The ark of the Testimony was constructed with two cherubim of hammered gold, who faced each other and touched wings. In this joining of the two, we are told, "There, above the cover between the two cherubim that are over the ark of the Testimony, I [God] will meet with you" (Exodus 25:22).

God's presence "between the cherubim" came to be a popular Old Testament image. In Samuel's time, the Israelites wanted to bring back the ark, referring to "the LORD Almighty, who is enthroned between the cherubim" (1 Samuel 4:4). The psalmist writes, "Hear us, O Shepherd of Israel ... you who sit enthroned between the cherubim" (Psalm 80:1). Isaiah uses the same imagery: "O LORD Almighty, God of Israel, enthroned between the cherubim" (Isaiah 37:16). This imagery even makes its way into the New Testament: "Above the ark were the cherubim of the Glory" (Hebrews 9:5).

The presence of God comes to us as two beings are joined. God "dwells" in the midst of this coming together. It's a beautiful picture.

There is a long tradition of seeking God in solitude, but clearly there is also biblical warrant to seek God in relationship and community. Consider Jesus' words in Matthew: "I tell you that if two of you on earth agree about anything you ask for, it will be done for you by my Father in heaven. For where two or three come together in my name, there am I with them" (Matthew 18:19–20).

Notice that Jesus says "where two or three come together *in my name. . . .*" The family that will enjoy Jesus' presence as a customary part of their union is a family that is joined precisely because husband and wife want to invite Jesus into the deeper parts of their marriage. They are not coming together in order to escape loneliness, more favorably pool their financial resources, or merely gain an outlet for sexual desire. Above all these other reasons, they have joined themselves to each other as a way to live out and deepen their faith in God.

Even if you didn't enter marriage for this reason, you can make a decision to *maintain* your marriage on this basis. The day you do this, you will find that marriage can be a favorable funnel to direct God's presence into your daily life. Marriage invokes the presence of God through prodding us to communicate, reminding us of our transcendent ache, helping us to behold the image of God, and allowing us to participate in creation.

Conversation

As a young man, I always thought silence was the preferred pathway to the heart of God. The church I attended put a comment in the weekly bulletin that went something like this: "Please maintain an attitude of reverence as we prepare our hearts for worship." And, indeed, there are deep roots in Christian tradition testifying to the spiritual value of silence. For instance, because it is a Trappist monk's duty to maintain silence, members of this order often communicate with sign language. There are records of ancient monks who didn't talk for three decades or more.

Just as the silence of the Trappist monks is a discipline designed to draw them into the realm of the holy, so the conversation of marriage can bend us toward God. Earlier in this century, there developed in France the idea that talk should be seen as a spiritual exercise. Out of this arose *le devoir de s'asseoir,* which literally translated means, "the duty to sit down."[4]

In marriage, it is our duty to communicate. To be sure, every marriage needs times of silence and meditation. But in our relationship with our spouse, communication is a discipline of love. Our reaching out to each other mirrors God reaching out to us, and as he does so, his presence and character becomes better known to us. The fact that God uses dreams to communicate in the Old and New Testaments reveals that he is reaching out to us at all hours of the day and night. God loves us with words, rather than physical arms with which to embrace us. We can love our spouses with those same words and grow more like Christ in the process.

Allender and Longman observe that "we are called to cultivate Christ in our spouses by the power of the spoken word."[5] How can words do this? This way—at least in part: "Good speech quells chaos and produces joy and life; bad speech produces chaos and leads to despair and death."[6]

In this view, our tongue invites God's presence or pushes him away. Every word spoken to a family member is either an invitation to the experience of the holy or to the experience of chaos.

The letter of James views controlled speech as one of the fundamental Christian disciplines:

> We all stumble in many ways. If anyone is never at fault in what he says, he is a perfect man, able to keep his whole body in check. When we put bits into the mouths of horses to make them obey us, we can turn the whole animal. Or take ships as an example. Although they are so large and are driven by strong winds, they are steered by a very small rudder wherever the pilot wants to go. Likewise the tongue is a small part of the body, but it makes great boasts. Consider what a great forest is set on fire by a small spark. The tongue also is a fire, a world of evil among the parts of the body. It corrupts the whole person, sets the whole course of his life on fire, and is itself set on fire by hell (James 3:2–6).

In James's view, our tongue serves as a spiritual thermometer inasmuch as its words register our spiritual temperature toward God.

The tongue can be cruel in two ways: by speaking evil, or by refraining from speaking good. We need to recognize the offensiveness of pervasive silence within marriage. There comes a time when silence is healing, but there is also a malicious silence. You know your heart. You know whether you are being silent in order to promote healing or whether you are being self-centered, cowardly, or malicious. When I refuse to speak out of cowardice, selfishness, or weariness, I am taking a step back as a Christian.

God calls me to speak, *but to speak carefully*. I had to learn how to communicate with my wife, to find out why I sometimes exasperate her either by not speaking at all or by speaking in the wrong way. In other words, to be lovingly married, I had to learn how to better tame my tongue.

Communication forces us to enter into another's world. To communicate with my wife, I have to get beyond my own frame of reference and understand how the same word can mean two different things to each of us. This is an ego-emptying exercise that harbors enormous spiritual benefit.

Words spoken with malice can cut deeply. Words can destroy, pummel, and build walls. Dan Allender and Tremper Longman remind us of that truth and encourage us to choose our words carefully:

> I am to sow words like seeds to bring a harvest of fruit that blesses God.... We must choose our words as if we were choosing an instrument of life or death. If we know the power of words, then we will neither refuse to speak because of fear nor speak often and sow seeds of destruction. We are to speak words of encouragement to draw forth the heart of God in those we love; we are to speak words of rebuke to disrupt the natural bent of our hearts to pride and self-righteousness.[7]

The other side of communication is learning to listen, and it is this area where I often struggle mightily. I'm often lost in my own thoughts and consequently resent the fact that someone wants me to stop my thinking and share hers. But when I married Lisa, I committed to communicate with her.

My wife is an inveterate reader of *Guideposts* magazine. She loves the stories of tragedy and near tragedy and the often teardrop-producing effects of the regular column, "His Mysterious Ways." As coincidence would have it—I'm not making this up!—just as I was typing these words, she asked me to take a break so she could read a *Guideposts* story to me.

Lisa knows this isn't really the type of thing I would read on my own. I read about thirty to forty books a year and numerous magazines, but usually not the personal-experience type of literature. Even so, listening to these stories has become part of my commitment to enter into my wife's world. Love is an intentional movement toward another.

How does listening invite God's presence? A significant part of prayer involves listening to God. I think back to chapter 3 when I quoted Dr. John Barger. An abbreviated reminder might be in order here:

[When women] love, they love quietly; they speak, as it were, in whispers, and we have to listen carefully, attentively, to hear their words of love and to know them.

Isn't God also this way?

Doesn't he intervene in most of our lives in whispers, which we miss if we fail to recollect ourselves and pay careful attention — if we do not constantly strive to hear those whispers of divine love? The virtues necessary in truly loving a woman and having that love returned — the virtues of listening, patience, humility, service, and faithful love — are the very virtues necessary for us to love God and to feel his love returned.

Communication calls us out of ourselves. Learning how to do this is as much a prerequisite for building a meaningful prayer life as it is for building a meaningful marriage. The act of communication invites God's presence into our daily existence. The truth of the matter is this: By our words, we either draw forth God's presence or we push him away.

Transcendent Ache

At some point in your relationship with the one who was to become your spouse, you were willing to leave all other possible suitors and cleave to this one person for the rest of your life. As a single man or woman, the options for a lifetime partner were virtually unlimited — as long as someone would have you, you could marry them. And yet, out of all the billions of people in the world, you chose this one person — your spouse.

As a spiritual exercise, remind yourself again that, regardless of the result of your choice, you *willingly chose* this man or woman. After considerable consideration, you asked this person to marry you — or you said yes when he asked you. At the time, your decision made perfect sense—you were literally willing to bet your life on it—and you had every reason to believe that being married to this person was a relationship you would cherish for years to come, till death intervened to separate you.

The marriage relationship creates the opportunity for us to be reminded of our need for God when we become disillusioned by the inability to receive all the love we need and desire from fellow humans. This inescapable disillusionment can lead to the anguish of serial (multiple) marriages. Instead of realizing that our true needs can be ultimately met only in and by God, some people keep trying to find their fulfillment in new relationships, thinking that what they really need is just to find the "right person," which, when translated, usually means a *new* person. Christianity does not direct us to focus on *finding* the right person; it calls us to *become* the right person.

Use your dissatisfaction—or even your boredom with life and with your relationships—as a compass that directs you to the True North of your heart's passion: God himself. Remind yourself that in serial marriage the same process will inevitably repeat itself—great excitement, the thrill of discovery, and then, on some level, severe and increasing disillusionment.

All this brings me back to that computer analogy I used in the first chapter. It would do me no good to trade in my 486 for another 486. The screen might look new for a couple weeks; it might be a little shinier, but eventually I'd find I was working with the very same limitations.

All of us humans are just 486s—and our hearts long for a Pentium III. Another person won't, in fact, can't complete us. They might look new for a couple years; they might be a little shinier with a few less wrinkles, but eventually, we'd discover they had many of the same limitations as the person we "traded in." Augustine's famous line has become such a cliché that I hesitate to mention it, but it is still so true: "Our hearts are restless until they find their rest in thee."

One caution here: While our hearts will find their rest only when

God is part of the equation, it is a stunning scriptural fact that soon after creating Adam God declared, "It is not good for the man to be alone" (Genesis 2:18) — even though God delighted in his relationship with the man. Clearly God created us with a need to enjoy other relationships besides himself exclusively,[8] but God must be at the center of our hearts, to which all our other relationships are then added.

Let your relationship with your spouse point you to what you really need most of all: God's love and active presence in your life. Above all, don't blame your spouse for lack of fulfillment; blame yourself for not pursuing a fulfilling relationship with God. Monks and nuns who have found delight in their solitary pursuit of God bear witness to the fact that lack of marital intimacy is not a guarantee of misery or a prohibitor of spiritual enjoyment. When you discover this truth, it's amazing how satisfied you can be, regardless of who you're living with.

Marital dissatisfaction, on whatever level, is best met with the prayer, "That's why I need *you*, O God." We are reminded of the transcendent ache in our soul that even this one very special person can't relieve entirely on his or her own. As odd as this may sound, I have discovered in my own life that my satisfaction or dissatisfaction with my marriage has far more to do with my relationship to God than it does with my relationship to Lisa. When my heart grows cold toward God, my other relationships suffer, so if I sense a burgeoning alienation from, or lack of affection toward, my wife, the first place I look is how I'm doing with the Lord. Lisa is, quite literally, my God-thermometer.

Beholding the Image of God

Every night, I sleep with a God-mirror lying beside me.

The Bible teaches us that both men and women are made in the image of God (see Genesis 1:26 – 27). Understanding this truth should remind us regularly of God's presence, for it allows us to realize that our mate is helping us to complete a fuller picture of God's nature and person.

Dan Allender and Tremper Longman point out how important it is for men and women to model elements of God's existence to each other: "Since a husband's strength helps him resonate God's strong qualities, he can help his wife understand that aspect of God's being more clearly by incarnating it, even though he does that imperfectly. On the other hand, a woman's tenderness and compassion can increase her husband's awareness of God's mercy (1 Peter 3:1–2)."[9]

I practically begged a close college friend not to get married. He and his girlfriend fought all the time when they were dating, in part because they were on opposite ends of the personality spectrum. Steve could be harsh, blunt, and amazingly tactless. His girlfriend Laura was one of the most sensitive women I've ever known. On one occasion, Steve "confronted" Laura with seven ways she was failing as a girlfriend. When I expressed my incredulity that he could dump so much on her at one time, Steve responded, "But Gary, I could have said so much more!"

And yet, as both Steve and Laura grew in their relationship with Jesus Christ, they both changed in many positive ways. Steve might have grown up without tact, but to his credit he began practicing the Christian virtue of humility, willingly learning from Laura's sensitivity. Laura respected Steve's courage to tell the truth, regardless of the consequences, and realized that always being "soft" wasn't appropriate in every circumstance. After thirteen years of wedlock, they have a marvelous relationship, in fact, one of the strongest marriage relationships I've seen. Each one has helped the other draw closer to God in character, as each represented respectively (almost to an extreme) God's strength and God's tenderness.

Not only can being married remind us of God's nature and character, but it also reminds us of his moral claims on our lives. One of the great problems of Christian spirituality is the seemingly simple problem of forgetfulness. God appeals to us to adopt and act on certain priorities, but we "forget" about these priorities and go our own way. God is always with us, yet we "forget" his immediate presence and treat our wives or kids in a way we would never treat them if our pastor or other church members were seated around our kitchen table.

Godly husbands and godly wives make God seem more real and active in the home. I've always loved movies, but movies are not always a "safe" recreation. So in this activity Lisa acts as sort of a conscience for me. For some reason that I'm not proud of, I suspect that my standards would be a bit lower if I knew that Lisa wouldn't be in the room watching the movie with me. Even after fifteen years of marriage, watching a movie with Lisa feels a little like watching it with God. I can imagine her thinking, "You rented *this?*"

Dietrich Bonhoeffer shocked the theological world when, as a Lutheran theologian in the early part of the twentieth century, he began advocating that Protestants reinstitute the practice of confession. He did so not because he felt confession to a human was necessary in order to gain forgiveness from God, but because human confession has a practical purpose — it makes our sin seem more real to us.

If you question the truth of this, ask yourself, why is it so much easier to confess sins to God than to your pastor? Why is there more shame when another sinful human being observes my weakness than when I pronounce them before an all-holy God?

Could it be because God's presence is so weak in our lives? If we truly understood and cherished the beauty and holiness of God, we would shake a little bit more when approaching him. But his invisibility often creates a buffer, thereby softening the impact of his presence.

In and through our spouse, God becomes real to us in human form. There is a flesh-and-blood person sitting next to me who flinches when she sees what should make *me* flinch, but doesn't — and I see my hard heart exposed by her soft one.

It goes both ways, of course. Sometimes I'll try to help Lisa understand how she sounds when she's tired and letting the kids have it verbally. When she sees the reaction on my face, she knows she's allowed the sins of others to incite her own sin.

We can help each other become aware of God's presence by gently encouraging each other toward growth in holiness. Yet we need to be sure to undertake this with extreme caution — *we want to bring God's presence into the other's life, not our own judgment.* But pointing each other to God's presence is certainly a fundamental spiritual discipline for spouses.

A spiritually discerning marriage will be a tool of sanctification. As we look at our spouse, we are reminded of God's presence and image. And in the presence of God, we long to become more holy. "Make every effort to live in peace with all men and to be holy," the author of the book of Hebrews writes. "Without holiness no one will see the Lord" (Hebrews 12:14).

It is no easy discipline, this cooperating in sanctification. My tendency is to *hide* my faults rather than work on trying to transform them. Every day I am choosing to either spend my energy covering up my mistakes and trying to create a false, glittering image, or I am repenting and cooperating with God to become a more holy person. Living with a woman made in the image of God calls me to honesty and to growth in sanctification — *provided I allow my marriage to remind me of God's presence and his claims on my life.*

Creating

I stood on the top of Marye's Heights in Fredricksburg, Virginia, site of a horrible Civil War battle in 1862, and kept whispering, "What a waste." On this spot, Union troops had foolishly tried to take an impenetrable wall, charging uphill in an effort to capture the city. It was nothing more than target practice for the Confederates. The first wave of the Union assault group was massacred. Ambrose Everett Burnside, the Union general, ordered another wave. The Confederates cheered their bravery, waited until the soldiers were in range, and then shot every last one of them.

Burnside sent yet another wave, with the same result. Every man lost was a son, husband, uncle, father, or brother. Every lost life was no doubt felt keenly by at least one other person. And these lives were virtually thrown away on a fool's errand.

Few things anger me more than wasted life. When I hear about high school kids who drive foolishly and end up dead before their nineteenth birthday; when I read about college students who go on a fatal drinking binge and die of alcohol poisoning before they reach their twenty-first birthday; when I read anything about a preventable loss of life, I feel an uncommon and profound sadness.

Part of this springs from my theological belief that as people created in the image of God, we have a responsibility to create. Whether we build a business, a house, a family, a book, a life (through education or medicine), or whatever else we choose to build, we shouldn't waste our lives but spend them productively.

Marriage leads us into the domain of creation. It goes without saying that there is no holy way to have children and help create a new life if you are not married. The sheer mystery, awe, and absolute wonder of birth is something that simply transcends this world. When that first bloody and naked baby was placed in my wife's arms, I felt emotions I had never known before. Overnight I quit being a passivist. I didn't rethink my intellectual positions on Christians being involved in military combat. I just knew, at the core of my being, that I would do whatever it took to protect this child and the wife who bore her.

Creating a family is the closest we get to sharing the image of God. Seeing this child, made partially in your image, is almost too frighteningly comparable to us being made in God's image. I'm an inveterate "teaser" with little kids. I love to play around and trick them. Now, my nine-year-old son does the same thing when he's with younger kids. And it amazes me how, when I sense a renewal of my faith, I can wake up and see that my son has also discovered a new thirst for God. It's sobering to realize that by my actions, I'm shaping three little lives.

But this kind of creation takes effort. I once visited a pastor's house, and his kids were almost unbelievably well-behaved. After his teenage daughter displayed her usual good grace, I turned to another friend and asked, "They *do* bleed if you prick them, right?" and the friend laughed.

But the next morning, as I was having breakfast with this pastor, he confessed that he had spent over an hour and a half talking through a tough issue with his daughter after I had left their house the night before. And he was participating in similar lengthy talks with his son *on a daily basis.* Something was always coming up that called for his attention.

I was shocked at the effort, time, and purposeful attention that this godly man was pouring into his family. He was engaged in a way that I wasn't. He was sacrificing enormous amounts of his own life to pour his efforts into helping create other lives. And I realized that building a family together isn't a side avocation. It takes enormous energy, concentration, and self-denial.

When this sense of creation is lost, marriage loses some of its spiritual transcendence. Dan Allender and Tremper Longman tell the story of a man named Jack to spotlight the consequences that the loss of this creative force has on purposeful living:

> [Jack] refused to imagine what he could be if God were to rule his heart more deeply. Jack's refusal to see his own soul as the prime ground for creation left him dreamless as he thought about his wife and children. He had no more vision of who they were and who they were meant to be than he had for himself. In harsh terms, Jack loved them, but he never dreamed about their existence. He was a creator in his job but not in his family. Therefore the family was left in middle-class chaos — moving aimlessly, circling in the tiresome, dark loneliness of the status quo.[10]

If we don't nurture a godly sense of creativity, we will experience an emptiness that we may perversely and wrongly blame on our marriage. The emptiness comes not from our marriage, however, but from the fact that we're not *engaged* in our marriage. We're not using this powerful relationship in order to create something.

In many of my seminars I tell my listeners that we were made to worship. If we don't grow in our worship of God, we will descend to worship something or someone else—power, money, our reputation, a sports team—it could be anything. In the same way, if we are not creating in our marriage—if we are not filling our souls with the meaning that comes from doing what we were made to do—we will become dissatisfied very quickly. Getting a promotion won't fill our souls—at least not for long. Keeping up with the latest sitcom or soap opera certainly won't create soul satisfaction either.

Have you ever noticed how our culture lives off other people's acts of creation? Consider how many "awards" shows fill the television schedule—the Grammys, the People's Awards, the TV Guide Awards, the Blockbuster Awards, MTV Awards, the Golden Globes, the Dove Awards, the Emmys—and the list goes on and on—as our culture lives vicariously through the achievements and recognition of others.

You were made by God to create. If you don't create in a thoughtful and worshipful manner—whether preparing meals, decorating a home, achieving a vocational dream, responsibly raising children —you will feel less than human because you are in fact acting in a subhuman mode. A life spent in a dead-end, joyless job with evenings spent in front of a television set and weekends spent "passing the time" will feel like hell on earth *because it is*. It's a wasted life, devoid of God's creative energy. There hasn't been a single marriage in all of human history that could fill a soul that has been emptied of purpose through noncreative living.

Marriage calls us to create—each and every day. It leads us into many and varied acts of creation. My wife throws some unbelievable parties for our kids. She recently set a table for my youngest daughter's valentine party that should have been featured in a magazine. We should embrace these opportunities and throw ourselves into them unreservedly. When we do, we may be surprised at the quiet fulfillment that the act of creating brings our way.

The creation, of course, must have a proper focus—namely, the glory of God. "Creating" children who are just as shallow as we are is not the same thing as creating children who are mature in the Lord and who live to serve him. Building a business to honor God is not the same thing as creating a monument to our success. Selfish hospitality—when it is done primarily to impress and elicit appreciation—is easily detectable and is far removed from genuine service.

But a man and woman dedicated to seeing each other grow in their maturity in Christ; who raise children who know and honor the Lord; who engage in business that supports God's work on earth and is carried out in the context of relationships and good stewardship of both time and money—these Christians are participating in the creativity that gives a spiritually healthy soul immeasurable joy, purpose, and fulfillment.

God has given us the privilege and opportunity to place ourselves and our families on a "glorious pursuit"[11]: becoming partakers of the divine nature (see 2 Peter 1:4), reflecting the very image of Jesus Christ. When we aggressively (and gracefully) lead our families in this pathway of progressive sanctification, we begin to reflect God's glory.

It's clear that marriage creates a context that ushers us directly into acts of creation. This is a spiritual duty and discipline of the highest order.

Purposeful Marriage

These realities should make it abundantly clear that marriage, on its own, should not and does not make it difficult to pursue God and enjoy his presence. What makes spirituality in marriage difficult is a laissez-faire attitude within marriage. When we don't seek to communicate; when we ignore the divine ache in our soul and try to soothe that ache with human companionship alone; when we fail to behold the image of God in our spouse and instead embark on a deceitful life; when we become disengaged as married people and do not revel in marriage's call for us to create — *this* is what can lead us ultimately to separation from God.

In many ways, marriage is a slippery slope. If we are not vigilant, we will fall backwards. If we are lackadaisical, our spiritual sensitivity will become frozen. But if we enter marriage thoughtfully, purposefully, and with godly intentions, our wedlock will shape us in a way that few other life experiences can. It will usher us into God's own presence.

Sacred Mission

Marriage Can Develop Our Spiritual Calling, Mission, and Purpose

Christianity has long called us to this truth:
Marriage must be about more than itself because
love that does not serve life will die.
EVELYN AND JAMES WHITEHEAD

ESTA LISA?" I ASKED.

There followed a gibbering of Spanish, none of which I could pick up.

"Esta Lisa?" I repeated, hoping the Mexican woman would catch the hint and put my girlfriend on the phone.

Finally Lisa was on the other end, but our connection was anything but a happy one. In all honesty, there was a long, mutual, and half-frustrated sigh — from both of us. It was the summer before we became engaged and Lisa was on a missions trip in Mexico City. Her letters had grown a little more distant over the summer — less and less about how she was doing personally and how she was feeling, with more and more information about *what* she was doing and that strong male assistant she was spending so much time with.

The virtual absence in her letters of any talk about us — or about missing me — had raised a red flag. Then, so casually that it hurt twice as much, Lisa dropped a line in one of her letters mentioning that she was thinking about extending her stay for an entire year. As I recall, the male assistant was pondering the same possibility.

245

I hadn't called Lisa before. This was back in the days when long-distance phone companies enjoyed a monopoly and international calling was frightfully expensive, especially for a near-penniless college student. E-mail was still the stuff of science-fiction novels as far as the general public was concerned.

I don't remember how the phone call started, but in the middle there was a long silence—more than a minute at least. I finally broke it with the not-too-gentle (and not-too-bright) comment, "Do you have any idea how much that silence just cost me?!"

Our struggle to be together *and* serve the Lord had begun before we were even engaged. I wanted Lisa to serve the Lord, all right—as long as she did it with me. At the time I wasn't open to any other possibility.

I could have learned a few things from one of my heroes at the time, the German pastor Dietrich Bonhoeffer, who was himself engaged to be married when he entered his Tegel prison cell after having been arrested for his part in a plot to overthrow Adolf Hitler. Flush with the passion of a new love and the confirmation of returned love, Bonhoeffer was no doubt tempted to reconsider the harsh effects of his personal mission to stop Hitler at virtually any cost. If he held back, he could expect a rather easy and enjoyable life—being married to Maria and living out his days as a seminary professor. Yet Dietrich willingly risked a life of relative ease for the uncertainty of revolutionary involvement.

Tucked away in his prison cell, Bonhoeffer asked some hard and fundamental questions. In one poem written during confinement, Bonhoeffer posed the question, "Who am I?" He observed how he was often complimented for being friendly and cheerful and agreeable. Yet inside himself, he was experiencing a different sense of who he might be. In the midst of anguish of spirit he proceeded to ask himself some heartrending questions:

> Who am I? This or the other?
> Am I one person today, and tomorrow another?

Am I both at once? A hypocrite before others,
and before myself a contemptibly woebegone weakling?...
Who am I? They mock me, these lonely questions of mine.
Whoever I am, thou knowest, O God, I am thine.[1]

It's this last line I would like to focus on: "Whoever I am, thou knowest, O God, I am thine."

The intimacy of the marriage relationship is something most of us desire, but how do we enter this union without sacrificing our sense of personal mission before God? How do we promise to be unreservedly faithful and continue to "fall forward" toward our spouse when we have already pledged to be unreservedly available for God's service?

It's not easy to balance the competing demands of an intense human relationship and an overarching, all-embracing spiritual devotion. One of the great (and often unexplored) challenges of marriage is maintaining a sense of individual mission while living in a cooperative relationship.

Not much has been written about this for the simple reason that most ancient Christian writings assume that "really" serious Christians will remain single. I've found one classical Christian writer, however, who addresses this challenge head-on — a man by the name of Francis de Sales (1567–1622). De Sales was learned in both law and theology and carried on an active spiritual-direction-by-letter ministry, making him somewhat of a seventeenth-century Ann Landers. His advice is so insightful, practical, and helpful that I want to devote an entire section in this chapter to his responses to letters sent from earnest Christians living "in the world."

Letters to Persons in the World

A married woman once wrote Francis to express her concern that her marital and spiritual devotion were at conflict. De Sales dismissed this concern out of hand, encouraging her, "Let us be what we are, and let us be it well." In other words, if we are married, we are married, and we must not try to live as if we were otherwise. Francis noted that by living with this attitude, we "do honor to the Master whose work we are."[2]

To accept this counsel entails that we do not make the mistake John Wesley made — get married, but then refuse to adjust his life accordingly. Wesley said he was adamant that he wouldn't let being married slow him down by even one sermon. This kind of vision is unrealistic, and even unfair to our spouse, to be sure. Being married brings obligations — some particularly intense ones for those who are by nature ambitious. There are times I must sacrifice my ambition to succeed in God's service so that I can be fully present and involved in the lives of my wife and children. Most assuredly the tension should lead us to ask the question, "If I ignore God's daughter [God's son] to do God's work, am I honoring God?"

Christian men in particular might be tempted above all others to let ambition erode their marital devotion, even to the point of using religious language to justify shortchanging their spouse, but de Sales warned that even spiritual devotion can be taken "out of bounds." When we get married, we make a certain promise to our spouse that we will devote a considerable amount of energy, initiative, and time into building and nurturing the relationship. It is spiritual fraud to enter marriage and then to live like a single man or woman.

To another woman with a similar concern — longing to become a nun but feeling yoked within her marriage, Francis counseled, "God does not regard his servants according to the dignity of the office they exercise," but according to the *faithfulness* with which they exercise it. Whether a woman is overseeing a hospital or running a homeschool makes little difference in God's eyes, as long as that woman is being faithful to her particular calling in life.

To yet another woman, who wrote that she had great difficulty harmonizing marriage and devotion, Francis wrote, "The means of gaining perfection are various according to the variety of vocations: religious, widows, and married persons must all seek after this perfection, but not all by the same means." He encouraged the woman by suggesting several spiritual exercises, but then he warned, "In all this take particular care that your husband, your servants, and your parents do not suffer by your too long stayings in church, your too great retirement [for prayer], or by your failing to care for your household.... You must not only be devout, and love devotion, but you must make it lovable to everyone."[3]

God is not served well if we turn off everyone around us in our selfish pursuit of devotion. "We must sometimes leave our Lord," Francis affirmed, "in order to please others for the love of him."

I've met women who, because they are married to unbelieving husbands, feel frustrated that they are not able to participate as fully in the life of the church as they might wish. This is a frustration that Francis would urge wives to live with; he would argue that it is not the better part of godliness to let one's spiritual duties eclipse one's marital responsibilities.

One of the great challenges of marriage for me is the seemingly endless tasks that accompany married life. How can I experience peace and serenity, focus on the presence of God, and devote myself to worship when the lawn needs to be mowed, the garbage needs to be taken out, the kids want time alone with me, laundry needs to be done, meals need to be cooked, cars need to be fixed....

To a woman who had this same concern, Francis was gentle rather than condemning. "I remember you telling me how much the multiplicity of your affairs weighs on you," he wrote—and then, rather than chide her, he encouraged her, "[This] is a good opportunity for acquiring the true and solid virtues."

According to Francis, the multiplicity of these concerns actually feeds rather than empties our spiritual growth *when* we approach them with an attitude of continually dying to ourselves and rising to inner growth: "The multiplicity of affairs is a continual martyrdom, for just as flies cause more pain and irritation to those who travel in summer than the traveling itself does, just so the diversity and the multitude of affairs cause more pain than the weight of these affairs itself."

De Sales wrote with the wonderful assumption, so lost to our culture, that the more difficult something is, the more spiritually beneficial we will find it to be, as it builds our character. It is only natural when facing all these responsibilities that our souls cry out for relief. But Francis urges us to draw maximum benefit from them by crying out for patience and virtue and growth in Christlikeness.

Here's the kicker: Patience can be formed only in the crucible of frustration—making marriage, with its multitude of tasks, one of the best schools of patience there is. De Sales entreats us to "resolve to restore yourself to patience throughout the day as many times as you sense yourself becoming distracted."

He encouraged this same woman to further practice "mortification" by not losing "any occasion, however small it may be, for exercising gentleness of heart toward everyone." The practice of this virtue of *gentleness* is particularly challenging (Francis admitted that his correspondent will be able to succeed only by the assistance of God), because it is one thing to do the right thing and it is another thing entirely to do the right thing *with the right spirit*—and our motives and character are surely being tested in marriage. Francis explained further: "I say 'gentle diligence,' because violent diligence spoils the heart and affairs, and is not diligence, but haste and trouble."

Francis accepted the presupposition that *becoming* a more mature person is just as honoring to God as is *doing the right things*. There is no question that marriage limits how much we can do, but it multiplies what we can become. If a man or woman focuses on spiritual growth rather than achievement and accomplishment, they'll see the marriage relationship as providing a wonderful environment for Christian mission.

Knowing that the juggling of many concerns can become burdensome, Francis encouraged the mother to persevere by remembering eternity:

> We will soon be in eternity, and then we will see how all the affairs of this world are such little things and how little it matters

whether they turn out or not.... When we were little children, with what eagerness did we put together little bits of tile, wood, and mud, to make houses and small buildings! And if someone destroyed them, we were very grieved and tearful at it; but now we know well that it all mattered very little. One day it will be the same with us in heaven, when we will see that our concerns in this world were truly only child's play.

This is *not* to suggest, Francis hastened to add, that these "affairs of this world" have no value at all: "I do not want to take away the care that we must have regarding these little trifles, because God has entrusted them to us in this world for exercise; but I would indeed like to take away the passion and anxiety of this care."[4]

On yet another occasion, de Sales addressed a pregnant woman who was very discouraged. She was disappointed with the heaviness in her spirit, but Francis comforted her: "A delicate body that is weighed down by the burden of pregnancy, weakened by the labor of carrying a child, and troubled with many pains does not allow the heart to be so lively, so active, so ready in its operations; but this in no way injures the acts of that higher part of the soul."[5]

He tenderly exhorted her, "My dearest daughter, we must not be unjust and require from ourselves what is not in ourselves.... Have patience with yourself."

Marital concerns necessarily give rise to more emotional swings than celibate living. I remember one Sunday morning in particular. I had spoken at a banquet the previous night, and now I was scheduled to preach at all four services at a local church. Two of my children decided to initiate World War III in my kitchen. Lisa was getting ready for church and I had to take care of disciplining the kids. I was so frazzled that I lost my temper.

"This is just *great!*" I wanted to scream. "How am I supposed to preach when I live in chaos?!"

I limped emotionally to church that morning and asked several people to pray for me, explaining what had happened. It wasn't until after the first service that I really got "warmed up." While I wished things had turned out differently that morning, looking back on it now, the entire experience was in all likelihood beneficial in the long run (as far as my character growth), though it certainly wasn't the best preparation for a "performance."

De Sales continually challenges me with his amazing ability to see every difficulty in life as an opportunity for spiritual advancement. When a woman whose husband was struggling with illness wrote to him, Francis replied to her feelings of distress: "Truly, if charity allowed, I could willingly love the maladies of your dear husband because I think them useful to you for the mortification of your affection and feelings.... How often the world calls good what is evil, and still oftener evil what is good!"

From all these letters and more, we can discern that de Sales did not view marriage as a compromise to our mission before God, precisely because if we are led into marriage, then marriage *becomes* an essential element of our mission—not our *only* mission, to be sure, but at least the front lines from which our mission is launched.

We can draw this conclusion because mission includes not just what we *do,* but what we *become.* Christianity is one of those rare religions that marries internal reality with outward obedience. We cannot simply focus on external adherence—doing that was the spiritually fatal mistake of the Pharisees. On the other hand, internal piety that shows no concern for service in and for the world is just as grievous an error. Our marriages *will,* as a matter of fact, be strengthened by an outward focus.

Outward Bound

A friend of mine named Mike is an unusually gifted man. He is one of the best oral communicators I have ever heard—one of those rare individuals who can leave you laughing until your sides ache, then slip in a spiritually penetrating challenge as well—and his written material is equally well done.

He built a college ministry from sixty participants to over six hundred in just a few years. He then surprised many people by leaving the ministry and launching a very successful management and consulting business. "On the side" he publishes a newsletter for college pastors, organizes a national campus pastors' conference, and writes articles and books and draws cartoons.

You get the picture—this is a very capable man!

Yet I remember one day, years ago, when he came into the church office (I was his associate at the time) raving about his wife. "You should have seen her last night," he gushed. "I was so proud of her!"

Sherri had approached her church board with an idea for a ministry to new mothers. Sherri recognized that if someone isn't won to the Lord in college, they may be most open to considering God's claims on their lives when they give birth to their first child. With that in mind, she drew up plans in which the church would send a small gift and letter to every woman in our community who gave birth, inviting her to worship and find fellowship at their church if the recipient didn't already have a church home. Because every birth is published in the paper, this plan would be surprisingly easy to carry out.

By focusing on extending God's kingdom, Sherri won her husband's heart. It's ironic, but true—by serving something *outside* her marriage, Sherri strengthened her own.

A spiritually alive marriage will remain a marriage of two individuals in pursuit of a common vision outside themselves. This has been true throughout history. I was particularly moved when reading the letters of another German hero, Count Helmuth James von Moltke —who, like Dietrich Bonhoeffer, was a conspirator against the Nazis.

Von Moltke's passion for his wife was obvious in his letters. Consider this:

> You are not one of God's agents to make me what I am, rather you are myself. You are my thirteenth chapter of the First Epistle to the Corinthians.... It is only in our union—you and I— that we form a complete human being. We are ... one creative thought.

While von Moltke loved his wife deeply, his life was equally charged by his participation in God's work on earth. Just hours before he was executed, von Moltke wrote another passionate letter to his wife. Before you read this, ask yourself, "What would I write to my spouse if I knew it would be my last letter?"

> My dear, my life draws to its close, and I can truthfully say of myself, "He died in fullness of years and of life's experience." That does not imply that I would not gladly go on living, that I would not gladly walk further at your side on this earth. *But for that I should need a new commission from God,* since the one for which he created me stands completed[6] [emphasis added].

Even with so passionate and rich and rewarding a marriage relationship, von Moltke says that to go on living, he would need a new commission from God. What a remarkable statement—by a man who was only hours from being hanged! What helped to make his marriage so rich was that von Moltke looked outside his marriage to find meaning—which, ironically enough, infused his marriage with even more meaning.

Earlier in this book I spoke about how essential it is that in marriage we view ourselves as "we" instead of "I." This "we," however, is not achieved through the absorption of one mate into the other —either the wife into the husband or the husband into the wife. The apostle Paul is clear that each of us is given our own gifts and our own role to play in the kingdom of God (see Romans 12:4–8; 1 Corinthians 12:1–11). Each of us must be passionately devoted to our own faithful service.

A mature marriage looks beyond itself, forfeiting not just the tyranny of individual desires, but also the tyranny of the couple's comfort. It has been described by one couple as the transition from "we are" to "we care. "Such a transition settles gradually. A couple's sex and recreational life is radically transformed when children are born; even such a simple act as getting ready for church can become an exhausting experience as the baby must have its diaper changed and the diaper bag packed. The selfishness of early infatuation and the virtual intoxication of young love are stretched to welcome this new tiny and demanding person.

In this early stage of rearing children, couples gradually begin to learn the value of serving. What they are able to do outside the home is limited. Ideally, as the children become independent and move out, the couple will continue to nurture the vitality of service. Freed from the demands of parenting young children, a man and woman are released to focus on a broader world.

I've seen my own parents go through this process. At seventy years old, my dad is just completing his tenth year of "retirement," but his vocational freedom has in reality become merely a redirection of service. My parents end up as servants even on vacation.

We once visited them at a remote campground, and they recounted how, the night before, they had spent two-and-a-half hours comforting a man who had recently lost his wife. They had never met this man before, but he sensed in them a listening ear, and they obliged, giving up participating in a "campground musical fest" to ease a grieving man's loneliness.

Soon thereafter, a young man—just released from a psychiatric ward—moved into the campground with his family. He homed in on my parents almost immediately, even to the point of calling them "grandpa" and "grandma" before his stay ended.

Retirement can be a lonely time, but my parents have plunged headlong into making that phase of life represent some of the most rewarding and even busy years of their lives. While it is appropriate to slow down and enjoy an occasional vacation or cruise, in the main their meaning and fulfillment has come from ongoing service. My dad has often remarked, "I don't know when I found the time to work!"

Without this involvement in and commitment to service, marriage gets very lonely very fast. A selfish marriage is a hollow marriage. We were made to serve God, and no human affection can appease that hunger for very long.

Two Visions, One Life

Ambition can be fatal.

Lou Kasischke joined a commercial expedition to climb Mount Everest in the spring of 1996. He was witness to one of the worst climbing disasters in history, a calamity that made worldwide news when several people perished on the world's highest peak. As that fateful day wore on, many climbers refused to turn back even though it was getting ridiculously late to be up so high. Lou decided to turn back, and that decision in all likelihood saved his life.

Although Kasischke was serious about reaching the top, he wasn't willing to put his life at grave risk in order to get there. He explains why:

> I didn't think I could get there and back alive or, best case, I'd lose some fingers and toes. And the other thing, too, is ... I wasn't really subject to a lot of the same pressures.... In my perspective of things, it wasn't life-and-death to me, it wasn't the most important thing in the world, and I wasn't going to have newspapers writing stories about me. And media, fame and fortune, world records, and all that kind of stuff, which were kind of the stakes for ... some of the others in our expedition.... It meant a lot to me, I don't want to suggest that it didn't. But ... my ambition to get there just wasn't suffocating every other thought that I had in my mind.[7]

That last line ("my ambition ... wasn't suffocating every other thought that I had in my mind") is particularly telling. I've seen men and women blinded by their own ambition, even religious ambition, and that kind of blind ambition *does* have the tendency to suffocate everything and everyone around them. They don't see the price they're making their loved ones pay for their blind, obsessive pursuit. If their spouse doesn't fall in line, a sort of spiritual murder often can result. Something will die—affection, the relationship, virtue. Some kind of casualty is certain.

Mixing ambition and relationships is like mixing fire and dynamite—an explosion is inevitable. If we are going to learn how to live out our mission in the marriage relationship, we must learn to be more selfless, and we have to become more connected with each other. We have to remember that our spouse is called, just as we are, and we have to be interested enough in *their* call to know what it is that moves them and gives them energy.

When Lisa and I got married, we were pursuing two seemingly disharmonious missions. More than anything, I wanted to be a writer, and most professional writers will tell aspiring writers what I typically say to such folks: "You really want to be a writer? Marry a spouse who can support you for ten years!"

Lisa has *never* wanted to work outside the home. She is dedicated to homeschooling and to creating a home environment that is conducive to the children's intellectual, cultural, and spiritual development.

On the face of it, you can easily see the potential for tension in the relationship, can't you? As a writer, I haven't earned a tenth of the money Lisa would need to make her dreams a reality. As a stay-at-home spouse, Lisa hasn't earned any money to help me build a self-supporting writing career.

I would be lying if I implied that this situation hasn't caused a few heated discussions in our household. Looking back, these "irreconcilable differences" can be seen as complementary, provided that neither of us insisted that the other "lose" the debate. By respecting what God has called each of us to do, we've been able to make progress —albeit more slowly than either of us would prefer. Yet, as we again look back, the seeming lack of speedy progress has helped to build patience and more selflessness in each of us—two extraordinarily valuable spiritual qualities.

The point is that *we* think we know best—*God, why can't you allow things to work out the way I want?*—but it just may be that our assumptions are wildly off-kilter. What we want may have the potential to destroy us. If our eyes are so set on the summit of Everest that we forget about having to come back down while there is still time, we may very well impale ourselves on our own desires.

Over two thousand years ago, a young governor of Spain walked up to a statue of Alexander the Great and openly wept at its base. This governor had just turned thirty, and he was filled with shame when he compared his accomplishments with what the great conqueror had achieved at the same age. Many of us might think that becoming a governor of Spain by the age of thirty is nothing to be ashamed about, but this young man was crushed.

Less than three decades later, the governor — Julius Caesar by name — had become one of the most powerful rulers and military commanders in history. In fact, he became so powerful that his closest friends and advisers conspired to kill him. They thought it was extremely dangerous for any one man — however noble — to have so much power.

The assassination attempt took place indoors. So that no one person could be accused of committing the murder (it's no easy business knocking off a ruler!), each conspirator had agreed to inflict at least one stab wound. The assailants tightened their circle around Julius, their knives positioned to stab him, but Caesar fought back fiercely, inflicting no little damage of his own. He was a strong man, and some of the conspirators paid dearly for their treachery.

Caesar kept fighting until the moment he turned and saw his good friend Brutus. The pain of recognition brought the fracas to a halt; there was an eerie moment of silence. It is within this context that Caesar uttered the now-famous words, "Et tu, Brute?" ("You too, Brutus?") Seeing Brutus before him, the urge to fight left Julius Caesar. It is one thing to be betrayed by colleagues. It is another thing altogether to be preyed on by your closest friend. Caesar ceased his struggle, covered himself with his cloak, and laid down, letting his conspirators stab him at will.

When Julius Caesar aspired to such fame, he never envisioned that it would turn his closest friends against him. I can imagine few things more agonizing than being attacked and betrayed by your dearest and most trusted friends.

Ambition is a violent undertaking, to be sure; what we sacrifice everything to achieve can turn around and bury us even as it reaches its fulfillment. It just may be that God gives us the marriage relationship to moderate and redirect our dreams. Forced to compromise, we learn to reevaluate what's truly important. We are asked to reconsider our priorities and slow down long enough to look at someone else's opinions or needs.

Few things have been sadder to me than reading Donald Trump's three autobiographies. Don't ask me why I've read all of them — I'm not sure myself! — but by the end of the third, you see a clear picture of a man who blindly pursued his financial dreams and lost the intimacy that could make such dreams meaningful. One of his problems with his first wife Ivana was that she wanted to talk about work at home, and Donald wanted to rest. On the rebound he married a young woman by the name of Marla, who had no interest in managing hotels and who wanted to build a home — but in this case, ironically, Donald became restless with a woman who wanted him home *in time for dinner*.

Instead of compromising and discovering what his wives might have had to teach him, Donald changed spouses. He's mined both ends of the spectrum — work ambition and domesticity — and found both of them wanting. One has to wonder how "warm" all those buildings and casinos he owns make him feel late at night when he sleeps alone or with a woman who has no significant history with him.

The duties of marriage call us out of ourselves to help us remember that ours is not the only vision in the world. God is building an entire church, and *each* member is crucial. The eye, the hand, the foot, the mouth — all have a role to play (see 1 Corinthians 12:14–31). We are just one cog in the machine, and — quite frankly — God could replace any one of us without hesitation.

When I was in college, I was deeply saddened by the tragic death of Keith Green, a powerful Christian musician who was amazingly effective in reaching teens. How could God let such a strong leader die? I wondered. But neither Dietrich Bonhoeffer, the great German writer and teacher, nor Blaise Pascal, a brilliant thinker and Christian apologist, lived to the age of forty. Jesus himself didn't even live for forty years here on this earth.

This reality teaches me plainly that *my faithfulness is important but my service isn't essential.* The Christian church can carry on very well if I never write another book or speak at another retreat. She won't miss a step.

I wish I could have given Lisa her dream house, and I know Lisa wishes I could have been a writer from the very beginning of our marriage. And both of us are probably weak enough that, if given the choice, we would go back and take the easy road. But I'm not sure that to do so would have been ultimately in our best interest. Like Caesar, achieving our early ambition might have destroyed us.

Looking Beyond Marriage

The importance of service—looking beyond the marriage relationship—is necessary because marriage itself is not eternal. When God provides us with a mate, there is no guarantee that this mate will be with us for life. We certainly hope this will be the case, but very few marriages end in a simultaneous death. Marriage is for this world, and this world is passing away—at different times for each and every one of us.

Otto Piper suggests that "the loss of a spouse is not simply a sad natural occurrence but ... it is a divine intervention by which a marriage is terminated so that the surviving partner may devote himself fully to the service of God in the Church."[8] Listen carefully to his conclusion: "Therefore, every stage of the individual's sexual development both depends on his being subject to the law of God and is also a partial execution of the divine plan of redemption."

When marriage is placed within the context of God's redemptive plan, we stay married, as far as it depends on us, as a means to express *God's* commitment to his people; when the marriage is ended by God's design — through death — our ultimate purpose hasn't changed. Now we are "free" to perhaps more actively serve God in bringing knowledge of his redemptive plan to others.

When marriage becomes our primary pursuit, our delight in the relationship will be crippled by fear, possessiveness, and self-centeredness. We were made to admire, respect, and love someone who has a purpose bigger than ourselves, a purpose centered on God's untiring work of calling his people home to his heart of love.

We allow marriage to point beyond itself when we accept two central missions: becoming the people God created us to be, and doing the work God has given us to do. If we embrace — not just accept, but actively *embrace* — these two missions, we will have a full life, a rich life, a meaningful life, and a successful life. The irony is, we will probably also have a happy marriage, but that will come as a blessed by-product of putting everything else in order.

Epilogue

The Holy couple

*In our marriage we tell the next generation
what sex and marriage and fidelity look like to Christians.
We are prophets, for better and for worse,
of the future of Christian marriage.*
EVELYN AND JAMES WHITEHEAD

*Our marriages are the testing ground for God
to win us to himself. Our marriages are basic training
for the one Marriage that will not disappoint.*
DAN ALLENDER AND TREMPER LONGMAN III

I WAS ALONE, TRAVELING IN MY CAR (HAVING BEEN SEPARATED FROM my family for over a week due to business travel), when I heard a song that stopped me short. After realistically portraying a relational struggle, the singer lifts the listener up with this chorus: "Ain't nobody gonna say good-bye, no, ain't nobody gonna walk away. This time, Baby, I'm learning how to love you, love you. Ain't nobody ... ever really tried to love you like I love you."

The poor grammar notwithstanding, this is a profound statement. It is undeniably biblical — focusing on "learning to love" rather than anything else. It struck me that if I could succeed in loving Lisa like nobody ever has or ever will, I will have been a "good" husband. My goal is that at the end of her life Lisa will be able to say, "Gary had his rough edges, and there were some struggles he faced his entire life, but for all his faults, Gary loved me like no one else ever could or ever has."

Lisa's parents have five children, so they can't give Lisa the exclusive love that I can. Our children have two parents, so they can't focus on Lisa like I can. It's my job, calling, and mission to walk through the travails and challenges of marriage and declare, "Hey, I'm never leaving, and furthermore (you can immediately see I lack the song-writer's poetic spirit; I can't imagine her using the word *furthermore* in a song), I'm going to love you like you have never been loved."

I'm getting better. After that disastrous birthday experience so many years ago, I've learned how to shop for Lisa. In fact, she is reluctant to give me ideas now, as she thinks I do a better job on my own—and she enjoys being surprised. Strolling through a store one recent holiday season, I immediately knew that Lisa would love a Japanese buckwheat pillow for Christmas—even though she had never heard of one. The kids thought I was crazy, but I knew she would like it and I knew it would demonstrate to her that I've studied her and that I know her better than anyone else.

I was right.

I've been wrong about so many things in my marriage. There have been moments of betrayal, apathy, unkindness, selfishness—but marriage is a long walk. We can start out a little slowly, even occasionally lose our way, and still salvage a most meaningful journey.

If we view the marriage relationship as an opportunity to excel in love, it doesn't matter how difficult the person is whom we are called to love; it doesn't matter even whether that love is ever returned. We can still excel at love. We can still say, "Like it or not, I'm going to love you like nobody ever has."

This mirrors Christ's own love, a love without compare, a love that is infinitely deeper than any human love we could ever know. It is a love pregnant with the opportunity for spiritual birth and rebirth. The Russian Orthodox priest Yelchaninov wrote that "a single vivid experience of love will advance us much farther, will far more surely protect our souls from evil, than the most arduous *struggle* against sin."[1]

We need to further explore the power of human love to feed our divine love. Rather than seeing marriage as a cosmic competitor with heaven, we can embrace it as a school of faith. Maximus the Confessor (580–662) observed that the love we have for God and the love we have for others are not two distinct loves, but "two aspects of a single total love."[2] Jesus suggested the same thing, when in response to a question about the "greatest" commandment he declared that there is not just one, but two — not only must we love God, but also our neighbors.

This is a love that can be practiced by either partner in a marriage relationship. If your spouse isn't a willing participant, you can still learn to grow by loving him or her.

But there's another challenge when two believers are both committed to pursuing a deeper spiritual reality in marriage — the formidable task of working to become not just a holy spouse, but a holy couple.

Pioneers

I once told a church that I would take it as a great compliment if someone told me, "That was the most unoriginal talk I've ever heard." My mission has been, and continues to be, to integrate Scripture, church history, and the Christian classics, and then to apply that wisdom to today. I am not as interested in breaking new ground as I am in recapturing the contemporary relevance of old ground that has been forgotten.

But clearly, while we may not be breaking new ground with the idea of marriage spirituality, we are certainly walking with the minority. Christian spirituality has undeniably been focused on celibacy and a solitary pursuit of God. This emphasis needs to change. Most of the church serves God within a family relationship; it stands to reason that ninety percent of the teaching regarding the spiritual life should thus be placed in a marital context.

I'm inspired by Mary Anne McPherson Oliver's words:

Conjugal saintliness is clearly an ideal from which most of what we see and experience is far removed.... If there are couple-saints around, we might not even recognize them, and if we have never looked for the work of the Spirit in sexuality, we probably haven't noticed it. Besides, saints are rare, and holy couples should be statistically rarer still. Logically one could expect a three-to-one ratio, since there are not only two human beings but their relationship to perfect.[3]

What if a few Christian couples took this pioneering challenge seriously and made it their goal to become a "couple-saint"? No longer defining their relationship to God in solitary terms, but working together to present themselves as a holy unit, a pair of cherubim in the middle of whom God's presence is radically enlivened?

It is, at the very least, an interesting invitation. Is there anyone who will take up that invitation for today—for such a time as this?

Acknowledgments

First, I'd like to thank all those who contributed their stories to this effort. Because some of you want to remain anonymous for your own reasons, and the publisher's lawyers want others of you to remain anonymous for their reasons, I can't thank each one of you individually, but I am deeply grateful.

I've been extremely well-served by Zondervan in writing this book. John Sloan did a marvelous job keeping the book on focus and well-structured. Dirk Buursma provided one of the most satisfying copy-editing experiences I've ever had. His gift at directing me toward a more precise word and his determination to still preserve my voice were greatly appreciated. Marketing director John Topliff has been a tremendous encouragement as well.

I'd also like to thank Scott Waxman, my agent, for providing the introduction to Zondervan; Rob and Jill Takemura for their friendship — both practical and spiritual (I don't know how Lisa and I coped when we didn't live within half a block of you guys); Dr. Bob Stone, my pastor, whose encouragement and teaching continue to inspire and challenge me; Carolyn McCulley of PDI, whose referrals, introductions, and friendship are greatly appreciated; Gene Breitenbach, for his insightful comments and patience with a non-techie writer trying to survive in a world that is being increasingly overrun by the Internet; and my children — Allison, Graham, and Kelsey — for the laughter, the hugs, the prayers, and your comments that light up my life (and for letting *some* of your stories entertain others).

Finally, this book has been lived out with a woman beyond compare. I have tested her and been tested by her; I have sinned against her and sought her forgiveness; I have laughed with her, cried with her, prayed with her, and conceived children with her. Lisa, I adore you more every day. I can't imagine life without you. Thank you for sharing this life with me. Your personality has put the celebration in our marriage; your faith has made it sacred. You are truly a treasure.

Notes

CHAPTER 1: The Greatest Challenge in the World

1. Francis de Sales, *Thy Will Be Done: Letters to Persons in the World* (Manchester, N.H.: Sophia Institute, 1995), 42.

2. Derrick Sherwin Bailey, *The Mystery of Love and Marriage: A Study in the Theology of Sexual Relations* (New York: Harper and Brothers, 1952), 4.

3. C. S. Lewis, *The Allegory of Love: A Study in Medieval Tradition* (New York: Oxford Univ. Press, 1985), 4.

4. Eventually, however, Frieda did leave her husband and children for Lawrence. The account of this and several other literary marriages are explored in John Tytell's book, *Passionate Lives* (New York: Birch Lane, 1991).

5. Katherine Anne Porter, "The Necessary Enemy," *The Collected Essays and Occasional Writings of Katherine Anne Porter* (New York: Delacorte, 1970), 182–84.

6. C. S. Lewis, *The Screwtape Letters* (New York: Macmillan, 1951), 94–95.

7. I've since come to understand that in this verse Paul is probably repeating a phrase offered by the Corinthians—but this is not the place to go into the complexities of the Greek language or the sentence structure. Gordon Fee's commentary on 1 Corinthians in the *New International Commentary on the New Testament* (Grand Rapids: Eerdmans, 1994) is the most thorough and well-reasoned account of this passage I've read.

8. From "The Goods of Marriage," quoted in Evelyn Eaton Whitehead and James D. Whitehead, *A Sense of Sexuality: Christian Love and Intimacy* (New York: Doubleday, 1989), 100.

9. Mary Anne McPherson Oliver, *Conjugal Spirituality: The Primacy of Mutual Love in Christian Tradition* (Kansas City: Sheed and Ward, 1994), 12.

10. Quoted in Oliver, *Conjugal Spirituality*, 12.

11. Gary and Betsy Ricucci, *Love That Lasts: Making a Magnificent Marriage* (Gaithersburg, Md.: PDI Communications, 1993), 95.

CHAPTER 2: **Finding God in Marriage**

1. Belden C. Lane, "Rabbinical Stories," *Christian Century* (12/16/81), quoted in Thomas N. Hart and Kathleen Fischer Hart, *The First Two Years of Marriage* (New York: Paulist, 1983), 117–18.

2. Bailey, *The Mystery of Love and Marriage*, 101.

3. C.J. Mahaney, "God's Purpose and Pattern for Marriage," *According to Plan* audiotape series (Gaithersburg, Md.: PDI Communications, 1994).

4. Philip E. Hughes, *The Second Epistle to the Corinthians: New International Commentary on the New Testament* (Grand Rapids: Eerdmans, 1962, 1982), 178.

5. C. K. Barrett, *A Commentary on the Second Epistle to the Corinthians: 2nd ed. Harper's New Testament Commentaries* (New York: Harper & Row, 1973), 175.

6. Quoted in Philip Yancey, *What's So Amazing About Grace?* (Grand Rapids: Zondervan, 1997), 263.

CHAPTER 3: **Learning to Love**

1. Porter, "The Necessary Enemy," *The Collected Essays*, 184.

2. Yancey, *What's So Amazing About Grace?* 266.

3. This excerpt and the following accounts are taken from the pamphlet *Do You Love Me?* by John Barger (Manchester, N.H.: Sophia Institute, 1987).

CHAPTER 4: **Holy Honor**

1. Quoted in Leon Morris, *The Gospel According to John: New International Commentary on the New Testament* (Grand Rapids: Eerdmans, 1971), 274.

2. Quoted in Oliver, *Conjugal Spirituality*, 38.

3. Ricucci, *Love That Lasts*, 70.

4. Quoted in Ricucci, *Love That Lasts*, 121.

5. John Owen, *Sin and Temptation*, edited and abridged by James Houston (Portland, Ore.: Multnomah, 1983), 29.

6. William Law, *A Serious Call to a Devout and Holy Life* (New York: Paulist, 1978), 294.

7. Dan Allender and Tremper Longman III, *Intimate Allies* (Wheaton, Ill.: Tyndale House, 1995), 287.

8. Allender and Longman, *Intimate Allies*, 281.

CHAPTER 5: **The Soul's Embrace**

1. This quote and the next four quotes are taken from Terry Glaspey, *Pathway to the Heart of God* (Eugene, Ore.: Harvest House, 1998), 16, 24–25.

2. This quote and the following quotes are taken from the article "McCartney on the Rebound," by Phyllis Alsdurf, *Christianity Today* (May 18, 1998).

3. Quoted in Yancey, *What's So Amazing About Grace?* 265.

4. My wife came up after I had written this, looked over my shoulder, read what I said, and offered, "Have I ever told you I think you're a saint?" The giggle that followed her question, however, left the subject clearly unresolved.

5. This rendering is based on the New International Version, which Dr. Fee alters slightly in his commentary. There is also an Old Testament verse that addresses the "marital obligation"—even in the midst of a polygamous society—see Exodus 21:10.

6. Jacques Ellul, *Prayer and Modern Man* (New York: Seabury, 1979), 56.

7. The citations regarding Heloise and Abelard are taken from a letter quoted in Bailey, *The Mystery of Love and Marriage*, 5.

CHAPTER 6: The Cleansing of Marriage

1. Oliver, *Conjugal Spirituality*, v–vi.

2. Pseudo-Athanasius, "The Life and Activity of the Holy and Blessed Teacher Syncletica," trans. Elizabeth Castelli, in *Ascetic Behavior in Greco-Roman Antiquity*, Vincent Wimbush, ed. (Minneapolis: Fortress, 1990), 284.

3. Saint Ambrose, *Concerning Virgins*, book 1, chap. VI, para 25–26.

4. C. S. Lewis, *The Four Loves* (New York: Harcourt Brace, 1971), 111.

5. Hart and Hart, *The First Two Years of Marriage*, 50.

6. Allender and Longman, *Intimate Allies*, 278.

7. Allender and Longman, *Intimate Allies*, 288.

8. Blaise Pascal, *Pensées*, trans. A. S. Krailsheimer (New York: Penguin, 1966).

9. François de Salignac de La Mothe Fénelon, *Christian Perfection* (Minneapolis: Bethany House, 1975), 205.

10. Law, *A Serious Call to a Devout and Holy Life*, 228.

11. Fénelon, *Christian Perfection*, 90.

CHAPTER 7: Sacred History

1. Hart and Hart, *The First Two Years of Marriage*, 15.

2. Oliver, *Conjugal Spirituality*, 26.

3. Oliver, *Conjugal Spirituality*, 33.

4. Quoted in Oliver, *Conjugal Spirituality*, 34.

5. Anne Tyler, *A Patchwork Planet* (New York: Knopf, 1998), 218–19.

6. Jerry Jenkins, *Hedges: Loving Your Marriage Enough to Protect It* (Brentwood, Tenn.: Wolgemuth and Hyatt, 1989), 142.

CHAPTER 8: Sacred Struggle

1. Ricucci, *Love That Lasts*, 50.

2. Otto Piper, *The Biblical View of Sex and Marriage* (New York: Scribner's, 1960), 114–15.

3. Piper, *The Biblical View of Sex and Marriage,* 134.

4. The Lincoln material was gleaned from several works: *Abraham Lincoln, Speeches and Writings, 1832–1858* (New York: The Library of America, 1989); Frederick Owen, *Abraham Lincoln: The Man and His Faith* (Wheaton, Ill.: Tyndale House, 1976); Shelby Foote, *The Civil War: A Narrative,* Vols. *1&2* (New York: Random House, 1958, 1963); and Dale Carnegie, *How to Win Friends and Influence People* (New York: Simon and Schuster, 1994).

5. The Lindbergh material was gleaned from several works: Anne Morrow Lindbergh, *Bring Me a Unicorn* (New York: Harcourt Brace Jovanovich, 1971); Anne Morrow Lindbergh, *Hour of Gold, Hour of Lead* (New York: Harcourt Brace Jovanovich, 1973); Dorothy Herrmann, *Anne Morrow Lindbergh: A Gift for Life* (New York: Ticknor and Fields, 1993); Roxanne Chadwick, *Anne Morrow Lindbergh: Pilot and Poet* (Minneapolis: Lerner, 1987); and A. Scott Berg, *Lindbergh* (New York: G. P. Putnam's Sons, 1998).

6. Eugene Peterson, *Take and Read* (Grand Rapids: Eerdmans, 1996), 44.

CHAPTER 9: Falling Forward

1. Based on a true story submitted by Pam Hoepner to *Reader's Digest* (July 1998).

2. Quoted in Oliver, *Conjugal Spirituality,* 126.

3. Quoted in Ricucci, *Love That Lasts,* 129.

4. I heard L'Engle recite this poem at a forum I attended in Bellingham, Washington, in 1998.

5. Hart and Hart, *The First Two Years of Marriage,* 19.

6. Quoted in Ricucci, *Love That Lasts,* 152.

7. Whitehead and Whitehead, *A Sense of Sexuality,* 197.

8. Quoted in Ricucci, *Love That Lasts,* 124.

9. The story is told in *The Jerusalem Post* (May 15, 1998).

10. Yancey, *What's So Amazing About Grace?* 84.

11. Quoted in Yancey, *What's So Amazing About Grace?* 281.

CHAPTER 10: Make Me a Servant

1. Piper, *The Biblical View of Sex and Marriage,* 153.

2. This and the following quotes are taken from an article by Robert Draper, "Death Takes a Honeymoon," *GQ* (June 1998), 232–35.

3. Ricucci, *Love That Lasts,* 5–6.

4. This account is taken from an article by Jack Friedman and Barbara Sandler, "Winning at Home," *People* (1/11/99).

5. This account is taken from an article by Elizabeth Gilbert, "Losing Is Not an Option," *GQ* (September 1999).

6. C.J. Mahaney, "A Husband's Responsibilities," *According to Plan* audiotape series.

7. Dietrich Bonhoeffer, *The Cost of Discipleship* (New York: Macmillan, 1963 rev. ed.), 149.

8. Oliver, *Conjugal Spirituality*, 1.

9. Piper, *The Biblical View of Sex and Marriage*, 157.

10. Allender and Longman, *Intimate Allies*, 317–18.

11. Quoted in Whitehead and Whitehead, *A Sense of Sexuality*, 13.

CHAPTER 11: **Sexual Saints**

1. Quoted in Whitehead and Whitehead, *A Sense of Sexuality*, 11.

2. Oliver, *Conjugal Spirituality*, 13.

3. Allender and Longman, *Intimate Allies*, 228.

4. John Calvin discusses this in his *Institutes of the Christian Religion*, book IV, chap. 12, para. 26.

5. Mary Anne McPherson Oliver, "Conjugal Spirituality," *Spirituality Today* 43, no. 1 (Spring 1991), 54.

6. Edmund Leites, *The Puritan Conscience and Modern Sexuality* (New Haven, Conn.: Yale Univ. Press, 1986), 12–13.

7. Quoted in Kathleen Fischer Hart and Thomas N. Hart, "The Call to Holiness in Christian Marriage," *Spirituality Today* 36, no. 1 (Spring 1984), 16.

8. Piper, *The Biblical View of Sex and Marriage*, 79.

9. Nahmanides, *The Holy Letter*, 60.

10. Ricucci, *Love That Lasts*, 159.

11. Harold Best, *Music Through the Eyes of Faith* (San Francisco: HarperSanFrancisco, 1993), 40.

12. Thankfulness is a fundamental Christian virtue that is essential for a healthy soul. I discuss this more thoroughly in my book *The Glorious Pursuit: Embracing the Virtues of Christ* (Colorado Springs: NavPress, 1988).

13. Piper, *The Biblical View of Sex and Marriage*, 215.

14. Piper, *The Biblical View of Sex and Marriage*, 216.

15. Thomas N. Hart, *Living Happily Ever After: Toward a Theology of Christian Marriage* (New York: Paulist, 1979), 44.

16. C.S. Lewis, *Letters to Malcolm* (New York: Harcourt, Brace & World, 1963), 89.

17. Lewis, *The Screwtape Letters*, 102–03.

18. Nahmanides, *The Holy Letter*, 116.

19. Whitehead and Whitehead, *A Sense of Sexuality*, 75.

20. See the discussion in Whitehead and Whitehead, *A Sense of Sexuality*, 150.

21. Whitehead and Whitehead, *A Sense of Sexuality*, 151.

22. Elton Trueblood, *The Humor of Christ* (New York: Harper & Row, 1964), 32.

23. Quoted in Oliver, *Conjugal Spirituality,* 28.

CHAPTER 12: Sacred Presence

1. Evelyn Eaton Whitehead and James D. Whitehead, *Marrying Well: Stages on the Journey of Christian Marriage* (New York: Doubleday, 1983), 187.

2. Fénelon, *Christian Perfection,* 4

3. Brother Lawrence, *Practicing the Presence of God,* trans. John J. Delaney (New York: Doubleday, 1977).

4. Oliver, *Conjugal Spirituality,* 61.

5. Allender and Longman, *Intimate Allies,* 89.

6. Allender and Longman, *Intimate Allies,* 99.

7. Allender and Longman, *Intimate Allies,* 101.

8. Allender and Longman put this best: "God does not exclusively fill the human heart. He made humankind to need more than himself. The staggering humility of God to make something that was not to be fully satisfied with the Creator and the creation is incomprehensible" (*Intimate Allies,* 146).

9. Allender and Longman, *Intimate Allies,* 161.

10. Allender and Longman, *Intimate Allies,* 78.

11. I discuss this in some detail in my book *The Glorious Pursuit.*

CHAPTER 13: Sacred Mission

1. Dietrich Bonhoeffer, *Letters and Papers from Prison* (New York: Macmillan, 1972), 347–48.

2. De Sales, *Thy Will Be Done,* 20.

3. De Sales, *Thy Will Be Done,* 46.

4. De Sales, *Thy Will Be Done,* 47–48.

5. De Sales, *Thy Will Be Done,* 85.

6. Count Helmuth James von Moltke, *A German of the Resistance: The Last Letters of Count Helmuth James von Moltke* (London: Oxford Univ. Press, 1946), 51.

7. Quoted in Anatoli Boukreev and G. Weston DeWalt, *The Climb* (New York: St. Martin's, 1997), 142.

8. Piper, *The Biblical View of Sex and Marriage,* 78.

EPILOGUE: The Holy Couple

1. Alexander Yelchaninov, "Fragments of a Diary: 1881–1934," in *A Treasury of Russian Spirituality,* quoted in Oliver, *Conjugal Spirituality,* 53.

2. Quoted in Oliver, *Conjugal Spirituality,* 24.

3. Oliver, *Conjugal Spirituality,* 75.

Questions for Discussion and Reflection

CHAPTER 1: The Greatest Challenge in the World

1. Why did you choose to get married (or why do you want to get married)? Is this a biblical reason?

2. How do you think most Christians would describe the purpose of marriage?

3. Were you encouraged or discouraged by the author's premise that marriage is a crucible in which we can learn more about ourselves and about God? What has been your personal experience in this regard?

4. What do you think of Gary's critique of romantic love as the basis — or measurement of success — for marriage? How have your attitudes toward romantic love changed over time?

5. Do you agree with Gary that, in one sense, moderns "ask too much of marriage?" If so, in what way?

6. What has your marriage revealed to you about your sinful attitudes, selfish behaviors, and other character flaws? Why do you think marriage brings so many character issues to the surface?

7. Gary says God is the One who ultimately fulfills us, not our mate. If this is so, what contribution does our mate make to our life?

8. How do you react to the idea that God may have designed marriage to make us holy even more than to make us happy?

CHAPTER 2: **Finding God in Marriage**

1. What aspect, event, or element of your marriage has taught you the most about how God loves us?

2. How can a discouraged spouse directly apply Gary's admonition to seek God in the midst of disappointments rather than to obsess over where the spouse falls short? What mental exercises would you suggest?

3. Can you think of any analogies that Gary doesn't mention about how marriage reveals God and his love to the world?

4. Gary contrasts a human-centered view of marriage (staying put as long as our desires and expectations are being met) and a God-centered view (preserving the marriage because it brings glory to God and points a sinful world to a reconciling Creator). What most motivates you to maintain and preserve your marital commitment?

5. In your own marital experience, are you motivated more by what makes you happy or by what pleases God? How can churches support and encourage this latter and higher motivation?

6. What aspect of God's character would you most like your marriage to reveal to the world? How can you accomplish this?

CHAPTER 3: **Learning to Love**

1. Compare and contrast what our culture usually means by the word love with how the Bible defines it.

2. Discuss some of the ways that marriage seems uniquely designed to train us in how to love.

3. If somebody tried to describe your love for God solely by how well you love your spouse, what would he or she conclude? What are one or two things you can do that would serve your spouse, strengthen your marriage, and please God?

4. How much time do you spend thinking about how to make your spouse happy, compared to the amount of time you spend thinking about how well your spouse is pleasing you? Do you think your answer is about right, or do you need to do better in this area?

5. Discuss how marriage can reveal men's poor attitudes and prejudices about women, and how it can also illuminate women's critical thoughts about men. Is your marriage confronting these stereotypes, or is it suffering from them? What can you do to uncover and renounce such negative attitudes?

6. God loves us in spite of our flaws. How does marriage teach us to love our spouse in spite of their imperfections?

7. You and your spouse are different in many ways. Which differences have you grown to appreciate? Which ones still annoy you? Are these differences something you can learn from with better understanding? How so?

CHAPTER 4: **Holy Honor**

1. How is any lack of respect or active contempt for your spouse negatively affecting your own life and the lives of your children?

2. Are you more apt to look for "evidences of God's grace" in your spouse, or is it your pattern to be consumed with your mate's flaws? What practical steps can you take to choose respect over contempt?

3. What evidences of grace can you see in your mate when you take the time to look for them? What are personal qualities of your mate and contributions your mate makes to your life for which you should regularly thank God?

4. How many of your marital disagreements are rooted in gender differences as compared to personal disagreements? How can recognizing such distinctions improve the quality of your relationship?

5. How does trying to understand our spouses — rather than judging them — help us to fulfill the biblical command to respect them?

6. Discuss some of the ways that you can actively honor your spouse.

7. How would your marriage benefit if you and your spouse became better at showing respect to each other?

8. Gary writes that "we're not married in a carefree Garden of Eden. We're married in the midst of many responsibilities that compete for our energy." In light of this, do you believe you give your spouse sufficient leeway and understanding?

CHAPTER 5: **The Soul's Embrace**

1. Do you know any married couples who seem unusually successful in prayer? If so, what stands out about their prayer habits?

2. Has your prayer life ever been hindered due to negative attitudes toward your spouse? Are there any negative attitudes hindering your prayer life today?

3. Gary writes, "We're told that if we want to have a stronger marriage, we should improve our prayer lives. But Peter tells us that we should improve our marriages so that we can improve our prayer lives." How can you imagine your prayer life improving if your marriage can be closer to the way God intended it to be?

4. How would you say the quality and quantity of sexual activity in your marriage affects the way you pray? The way your spouse prays?

5. Gary writes, "Dissension is a major prayer-killer. Looked at from this perspective, the institution of marriage is designed to force us to become reconcilers. That's the only way we'll survive spiritually." How well do you and your spouse resolve disagreements in a timely manner? What happens to your praying when you are upset with your spouse?

6. What idea about sexual activity and prayer intrigued you the most? What other aspects of being married might contain "hidden" lessons about prayer? How has your marriage helped you grow in prayer?

CHAPTER 6: **The Cleansing of Marriage**

1. What most surprised you about your own sin during the first year or two of your marriage?

2. What is your overall reaction to the idea that God intends to use your marriage to expose your sin and help you grow out of it?

3. Is your marriage a safe place for your sin to be revealed? How can it become more nurturing in this regard?

4. How might Gary's comment, "Couples don't fall out of love so much as they fall out of repentance,' " help restore a troubled marriage?

5. Do you agree with Gary that "much of our marital dissatisfaction stems from self-hatred"? How can we avoid the "flight" mentality — running from what we've done or become — and instead use our marriage to fight the sin that's revealed?

6. Why do you think spouses are often afraid to confess their sins or admit their faults? What needs to happen in our marriages so that it's safe to be more transparent? (Or what is true of your marriage that has helped you become transparent?)

7. Identify the top two weaknesses in the way you relate to your mate. What are the positive virtues that are the moral/spiritual opposites of those two weaknesses (for example, harshness/ gentleness; criticism/encouragement)? Which one will you work on this week?

8. Have you ever used your knowledge of a weakness in your mate to shame or punish him or her? How could you have used that situation to build up your spouse and encourage spiritual growth?

CHAPTER 7: **Sacred History**

1. How can understanding Israel's history with God (times of celebration, anger, infidelity, and silence) help couples grow in all seasons of marriage? What lessons have you learned that will help you face the "angry" or "silent" seasons?

2. Do you agree with Gary that "we live in a nation of quitters"? How can the church more effectively teach about the benefits of perseverance when addressing such a culture?

3. What do you see as the relationship between perseverance and personal holiness? What "messages" of modern life are hostile to perseverance and holiness?

4. How can the concept of perseverance and persistence help you be patient with your spouse's growth in holiness?

5. What would you lose if the sacred history of your marriage was ended? What would your spouse lose? Your children? Your church?

6. Spend some time talking with your spouse about which stories should go into the sacred history of your marriage, to be told to your children, family, and friends.

7. Discuss how respecting and telling the sacred history of your marriage can foster community with other couples you know.

8. How can you make the idea of eternity and its rewards a practical motivation for perseverance in the daily grind of married life?

9. How do you want people to describe your marriage at your golden wedding anniversary?

CHAPTER 8: **Sacred Struggle**

1. Whom do you admire for the way they handled difficulties in their marriage? What do you admire most about these individuals?

2. What is the difference between productive, spiritually profitable marital struggle and debilitating marital struggle? How can the difficulty in your marriage produce positive spiritual results?

3. How did you answer Gary's question, "Would I rather live a life of ease and comfort and remain immature in Christ, or am I willing to be seasoned with suffering if by doing so I am conformed to the image of Christ?"

4. Gary says that a good marriage "takes struggle. You must crucify your selfishness. You must at times confront, and at other times confess." Do you think this is overstated? Are there any exceptions? How might this belief provide perspective for couples going through difficult times?

5. How can sorrow "set us free," as Anne Morrow Lindbergh wrote? How can we encourage each other — as Anne urges — to add "understanding, patience, love, openness, and the willingness to remain vulnerable" to our disappointments and sorrow?

6. Do you think Abraham Lincoln and Anne Morrow Lindbergh would have accomplished what they did if both had been in relatively "easy" marriages? Why or why not?

7. How can the Christian belief in heaven encourage couples to persevere?

8. How do you think God can use the specific difficulties in your marriage to refine your character and prepare you for future ministry?

9. Why are difficulties and suffering inevitable in every marriage? What happens if we run from them? What happens if we face them head-on?

10. Do you and your mate face the difficulties in your marriage differently? What can you learn from your spouse's approach? What can your spouse learn from your approach?

CHAPTER 9: **Falling Forward**

1. Donald Harvey argues that intimate relationships "are the result of planning. They are built. The sense of union that comes with genuine spiritual closeness will not just happen." Over the past year, how much thought, prayer, and effort have you put into building "genuine spiritual closeness?"

2. What makes you feel like your spouse is "falling forward" toward you? What makes your spouse feel like you are falling forward toward them?

3. In which arena is it most difficult for you to grow toward your spouse: physical intimacy, emotional intimacy, or spiritual intimacy? Ask your spouse what you can do to improve in your weakest area.

4. What accommodation can you make in your marriage in order to foster deeper fellowship and intimacy?

5. Is there a "file cabinet" in your marriage's "confessional"? What do you have to do to forgive your spouse and get rid of the filing cabinet?

6. Christian marriage expects that you give the "gift of self" to your mate. What are some ways in which you think your spouse truly wants to receive you? How can you give more of yourself in these ways?

7. Fellowship is fostered by three spiritual practices: learning not to run from conflict, learning how to compromise, and accepting your mate's weaknesses. Which of these disciplines is your strongest? Weakest? What can you do to build on your strength and overcome your weakness?

8. Where do you fall on the spectrum of running from conflict to being brutally harsh during conflict? How can you work toward a healthier response?

9. Would you say that in the past you have been a "falling forward" or a "pulling away" spouse after you were offended? Based on the teaching here, what steps can you take to learn how to fall forward? What can you do to make it easier for your spouse to fall forward?

CHAPTER 10: Make Me a Servant

1. When is the last time you loved your spouse in such a way that it cost you something? What can you do for your spouse in the next few days that will fulfill this level of love?

2. Do you agree with Dietrich Bonhoeffer that "Christian marriage is marked by discipline and self-denial"? How does this view compare or contrast with the view you held before you got married?

3. Kathleen and Thomas Hart write of the "paschal mystery of marriage — the process of dying and rising as a pattern of life for married people." What does your marriage call you to die to? What might it be calling you to rise to?

4. When you think back to why you decided to get married, were your motivations more selfish than selfless? In what way? How has this changed (or does it need to)?

5. Do you sometimes find it difficult to serve your spouse by letting him/her serve you? What can you do to grow in this area?

6. What are some of the world's messages to men that keep them from serving their wives? What are some of the world's messages to women that keep them from serving their husbands? How can we counteract these messages in our marriages?

7. When you think of your marriage, do you agree that "quarrels over money and time usually reflect a demand to 'own' our life rather than to serve the other with our wealth and existence?" How can you use your money and time to better serve your spouse?

8. Is your attitude toward the sexual relationship marked more by service or by the exercise of power? What can you do to grow in this area?

9. What do you think would be the greatest benefit for your marriage if you and your spouse became better servants of each other?

CHAPTER 11: Sexual Saints

1. In what ways has your past had a negative impact on your marriage's sexuality? How may seeking spiritual counsel or care help you deal with this past?

2. Were you shocked by Gary's assertion that "God doesn't turn his eyes when a married couple goes to bed?" How does this make you feel? Consider praying with your spouse, specifically thanking God for the gift of sexual intimacy.

3. Has sex been more of a blessing or a burden in your marriage? Was it always this way? If not, what may have changed and why?

4. How well have you "cultivated" holy appetites? How may this be affecting your physical intimacy?

5. Has shame kept you from giving what you do have to your spouse? What is one small thing you can do to begin confronting this selfishness?

6. How much do you think selfishness affects the average married couple with regard to their sex life? In what ways can an attitude of service transform the experience of marital sexuality?

7. How can gratitude for the marital sexual experience help a couple overcome guilt about previous sexual experience prior to marriage?

8. According to Gary, "Abstinence is not a cul-de-sac or dead end; it is a long on-ramp.... I am not truly saying no, but rather, wait." What can you learn from the rhythm of abstaining and enjoyment inherent in married sexual expression? In other aspects of married life? In life in general?

9. How are you growing in the spiritual side of your sexuality (generosity and service)? What would you like to become more true of you? What would you like to stop being true of you?

10. What one thing can you do in the next month to demonstrate to your spouse your desire to grow in the area of physical intimacy?

CHAPTER 12: **Sacred Presence**

1. How can a husband and wife more consciously invite the presence of God into their marriage?

2. Are your spoken words inviting God's presence into your home, or are they pushing him away?

3. Have you ever experienced "malicious silence" in your marriage? How is this an offense to God?

4. How does listening invite God's presence into our homes?

5. How can marital dissatisfaction remind us of our need for fellowship with God?

6. Did you agree with Gary when he wrote, "I have discovered ... that my satisfaction or dissatisfaction with my marriage has far more to do with my relationship to God than it does with my relationship to [my wife]?" How so?

7. How does your spouse mirror a quality of God that you might be somewhat lacking in? What can you learn from this?

8. Gary suggests that if our pastor lived with us, we might treat our spouse differently in his presence — yet God is always present! How can we become more aware of God's presence, creating a more nurturing and encouraging environment at home?

9. Gary warns, "There hasn't been a single marriage in all of human history that could fill a soul that has been emptied of purpose through noncreative living." Has life's busyness kept you from being fully engaged in creating a family together? What can you do to become more creative in your family?

10. "The family that will enjoy Jesus' presence as a customary part of their union is a family that is joined precisely because husband and wife want to invite Jesus into the deeper parts of their marriage." What are some of the deeper parts of your marriage that you've never thought about asking Jesus into? How would you go about inviting him there? What would be the implications of such a step?

CHAPTER 13: **Sacred Mission**

1. Before you got married, what did you sense that God wanted to do with your life? What was your mate's life mission before you got married? How has marriage affected these life missions? How do you feel about this?

2. Have you, in any way, committed what Gary calls "spiritual fraud" — agreeing to get married but then acting like a single man or woman after the wedding? What do you need to do to renounce this?

3. How can we find the right balance between faithfulness to our calling and faithfulness to our marital vows?

4. Do you believe that either your or your spouse's ambition may be suffocating your relationship? If so, discuss the best way to confront this.

5. Honestly consider how an early ambition — had it been fulfilled — might have harmed you and/or your marriage.

6. What ministries at church or in your community are you engaged in? What ministries is your spouse engaged in? Which do you share? How is your marriage healthier (or weaker) because you serve in contexts outside of your home?

7. Consider the effects that these stages of family life can have on ministry:
   • newly married, without children
   • married with toddlers
   • raising teenagers
   • empty nesters

   What are the advantages and challenges of each phase of life as it relates to living out your ministry calling?

8. What do you think would happen in a marriage if a couple focused only on their emotional satisfaction with each other to the exclusion of any involvement or service to God's work?

9. How has being married shaped and strengthened the way you engage in ministry?

EPILOGUE: The Holy Couple

1. Will you commit to praying, at least several times a week, "Lord, how can I love my spouse today like she (or he) has never been loved?"

2. What appeals to you about Gary's challenge to become a "couple saint" with your spouse? What concerns you about such a challenge?

3. As you consider everything you've read, what one or two areas will most help you begin remaking your marriage into a God-honoring one?

DEVOTIONS
FOR A
SACRED
MARRIAGE

1

The God-Centered Spouse

*Let us purify ourselves from everything
that contaminates body and spirit,
perfecting holiness out of reverence for God.*
2 Corinthians 7:1

Greg Nettle, pastor of the RiverTree Christian Church in Massillon, Ohio, was walking to his car after a golf tournament when he realized the remote trunk opener wasn't working. Neither were the automatic door locks. When he finally got inside the car, he saw the fuel gauge reading empty, even though he had filled up on gas less than twenty-four hours before. More frustrating yet, the car would turn over but then immediately die.

After a tow truck delivered the disabled vehicle to the dealership, a mechanic came out to Greg and told him the problem: a bad BCM.

"What's a BCM?"

"The basic control module. It's essentially the car's brain, and once it goes bad, everything starts malfunctioning."

Greg could have insisted on "fixing" the trunk, the door locks, the gas gauge, and any number of problems—but those were merely the symptoms of an overall malfunction.

How often do we do the same thing with marriage! We focus on the symptoms:

- "We need to improve our communication."
- "We need to get better at handling conflict."
- "We need to show more appreciation for each other."

- "We need to have a more unified plan with the children."
- "We need to work harder at keeping the romance alive in our relationship."

We can spend a lifetime focusing on the symptoms, or we can replace the BCM—the basic control module. I believe the BCM for marriage is our *spiritual motivation*.

It all comes down to this: Are you a God-centered spouse or a spouse-centered spouse? A spouse-centered spouse acts nicely toward her husband when he acts nicely toward her. She is accommodating, as long as her husband pays her attention. A spouse-centered husband will go out of his way for his wife, as long as she remains agreeable and affectionate. He'll romance her, as long as he feels rewarded for doing so.

But Paul tells us we are to perfect holiness *out of reverence for God*. Since God is always worthy to be revered, we are always called to holiness; we are always called to love. A God-centered spouse feels more motivated by his or her commitment to God than by whatever response a spouse may give.

Spouse-centered Christians try to make excuses to stop loving their spouses because of their spouses' sins. But if this were a valid excuse, every one of us could avoid the call to love, since every one of us married a sinner!

One woman came up to me after a seminar and said, "It would be easy to be married if my husband were half as holy as you." I managed to contain my laughter and pointed out that she had no idea how "holy" I was; my wife feels pushed beyond her limit in many areas while trying to love this sinful man.

But that's not the point! I am not called to love my wife because she is holier than other wives (though I'm deeply thankful for her godliness). I am not called to love her because she makes me happy (though I am grateful for the many good times we share). I am not called to love her because she makes me go all gooey inside (though sometimes she still does). I am called to love her *out of reverence for God*. Any other motivation is less than Christian.

If I am to rid myself of anything that may contaminate body or spirit, then I can give no place in my life to jealousy, bitterness, resentment, or selfishness. I am always called to practice gentleness, kindness, goodness, faithfulness, and self-control. Someone else's sin — even the sin of my spouse against me — never gives me the license to respond with sin. I am called to just one motivation, and one only: reverence for God.

In one sense, what my spouse says or does or doesn't do is almost irrelevant. Every decision I make, every word I utter, every thought I think, every movement I perform, is to flow out of one holy motivation: reverence for God.

Are you a God-centered spouse?

2

A Prayer to Remember

Be imitators of God, therefore, as dearly loved children
and live a life of love, just as Christ loved us and gave himself up
for us as a fragrant offering and sacrifice to God.
EPHESIANS 5:1–2

WHEN I COME INTO TOWN FOR "SACRED MARRIAGE" SEMINARS, I
often get taken out to dinner beforehand. The organizers sometimes
invite an engaged couple to join us. I always like this, particularly if
I feel tired from traveling, because I know I can ask one question of
the engaged woman that will reward me with a good rest. I know
this because she will likely take at least ten minutes to answer. The
question is this:

"Tell me about your future husband."

The bride-to-be's eyes light up, and she starts to gush with enthusiastic and unqualified praise: "Oh, I so appreciate this about him,
and he's so good at that, and he's so wonderfully thoughtful in this
area, and in that area he's absolutely the best ..."

Then, later in the weekend, I'll be with a group of wives and say,
"Tell me about your husbands." I still get a rest, but I don't find it
nearly as pleasant. The chorus goes like this: "He doesn't do this.
He never does that. He wouldn't know how to *spell* 'spiritual leader,'
much less act like one."

I go back to my hotel room and ask myself, "Where is the bridge
that leads a woman to stop defining a man by what he *is* and start
defining him by what he *is not?*"

The sad answer, unfortunately, is *marriage.* All our hopes, expec-

296

tations, dreams, and ideals get poured into this real relationship. Because we marry a sinner, each day brings a new and often legitimate disappointment. Before long, we stop seeing what attracted us and instead become consumed by what disappoints us. Whereas before marriage our eyes filled with the glory of the person we had chosen to spend our lives with, now our eyes get filled only with their shortcomings.

I end the "Sacred Marriage" seminar with a story about a woman who decided to marry a man who was severely disabled in a work-related fire. While he could certainly offer emotional, relational, and spiritual support, such a man obviously will lack a lot of other things women typically seek.

"Ask yourself what a blind man with no arms and only one leg can't do for himself, much less for you," I'll say, "and then tell me what your husband *isn't*. Tell me how your wife disappoints you, or how your spouse doesn't live up to your highest ideals."

Every day, millions of couples wake up and evaluate their marriages by asking themselves, "Am I happier today than I was yesterday?" but I think there's a much better question we could ask. It comes from a song I heard on the radio, with one line that goes like this: "Ain't nobody gonna say good-bye, ain't nobody ever really tried to love you like I love you."

The poor grammar aside, there's some good theology in there. I'm called to love my wife like nobody ever has and nobody ever will. I am called to be the one person so devoted to her overall good that I commit myself to being there on her behalf, regardless of any disappointments or faults, so that on the day I die, while my wife may well remember the many bad habits I carried with me to my grave, she might yet say, "But you know what? That man loved me like I've never been loved; I can't imagine ever being loved like that again." If she can say this, then I'll know I've "succeeded" at this thing called marriage. It won't be about dying happier than other men; it'll be about whether I have truly loved.

So here's the question — more of a prayer, actually. Instead of waking up and asking yourself, "Am I happier today than I was yesterday?" how about praying, "Lord, how can I love my spouse today like she [or he] has never been or ever will be loved?"

You know what I've found? That's a prayer God *loves* to answer in very practical ways. He delights in loving his children, and he searches the earth to find someone willing to be his agent to fulfill this quest.

Just imagine how your marriage might change if, before your husband or wife returned home from work this evening, you spent some time asking God—and listening for his response—"Lord, how can I love him [or her] today like he [or she] has never been loved?" The answer may be very practical: take over a chore, speak a word of encouragement, take care of something that needs fixing. Or it may be romantic, or over-the-top creative, or generous, or very simple.

But ask God to help you. Partner with him to build up and encourage the person with whom you've chosen to spend the rest of your life.

Ask.

"How can I love my spouse today like he [or she] has never been or ever will be loved?"

When we focus on what *we* can do, it's amazing how little time we have left to become consumed by our disappointments.

3

Keeping the Focus
Where It Belongs

*"Why do you look at the speck of sawdust in your brother's eye
and pay no attention to the plank in your own eye?
How can you say to your brother, 'Brother, let me take the speck out
of your eye,' when you yourself fail to see the plank in your own eye?
You hypocrite, first take the plank out of your eye, and then
you will see clearly to remove the speck from your brother's eye."*
LUKE 6:41–42

"GARY," THE EMAIL READ, "WHAT DOES A WIFE DO WHEN HER HUS-band doesn't love her like Christ loves the church?"

I responded by pointing out that no husband alive loves his wife this well. While all Christian husbands should aspire to it, the truth is that we all fall short.

I soon received a second email.

"Here's my story," she wrote. "Before I got married, I read ten Harlequin romances a day, and I thought marriage would be like that. For a while it was, but then things cooled off. A couple years later, I found that exciting love once again by having an affair; but after a number of months, that cooled off as well."

At that point, she had thrown herself into the church, but after a while even God became boring. That's when she "fell" into yet another affair, which—no surprise here—also eventually cooled off. In the aftermath of those two affairs, in which she wounded and humiliated her husband about as deeply as a wife can, she wrote to me, consumed with how her husband wasn't loving her like Christ loves the church.

Admittedly, this is an extreme example, but all of us have hearts that tend toward dismissing our own faults while magnifying the flaws of our spouses. Sometimes we need an extreme example to show us how dark our own hearts really are.

Jesus could not have been clearer: "Why do you look at the speck of sawdust in your brother's eye and pay no attention to the plank in your own eye? How can you say to your brother, 'Brother, let me take the speck out of your eye,' when you yourself fail to see the plank in your own eye? You hypocrite, first take the plank out of your eye, and then you will see clearly to remove the speck from your brother's eye" (Luke 6:41–42).

If you're thinking, "But in my case, my spouse really *is* the worst sinner," then know this: Jesus is talking specifically about *you*. This is precisely the attitude he finds so offensive.

Humans arguing about who is holier is like a couple of twenty-five handicap golfers fighting over which one of them can drive the ball farther—while Tiger Woods watches over their shoulder. We're all so many degrees below God's standard of perfection that even the holiest of humans is in desperate, aching need of God's gracious mercy and forgiveness.

While we tend to rank certain sins, in the glory of God's goodness every mark of sin—whether an errant attitude, a prideful spirit, or a lust of the flesh—is vile and offensive in his sight. I've seen wives who abuse food disdain husbands who struggle with pornography; I've seen controlling and arrogant husbands disdain wives who watch too much television. Both seem completely blinded to their own shortcomings.

We're not called to judge our spouses—ever; we are called to *love* them. We are not called to recount their failures in a Pharisaic game of "I'm holier than you"; we're called to *encourage* them. We are not called to build a case against them regarding how far they fall short of the glory of God; we are called to *honor and respect* them.

A final thought: You might never talk to another person about your spouse's weaknesses, but when you pray for or about him or her, how do you sound to God? Are you spending more time asking God how you can love your spouse like he or she has never been or ever will be loved, or are you endlessly repeating your spouse's failures and presenting God with a laundry list of things you want him to change?

If God seems silent, maybe he's hoping you'll catch a clue and turn the mirror on yourself. For the next week, revolutionize your marriage by asking God where *you* fall short. Every time you're tempted to turn the spotlight on your spouse, ask for God's gentle correction: "Lord, where am I falling short of your will for me to be a loving husband [a loving wife]? Where do I need to grow? Am I loving my spouse with the extravagant love displayed by Jesus?"

Growing Old Together

O Lord, you are my God;
I will exalt you and praise your name,
for in perfect faithfulness
you have done marvelous things.

Isaiah 25:1

Hollywood actor Al Pacino once talked about attending a Frank Sinatra concert in the early 1980s. When he arrived, he discovered that the opening act featured Buddy Rich, the famous drummer. Suddenly, it dawned on Al that Buddy was in his sixties — and he was going to play the drums? Al confessed, "I'm thinking, now I'm going to sit here and listen to him drum for a while and twiddle my thumbs until Frank Sinatra comes out."

And then something totally unexpected happened. Buddy Rich sat down and pulled sounds, rhythms, and cadences out of that set of instruments the likes of which Al Pacino had never heard. He sat mesmerized, confessing that Buddy Rich "transcended what I thought he was gonna do tenfold. And it became this *experience.*"

Rich amazed the entire audience. Everyone stood up in unison and started screaming, at which point Frank Sinatra came out and said, "You see this guy drumming? You know, sometimes it's a good idea to stay at a thing." [1]

Sometimes it's a good idea to stay at a thing.

Persevering in a marriage creates something that nothing else can match. A deep marriage takes time to build, as well as tremendous effort, but something about a love that has endured surpasses even the thrill of newly discovered affection and infatuation. Hollywood likes to celebrate the couples who have just met and can't keep their hands off each other, who talk baby talk incessantly and practically smother each other with their affection. But Lisa and I have developed a much greater appreciation for those couples in their sixties and seventies who have all but melted into each other.

A 1996 study in *Social Psychology Quarterly* found that the happiness of most couples declines somewhat for the first twenty years of marriage, but those who make it to their thirty-fifth anniversary find themselves as happy with each other as they felt when they were newlyweds. [2] Why is this so? Romance in the early years of marriage quickly gets assaulted by unmet expectations, the duties of child rearing, financial concerns, and the busyness of life. But during that emotional winter, unseen roots sink deep into the ground, ready to produce a fruit that a new but untested love can never match. A certain intimacy begins to develop, provided we don't kill it with divorce.

I see this in my parents, and I see it in couples I don't even know. You've seen them, too — in their seventies or eighties, frail creatures physically but strong in love, who walk together as a unit. They've become one in almost every sense of the word — in the way they order their hamburgers, find a table, eat their lunch, and walk back to their car. They have perfected the dance, and every step comes in unison.

People who flit from relationship to relationship as their infatuations lead them aren't really happy; they're desperate — and they'll never find what they're looking for as they allow their desperation to bury potential life partners. There is no perfect "soul mate," either for them or for us. There will be only sinner after sinner after sinner. But when you learn to accept and love one particular sinner over several decades, you can slowly build an alliance and intimacy that nothing else can match.

Love doesn't have to slowly fade away like a snowman on a warm day. It can grow like an avalanche in power and force, picking up strength along the way.

Sometimes it's a good idea to stay at a thing.

5

God's Son, God's Daughter

Can a mother forget the baby at her breast
    and have no compassion on the child she has borne?
Though she may forget,
    I will not forget you!
See, I have engraved you on the palms of my hands.
ISAIAH 49:15–16

ONE DAY IN PRAYER, I SENSED THAT GOD WAS TELLING ME VERY directly that Lisa wasn't just my wife; she's also his daughter, and I was to treat her accordingly.

This was a moment of revelation for me, and the force of this insight grew once I had kids of my own. If you want to get on my "good side," just be good to one of my kids. A wonderful young woman at our church became Allison's "big sister," taking her out to Starbucks or for ice cream and being a positive influence. And my wife and I will love Amy for the rest of our lives. Why? She was generous and kind to one of our children.

Conversely, if you really want to make me angry, pick on my kids. Be mean to them. Bully them. You'll fire up my righteous anger faster than anything you could possibly do to me.

So when I realized I am married to *God's daughter* — and that you, women, are married to *God's sons* — everything about how I view marriage changed overnight. It was no longer about just me and one other person; it was very much a relationship with a passionately interested third partner. We have been encouraged to contemplate the Fatherhood of God, a wonderful and true doctrine. But if you want to change your marriage, extend this analogy and spend some time thinking about God as Father-*in-Law*. Because he is!

When I fail to respect my wife—when I demean her or trouble her, when I'm condescending toward her or mistreat her in any way—I am courting trouble with the heavenly Father, who feels passionately about my spouse's welfare.

Most of us fail to grasp just how fully God loves the person we married. Even if you were to spend ten years thinking about it, you'd still fall short of how much God truly cares about your spouse. He designed and created the person to whom you are married. He wooed him or her to regeneration. He adores and feels passionately about him or her. If any doubt remains as to his care and concern, consider this: he sent his Son to die on his or her behalf.

As the human father of three children, I fervently pray that each one of my children will marry a spouse who will love him or her generously and respect and enjoy him or her. I realize each of my children has certain quirks or limitations that might test a future spouse, but I pray that their spouses will be kind in these areas rather than use them to belittle my children or make them feel smaller. I hope with all my heart they'll find partners who will encourage them with a gracious spirit. I pray they won't marry someone who will be stingy or selfish or who might abuse them. I know my kids aren't perfect—but I want them to have spouses who will love them despite their imperfections.

In the same way, God is fully aware of our spouses' limitations—and he is just as eager for us to be kind and generous with these faults as we are for our kids' future spouses to be kind to them.

Think about how you treated your husband or wife this past week—is that how you want your son or daughter to be treated by his or her spouse? Never forget: you didn't just marry a man or a woman; you married God's son or God's daughter.

Treat him, treat her, accordingly.

6

The Gift of Fear

I feared the anger and wrath of the Lord.
DEUTERONOMY 9:19

IF I COULD PREACH ONLY ONE SERMON TO THE CHURCH TODAY, IT wouldn't be about faith. We hear more about faith today than ever before in the history of the church.

It would be about fear.

Moses felt motivated by a godly fear of a holy God: "I feared the anger and wrath of the LORD" (Deuteronomy 9:19). According to the book of Isaiah, Jesus had more than mere wisdom and understanding and knowledge; he also lived with a healthy fear of the Lord (Isaiah 11:2–3).

Biblical fear is more complex and profound than what we usually think of when we use the English word *fear*. It isn't defined fully by the words *terror* and *dread*. Although it encompasses these emotions, it also carries the idea of a passionate love, the positive desire to please God, and a worshipful awe.³

God is gracious—yes! God is merciful—absolutely! God is kind and good and loving and caring—no doubt! But it is still a fearful thing to offend God, to fall into his holy hands, for he is a just God with the power and might and will to carry out judgments against those who offend him. Our Lord used this godly fear to root the early church in a proper attitude toward him. Ananias and Sapphira lost their lives when they tried to deceive the apostolic leaders. The surviving community responded just as God intended: "Great fear seized the whole church and all who heard about these events" (Acts 5:11). Keep

306

in mind, this is the church *after* Pentecost, filled with the Holy Spirit but still needing an appropriate fear to help its members live godly lives.

How does this relate to marriage? It's directly tied to last week's devotion. Your heavenly Father-in-Law never takes his eyes off his beloved child. He hears every word uttered in anger toward his children. He sees every act of violence; he witnesses every act of denial, manipulation, and control. Never imagine that he witnesses such assaults with a dispassionate apathy; on the contrary, he feels each slight as though you were persecuting Christ himself.

That's the truth of Acts 9. Saul thought he was persecuting the Christians, but Jesus made it very personal: "'Who are you, Lord?' Saul had asked after Jesus called out to him. 'I am Jesus, whom you are persecuting'" (Acts 9:5).

You didn't marry an orphan; you married a man or woman with a very influential, very powerful, and all-seeing Dad. Based on how you're loving and caring for your spouse, how happy do you think your heavenly Father-in-Law feels with you? Is he smiling over your extravagant love? Or are you storing up his anger and wrath because of how you're mistreating his precious son or daughter?

I fully realize that talking about the fear of God seems outdated. Recently a pastor told me outright he didn't believe he should "fear" God but rather "love" him. And yet the Bible is clear that "[the church] was strengthened; and encouraged by the Holy Spirit, it grew in numbers, living in the fear of the Lord" (Acts 9:31).

Listen, I adore God. I feel safe with him. But I also fear him. The biggest changes in my marriage have come from listening to God in prayer, from being chastised and rebuked and encouraged directly by him. Most of us know by now that physical attraction won't hold a marriage together. We also realize that the trials of living with a sinner will, in time, temper our romantic affection.

But the fear of God — that's eternal. That lasts. That's a solid foundation on which to build a lifelong marriage. God hears every conversation. He sees every act of every day. He even reads our thoughts. I might be three thousand miles away from my wife, far from her sight, but the God before whom I promised I'd be faithful is in that hotel room with me.

I've come to view the fear of God as a shelter, a covering, a mighty force. I know I'm sinful. I know my own good intentions are far too weak in the face of way too many temptations. I've broken promises before, so I know I can break them again. But I've also found that my fear of God is growing greater than my rebellion; it reins in my baser instincts. It helps me to make choices that lead me to become the type of man I want to be rather than the type of man I despise.

I can't imagine living a single day without the fear of the Lord—and there's no way I could contemplate trying to be married without that same covering. The best gift you can give your spouse is to fear the God who made him or her. That's a gift that *truly* keeps on giving.

Don't Look Back

Therefore, if anyone is in Christ, he is a new creation;
the old has gone, the new has come!
2 Corinthians 5:17

A RELATIONSHIP FROM MY TEEN YEARS STILL MAKES ME WINCE whenever the girl's name comes to mind and I think about the hurt I caused her. One day recently I was wondering and praying about looking her up to tell her how sorry I felt for how I acted twenty-five years ago.

One of my best friends — a marriage and family therapist from San Diego — adamantly opposed the idea. "Gary," Steve said, "I'm thinking this is more about you than it is about her." In his counseling experience, Steve has discovered that looking up someone after two and a half decades can be dangerous; you don't know where he or she is coming from or what's happening in his or her life. The potential for hurt is just as great as the potential for healing.

But the clincher came when he said, "Look, why don't you take all the energy you're using thinking about this and spend it on planning how you can love your wife *today?*"

That's when it dawned on me: Guilt attacks us by using a dead relationship to distract us from a living one.

I remember the time a woman approached me after I had taught on the topic of sacred history — the meaning two people build together when they persevere through the difficult seasons in life. After hearing me talk, she felt convinced she had sought an unbiblical divorce with her first husband — but it was too late to go back. She had remarried and her ex-husband had remarried, and now she was poisoning her current marriage with the dead relationship from the past.

"The real danger here," I said, "is that through this guilt about the past, you'll fail to love your second husband, just like you failed your first husband. It seems to me your charge is to focus on loving your current husband like he's never been or ever will be loved. You need to stop thinking about your first husband, and focus on the husband you're called to love *now*."

I saw a light go on in her countenance when I said this — and I could see visible relief on her second husband's face. Clearly, he had been feeling cheated.

Some things in our past can't be "fixed." You can repent, you can ask for forgiveness; but you can't always go back — nor should you try. Some of us are more introspective and hold on to our guilt in such a way that we become blinded to our present obligations.

When guilt comes knocking on your door about a failed relationship from the past, start praying about how to love your spouse today. Don't let a dead relationship pollute or weigh down a living one.

For others, the dead relationship isn't about guilt but about fantasy. These folks allow a relationship that never worked out to steal the energy they should be pouring into their marriage. "If only I had married him instead!" they think, or, "I wonder what so-and-so is doing right now?" So instead of praying about how to love his or her spouse, he or she daydreams about being married to this other person.

There are few things so destructive and self-defeating as giving way to such fantasies — fantasies that can't be fulfilled in a biblically appropriate way. Since there's little chance this relationship can happen (I've even heard people confess they've tried to justify these thoughts by wondering what might happen if their current spouse died), it is simply wasted time — time stolen from what you could be using to make your current marriage more meaningful.

Besides, there's a reason behind why this dead relationship isn't a living one! Our memories tend to be very selective. We forget the negative and fixate on the positive — and every such fantasy robs our spouses of energy and thought that should be expended on them.

Don't look back. You're cheating your spouse — and ultimately yourself — when you do. Pour all your energy into something current and real.

8

Fame Is Trumped
by Intimacy

*I belong to my lover,
and his desire is for me.*
SONG OF SONGS 7:10

JOHN WOODEN IS THE UNDISPUTED BEST AT WHAT HE DID. YOU CAN
debate the greatest college football coach of all time; you can debate
the best professional basketball coach. But there's no debating the
best college basketball coach of all time.

It's John Wooden, hands down.

Wooden's UCLA Bruins won ten NCAA championships. No
other coach has won more than four. In an incredible three-and-a-
half-year run, his Bruins went undefeated for eighty-eight straight
games. Now that it seems as though twelve-year-olds are entering
the NBA draft, it's highly unlikely any other coach will ever have a
program stable enough to match that string.

Wooden retired in 1975 but remains so respected that he can
hardly enter a room without getting a standing ovation. Many pub-
lishers would eagerly throw a six-figure contract at him if he would
write another book. He could command speaking fees in the tens of
thousands.

But Coach Wooden has his eyes on something other than popular acclaim. Rick Reilly, a writer for *Sports Illustrated*, paid Coach
Wooden a visit and soon found himself in something of an awkward
situation. How do you tactfully tell a man in his nineties that you

hope he doesn't die because this world still needs him and there's nobody else like him waiting in the wings?

Coach Wooden picked up on Rick's message and finally said, "I'm not afraid to die. Death is my only chance to be with her again."[4]

The "her" John referred to was his wife, Nellie, who died in 1985 after fifty-three years of marriage. John is still very connected to this woman. On the twenty-first of every month, he writes a passionate letter to Nellie, telling her how much he misses her, loves her, and values the time they had together. Then he folds the letter and puts it on a pile near where he sleeps.

That stack now has over two hundred letters.

By his own admission, John would gladly leave this world of acclaim if in doing so he could be reunited with the love of his life.

I don't believe I'm insulting you by saying you'll never achieve the acclaim of John Wooden. You may be very, very good at what you do —but can you ever honestly hope to be considered the absolute best of anyone who has ever pursued your profession?

So often, we ignore our marriages in pursuit of high acclaim — but John Wooden, a man who received that acclaim, would gladly give it up for more time with his wife: "I'm not afraid to die. Death is my only chance to be with her again."

Sadly, many of us learn this lesson too late. We spend our entire lives ignoring the glory and power of true love and intimacy with one person for the elusive elixir of fame. Let's learn a lesson from a man who has been there—who has seen both sides and who remains convinced that a relationship with a spouse who truly knows you and loves you and who walks with you is far more fulfilling to the soul than receiving applause from the crowd or adoration from afar.

Of course, most of us won't even smell national acclaim. Even so, we shortchange our spouses for something much smaller: a corner office, a pay raise, the esteem of our neighborhood friends, two strokes off our golf handicap, fear that others will look down on our family-centered lifestyle ...

If you're a wife, you may be chided for showing such concern and attention to your husband. It's certainly out of fashion to even think about being a devoted wife. Just witness the controversy surrounding the release of Dr. Laura Schlessinger's book *The Proper Care and Feeding of Your Husband*. Some will mock you for "degrading" yourself and urge you to "get your own life."

And yet, if you will ignore this disdain and truly dedicate yourself to loving this man, you will receive far more in the end than you ever will from others' approval. Consider the poem "To Her Loving Husband," written by the Puritan wife Anne Bradstreet:

> If ever two were one, then surely we.
> If ever man were lov'd by wife, then thee;
> If ever wife was happy in a man,
> Compare with me, ye women, if you can.[5]

Have any of your mockers ever felt such a sentiment about their husbands? Have they ever known such a love?

You can.

Go for something real. Develop an appetite for authentic intimacy. Dive into your marriage, and discover the quiet but profound pleasure of loving and being loved, of truly knowing and being known. To be loved well and to be known completely by one is far more fulfilling than being adored by many and truly known by none.

9

A Soul Filled with God

One thing I ask of the Lord,
this is what I seek:
that I may dwell in the house of the Lord
all the days of my life,
to gaze upon the beauty of the Lord
and to seek him in his temple.

PSALM 27:4

PERSONAL WORSHIP IS AN ABSOLUTE NECESSITY FOR A STRONG MARRIAGE. It comes down to this: If I stop receiving from God, I start demanding from others. Instead of appreciating and loving and serving others, I become disappointed in them. Instead of cherishing my wife, I become aware of her shortcomings. I take out my frustrations with a less-than-perfect life and somehow blame *her* for my lack of fulfillment.

But when my heart gets filled by God's love and acceptance, I'm set free to love instead of worrying about being loved. I'm motivated to serve instead of becoming obsessed about whether I'm being served. I'm moved to cherish instead of feeling unappreciated.

Madeleine complains about a lack of spiritual intimacy in her relationship with her husband, Martin. "He's never been what you might call a spiritual leader," she says, and this has become almost an obsession for her—as though her own spiritual health depends on her husband suddenly becoming mature.

"Did Teresa of Avila have a spiritual leader?" I asked her. "Madame Guyon? Mother Teresa of Calcutta? What about the countless widows who now pursue God on their own? Were—and are—their lives empty simply because they aren't married to a spiritually mature man?"

Tim is upset because his wife never initiates physical intimacy. Like Madeleine, he's become fixated on one issue in his marriage, so that he can hardly even pray—which makes him feel even more emotionally dependent on the sexual intimacy he's not getting. "Tim," I said, "I remember praying with a husband whose wife was in the last stages of severe multiple sclerosis. It had been years since they could enjoy anything even approximating normal sexual relations. Do you think God has wired this world in such a way that her husband has no chance to be happy and fulfilled because his wife can't initiate —or even perform?"

Tim had expected me to preach only to his wife, not to him. "In fact," I added, "he found great joy in taking care of her—and that meant cleaning out a bedpan on a regular basis."

Certainly, spiritual intimacy and sexual relations are legitimate desires, but you know what? Whenever I place my happiness in the hands of another human being, I'm virtually guaranteeing some degree of disappointment. It can be as frivolous as a barista not getting my chai at Starbucks just the way I like it, or it can be as profound as some pastor I really admire falling into sin.

That's why worship sets me free. It meets my most basic need—to rest in the fact that I am known and loved, that I have a purpose, and that my eternal destiny and delight are secure—so that lesser needs (including spiritual companionship and sexual desires) serve the role of an occasional dessert rather than my main meal.

It's simply not fair to ask your spouse to fulfill you. No one can. If you expect your spouse to be God for you, your spouse will fail every day and on every account. Not only that, should your disappointment lead you to divorce, your second, third, and even fourth spouses will fail you too!

Only one can love you like God, with a perfect, constantly steady, and giving love—and that is God himself. When the "one thing" we seek is to dwell in God's house, to gaze upon his beauty, and to seek him in his temple, our soul's sense of desperate need is met in our heavenly Father's arms. Then we leave this temple and find tremendous joy in giving, in loving, and in serving rather than in keeping close accounts as to whether we're being loved or being served.

Maybe it's just me, but I've seen a constant formula at work in my life: the less I receive from God, the more I demand from my wife; the more I receive from God, the more I am set free to give to my wife.

The best thing you can do for your marriage is to fill your soul with God. Start defining disappointment with your spouse as spiritual hunger, a cosmic call to worship. Marriage is a wonderful institution, but it is limited. It can't replace God. Don't ask it to.

10

The Foundation
of Fellowship

But if we walk in the light, as he is in the light,
we have fellowship with one another,
and the blood of Jesus, his Son, purifies us from all sin.
1 JOHN 1:7

AN ACTRESS WHO ONCE HAD ONE OF THE MOST POPULAR SHOWS ON cable television wrote a sex manual with her husband, praising him as an "artist" and liberally sharing the delight the two of them experienced in bed.

Barely a year after the book came out, the actress announced that she and her husband had separated. Later, the two divorced.

Couples won't save their marriages by becoming athletes in bed. They won't stave off divorce by increasing their income. They won't find that having children will reinvigorate a dead marriage. All these efforts have been tried and found wanting, because what most frustrated marriages lack is what the Bible calls *fellowship*.

I know, fellowship sounds like a pretty mundane word. How can fellowship ever hope to compete with sex?

It doesn't have to. That's the beauty of Christian marriage: we can completely embrace the intoxicating pleasure of physical passion, while also appreciating the profound but quieter fulfillment of fellowship.

God made us social beings, and a lot of couples do "social" things: go out to dinner, watch a movie or television, take a vacation, and,

318

yes, have sex. But these social things fall short of the biblical meaning of fellowship. What often gets left behind is the deeply meaningful interaction between two believers, both filled with the Holy Spirit, who encourage each other by their mutual passion for God and who use their God-given spiritual gifts to build each other up as together they seek first the kingdom of God.

This is the heart of biblical fellowship. It is sharing spiritual struggles, being open to loving confrontation and rebuke, and submitting ourselves to the correction of God's Word, appropriately applied. It is praying for and with each other. It is encouraging each other to fully use the gifts God has given us, testifying to the risen Christ through his work in our bodies. It is cultivating *together* an increased passion for God. Such a fellowship will maintain loyalty between the peaks of physical passion.

I have been married for almost two decades now, and the longer I'm married, the more convinced I become that my primary relationship with Lisa — even above being married to her — is as her brother in Christ. This is an eternal bond we'll share for the next ten million years (and beyond). As her brother in the Lord, I am committed to her well-being, even apart from how we are doing in our marriage. I want the best for her. I want her to grow in holiness — not so *my* life will be easier (God's work in her may, in fact, inconvenience me), but so she will surrender to God's will for her life.

When our marriages have an empty spiritual core, we put too much emphasis on things that can't sustain or nurture a marriage — like sex. Sex is a wonderful gift, but it can't fill an empty spiritual core. The emphasis we place on it can be almost comical. Here's an example: Lisa and I love to go on walks in the woods; it's one of our favorite things to do together. It would never occur to me after such a walk to immediately pelt Lisa with the question, "So, was that an especially good walk?"

"What are you talking about?"

"Well, was that walk as good for you as it was for me?"

"Gary, have you lost your mind?"

"I want to know! Was that walk better than the last walk? Was it maybe the best walk you've ever had?"

Such talk would cheapen an activity we greatly enjoy doing together, and it would put absurd pressure on each episode.

Without a strong spiritual core, we give certain activities an emphasis they don't deserve, while ignoring the things that really do create long-term intimacy.

Improving your skills in bed may have its place, but good sex alone won't create a good marriage, and good sex doesn't necessarily — by any means — lead to better fellowship. On the other hand, strong fellowship almost always leads to better sex. Sex is, inherently, a spiritual activity, even though it is expressed in very physical terms. In his book *Sex, Romance, and the Glory of God*, C. J. Mahaney puts it this way:

> When Carolyn and I are behind closed doors and locked in a passionate embrace, that moment is either enhanced or diminished by how well I have been leading in the area of loving communication. So, to talk about romantic communication and creativity is not to delay talking about sex. It is to talk about what makes for the best sex. Communication and sex are inseparable. It's not as though sex is one thing and communication is something else. Life doesn't divide up into neat little compartments like that, especially in the oneness of marriage. It's all one thing.[6]

Most of us don't need to spice up our marriages so much as we need to dig deeper in the Lord. Are you asking your sexual relationship to compensate for a lack of spiritual intimacy? That's backwards! Spend some time this week thinking about how the two of you can better express what it means to be a brother and sister in the Lord. How can you pray for each other? How can you share more honestly and more intimately? How can you encourage each other in your individual passion for God?

Nothing else on this earth rivals the inner satisfaction of a relationship built on biblical fellowship.

11

The Heart To

Above all else, guard your heart,
for it is the wellspring of life.
PROVERBS 4:23

MARK, A MIDWESTERN FAMILY PHYSICIAN WITH A GOOD EYE FOR investments, has lifted his family into affluence through hard work. He's provided his wife—who comes from a poorer background—with a good living, and he's the type of husband who does the dishes, puts the kids to bed while his wife reads or takes a bath, and is the first to volunteer for "car duty" (taking the kids to their sporting and church events).

Because of his job, Mark needs to literally leave the city to get away from his work—otherwise, someone stops him after church to ask about a sore shoulder or an irregular heartbeat. At the grocery store, he can be asked to diagnose a rash, and at the library he might be stopped to give his opinion on a daily aspirin regimen that someone just heard mentioned on the radio.

More than anything, Mark appreciates getting away with his wife, so the two of them can enjoy each other's company without interruption. It would mean even more to him if his wife would plan a weekend, or even just a night away, six to eight times a year. It's not as though Charlotte (Mark's wife) isn't equipped to handle this. Before the investments came in, she used to work in the travel industry; but she now has the opportunity to do basically whatever she wants.

Even so, by the time I spoke with Mark, it had been almost a year since Charlotte had planned anything like this. Mark reminds

Charlotte of this every five months or so, which usually results in a heated argument that ends with Charlotte saying, "Fine, go get your calendar and we'll plan something right now."

"That *really* makes me want to get away," Mark says sarcastically.

While how-to marriage books and seminars certainly have their value and place, on their own they miss the key issue. It's not really about *how* to; far more often, it's about whether we have the *heart* to. Charlotte knows how to please her husband; she just lacks the heart to do it.

Motivation is more than half the battle. You don't have to teach an infatuated couple how to communicate. Infatuated couples don't read books about resolving disputes; they don't watch instructional videos about making time for each other. Why not? Because when you possess the heart to do these things, the how-to takes care of itself.

If the two of you used to communicate, used to keep romance alive, used to find ways to maintain intimacy in spite of differing opinions, that's evidence enough that, somewhere, you already possess these basic skills. It's not like you lost the skills you had as a younger man or woman. The real issue is whether you're willing to exercise those skills.

If I have the heart to romance my wife, I'll find a way to romance her. I was great at romancing her twenty years ago. In fact, I wrote her cards and letters, taped little notes around her room, planned creative dates—the works. Now, in my forties, do I have fewer romance skills than I possessed in my twenties?

Of course not. The real issue is, do I have less heart for such activities in my forties than I had in my twenties? Am I acting "out of reverence for God" (2 Corinthians 7:1), pursuing Lisa just as aggressively out of a motivation of faith as formerly I felt motivated by mere emotion? Or am I allowing daily duties to take time and energy away from loving my wife?

Charlotte knows she is married to a loving, godly man who is a good provider. She also knows he doesn't ask much in return—but she has lost the heart to give him even that. She knows how to plan an outing, but for whatever reason, she has lost the will.

In the same way, most wives know what their husbands want. Most have a basic understanding of how to please him. That's not to say you can't pick up a few helpful tips along the way, but you know most of what you need to know to make your husband a satisfied spouse. The real question is, do you have the heart to do what you know how to do?

Sometimes, we hide behind the how-to because it doesn't feel as shameful as purposefully withholding on our spouses. Men say, "I don't know how to romance my wife. After all, I'm a guy!" But what we really mean is, "It's more acceptable to play the 'stupid male' role than to admit I'm so self-centered that I fail to take the time to show my wife how much I cherish her."

Can I challenge you to spend just as much time examining your heart as you do filling your head? Will you sit before the Lord for as long as you pore over the latest self-help book? Will you allow the Holy Spirit to convict, instruct, chasten, and encourage?

Be quiet throughout this week. Listen to the Lord's still, small voice. Let him name your true motivation. I hope those motivations will be charity, kindness, goodwill, patience, and love. But mixed in with such attitudes may be spite, bitterness, resentment, selfishness, or sheer laziness. Ask the Lord to show you where you're withholding on your spouse. Let him hold up a mirror to your heart's true condition.

Keep in mind that it's not as though the heart is ever fixed once and for all. While I may have the "heart to" today, it doesn't guarantee I'll have the "heart to" tomorrow. We need to regularly examine our hearts.

Listen: when we first laid eyes on our spouses and decided to make them ours, we found a way to attract and maintain their attention. We had far less knowledge of our spouses then than we have today —but we also had the heart then, and that made all the difference. If you've fallen into a silent season, nine times out of ten it's an issue of the heart, not of a lack of knowledge.

Fire up that will! Let God charge your motivation. You already know most of what you need to know. Now, you just have to get busy doing it. What one thing can you do today?

$$12$$

The Preyer

Be self-controlled and alert.
Your enemy the devil prowls around like a roaring lion
looking for someone to devour.
1 PETER 5:8

PREVIOUS GENERATIONS OF CHRISTIANS MAY HAVE PAID TOO MUCH attention to the devil, but our age tends to pay him too little heed. The severe truth is that Satan hates your marriage and makes its destruction a nearly daily aim.

It is said that while Francis of Assisi prayed for his Order, "by divine revelation he saw the whole Place surrounded and besieged by devils, as by a great army." Much to Francis's satisfaction, the demons couldn't find a place to enter, until one of the friars was stirred to anger and began to plot revenge on a brother. "As a result, the gate of virtue being abandoned and the door of wickedness being open, he gave the devil a way to come in."[7]

Francis called for the offending brother and confronted him. The brother confessed that he had, indeed, been making vengeful plans; he repented, and the gate to hell slammed shut.

While many today might snicker at such a "primitive" world-view presented in a classic book written almost seven hundred years ago, our modern naïveté concerning spiritual realities is at least as pathetic. When we quarrel with each other; hold resentments; allow bitterness to simmer; play petty games of control, manipulation, and revenge, we do, in fact, open up the door to spiritual beings who seek to destroy the holy family God has called us to create.

Jesus taught constant vigilance when he told his disciples how to pray. The Lord's Prayer includes these words: "And lead us not into temptation, but deliver us from the evil one" (Matthew 6:13). Notice, Jesus didn't say, "deliver us from evil" but from "the evil one." Jesus told his followers to regularly petition God so that they wouldn't fall prey to the evil one's schemes.

A married couple's relationship is the inner fortress in a cosmic spiritual battle. This fortress is not limited to just a man and woman; it also protects the children who result from that union. Even more than that, it protects generations of grandchildren and great-grandchildren, who will be influenced by their ancestors.

With so much at stake, can we afford to be lackadaisical? Dare we forget that a powerful, pernicious being has made it his aim to wreck what God is trying to build? Even worse, are we cooperating with his agenda? By our actions, whether physical (flirting with an office mate, viewing pornography, getting so busy we have little or no time to work on our marriages) or spiritual (refusing to forgive, holding a grudge, neglecting to build spiritual intimacy), are we foolishly and recklessly putting our marriages at risk?

Because Satan exists, we must remain vigilant over our souls and our relationships and refuse to provide any open doors that can invite Satan to work his wiles. One "little" thing, left untended, can be nursed and built up to become a major issue.

Flush out all of it today. Ask God to give you a forgiving heart, a loving heart, and a pure heart. Keep moving toward your spouse. Ask God to close any doors you have foolishly left open. Guard what God has given you; give Satan no place to enter.

13

Love Mercy

Love mercy.
MICAH 6:8

A COUPLE ASKED TO SPEAK TO ME AFTER A "SACRED MARRIAGE" seminar. The husband had done some truly heinous things, and their marriage seemed on the verge of breaking up. The wife rightfully desired to call him to account. We talked for over an hour, and both of them left in tears — good tears that were bringing healing and restoration.

I gave the sermon at their church the next morning, and the husband sheepishly approached me after the services. "I bet I'm the worst man you've ever preached to," he said.

"You've certainly done some awful things," I admitted, "and you and your wife invited me into some of your worst moments — but I know that's not the whole story. If someone created a video of *my* worst moments, and that's all you were to see about me, you'd be tempted to kick me out of this church before you'd shake my hand."

Because we married a sinner, we're going to see some ugly, ugly things. That's why our attitude toward another's sin will determine, in large part, the degree of intimacy we can achieve in marriage. A Pharisee might impress a mate, but he'll never get truly close to her, because judgment repels intimacy as surely as heat melts ice.

One glorious day, God used a Bible verse to open my eyes to a reality so large that it changed everything about how I view my marriage and my standing before God, as well as how I am to treat others.

326

Micah 6:8 tell us to "love mercy." That short phrase—"love mercy" —kept playing in my mind.

Love mercy. Micah isn't telling us merely to "demonstrate" mercy or only to "practice" mercy; he tells us to fall in love with it!

The wide, biblical concept of mercy includes forgiveness but also has roots in loyalty. One commentator notes, "This steady, persistent refusal of God to wash his hands of wayward Israel is the essential meaning of the Hebrew word which is translated loving-kindness [or mercy]."[8] This is a loyalty and forgiveness seasoned with graciousness and kindness—particularly to those who don't deserve it. It is one of the most beautiful words in the English language and certainly one of the most precious truths in the Christian faith.

What does it mean to fall in love with mercy? It means I am to become mercy's biggest fan. Having received mercy from God, I am to walk in assurance and thankfulness, using my own gift of mercy as the lens through which I view anyone else's sin—including that of my spouse.

Mercy is wonderful. Without mercy, I'd be damned for all eternity. Through his mercy, God made a way for me to enjoy eternal happiness instead of never-ending pain and torture. Mercy also allows me to minister. As a fallen man who sins daily, I could never even begin to reach out to others with God's perfect gospel unless every hour I live in the joy of knowing that Jesus Christ's sacrifice on my behalf has set me free and washed me clean. In short, without mercy, I'd be toast; but with mercy, the celebratory toast never ends!

Falling in love with mercy means I love everything about it. It means I also love the way it applies to the person I married. Just as I love my wife when she's in the kitchen, the living room, and the bedroom, so I love mercy when it's applied to me, my wife, and my children. There is no arena where I don't delight in mercy. People who love mercy feel eager to show mercy to others. Like God, they not only *want* to forgive, they are *eager* to forgive. You don't have to convince them to show mercy; they love to show mercy!

A Christian spouse who understands mercy is a husband or wife who looks forward to another opportunity to demonstrate God's grace. It is a believer eager to forgive, whose first thought leaps toward reconciliation rather than revenge. Mercy isn't an obligation grudgingly given in to — it's the love of his or her life! It's his or her favorite practice.

Listen to one of the most practical applications of mercy I've ever read about. A wife got in an accident while driving a brand-new car. She felt understandably upset, fretting about what her husband would say when he found out. As she retrieved the insurance papers from the glove compartment, she found this note in her husband's handwriting: "Dear Mary, when you need these papers, remember it's you I love, not the car."[9]

You are an imperfect, very fallible, prone-to-mess-up sinner saved by mercy. You married a fallible sinner who needs the same remedy. The intimacy of marriage cannot be sustained without mercy. Our sin and guilt are so powerful that, absent mercy, every human relationship will fall before their might. You can self-righteously judge every spouse who has ever lived. You can prove his or her guilt in a court of law. You can compellingly state your case and clearly demonstrate how far your spouse has fallen short — but the judgment you render will kill intimacy in your own life; it won't kill sin in your spouse's life. It will also herald your spiritual poverty and destruction: "Judgment without mercy will be shown to anyone who has not been merciful. Mercy triumphs over judgment!" (James 2:13).

This week, meditate on mercy. Fall in love with it. Seek to understand what a gift you've been given in God's mercy. And then, from that foundation, explore the riches of extending this same mercy to others, beginning with your spouse. Commit to memory the theologically crucial phrase "Mercy triumphs over judgment," and seek to build your marriage anew on the back of God's gift rather than on the failed policies of the legalistic Pharisees.

14

One Bad Habit

Be perfect, therefore, as your heavenly Father is perfect.
MATTHEW 5:48

I WASN'T HAPPY WITH MY WIFE.

Our family had talked about observing Lent, and without a moment's hesitation, both Lisa and my son, Graham, had it planned for me: "You need to give up Pepsi."

What, they think I couldn't do it? What is Lent — forty-six days? (We don't observe Lent like the Roman Catholics, who get to imbibe on Sunday; our family goes for an "absolute" Lent, from Ash Wednesday all the way up to Easter morning.) I could handle six and a half weeks, no problem.

Two weekends into the ordeal, I called Lisa from the Chicago airport. "Look," I complained, "I don't have a lot of diversions on the road. I don't look at *Playboy.* I don't rent dirty movies at the hotel. I don't get drinks at the bar. I don't even enjoy the occasional cigar on the golf course. What's so bad about a daily Pepsi? Why did you say I should give that up?"

"Those drinks are so bad for you," Lisa answered.

"Can't I have just one stinking vice?" I protested. "Just one?! You encouraged me to give up the one thing I can enjoy when I'm traveling and tired and stuck in an airport. Thanks a lot."

But you know what? Forty-six days later, after breaking the habit, I realized I really don't need a daily Pepsi. And how pathetic, anyway, that I count my one pleasure on the road sitting down with a sugary soft drink to get a caffeine pick-me-up? Breaking away from that "one stinking vice" helped me see that, in the long run, I might feel a lot better if I occasionally settled for an iced tea.

Admittedly, whether I drink a daily Pepsi is a very trivial matter —but the principle behind it goes much deeper. My statement "Can't I have just one stinking vice?" has infected my own and many other marriages on a much more significant and profound level. Husbands may say, "Look, I don't have affairs. I don't gamble with the mortgage money. I'm home in the evening. Yeah, I occasionally lose my temper and wound you with a few careless words, but am I not allowed one vice?"

Wives may say, "I've been a faithful wife. I don't bust the family budget. I'm there for my family. Maybe at times I talk negatively about my husband behind his back when he really ticks me off, but all in all, I think he has it pretty good."

And so we excuse something we know we should change, but we ignore it, based on the faulty assumption that, since we are generally good husbands and wives, we can maintain our "one little vice."

But the Bible doesn't give us permission to ignore "one little vice." Second Corinthians 7:1 urges us to "purify ourselves from *everything* that contaminates body and spirit, perfecting holiness out of reverence for God" (emphasis added). When we say, "All in all, my spouse has it OK," we're not perfecting holiness; we're excusing wickedness.

I have a tendency to get a little short with my wife when a publishing deadline approaches—and this book was no exception. Just days before my editor needed the manuscript, Lisa and I had a misunderstanding, to which I responded in a less-than-gracious manner. I can excuse these episodes with, "Well, I'm under a lot of pressure right now, so it's to be expected," or I can take the attitude of perfecting holiness, resolving that I don't want to treat my wife like that—*ever*. Being generally gracious to her during the eleven and a half months of the year where I'm free of a deadline (not that I always am) doesn't mean I've stored up the right to neglect her or get short with her for those other two weeks. Instead, I can learn to recognize the temptation and more effectively prepare to deal with the stress in a way that won't wound my wife.

We fail to see that one hole can sink a ship as effectively as can ten holes; it may take a little longer, but the ship will still sink. Since any hole can threaten a marriage, such cavalier thinking has to be challenged.

The truth is, I'm *not* granted "one little vice." Jesus said, "Be perfect, therefore, as your heavenly Father is perfect" (Matthew 5:48). If something injures my relationship with Lisa, out of love I will work with God's Spirit to root that habit out of my life. I won't make excuses by pointing to the lack of other negative things about me, and I won't try to hide behind my strengths. A weakness is a weakness, regardless of any strengths that surround it. Sin is sin, regardless of how many virtues accompany it.

Doing good doesn't create marital "bank deposits" that allow us to make vice-ridden "withdrawals." Don't excuse that one little vice. Keep in mind that, apart from Christ's sacrifice, just "one little vice" would keep you out of heaven for all eternity.

This week, stop yourself when you start making excuses or try to explain away personality faults by thinking, "All in all, my spouse has it pretty good." Instead, challenge yourself with Scripture: "Be perfect, therefore, as your heavenly Father is perfect."

15

Soul Mate
or Sole Mate?

Greater love has no one than this,
that he lay down his life for his friends.

JOHN 15:13

WELL OVER TWO THOUSAND YEARS AGO, THE GREEK PHILOSOPHER
Plato surmised that a perfect human being was tragically split in two,
resulting in a race of creatures sentenced to spend the rest of their
lives searching for that missing other who can complete them.

Thus was created the notion of the "soul mate."

Despite its bizarre historical underpinnings, the notion of a soul
mate has rooted itself in our culture, inspiring countless movies, novels,
and Top 40 songs. One Rutgers University study found that 94 percent
of people in their twenties say that the first requirement in a spouse
is being such a soul mate. Just as surprising, 87 percent think they'll
actually find that person "when they are ready."[10] A culture suspicious
of God has nevertheless brazenly embraced some sort of forceful and
intelligent destiny that brings two lovelorn souls together!

But there's a danger in this line of thinking. Many people mistake
a storm of emotion as the identifying mark of their soul mate. A student of my friend Byron Weathersbee once declared that she wanted
to marry a man because "he gives me butterflies."

While we may laugh at this, I've seen far too many couples want
to end a marriage simply because the butterflies have left. Individuals
captivated by the "soul mate" line of thinking marry on an infatua-

332

tion binge without seriously considering character, compatibility, life goals, family desires, spiritual health, and other important concerns. Then when the music fades and the relationship requires work, one or both partners suddenly discover that they were "mistaken": this person must not be their soul mate after all! Otherwise, it wouldn't be so much work. Next they panic. Their soul mate must still be out there! Such people can't get to divorce court fast enough, lest someone steal their "one true soul mate" meant only for them.

When we get married for trivial reasons, we tend to seek divorce for trivial reasons.

Can I suggest a more biblical pattern? Instead of following Plato in a wild pursuit of our soul mate, we should seek to find a biblical "sole mate." A sole mate is someone who willingly does the shoe-leather application of living out biblical love. The most accurate definition of true love is found in John 15:13: "Greater love has no one than this, that he lay down his life for his friends."

This love isn't based on feelings but on sacrifice. It pictures love, not as an emotion, but as a policy—a commitment we choose to keep. Such a love is not based on the worthiness of the person being loved —none of us deserve Christ's sacrifice!—but on the worthiness of the One who calls us to love: "We love because [God] first loved us" (1 John 4:19). This takes us back to the very first devotion: loving our spouses "out of reverence for God" (2 Corinthians 7:1).

A "sole mate" appreciates the truth that marriage is a school of character. He cherishes his spouse as an imperfect sister in Christ who is helping him develop the biblical skill of love. Clement of Alexandria, an early church father (ca. 150–215), captures this thinking marvelously when he writes, "The prize in the contest of men is shown by him who has trained himself by the discharge of the duties of marriage; by him, I say, who in the midst of his solicitude for his family shows himself inseparable from the love of God."[11]

Such sole mates are women or men who, through the duties and sacrifices of marriage, have trained themselves to love with God's love. They live out the gospel on a daily basis, forgiving, serving, and putting others first in the most ordinary issues of life (putting on a new roll of toilet paper instead of leaving a tiny shred, complimenting others for tasks instead of taking them for granted, being gracious instead of condemning when someone has had a hard day) in such a way that they see themselves as being in training to be godly (1 Timothy 4:7).

As Christ's follower—as a true sole mate—I'm called to take his example and his definition of love and apply it to my spouse. It really doesn't matter whether my spouse is a "soul mate," as much as it matters that I choose to love her with Christ's love. It means having a sacrificial mind-set marked by generosity, kindness, and mercy—for she certainly is my sole mate, my precious sister in Christ.

Become a biblical sole mate who walks in this truth, who daily travels God's journey of sacrificial love, and who willingly goes into training to be godly. This is a far more stable foundation on which to build a lifelong partnership than the theory of the philosopher Plato.

"Greater love has no one than this, that he lay down his life for his friends." It may not always be the most exciting love, but it is certainly the truest love.

16

Enjoying Each Other

[God] redeemed my soul from going down to the pit,
and I will live to enjoy the light.
Job 33:28

I was on Jekyll Island, Georgia, speaking at a benefit for a pregnancy care center. The center put me up in a beautiful resort Jacuzzi room (alas, Lisa wasn't with me), right on the beach. I spent the bulk of my forty-eight hours there working, wanting to make full use of my time away from my family. But the afternoon of the benefit, God seemed to call me outside. The Lord and I went for a walk on the beach, and I had time to clear my thoughts and enjoy a quiet moment with him.

Sadly, I almost missed that walk. I love the ocean—it reminds me of how small I am, and the wind that invariably greets me I consider a welcome companion. But I felt so preoccupied with getting a lot done that, had it been up to me, I would have left Georgia without so much as touching a single grain of sand. God reminded me that, though work is important, he wants us to enjoy life, too.

The same principle holds true in marriage. We can become so consumed with the challenges of marriage—growing in character, doing the right thing, being a servant, getting all the tasks done, paying attention to our children (the list is endless)—that we forget to enjoy each other.

While I firmly believe growth in holiness is one of God's primary purposes behind marriage, it's not the only one. In fact, God's first stated reason for putting Eve with Adam was that "it is not good for the

335

man to be alone" (Genesis 2:18). This points to companionship. And Deuteronomy 24:5 gave young men an entire year to focus on their wives' happiness: "If a man has recently married, he must not be sent to war or have any other duty laid on him. For one year he is to be free to stay at home and bring happiness to the wife he has married."

We give God glory when we learn to "enjoy the light" (Job 33:28). Accordingly, the Lord calls us into marriage so that we might enjoy each other. Please, let's not allow the realities of life—work, responsibilities, obligations, or even spiritual growth—to blind us to the necessity of enjoying each other's company.

You can't pick up a magazine without reading warnings that a couple shouldn't allow their sex life to wane—but why not just as many warnings that we shouldn't allow our enjoyment of each other to grow lukewarm? Certainly, sex can be part of this enjoyment, but I'm talking about the more common elements of appreciating each other. God could have decreed that I walk this earth by myself—but he has blessed me with a companion whose smile and occasionally giddy nature bring delight into many otherwise dreary days.

And yet our weeks and our evenings can get so busy that we miss times set aside for pure enjoyment. I used to laugh off "date nights" as impractical, but I've since come to see their essential place. A couple needs to set aside some regular time—and the "date" doesn't have to occur in the evening—when they get together simply to enjoy each other. This is God's good plan and design, his gracious gift to us.

When a couple tells me they've fallen into constant quarreling, nine times out of ten it's because their marriage has become utilitarian—who will pick up the kids, did you pay the bills, it's your turn to cook dinner tonight. And the element of enjoyment for pure pleasure goes sadly lacking.

When did you last take a step back and admire your spouse, thanking God you don't have to walk this life alone? When have you taken the time to enjoy a good conversation or a shared walk, or even watched a movie or read a book or went sailing together?

Jesus warned that some miracle workers can get so busy serving him that they cease to know him (Matthew 7:21 – 23). How utterly sad! In the same way, we can get so caught up in the "business" of marriage that we stop relating to, loving, and enjoying each other.

Some evening this week, why not shelve all the discussion about what needs to change, what needs to be done, who's at fault, who's going to drive the kids to soccer — and instead just go out and do what you like to do together? As you do so, recognize God as the author of this enjoyment. He designed us to enjoy each other, and we honor him when we experience this quiet pleasure.

"He redeemed my soul from going down to the pit, and I will live to enjoy the light."

17

Thoughtlessly Cruel

*Remind the people to be ... peaceable and considerate,
and to show true humility toward all men.*

Titus 3:1–2

A COUPLE OF YEARS AGO, MY WIFE PLANTED BLUEBERRIES BESIDE OUR house, about seventy feet away from the nearest faucet. We had a cheap hose at the time that kept splitting as I hauled it across the lawn to water the blueberries. I had to cut the hose and reset a new nozzle every time it split, so I finally got fed up and went to the hardware store and got a "heavy-duty, industrial-strength" hose, *guaranteed* not to split.

I felt so happy with my purchase—finally, a decent hose! It made me smile, just looking at it. I'd pick it up, feel its weight, and say to myself, "No way this baby is *ever* gonna split."

Imagine my chagrin when Lisa barged into the house one evening and exclaimed, "I *hate* that stupid hose!"

My superindustrial-strength beauty proved far too heavy for my poor wife. When she tried to lug it across the front yard and the driveway to reach the side of our house, it felt like she was trying to pull a stubborn mule. I bought that hose thinking of me; I never even considered whether Lisa would be able to lift it.

Although some might consider this a simple inconsiderate act, at a deeper level it revealed my prideful self-centeredness. I didn't mean to act intentionally cruel, but I did act *thoughtlessly* cruel. I simply didn't pay attention to what was best for Lisa. Worse, I hadn't even thought about Lisa when I made the purchase. I had grown tired of repairing the hose, so I determined to make my own life better—as it turned out, at her expense. (We ultimately found a coiled hose that weighed much less but still stretched the necessary distance.)

Spiritual humility—what the ancients called "the queen of the virtues"—invites us to become more thoughtful, more aware, and more sensitive to others. In our arrogance, we can get so wrapped up in our own world that we can't see anyone else.

Humility is often built on the little things in life, and marriage is 90 percent small stuff. These small occurrences are, as writer Andrew Murray puts it, "the tests of eternity" because they reveal what's in our hearts.[12] We don't build humility on giant gestures as much as forge it with consistent, thoughtful actions, day after day.

This "queen of the virtues" so often gets misunderstood. We don't find humility by demeaning ourselves or criticizing ourselves or denying that God has given us obvious gifts and talents. Vertically, we find biblical humility by pointing others to the one true hero of Scripture, namely, God himself: "He must become greater; I must become less" (John 3:30). Horizontally, we find it by thinking less about ourselves and more about others (Philippians 2:4). We embrace humility when we refuse to get so wrapped up in our own worlds that we can examine what we are doing and saying in light of how our actions affect those around us. We find it when we stop pretending we are at the center of the universe, and instead adopt Jesus' attitude of becoming a servant of all (Mark 9:35)—which requires us to start *actively* thinking about others.

What better arena to learn this than in marriage? What relationship seems designed to confront our self-preoccupation more than living with a spouse?

In what areas in your marriage are you being thoughtlessly cruel? Where are you not even considering how your actions (or inactions) are making life difficult for your spouse?

Learn the joy of consideration. Free yourself from the constraints of being focused on yourself. Allow God to use your marriage to teach you to think of others.

18

You Deserve
a Break Today

*Remember the Sabbath day
by keeping it holy.*
Exodus 20:8

SHEILA WAS MARRIED TO A NON-CHRISTIAN FOR ALMOST TWENTY-FIVE years. Though initially she tried to pray fervently and every day for her husband's salvation, she eventually discovered that constant praying without a break was wearing her out. Through trial and error, Sheila found that she simply couldn't pray with equal fervor every day, but at various times, at the prompting of the Holy Spirit, she would enter renewed seasons of intercession—what she now calls her "seasons" of prayer. At the end of one such season, her husband became a believer—more than two decades after they had exchanged their wedding vows.

Sheila's "seasons" make sense to me. Very few spouses can pray intensely over one issue for twenty years. Marriage is a marathon, not a sprint, and at times we have to pace ourselves. That's why an "emotional Sabbath" can be your marriage's best friend.

A biblical view of marriage stresses the heart as a muscle more than as the center of emotion, and muscles need to rest and recover. When I returned to running after my fortieth birthday, I started reading up on modern training techniques. The biggest development over the past two decades seemed to be the crucial aspect of recovery time, as well as the idea of tapering before a long race. You work hard, and then you rest to give your muscles time to recover.

Relationships are no different.

If you're married to an unusually selfish or narcissistic person, a controlling person, a depressed spouse — or even if you're just wed to an average sinner — on some days you may say to yourself, "Today, I just need to survive."

That's OK. The idea of a Sabbath was God's, after all. If you truly are doing most of the giving in your marriage and rarely receiving, you may need to take a short breather — maybe you'll just go shopping, go out for a jog, watch a movie, or slip away for a long walk in the woods.

I'll admit, being married to Lisa, I have it easier than most. But even though I'm married to an agreeable person, on occasion the two of us will butt heads, which usually leads me to fret. My mind is sort of like a Crock-Pot — cooking up a slow-burning mess of stew. It's been a personal fault throughout my life.

On one occasion, I realized I needed, more than anything, just to turn my mind off. I went out by myself (many wives will hate me for suggesting this) and played eighteen holes of golf. Whenever a stray thought would come up, I forced myself to think about the tee shot, the approach shot, or the putt. I wasn't running from my problem — I was taking a break, so that I could look at the situation with fresh eyes and renewed energy.

There's a big difference between escape and refreshment. A genuine, biblical Sabbath of refreshment points back to work; we rest so that we can become even more engaged in the future. We take a break with a view toward returning to the task, asking God to refresh us in order that we might fulfill his high call to love our spouses. It's like sharpening the saw — we're doing something besides the direct work we're called to because in the end it will help us complete that work even better.

If you're in a difficult time in your marriage (and again, every marriage has such seasons), one of the best things you can do is to get out and laugh — find a few friends, rent a comedy, play with your kids, read a long novel, go on a men's or women's retreat. We are limited human beings with finite resources, yet the Bible calls us to a supernatural love beyond our strength. This should teach us two things: we need to radically depend on the Holy Spirit's empowerment, and we need to take breaks. Charles Spurgeon once said that many spiritual ills could be solved if we'd simply get a good night's sleep. Tiredness makes us resentful, bitter, petty, angry—and worse.

Good for you for being so conscientious about your marital responsibilities! God bless you for wanting to love your spouse like no one ever has and no one ever will. But remember—you're running a marathon. You can't keep sprinting. Sometimes you need true Sabbath rest.

19

Shaped by Sharing

Do not judge, or you too will be judged.
For in the same way you judge others, you will be judged,
and with the measure you use, it will be measured to you.
MATTHEW 7:1–2

IN COLLEGE, I HAD A PRETTY STRICT VIEW ABOUT A "QUIET TIME." I believed you were supposed to do certain things, and certain times of the day were better than others to do them in.

Then I started dating Lisa. Here was a woman who had a dynamic relationship with God but who rarely had a quiet time first thing in the morning. For starters, Lisa usually got out of bed just in time to make her first class. Not until later in the day would she go up on the roof of our dorm to lie in the sun during the afternoon. She brought her Bible along and called it a quiet time.

"At least be honest," I kidded her. "I mean, who goes up on the roof after lunch to pray and lay in the sun and calls that a quiet time?"

Then one day there was a loud knock on my dorm room door. I opened it up, Lisa marched in, and threw open my Bible to Acts 10:9: "About noon the following day ..., Peter went up on the roof to pray."

Score one for Lisa.

Eventually, this insight — that different people pray in different ways — led to the writing of *Sacred Pathways*.

Fast-forward a few years. I sinned against Lisa deeply, hurting her about as much as I've ever hurt her — and probably as much as she's ever been hurt. Even so, Lisa stuck with me. I realized I had some enormous holes in my soul and some gaping tears in my spiritual fabric. After much prayer and study and repentance, the key truth of *Sacred Marriage* emerged. Though I didn't write the words for another decade, the groundwork for that book had been laid.

Many audiences have laughed about Lisa's and my different views of what constitutes food. Some of my college buddies still can't believe I can eat—and actually enjoy—a good tofu casserole, but I do every now and then. Lisa was one of the first people on the bandwagon of decrying the danger of trans fat, getting rid of everything in our house that included partially hydrogenated oil—and though I initially thought she was going off on another health food–magazine scare, it turned out she was right.

It stuns me to look back, in ways both profound (spiritual truth) and earthy (tofu versus Tator Tots casseroles), how much being married to Lisa for twenty years has changed me. We are who we are in part because of the persons we married. You've done what you've done in good measure as a couple. Sharing our lives shapes us.

Pause for a moment, and think about how living with your spouse has helped make you into the person you are. This is true even if your spouse isn't a believer. I've talked to many women who are married to some difficult men, and these wives have been astonished at the wisdom that sometimes slips out of their husbands' mouths, or at how God has used a particular issue to point out failings in their own lives. Yes, these women may have lacked spiritual intimacy, but they've learned to appreciate the strength, or the provision, or the loyalty of even an unbelieving man.

I think it's helpful to take a step back and let yourself be amazed at how God has used your wife or husband to help you become who you are. It's also essential for future growth. Once I recount how God has already used my spouse to help me grow, then I'll be more open to how he might continue using my spouse to help me grow in the present and the future. But one thing kills this learning process more than anything else: our tendency to judge our spouses rather than listen to them (and this may be especially true if your spouse isn't a believer, or if you perceive your spouse to be less spiritually mature than you are).

What strengths does your spouse possess that you lack and can learn from? Your spouse may be far from perfect; even so, what character quality does he or she have that you can admire and emulate? We're always so aware of the areas in which our spouses seem to be lacking; this week, concentrate on the strengths that can inspire you.

When I judged Lisa about her quiet time, I wasn't learning from her; I was building prejudice. When I faced challenges early on in our marriage, I blamed her instead of confronting my own sin and unrealistic expectations. When I ate what tasted good, regardless of what it contained, I was poisoning my body. I have been radically shaped, in matters both small and large, by sharing this life with Lisa.

I can't even imagine where or what I'd be if I hadn't asked Lisa to marry me. Although she's so different from me, and our strengths often come from opposite ends of the spectrum, God has used this curious mix to help both of us become what we are and accomplish what we have. Through the difficult and the easy, through the fun and the pain, through the encouragement and the repentance, God has shaped us—and he is shaping you as well.

Share—and be shaped!

20

I Hold You Responsible

Peter turned and saw that the disciple whom Jesus
loved was following them. . . . When Peter saw him, he asked,
"Lord, what about him?" Jesus answered, "If I want him
to remain alive until I return, what is that to you?
You must follow me."
John 21:20–23

ONE OF MY BEST FRIENDS IS A MARRIAGE AND FAMILY THERAPIST.
One summer, our families took a vacation together. When you do
that, you see the good *and* the bad.

On one occasion, he saw the bad. He and I had been talking about
a situation in my marriage in which I was struggling with an appropriate response. My friend knew this issue had been simmering in my
relationship with Lisa for some time, but now he saw it firsthand.

"So you see what I'm trying to deal with?" I asked him.

"I do. But, buddy, I hold you responsible."

My friend then helped me see how a weakness of my own had
exacerbated the situation. In fact, I think that's why this issue bugged
me so much — it regularly pointed out to me where *I* was falling
short, and I resented that.

We can't control how our spouses react, but we always remain
responsible for how *we* react. One person's sin never excuses our own.
In my case, I realized I was acting like a wimp. There's no more noble
way to put it! I was so consumed with being a "nice" husband that I
had become less than a good husband.

The next day I went on a long run, which is how I like to process things. I remember praying, "OK, God, we've established that I'm a wimp — but I don't know how to change. I've been like this my entire life. What should I do?"

Looking back, I'm amazed at how, just a day or two earlier, I had focused completely on what I thought Lisa was doing wrong and how Lisa needed to change. I felt sorry for myself and was more than a little frustrated. But my friend helped me see I could better spend my energies addressing the weakness that this situation was revealing in me.

Like Peter, I had insisted on saying, "Lord, what about *her*?" But just as Jesus challenged Peter, so he challenged me: "What is that to you? You must follow me." It was as if God was saying, "I'll deal with Lisa; right now, concern yourself with what *you* need to change."

I honestly believe just about every case of marital strife has this dynamic at work. God allows us to come together as two sinners, knowing we will be sinned against. Marriage is about learning how to respond to a sinful human being in a holy way. It's also about letting someone else's sin reveal our own.

Because we all marry sinners, I can't see any other way to look at it. None of us are married to perfect human beings. (The one perfect human — Jesus Christ — never married.) The reality of coping with someone else's sin never excuses us from fulfilling God's high call to keep on loving.

That's why Lisa and I have chosen to remain relatively transparent even to outsiders. I can't count the times someone has come up to us and said, "I just can't believe how transparent and vulnerable you and Lisa are in *Sacred Marriage*!" After hearing this a dozen or more times, Lisa and I went back and read through what I had written, worried that maybe we had been too vulnerable!

But after doing that, we still regretted nothing we said. We both acknowledge that we deal with sin every day, because we know that every couple deals with sin every day. It's time for all of us to acknowledge the reality of sin, and then to learn how to deal with it, rather than to pretend that some ugly realities don't exist, or that they can be solved in ten easy steps.

You may feel frustrated by an issue in your own marriage, and legitimately so. I know you're being sinned against, because I know you married a sinner. You're not the first in this situation, and you certainly won't be the last. Feeling sorry for yourself won't change anything. Changing spouses won't stop you from being sinned against either—all it will do is change the way you're sinned against!

One productive thing you *can* do is to take an honest look at how a character flaw of your own is contributing (notice, I didn't say "causing," which is too strong) to the situation, and ask God to help you overcome it. Seek godly counsel, listen to God in prayer, study what the Bible says about it. Use marital strife as a "mirror moment" that points out an area where God wants to change you.

Whenever you catch yourself saying, "Lord, what about him? What about her?" listen to Jesus responding, "What *about* them? *You* must follow me."

21

The Big Picture

But seek first his kingdom and his righteousness,
and all these things will be given to you as well.
MATTHEW 6:33

SCENE 1: WHILE ON A FAMILY VACATION IN HAWAII, LISA WAS look-ing at me as if I had just lost my mind. We woke up very early that morning to go snorkeling, and everyone was feeling pretty tired by early afternoon. When I realized we had a few hours before we planned to be anywhere else, I announced that I intended to squeeze in a run.

"It's ninety degrees out!" Lisa exclaimed. "And the humidity is brutal. You want to kill yourself?" She couldn't understand why I wanted to pound the hot pavement instead of lie on the beach.

Scene 2: July 4th, back in Bellingham, Washington. Though I really love fireworks, I volunteered to stay home and do the dishes and watch our terrified dog while Lisa and the kids found a strategic place to view the city fireworks. As I lay next to our golden retriever (some-thing that happens *only* on the Fourth of July), I heard the "grand finale," the cascade of explosions signifying the end of the show, and it dawned on me: I had just missed something I really enjoy seeing.

What was going on?

A greater dream fueled both scenarios. For a good bit of my adult life, I've harbored the dream of completing a marathon. Now that I'm in my forties (a fact my body reminds me of almost daily), I realized that if I didn't get this done soon, it would only become increasingly difficult. So I joined a local training group that prepared weekend athletes to run the Seattle Marathon. I followed their training schedule religiously—even in Hawaii.

I missed the fireworks because I had planned to do a group run early the next morning—July 5—and I thought that if I stayed up late, I wouldn't be ready to do a hard training run.

Because I had the bigger picture in mind—finishing a marathon—the little sacrifices barely registered. The fact that the thermometer in Hawaii registered ninety degrees didn't carry as much weight as the fact that I needed to get in an hour run that day. The fact that I enjoy fireworks and would really miss them didn't even register until I heard, through the walls, what I was missing because I had been so focused on accomplishing this one goal.

If we ever lose the "bigger picture" in our marriages, we're headed for trouble. The big picture—glorifying God—will keep us from becoming consumed by the regular challenges marriage presents to our comfort. We become obsessed with not getting to do what we want to do or with our obligations, and soon, that's all we see. But when we keep the big picture in mind, we willingly endure the difficulties because the greater good—the future good—is even more important to us.

I can't tell you how many times I've reminded myself of one of the most important verses in the Bible: "But seek first his kingdom and his righteousness, and all these things will be given to you as well" (Matthew 6:33). When I strive to put God's kingdom first and focus on growing in his righteousness, it amazes me how quickly everything else falls into place.

Living in a marriage is sort of like putting together a jigsaw puzzle. You can become so myopic—just examining individual pieces—that occasionally you need to take a step back and look at the picture on the cover of the box to remind yourself exactly what you're trying to create. Likewise, we can become so fixated on the problems and challenges of marriage that we miss the ultimate purpose of every believer's life: seeking first—above all else—God's kingdom, and growing in righteousness and godly character.

A person who married solely for the sake of his or her marriage won't last if the marriage turns sour. If your primary purpose in being married is to be happily married, what will keep you in that marriage when your relationship becomes tough or distant or less than satisfying?

But when you decide to stay married to glorify God and to become more holy in his sight by remaining joyfully married to a sinner, you tend to view the smaller sacrifices as merely steps along the way to a much greater and glorious purpose. I didn't run in ninety-degree heat with high humidity because I considered it fun; I ran in sweltering weather because I wanted to complete a marathon several months later. I gave up watching fireworks in July because I had focused on what would happen in November — the Seattle Marathon.

Author and educator Elton Trueblood once made this insightful observation:

> Family solidarity takes hard work, much imagination and constant self-criticism on the part of all the members of the sacred circle. A successful marriage is not one in which two people, beautifully matched, find each other and get along happily ever after because of this initial matching. It is, instead, a system by means of which persons who are sinful and contentious are so caught by a dream bigger than themselves that they work throughout the years, in spite of repeated disappointment, to make the dream come true.[13]

Don't get bogged down in the minutiae of marriage. Keep the bigger picture in mind. Such a view will carry us through the challenges marriage regularly brings our way.

22

If It's Not Sin ...

Accept one another, then, just as Christ accepted you,
in order to bring praise to God.
ROMANS 15:7

WENDY AND DON JOINED EIGHT OTHER COUPLES IN THEIR PREMARI-
tal class. During one session, everyone wrote down a list of their
differences. Much to Don and Wendy's chagrin, their list ran longer
than any other couple's—three full pages! "We were the one couple
the counselors didn't think would survive," Wendy remembers, "but
we knew we would."

After they got married, their personal differences started to
become irritants. "I was always in a hurry," Wendy says, "and Don
was so methodical. I flew by the seat of my pants, and he was so
organized. I let things slide, but he had to know every little detail."

Inevitably, these personality differences created moments of tension
—little frustrations that crept up at the grocery store, while sitting
around at home, or as they carried out the basic rituals surrounding
dinnertime. In the aftermath of one such moment, Wendy found herself praying, "God, what do you want me to do here? Show me what
my response is supposed to be."

The tension had been building and now seemed about to boil
over. Wendy felt "really frustrated and angry," but she had learned
enough to ask God for his perspective on all of it. His insight sent
Wendy to her knees. She felt suddenly overcome by peace, and God,
in his gentle, quiet voice, whispered, "Wendy, if it's not sin, you can't
demand that it change."

Wendy realized she could *ask* her husband to change, but she couldn't demand that he change or nag the change out of him. If the irritating action or character quality wasn't sin, she'd have to learn to put up with it—unless Don decided to change it voluntarily.

That quiet conversation with God radically changed Wendy's attitude toward her husband. "Just because Don is organized and methodical and meticulous and can take his time when I want him to hurry up, well, that's not sin," she said. "Yeah, it can be frustrating shopping with him sometimes, but I can't demand that he become like me. Accepting this really freed up our relationship, and I stopped being such a nag. After all, it was really *my* problem, not Don's. Once I accepted this, our marriage started to come together, and everything became easier. We still have our struggles and our moments, but when I hear others talk about their marriages, I think Don and I have an unusually good one."

In fact, though Wendy and Don were pegged as "least likely to succeed" out of the nine couples taking the premarital class, eighteen years later, they are the only couple still together.

God has used Wendy's insight to reach out to others as well. She works at a preschool, where a young mom confessed she was about to leave her husband.

"Why?" Wendy asked.

When the woman shared her reason, Wendy responded, "*All* men are like that. All you're going to do is leave a man who loves your kid to marry a different man who hates your kid, and eventually he'll do the same thing. Why in the world would you want to do that?"

Wendy later said she "feels horribly sad for men, because women don't understand them and fault them for not doing things they usually aren't equipped to do."

God's words to Wendy can revolutionize any marriage. The man or woman you're married to is his or her own person. Some things about him or her may not be to your liking, but if the things that bug you aren't sin, you have no right to demand that he or she change.

You may wish your husband would be more spontaneous or your

wife less gregarious (or vice versa), but those are personality traits, not characteristics of sin.

If you persist in trying to change things that aren't sin issues, you're going to make your marriage life miserable. Dr. John Gottman, a leading marriage researcher, points out what he calls "one of the most surprising truths about marriage":

> Most marital arguments cannot be resolved. Couples spend year after year trying to change each other's mind—but it can't be done. This is because most of their disagreements are rooted in fundamental differences of lifestyle, personality, or values. By fighting over these differences, all they succeed in doing is wasting their time and harming their marriage.[14]

If you've been working on an issue for ten years or more, and the issue is one of annoyance rather than morality, here's my how-to advice: Let it go. Repeat to yourself, "This will never change."

Instead of trying to resolve these differences, find harmony in accepting them and learning to live with them. Such a response calls us to humility, where we no longer assume that our way is the only way or even the best way.

Different people have different quirks. We married people with different backgrounds, different outlooks, and different personalities from ours. In fact, those very things often attracted us to our spouses in the first place. Even so, at times these backgrounds, outlooks, or personalities may frustrate us, anger us, or inconvenience us, but *if it's not sin, we can't demand change.*

"Accept one another, then, just as Christ accepted you, in order to bring praise to God" (Romans 15:7).

23

Greater Than the Sum
of Their Parts

Two are better than one,
because they have a good return for their work:
If one falls down,
his friend can help him up.
But pity the man who falls
and has no one to help him up!

ECCLESIASTES 4:9–10

WITH A 30 HANDICAP, BOB ANDREWS MAY SOUND LIKE AN AVERAGE golfer.

Until you learn that he's blind.

Bob lost his eyesight during an attack while walking a Marine Corps patrol in Vietnam. Though he returned stateside stuck in a coma, his girlfriend, Tina, stayed by him. "I had to," she said. "My whole life was lying in that bed."[15]

When Bob came out of the coma, he felt little excitement about life, wondering what a blind man could possibly do. Tina challenged Bob's unilateral thinking; if he were to think in team terms — he and Tina together — the limits would vanish. "Look," Tina assured him, "we're two people. We're a team. We can do anything we want!"

Bob and Tina got married within two months of his return and immediately embarked on a life more active than most couples could imagine. Together, they have a business as building contractors. They have three sons, they sail, they fish, they bodysurf, and yes, they even

355

golf. Tina lines up Bob, tells him how far to hit it, and Bob lets fly. When he putts, Bob reads the greens with his feet.

After caddying for Bob one time, sportswriter Rick Reilly watched as Bob and Tina "sat next to each other like high school sweethearts. I half expected them to put two straws in his beer."

What's the secret to their happiness? Tom Sullivan, a blind actor and recording artist, gave Rick Reilly a clue:

> Every blind person is told at first that he's going to be dependent on others his whole life, and so they react wildly. They do anything they can to be independent. You know, walk into traffic, take up dangerous sports, stuff like that, stuff that will prove to the world that they don't need them. But it only makes them unhappier. Eventually, through love, they recognize that the only way to be happy and at peace is to live interdependently, to live knowing that they need others and others need them. And that's what blind golf is, a symbol of that lesson. The notion that we all need each other, blind or sighted.[16]

Rick's own reflections are equally touching: "I saw then what a team they had become — the broken soldier and the lost girlfriend. They were so much greater than the sum of their parts."

So many married couples resist this interdependence. They don't necessarily resent the person as much as they resent the relationship and its assumption of two people being shaped into one. They start doing selfish things to assert their independence, and they begin saying things like, "I can go do whatever I want! Why should I have to check with you?" "Who are you to tell me how I can spend my money?" "Look, you're not my mother [or father]. Get off my back!"

These and similar statements are cries for independence — but we gave that up the day we got married. We're part of a team now, and we have to think like a team. Maybe it's fear that makes you lash out like this; maybe it's pride, or maybe it's selfishness — whatever the cause, the effect is the same: disaster for the marriage.

You'll find true joy only in learning to work together and play together, and even in becoming dependent on each other. Burn your boats! Throw yourself recklessly into this marriage, as if there were no way out. That's the way to build interdependence and to experience the oneness the Bible describes as characterizing husband and wife. May this be said of every married couple: "They were so much more than the sum of their parts."

24

You're Prime!

Therefore encourage one another and build each other up.

1 Thessalonians 5:11

In the classic novel *Freckles* by Gene Stratton-Porter, a kindly couple gives a young man who is "intensely eager to belong somewhere" a new chance in life by offering him employment.[17] The boss's wife treats Freckles like a son, becoming the mother he never had. When Freckles's boss sees how this kindness leads the young boy to tears, he praises his wife:

> Sarah, you're a good woman, a mighty good woman. You have a way of speaking out at times that's like the inspired prophets of the Lord.... Did you see his face, woman? You sent him off looking like a white light of holiness had passed over and settled on him. You sent the lad off too happy for mortal words, Sarah. And you made me that proud of you! I wouldn't trade you and my share of the [forest] with any king you could mention.[18]

Pausing, the man looks straight into his wife's eyes and adds, "You're prime, Sarah, just prime!"

The same day my wife read that passage to our children on a long car ride, I had watched her come to the car and told her, "You know, you look *really* good today," and my wife responded with the typical wifely response: "You think so? Because my hair didn't quite turn out the way I had planned it, and I'm not sure about this shirt. It doesn't look quite right when I leave it out, but I'm not sure it works tucking it in, either, and—"

358

"Well," I added, cutting her off, "I think you look fantastic."

The Bible calls us to encourage each other, which is an active, ongoing obligation during times of challenge, stress, and even just everyday living. Consider how widely encouragement is urged and reported in Scripture:

- God to Moses: "Encourage [Joshua], because he will lead Israel" (Deuteronomy 1:38).

- Soldiers in the midst of battle: "The men of Israel encouraged one another" (Judges 20:22).

- Joab to Saul before a battle: "Now go out and encourage your men" (2 Samuel 19:7).

- Josiah to the priests: "[Josiah] appointed the priests to their duties and encouraged them in the service of the LORD's temple" (2 Chronicles 35:2).

- Paul and Silas to the early church: "After Paul and Silas came out of the prison, they went to Lydia's house, where they met with the brothers and encouraged them" (Acts 16:40).

- Paul to the disciples: "When the uproar had ended, Paul sent for the disciples and, after encouraging them, said good-by and set out for Macedonia" (Acts 20:1).

Consider a few general exhortations to encouragement:

- "But my mouth would encourage you; comfort from my lips would bring you relief" (Job 16:5).

- "Encourage the oppressed" (Isaiah 1:17).

- "Therefore encourage one another and build each other up, just as in fact you are doing" (1 Thessalonians 5:11).

- "But encourage one another daily, as long as it is called Today, so that none of you may be hardened by sin's deceitfulness" (Hebrews 3:13).

- "Let us encourage one another" (Hebrews 10:25).

Yet, in our selfish humanness, instead of thinking about encouraging, we may be tempted in our marriages to ask if *we're* being encouraged. In fact, I'll bet there are many wives who, after reading the quoted passage from *Freckles*, may even have thought, "Why doesn't my husband talk to me like that?" instead of asking, "Do I encourage my husband like that?" My friend Lisa Fetters observes that "women think we deserve this encouragement, and that men don't need it, but men *do* need to hear much encouragement."

When was the last time you looked in your lover's eyes and said (to use old-fashioned language), "You're prime, you know that? You're really prime!"? When was the last time you didn't take your spouse's hard work for granted—inside the home or outside it—and specifically thanked him or her for what he or she contributes to your life? Has it been so very long since you've put words to your thoughts and told your spouse specifically what you're feeling?

Don't measure yourself merely by what you *don't* do ("I don't come home drunk, I don't get into affairs, I don't waste our money"). Love is an *active* duty, and encouragement, as a biblical command, requires us to take the initiative. We live in a world that beats us down on an almost daily (if not hourly) basis. Marriage is designed as an oasis of encouragement, a way station where we can get renewed and refreshed with loyalty and kindness.

It's so easy to be complacently married, forgetting the need to unleash the active force of encouragement—but take this gentle reminder. Think of a few things, even now, and make sure another day doesn't go by before you look your spouse in the eye and say, "You're prime, just prime!"

25

Marital Ruts

See, I am doing a new thing!
ISAIAH 43:19

ONE OF THE BEST THINGS THAT HAPPENED TO MY MARRIAGE WAS breaking my wrist. The break was serious enough to require surgery, and suddenly, Lisa and I got thrust out of our routine. We did almost everything together, in part because I needed so much help. Since I had to limit my exercise to walking, we took near-daily strolls together. We shopped together. We answered email together (at first, I couldn't type). For a while, Lisa even helped me get dressed (OK, *you* try tying your shoe with one hand!).

Forced out of our routine, Lisa and I discovered a deeper and newer love. The romance was always there; it had just lain buried under layers of always doing the same thing. Isn't this really one of the greatest challenges many marriages face: the mind-numbing routine?

Theologian Paul Evdokimov insightfully fingers this reality in his classic work *The Sacrament of Love*: "The day-to-day profanes the sacred.... It is in the fearsome struggle against the duration and murderous repetitions that the human being appears most vulnerable. The prosaic in life brings him down to the infernal element of boredom."[19]

You don't have to break a wrist to rouse yourself from this boredom; sometimes just getting away will do the trick. Years later, Lisa and I spent a long weekend in New York City. Being together nonstop for five days suddenly made it seem strange the first time I left the house upon our return — something I had taken for granted so many times before. I got so used to having Lisa by my side — eating every meal with me, no kids asking us questions, no errands pulling us apart—that it seemed strange when we returned to the "real world." I noticed for several days afterward that I acted far more affectionate with Lisa—even better, I acted that way without even thinking about it.

Marriage is a long journey, and any long journey requires occasionally getting off the road to eat, to fill up the car with gas, or simply to rest. Has your love fallen into a rut? Is your marriage slowly getting buried under the daily routine? What can you do differently to break out of the box and renew your love for each other?

Maybe your rut is more behavioral—you've learned to tune out your spouse's voice, or you always make love in the same, predictable way or on the same, predictable night. Maybe you've completely stopped trying to find creative ways to demonstrate your affection and care. Perhaps you've become so ensconced in the workweek routine —the early-morning departure, the commute, the time away from home, coming back in the evening tired and grouchy—that you're completely missing opportunities to affirm and reconnect with each other.

Never underestimate the element of occasional surprise in delighting your spouse and building up your marriage. It can be so simple —a wife going to the trouble of picking out a book on tape that her husband can listen to on his morning commute; a husband buying his wife a completely unexpected gift, unconnected to any holiday or anniversary, for no other reason than to tell her he loves her. What would it mean to your spouse if you took an afternoon off—from work or watching the kids—to go to a matinee, take a walk around the lake, or go on a picnic? Sometimes all it takes is something out of the ordinary, something that says, "I don't take you—or us—for granted. I've put some special thought into this. I want to fight the 'murderous repetitions' and 'infernal element of boredom.'"

Through Ezekiel, God promised Israel, "I will give you a new heart and put a new spirit in you; I will remove from you your heart of stone and give you a heart of flesh" (Ezekiel 36:26). In the same way we can become calloused toward God, so we can become calloused toward each other. Pray for a new spirit and attitude toward your spouse, that your "heart of stone" will become a "heart of flesh."

Occasional ruts are inevitable in any long-term relationship, but they're never insurmountable. We can break out of them if we really want to.

26

To Make Her Holy

Just as Christ loved the church
and gave himself up for her to make her holy.
EPHESIANS 5:25–26

WHEN AIR TRAVEL RESUMED AFTER THE 9/11 TERRORIST ATTACKS IN the United States, commutes got a lot more difficult. Gone were the days when I could show up at our small regional airport thirty minutes before my flight. In fact, the airline I usually fly closed down all flights from Bellingham, meaning I now have to drive ninety miles to the Seattle airport.

To wait in lines.

To be asked to take off my shoes and walk in my socks through a metal detector.

To have a complete stranger open my suitcase, riffle through my underwear, and ask me what a particular medication is for (I'm not kidding). How I could possibly bring down or hijack an airplane with sinus medication ("Get back; I've got Tylenol, and I'm not afraid to use it!") is beyond me, but there you have it.

I grew irritable at the constant harassment. I just wanted to get through the airport, catch my flight, and reach my destination.

Several months later, Lisa was traveling with me to go to a conference—the first time we had flown together after the attacks. Lisa saw the brusque way I pushed through the airport, the lack of grace evident in my life as I muttered under my breath, and my overall demeanor—and she was appalled.

"Gary, would you just dial it back a bit? I've never seen you like this. What's the matter with you?"

I thought about what she said and realized she was right. I had become a practical atheist. I wasn't praying for people I saw. I wasn't looking for ministry opportunities. I was trying to survive—and doing so with a mean and critical spirit. Biblically, I believe a Christian without a mission is only half a Christian, but that's exactly what I had become—at least in the airport.

All that changed over the next several trips. Because Lisa had held up a mirror to my sin, I started praying for people I passed. I tried to be open to any opportunities where God might want to use me. And a certain joy entered my life, even while traveling.

I'm so thankful for this mirror God has given me in my wife. Please don't resent it when your spouse brings up an area that really *does* need to be addressed. We become blinded to our faults all too easily, and our spouses, who know us best, can lovingly point them out.

God calls believers to grow in righteousness: "You were taught, with regard to your former way of life, to put off your old self, which is being corrupted by its deceitful desires; to be made new in the attitude of your minds; and to put on the new self, created to be like God in true righteousness and holiness" (Ephesians 4:22–24). In the original Greek, the "putting off" is in the aorist tense—it is done once for all. But the "being made new" is in the present tense—it's an *ongoing* action. Marriage can feed this like nothing else.

In fact, Paul says that Christ loved the church by giving himself up for her "to make her holy" (Ephesians 5:26). If your spouse is a believer, she or he is your sister or brother in Christ; as fellow believers, we're called to encourage each other to grow in character. We express our love by being part of the ongoing process of renewal and growth in righteousness.

I'm so thankful that Lisa spoke up at the airport and continues to speak the truth in love. I'm grateful that her love for me is strong enough to confront me. I'd be a lesser man if I weren't married to her.

In her book *The Good Marriage*, psychologist Judith Wallerstein draws this wonderful conclusion:

> A good marriage, I have come to understand, is transformative. The prevailing psychological view has been that the central dimensions of personality are fully established in childhood. But from my observations, men and women come to adulthood unfinished, and over the course of a marriage they change each other profoundly. The very act of living closely together for a long time brings about inner change, not just conscious accommodation.... As the men and women in good marriages respond to their partners' emotional and sexual needs and wishes, they grow and influence each other. The needs of one's partner and children become as important as one's own needs. Ways of thinking, self-image, self-esteem, and values all have the potential for change.[20]

Marriage is a mirror. At times, we may not like what we see, but if we resolve not to shy away from the reflection — or worse, crack the mirror — it can be a very valuable spiritual tool.

27

Marriage Is Movement

Behold, I am coming soon!
Revelation 22:12

Lisa and I went to see the movie *Seabiscuit* with Rob and Jill, two of our closest friends. At the start of the movie, I sat by Rob and Lisa sat by Jill, so that Lisa and Jill could share the unbuttered popcorn and Rob and I could assault our arteries with the buttered kind. But halfway through the movie, Lisa had to get up for a moment, and Rob slipped over to sit by his wife.

There was something wonderfully refreshing in seeing a man who has been married for eighteen years still eager to sit by his wife for the last hour of a movie. That simple movement said a great deal about Rob and Jill's marriage, and it personifies a biblical truth.

I heard of one wedding in which the *bridegroom* actually walked down the aisle instead of the bride, in order to capture the biblical picture of Christ—*the* bridegroom—going to his bride, the church. As Christ pursues the church, so the husband is to pursue his wife. (Note to future husbands: it's the rare woman indeed who would even *consider* giving up that famous walk down the aisle; I wouldn't recommend trying this at home!)

Marriage is more than a commitment; it is a movement toward someone. Husbands, are you still moving toward your wife? Or have you settled in, assuming you know her as well as she can be known, and thus turning your sights to other discoveries and challenges? Even worse, are you violating your vows with the "silent treatment" or a refusal to communicate?

Wives, are you moving toward your husband? Are you still pursuing him, seeking to get to know him, trying to draw closer to him? Have you considered new ways to please and pleasure him, or have you become stagnant in judgment, falling back to see if he'll come after *you*?

Jesus moves toward us even in our sin; will we move toward our spouses even in theirs?

Movement is about more than communication; it's about the force of our wills. Are we choosing to pursue greater intimacy in our relationship? Do we seek to resolve conflict, or do we push it aside, assuming it's "not worth the hassle" while letting our love grow colder? Are we still trying to understand our spouses' worlds — their temptations and trials, their frustrations and challenges — or are we too consumed with our own? Are we praying for our spouses, encouraging them to grow in grace and holiness, or are we tearing them down behind their backs, gossiping about them so that everyone will feel sorry for how difficult we have it?

Honestly ask yourself, "Do I know my spouse any better today than I did three years ago?" If not, maybe you've stopped moving toward your spouse. And if you've stopped moving toward your spouse, you've stopped being married in the fully biblical sense of the word.

This week, why not launch yourself on a new exploration — your spouse? Why not see what new things you can learn — how you can grow even closer to each other, how you can give up a little more independence and embrace a little more interdependence? Why not make a renewed attempt to study your spouse every bit as much as a biology student studies the movement of cells under a microscope or a seminary student pores over thick reference books late into the night?

So many people say the "excitement" has left their marriage. Well, exploration is one of the most exciting journeys known to humankind. Most of the globe has been mapped, many times over — but that person who wears your ring? There are still secrets yet unknown and yet to be explored on that side of the bed.

Get busy.

28

Earthly Education
for Heavenly Heights

And now these three remain: faith, hope and love.
But the greatest of these is love.
1 CORINTHIANS 13:13

HENRY DRUMMOND (1851 – 1897) WROTE A REMARKABLE LITTLE classic titled *The Greatest Thing in the World* in which he points out that when Paul defines love in his letter to the Corinthians, he's referring to how we treat people. This emphasis on loving other people, Drummond believes, is a thread throughout the New Testament: "We hear much of love to God; Christ spoke much of love to man."[21]

Drummond argues that if love is the greatest thing, then it should be the primary pursuit of our lives:

> The supreme work to which we need to address ourselves in this world [is] to learn Love. Is life not full of opportunities for learning Love? Every man and woman every day has a thousand of them. The world is not a playground; it is a schoolroom. Life is not a holiday, but an education. And the one eternal lesson for us all is *how better we can love.*[22]

Marriage is a primary place where people learn this — through lots of practice. People improve in athletics through practice; we improve in music, writing, and cooking through practice. We practice in order to overcome our failure and inadequacies. Drummond stresses the importance of practice:

If a man does not exercise his arm, he develops no biceps muscle; and if a man does not exercise his soul, he acquires no muscle in his soul, no strength of character, no vigor of moral fiber, nor beauty of spiritual growth. Love is not a thing of enthusiastic emotion. It is a rich, strong, manly, vigorous expression of the whole round Christian character—the Christ-like nature in its fullest development. And the constituents of this great character are only to be built up by ceaseless practice.[23]

This is so good I have to repeat it: the love we seek is not "a thing of enthusiastic emotion" but rather a Christlike character "built up by ceaseless practice." Thus, marriage is about learning to adopt "the greatest thing in the world" by practicing our ability to love while living with a sinner.

In the first flush of infatuation, lovelike activity comes spontaneously. It gushes out of us. We say nice things, we buy presents, we write encouragements, we are eager and creative lovers, we do all the things that make someone feel special. Why? Because "enthusiastic emotion" moves us to do so. But if we stop loving when the feelings fade, we reveal that we are motivated by mere emotions more than by God's call on our lives, that we pay more attention to feelings than to Christ's glorious invitation to love as he loved.

If we dodge this character-producing practice by running to divorce court or by pouting and withdrawing into silent marriages, our hearts start to calcify spiritually. Our hearts shrink instead of enlarge, and we reinforce the selfishness that already screams for pride of place. But if we *practice* loving—even when we don't feel like it—our hearts bulge with God's goodness and generosity until love becomes the natural expression and response to God's work in our lives.

That's why infatuation doesn't really teach us to love. Only marriage can do that. Infatuation comes naturally—it is innate, no practice required. But a marriage is built on the bedrock of many considered decisions: Will I love, or will I hold a grudge? Will I serve, or will I be selfish? Will I notice this person, or will I retreat into my own world? Will I please my spouse, or will I draw pleasure from ignoring him [or her]? Marriage reveals and then purifies our motivations in a way that infatuation never can.

In fact, if our hearts are right and if we truly desire to become like Christ, we won't resent the challenges of marriage but will welcome them instead. Drummond gives this sound advice:

> Do not quarrel ... with your lot in life. Do not complain of its never-ceasing cares, its petty environment, the vexations you have to stand, the small and sordid souls you have to live and work with.... That is the practice which God appoints you; and it is having its work in making you patient, and humble, and generous, and unselfish, and kind, and courteous. Do not grudge the hand that is molding the still too shapeless image within you. It is growing more beautiful though you see it not, and every touch of temptation may add to its perfection. Therefore keep in the midst of life [and marriage!]. Do not isolate yourself. Be among men, and among things, and among troubles, and difficulties, and obstacles.[24]

Certain elements of the Christian faith must be developed in solitude. The traditional disciplines of fasting, prayer, study, and meditation are necessary building blocks—but Christian character requires *community*. Marriage can give us this community, and more. It can usher us into the greatest thing in the world—by providing us, every day, the practice field on which we can learn how to love. The mundane and often routine duties of life provide an earthly education that can take us to heavenly heights.

29

One

*We who are strong ought to bear with the failings
of the weak and not to please ourselves.
Each of us should please his neighbor for his good, to build him up.
For even Christ did not please himself.*

Romans 15:1–3

LISA AND I WERE TALKING WITH A COUNSELOR ABOUT ONE OF OUR children, who can be greatly affected by tension. In talking with the counselor, this child identified me as the laid-back one, while admitting that Lisa can occasionally get tense. I'm ashamed and embarrassed to admit that part of me expected the counselor to really let Lisa have it, but in a stroke of genius, the counselor turned to me and said, "So, anything you can do, Gary, to release the pressure off Lisa would be really helpful."

Like Jesus, she dropped the responsibility right back into my own lap.

Too many times in marriage we forget we're one. We start operating as individuals, even occasionally setting ourselves up against each other, forgetting that God is making us into a single unit. We may not go so far as to have a financial prenuptial agreement (which mocks the marriage before it even begins), but we carry an *emotional* prenuptial agreement—looking out for ourselves at the expense of the union.

If you sense your spouse lacks something, rather than criticize or judge him or her, your job is to pick up the extra load. I hear many wives complain that their husbands aren't as spiritually mature as they are; they use this fact as a club to make their husbands feel guilty and inferior. But Paul says we should do the opposite: "We who are strong ought to bear with the failings of the weak and not to please ourselves. Each of us should please his neighbor for his good, *to build him up*. For even Christ did not please himself" (Romans 15:1–3, italics added).

If we're so "strong," then our calling is to bear with the "weak." Now, it's never the case that one person is always strong in everything while the other spouse is always weak in everything. At times Lisa feels frustrated that I'm *too* laid-back and not forceful enough. Lisa and a counselor would have many opportunities to pick apart my own faults if we discussed other issues in our family. But rather than point fingers, we're called by God to fill in the cracks.

Marriage as an institution is a stroke of genius on God's part. As sinful humans, all of us lack certain skills, and all of us enter this relationship with myriad limitations and faults. By joining two individuals, God creates a much stronger unit on which he can build a family. It truly is a wondrous work: two individuals coming together to fill in where the other lacks. But this dynamic will take place only when we stop using our spouses' shortcomings as ammunition and instead use them as a call to step up. United in God, we are one.

If you were at a ball game and the batter hit a foul ball that was headed straight for your nose, your arm wouldn't sit back and say to itself, "It's about time the nose got what was coming to it. That nose gets so much attention, while I just hang here on the side of the body. I hope that ball really hurts!" On the contrary, without even thinking, you'd raise your arm to cover your face. You'd do it instinctively, even if your arm was broken and in a cast. Why? Your body acts like a single unit.

Marriage thrives spiritually when we die to our singleness and are resurrected to a divine union. We are to support our spouses in all they lack, and they are to support us in the same way. And if you're tempted to say, "But my spouse doesn't watch my back, so why should I watch his [or hers]?!" go back and read the first three verses of Romans 15 one more time: "We who are strong ought to bear with the failings of the weak and not to please ourselves. Each of us should please his neighbor for his good, to build him up. For even Christ did not please himself."

The day you exchanged vows, you promised to join your finances, your future, your family, your welfare — everything you have — with this one other person. It's a waste of spiritual energy to obsess over a spouse's fault; instead, we're called to figure out what we can do to make this sacred relationship work.

30

The Happiness
That Follows Holiness

Remembering the words the Lord Jesus himself said:
"It is more blessed to give than to receive."
ACTS 20:35

ON RADIO PROGRAMS, AT SEMINARS, AND IN CHURCHES ACROSS THE country, I'm often asked what I mean by the subtitle of my book *Sacred Marriage*: "What if God designed marriage to make us holy more than to make us happy?"

Please note, I didn't write "*instead of* to make us happy" — Christians, of course, seek happiness like everyone else. The difference is the *means* by which we pursue happiness, and what we find our happiness *in*. Holiness and true happiness are not adversaries; they are allies. They do not go to war with each other but rather build each other up. This is not to say, however, that they are equals. Biblical happiness is the offspring of holiness, giving holiness the pride of place as the parent.

Henry Drummond, whom we met on pages 97 – 99, writes, "There is only one thing greater than happiness in the world, and that is holiness; and it is not in our keeping; but what God has put in our power is the happiness of those about us, and that is largely to be secured by our being kind to them."[25]

What a profound thought! We can't fully determine how others treat us, but we can determine how we treat others — and God has made us in such a way that how we treat others in the little routines of life lays the foundation for our own happiness.

I fear, though, that the contemporary meaning of *happy* doesn't do justice to either Scripture or Drummond. Perhaps *joy* is a better choice for modern readers, as I've heard many people say, "Doesn't God want me to be happy?" as justification for leaving their spouses and taking up with someone else. In today's society, "happy" has been reduced to "euphoria."

Drummond takes us deeper, telling us to find our happiness not in an emotional response but in a sacrificial policy called love:

> Where Love is, God is. He that dwelleth in Love dwelleth in God. God is love. Therefore *love*. Without distinction, without calculation, without procrastination, love.... Lose no chance of giving pleasure. For that is the ceaseless and anonymous triumph of a truly loving spirit. I will pass through this world but once. Any good thing therefore that I can do, or any kindness that I can show to any human being, let me do it now. Let me not defer it or neglect it, for I shall not pass this way again.[26]

Can anyone doubt that such an attitude would refresh, reenergize, and revolutionize virtually every marriage on the face of this earth? If each spouse would honestly say, "Any kindness I can do to my spouse, any act of affection, any motion of goodwill, let me do it now. I don't know how long I have left to live, so let me not defer or neglect any act of kindness, but let me truly *love*."

Each of us can choose to do this individually, regardless of how our spouses respond. Their actions toward us are not in our keeping, but our ability to be kind and giving lies entirely within our realm. And the beauty of God's creation is that when we love, we experience God—and that's what brings true happiness. When we act in love, we invite God into our house, and God brings a soul-fulfilling joy that transcends contemporary notions of mere euphoria.

When marriages break down, they often do so in a context of resentment and a feeling that we're not getting what we need or want. But looked at in the light of love, this enemy loses all its power and place: "The most obvious lesson in Christ's teaching," Drummond writes, "is that there is no happiness in having and getting anything, but only in giving. I repeat, *There is no happiness in having, or in getting, but only in giving.* And half the world is on the wrong scent in the pursuit of happiness. They think it consists in having and getting, and in being served by others. It consists in giving and serving others.... He that would be happy, let him remember that there is but one way — it is more blessed, it is more happy, to give than to receive."[27]

Great minds think alike. Albert Schweitzer once told a group of graduating seniors, "I don't know what your destiny will be, but one thing I know: the only ones among you who will be really happy are those who have sought and found how to serve."

Do you seek happiness? Then seek to love. Move toward your spouse. Serve him. Love her. Cherish him. Sacrifice for her. Don't miss a single opportunity to demonstrate a kindness or to speak some word of affirmation. In doing so, you will invite God into your life, home, and soul, and you will find true biblical happiness.

31

Running from Yourself

For by the grace given me I say to every one of you:
Do not think of yourself more highly than you ought,
but rather think of yourself with sober judgment.
ROMANS 12:3

EVER WONDER WHY HOLLYWOOD ROMANCES RARELY LAST EVEN thirty-six months? I have a theory.

Our culture virtually worships actors. They receive constant adulation, praise, and admiration, and they know they are the objects of many fantasies. But marriage unleashes reality. Within a real relationship, a spouse discovers that an actor smells just like the rest of us. They can be just as petty, just as selfish, just as demeaning, and just as despicable (sometimes even more so).

One time, after a nearly sleepless night in a hotel, tossing and turning all night long, I finally glanced in the mirror and was shocked at what I saw: the tired eyes, the messed-up hair, the pale color. I said to myself, "Gary, at this moment you may well be the ugliest person on the face of this planet."

Looking at our reflection through the mirror of our marriage can be equally hard to take. We feel horrified by how we've acted —astonished by our own selfishness, pettiness, laziness, or even cruelty. Satan can use this awareness to tempt us to run. In truth, we don't want to run just from our spouses; we also want to run from ourselves, the persons we were in our marriages. We want to be with someone new who hasn't seen our bad side. Some may even try to deceive themselves into thinking their spouses were at fault for bringing out the flaws in them. We think we can just start over, and the bad side won't follow.

This, of course, is the great myth. We have enough energy either to run from who we are, or to cooperate with God's Holy Spirit in changing who we are, but we never have enough to do both. It will always be one or the other.

Actors who love to receive praise may have a particularly difficult time coping with someone who looks at them with unjaundiced eyes. What must it feel like to be shown larger than life on fifty-foot screens, then to go home and see a look of absolute disdain on the face of your spouse? To have photographers beg you to stop for a picture after you've spent hours fixing your hair, getting into your clothes, and creating that look, then to go home and take off the makeup, sleep on the hair, and wake up in a T-shirt instead of a tuxedo or a Vera Wang dress?

This is slightly more than a theory—I read the words of a top Hollywood actor who said, "Here's the great thing about dating. You get to start over and go, 'I'm a really nice guy.' " He freely admitted he wasn't a consistently "nice guy" in his earlier relationships, but dating someone new gave him a chance to start over—until the real man acted out once again.

But the permanence of marriage forces us to admit we haven't been as nice to our spouses as we wish we had been. It encourages us to evaluate ourselves with, in Paul's words, "sober judgment." Some painful memories will tempt us to run. Some snapshots will make us wince and cause us to think, "I wasn't a really nice guy; I was a *horrible* guy."

But if we accept that God designed marriage to help us grow in holiness, we know, going in, that we're a work in progress. Instead of running from these hurtful revelations, we can welcome them, realizing that our marriage is showing us what we need to know and pointing out where we need to grow.

Rather than run from ourselves, we can focus on *changing* ourselves! Let's be honest—some things about you and me are ugly. If we marry, our spouses will see that ugliness, whether it's an attitude, a habit, a disposition—whatever. After marriage does its work and this weakness gets exposed, we'll have a decision to make: Will we run from this revelation into the arms of another person who doesn't yet know our weakness, or will we embrace the call to grow in holiness, accepting Scripture's admonition to "think of [ourselves] with sober judgment"?

Don't run from yourself. Be humble, stay where you are, and focus on changing your attitudes and actions instead of your spouse.

Good in Bed

Thus I have become in his eyes
like one bringing contentment.
<small>SONG OF SONGS 8:10</small>

"DON'T LET THIS LAWYERLY FACADE FOOL YOU," SANDRA BULLOCK warned Hugh Grant in the movie *Two Weeks' Notice*. "I'm actually really good in bed."

I was eating an airline dinner, flying somewhere over the Midwest, when I put on the headphones and caught this piece of dialogue. In a Christian worldview, a single person wouldn't know whether he or she was "good in bed." But since I was stuck in an aluminum tube 30,000 feet above the ground, I had plenty of time to think, and the question challenged me in another context.

When did I last ask myself whether *I* was good in bed? While it's a grave mistake to reduce sex to mere mechanics, the question can go much deeper: When did I last *care* about that question? And why do so many women's magazines that cater to singles feature this question, while publications reaching out to married couples almost never even raise it?

How sad, I thought, that a single woman who has no long-term interest in a man could be more determined to please her boyfriend sexually than a married woman would be in pleasing her husband. Shame on me if I spend less time thinking about how to pleasure my wife than a single man might think about how to keep his girlfriend interested!

We have to fight against taking our spouses—and our responsibilities

—for granted. And taking them for granted is easy to do, because on the day we marry, we gain a monopoly of sorts. Our spouses commit to have sexual relations with no one else. In a faithful marriage there exists no competition or even comparison. The only intimate life our spouses can and will enjoy is the intimate life we choose to give them. Regardless of whether we act thoughtfully, creatively, or selfishly in bed, they receive *only* what we provide. It's sheer laziness if I give less attention and care to the mother of my children than some twentysomething kid gives to a young woman he met mere weeks ago.

Rather than make us careless, this exclusivity should make us grateful, and therefore even more eager to please our mates. The principle goes well beyond the bedroom, of course. You're the primary person for intimate talk and encouragement. Are you "good in communication" too? You're the first person who should be supporting your spouse in prayer. Are you "good in prayer"?

But let's not act as though the bedroom is unimportant: When did you last ask yourself, "Am I endeavoring to please my spouse in bed?" If we're slacking in this area, our spouses can't really do much about it—but *we* can, and we should.

Here are some questions to ask: Do I want to reward my wife's commitment to me, or do I want to make her regret it? Do I want to bless her, or will I take her for granted? Do I want to be a generous lover, or am I content to be a miser who reluctantly doles out occasional "favors"? Am I creative? Am I enthusiastic? Am I initiating?

Honestly ask yourself, "Am I good in bed?"

33

Divine Detachment

For without [God],
who can ... find enjoyment?
ECCLESIASTES 2:25

I'M CONVINCED ONE OF GOD'S PURPOSES FOR MARRIAGE IS TO CREATE a divine disillusionment. He needs to bring us to the end of our belief that anyone other than God can ever fully satisfy us. I've talked to countless couples whose problems remain throughout the years — often discussed, yet never resolved. In such cases, a sense of betrayal almost always comes to the surface: "He won't do what I *need* him to do," or, "She just won't do what I *want* her to do."

When the desires are legitimate (better communication, more support, more sexual availability), the pain of denial is keenly felt; but demands — even legitimate ones — still represent the Achilles' heel of every person's contentment. Spiritually, demands place us at the mercy of sinful persons who are limited in their ability to love. If we look to anyone other than God to meet our deepest needs, we are guaranteeing frustration.

You might feel frustrated because of far too little action in the bedroom — but what will you say to the couple who wrote to me after the husband had an industrial accident, a pair now facing a future without *ever* experiencing sexual intercourse again? Should the wife be free to pursue someone else sexually?

Of course not.

She has a legitimate desire for sexual intercourse — but it must remain unfulfilled.

You may well feel frustrated that your husband doesn't support you emotionally the way you'd like him to—but what about the wife whose husband gets kidnapped on the mission field and who doesn't even hear from him for two full years?

She has a legitimate desire for support, a listening ear, an aptly spoken word—but it can't come from her husband.

Any desire can be obstructed and thereby bring frustration. We do not have an absolute right to anything. Rather, we have an obligation to trust that God, in his providence, will ultimately provide what we need—or will give us strength to do without.

I can already hear many of you arguing the point. The Christian virtue of detachment—which means we stop finding our meaning and security in people, things, position, money, and power and instead focus our needs on God—scores little popularity in today's culture, but it remains as true today as when the ancients touted it and Jesus taught it.[28]

In fact, I'll go out on a limb and claim it's somewhat healthy to feel a little disillusioned in your marriage, because it's at that point you'll realize you need to look to God for your highest joy. You may feel tempted to respond to disillusionment by searching for another spouse who promises to "fulfill" you more, but eventually you would find that, while she had strengths your spouse lacked, she was missing some of your spouse's better qualities. Life with that new person would inevitably bring its own disillusionment, until one day you'd wake up to the fact that your soul's happiness really does depend on a holy, perfect God—not a sinful human being.

John 15:13 says that Jesus, on the cross, demonstrated the greatest love ever known—laying down his life for his friends—but for every movie made about that kind of sacrificial act of love, thousands more extol romantic love. The fact is, our culture idolizes romantic love and looks teary-eyed at the meeting of "soul mates," and it yawns at Christ's work on the cross. May God save us from this idolatry! As wonderful as romantic love may be, it should never compete in my heart with Jesus' work of redemption where my deepest needs were fully met. Any other love—including every kind ever portrayed by Tom Cruise or Julia Roberts—is a far lesser love; it's an inferior love, the value of which assumes meaning only because of Jesus' preeminent love.

So your spouse has disappointed and continues to disappoint you? Thank God. You're in a great place. You're in the doorway of detachment, where you can learn to let go of the expectations of the created and fall into the arms of the Creator. Our Lord took the same journey. Jesus "detached" himself from heaven to come to earth. He left his earthly parents to assume his ministry as the Messiah. He died to currying favor with the crowds so that he could become the crowd's Savior. He even detached himself from spiritually experiencing his Father's presence so that he could bear our sin. And then he willingly detached himself from life on earth so that he could die for our sins.

Would you be like this Savior? Then die to your demands. Be resurrected to utter dependence on your heavenly Father, who has loved you, is loving you, and will always love you like no one else can, including your spouse.

34

Make Someone Happy

A happy heart makes the face cheerful,
but heartache crushes the spirit.
PROVERBS 15:13

A CRUEL AND ABUSIVE FATHER TOWERED OVER THE CHILDHOOD OF
Pat Conroy, author of *The Great Santini* and other popular novels.
Pat's earliest memory is sitting in a high chair, watching his mother
go at his father with a knife, while his father laughed and knocked
her away.

Pat went on to attend a military college, where in his plebe year
he suffered malicious attacks, degradation, pain, and embarrassment.
During this difficult time, Pat got to know a married couple, who
provided him with an island of sanity in an otherwise chaotic and
hostile world. Pat recounts that during one visit, he felt transfixed
by the healthy and adoring attitude the husband and wife expressed
toward each other, something he had never witnessed at home. He
wrote, "It made me happy to see how much she loved him."[29]

It made me happy to see how much she loved him.

While so many couples obsess about whether their spouses are
making *them* happy, many of us don't realize how we can make *others* happy by loving our spouses well. We can't control whether our
spouses act in a way that brings us happiness, but we can control how
we love—and how we love can bring great happiness to others.

For starters, loving his daughter or son well will certainly bring
happiness to the God who created him or her. In the same way that
my children's future spouses can make me happy by being generous

386

with their love and tolerant toward my kids' faults, so God delights in watching how I treat my wife — his daughter.

We also make our children happy when we treat each other with affection and kindness. I remember one time, while on a walk with my wife, Lisa and I held hands and laughed. Our oldest daughter came up behind us and said, "You two are so cute!" Seeing us love each other put a smile in her heart.

Loving our spouses well will certainly bring happiness to our in-laws, to our pastors, to our community, to young couples desperately searching for hope in their own marriages and thus eagerly on the lookout for role models, and to many others who watch us without our even knowing about it. People love it when they see adoring love, generous love, kind love, and committed love displayed in this jaded, fallen world.

I remember watching the Academy Awards as an Oscar-winning actor paid tribute to his wife during his acceptance speech. I know exactly where this man stands on virtually every political issue, in large part because our views are so radically different that I can pretty much assume we'll be on the opposite side of any debate. From the public comments he's made, I doubt we'll ever vote for the same candidate for president (or even dogcatcher). Yet when I saw him acknowledge his wife — genuine tears filling his eyes, and true, sincere affection in hers — I felt surprisingly moved. This couple's outspoken political activism may make me nauseous, but their love makes me smile.

This phenomenon — making others happy by our love — has remained true throughout the centuries. Almost three thousand years ago Homer wrote, "There is nothing nobler or more admirable than when two people who see eye to eye keep house as man and wife, confounding their enemies and delighting their friends."

Make someone happy today — by loving your spouse. You may not realize who is watching, but I'll guarantee you this: someone is.

35

I Love Him Anyway

"If you love those who love you, what credit is that to you? Even 'sinners' love those who love them. And if you do good to those who are good to you, what credit is that to you? Even 'sinners' do that. And if you lend to those from whom you expect repayment, what credit is that to you? Even 'sinners' lend to 'sinners,' expecting to be repaid in full. But love your enemies, do good to them, and lend to them without expecting to get anything back. Then your reward will be great, and you will be sons of the Most High, because he is kind to the ungrateful and wicked. Be merciful, just as your Father is merciful."
LUKE 6:32–36

MEG AND PETER HAVE BEEN MARRIED FOR MORE THAN TWENTY years. On Valentine's Day, Meg went all out, giving Peter his favorite candy, tickets to an upcoming hockey game, and later at night, she wrapped herself in a special outfit purchased for just that occasion.

Peter got her a card.

At the grocery store.

That he purchased on the way home from work.

He didn't add anything to it either. He just signed it: "Peter." He even forgot to write the word "Love."

A couple of days later, Meg tried to explain that she felt a little taken for granted. Apparently, Peter misunderstood her intent because when, two months later, they celebrated their twenty-second anniversary, Peter didn't get Meg *anything*.

Meg waited throughout the day, wondering when Peter would bring out the present—but the present never came. Since she had given Peter *her* present—some rather expensive fishing lures—she knew Peter had to know it was their anniversary. So as they got ready for bed, Meg waited in anticipation, but Peter slipped in beside her and promptly went to sleep.

The next morning, Meg was beside herself. She fretted all day until Peter came home from work, and then she asked, "How could you not get me anything for our anniversary—especially after our conversation about Valentine's Day?"

"Well, I thought about getting you something, but it didn't work out," he replied. "And I knew not to get you a card because you said you didn't like it last time."

"It's not that I didn't like the card. It's just that the card alone seemed a little *sparse*. But even that's better than nothing."

Several months later, Meg had a birthday. This time, Peter got her a present—a kitchen tool set. Several weeks before, Meg had asked to borrow Peter's tape measure and screwdriver. Peter figured Meg should have her own small set of kitchen tools so she didn't have to borrow his.

Meg recounted all this, then explained how she had tried to get her husband to read several how-to books on loving your spouse, but it just didn't interest him. He'd read the first few pages, lose interest, and never pick up the book again.

"I've realized it's never going to change," she confessed. "But I love him anyway."

That last statement—"But I love him anyway"—is one of the most profound theological statements on marriage I've ever heard. Most of us base love on "because," not on "anyway." I love you "because" you're good to me. I'll love you "because" you're kind, because you're considerate, because you keep the romance alive.

But in Luke 6:32–36, Jesus says we shouldn't love "because"; we should love "anyway." If we love someone because he's good to us, or she gives back to us, or he's kind to us, we're acting no better than your average, everyday, common sinner who lives without the regenerating influence of the Holy Spirit. In essence, Jesus is saying, "You don't need the Holy Spirit to love a man who remembers every anniversary — not just the anniversary of your marriage but the anniversary of your first date and your first kiss — or who even remembers what you were wearing the first time you saw each other. Any woman could love a man like that. And if you love a husband who is kind and good to you — who lavishes you with gifts, who reciprocates with back rubs, who goes out of his way to get you time off from around-the-house duties, and who is physically affectionate even when he doesn't want sex in return — well, you're doing what any woman would do. There's no special credit in that!

"But if you love a man who disappoints you, who may forget an anniversary or two, who can be a little selfish or a little self-absorbed — now you're loving 'anyway,' and that's what I call my followers to do. In doing that, you're following the model of the heavenly Father, who loves the ungrateful and the wicked."

Will you love only "because"? Or are you willing to love "anyway"? Will you love a man or woman who doesn't appreciate your sacrifice on his or her behalf? Will you love a husband or wife who takes you for granted? Will you love a spouse who isn't nearly as kind to you as you are to him or her?

If your answer is "No," then at least admit this: You're acting just like someone who has never known the Lord. Almost every faithless marriage is based on "because" love. Christians are called to "anyway" love. That's what makes us different. That's what gives glory to God. That's what helps us appreciate God's love for us, because God loves *us* "anyway." He loved us when we rebelled against him. He keeps loving us when we continue to sin against him. He gives and gives — and we take him for granted, the height of ungratefulness. He is eager to meet with us, and we get too busy to slow down and notice him. He is good to us, and we accuse him mercilessly when every little thing doesn't go just the way we planned it; in other words, we can be wicked.

But God loves us anyway. To love anyway is to love like God and to learn about God's love for us, who loves the "ungrateful and wicked."

That's love, Jesus style.

Let's love like that.

36

A Spiritually Tight Marriage

Let love and faithfulness never leave you;
bind them around your neck,
write them on the tablet of your heart.
PROVERBS 3:3

HAVE YOU EVER PAUSED TO CONSIDER THE ALMOST HEROIC VULNER-
ability we assume when we get married? We pledge to be sexually
and spiritually faithful to a person whose body can easily succumb to
disease, accident, and corruption—and the Bible doesn't offer sexual
prenuptial clauses! If your wife were to have a medical accident and
end up in a coma and on a feeding tube, you would still be obligated,
out of reverence for God, to remain absolutely faithful to her. No
leering glances at other women. No pornography. No inappropriate
relationships with any other female. Your Christian obligation would
call you to remain true to your wife until the day she died. Like some
of the couples who have written to me, you might well be facing
the possibility of *never again* experiencing sexual intercourse—but
still, your Christian duty calls you to remain completely and utterly
faithful. That's the commitment you made on the day you entered
Christian marriage and promised your wife that, as long as both of
you live, she will be the only, the sole, the exclusive, object of your
sexual desire.

You might think a Christian wife, recognizing how vulnerable her
husband has made himself on her behalf, would feel beside herself with
gratitude. You might think, from a spiritual perspective, she'd go out
of her way to be a generous and grateful lover. If she really understood

the risks this man was taking on her behalf, you might imagine she'd naturally respond by becoming an extravagant and enthusiastic lover.

But why is this so often not the case? Why, in fact, is it usually the exception? The answer: We don't have spiritually "tight" marriages.

Most men, even Christian men, don't truly make themselves this vulnerable. They opt for a conditional faithfulness, like the French count who responded to the question, "Are you faithful to your wife?" with a droll, "Frequently." If their wives cooperate in the bedroom, then they'll remain mentally faithful. But if their wives cool down, ignore them, get too busy, or the men themselves just get bored or restless while traveling on business or away with their buddies, then they make exceptions and allow themselves to look, to fantasize, to take sexual pleasure (either directly through an affair or indirectly through the eyes or mind) from another woman.

Women, spiritually intuitive as they are, know this. And the marriage enters a gray wasteland. The husband is neither faithful nor vulnerable, so the wife feels no gratitude. Together, they never experience the true heights of sexual fidelity and faithfulness.

It's no coincidence that the stereotypical sin for men is to become voyeurs, while for women it's to become exhibitionists. Both sins assault God's perfect plan for the exclusivity of marriage. Though God calls a man to focus all his sexual attention on one woman, he decides to seek sexual satisfaction from women in general. He looks wherever he wants to look. Sometimes he even touches whomever he wants to touch. He has spent his entire life seeking satisfaction from the female gender instead of waiting and then setting his desire on one female in particular. This makes him less inclined to move toward one particular woman, and it rips apart the exclusive foundation on which an intimate marriage is based.

In the same way, a woman gets tempted away from biblical modesty to seek approval from men in general. Instead of finding her sense of fulfillment in pleasing one man, a wife may dress in such a way that she knows excites sexual interest from men in general. Receiving this attention—and perhaps even comparing it to the lack of attention she gets from her husband—a woman feels less concerned about her husband's connection to her. As long as she feels appreciated, she doesn't need any particular man's affection. Once again, the intimate wall has been breached.

The man is not faithful, the woman is not grateful, and they never experience a spiritually healthy sex life.

Consider this analogy. If I snack all afternoon long, when I come to the dinner table, I'm not going to eat with relish or with thankfulness. I'll nibble—if it tastes good. I'll notice it—if it's special. But I won't feel hungry. I won't truly *desire* that meal. And it won't cross my mind to express gratitude that my wife has gone to the trouble to prepare it. My wife will sense this meal isn't really important to me. Over time, she'll learn that she wastes her efforts in trying to make it special, so the quality of the meals plunges. Eventually, she may understandably ask, "What's the use?" and throw a TV dinner my way—and I may have become so used to snacking that, in one sense, I hardly even notice and, worse, really don't care. I'll just be thinking about the snacking I can do later.

How sad—but that's the truth in many a marital bedroom.

What's the way out? Become more absolute. Become more extreme. Keep the marital circle completely tight.

Listen: God designed marriage based on *need*: Adam needed a helper (Genesis 2:18). God also said that Eve's desire would be for her husband (Genesis 3:16). The language is so explicit here that one commentator calls it a spiritual desire "bordering on disease."[30] Voyeurism and exhibitionism destroy the psychological and spiritual basis of pure desire. A diluted focus creates a diluted desire. Husbands and wives who nibble all day long stop needing each other. Not needing each other, they show no particular gratitude when sexual desires are met—because the marital bed becomes just one place among many where sexual desires get fulfilled.

Repentance is the first step on the way back to Eden. Men need to remain absolutely, utterly, and completely faithful. A man should focus 100 percent of his sexual desire on his wife. He should recognize that she is the only appropriate person on whom he should lavish his mental, physical, and spiritual affection.

In return, a woman should dress in public as Paul tells her to dress —attractively but modestly ("I also want women to dress modestly, with decency and propriety" [1 Timothy 2:9]). In private, however, a wife should take great pleasure in arousing her husband's interest. She should revel in that power—God gave it to her! She should delight in the hold she has over this man. She should be generous and grateful that he would make himself so completely vulnerable on her behalf. And she should be eager to reward his exclusivity, for as long as it is in her power to do so (as he should eagerly reward hers).

Spiritually, a woman will find it far more fulfilling to be exclusively desired, adored, enjoyed, and practically worshiped by one man than she ever will from eliciting leering, lascivious looks from men in general. Why? Because that's the way God made us.

God's call is certainly extreme! One man experiencing sexual relations with just one woman—for an entire life. No sex before marriage. No sex with anyone else during marriage. Not even thoughts of sex with someone else. If, for any reason, sex as a couple becomes impossible, each partner remains obligated to maintain the exclusive sexual relationship.

While this sounds extreme and absurd to a lust-riddled society, I'd put the sexual satisfaction of a couple who lived their life this way against that of someone with wandering eyes or immodest appearance any day of the week. A couple focused on each other experiences something other couples never do: a satisfaction that touches the depths of the soul. God knows how he made us; his instructions for how we should relate are based on knowledge the world denies. We are not evolutionary accidents for whom the sexual urge is merely a naturalistic response. We are intricate spiritual beings, created for God's pleasure and designed to give each other pleasure. This design goes far beyond physical nerve endings to include the spiritual and emotional reality of being created in the image of God. Therefore, in the more transcendent part of our souls, we value fidelity, belonging, and holiness over the mechanical eruption of an orgasm. Not that we disdain orgasms. Far from it! But we recognize the appropriate place for sexual climax. Outside its proper context, "the act" loses its spiritual beauty, its emotional meaning, and its ultimate purpose.

Keep the marriage "tight." Become extreme. Throw yourselves at each other while becoming blind, sexually, to everyone else. Only then will you know God's full design and intentions for true sexual satisfaction.

37

The Great Escape

Do not fret because of evil men
or be envious of those who do wrong....
Trust in the LORD and do good;
dwell in the land and enjoy safe pasture.

FRANK HAS BEEN A DRUG ADDICT FOR A DOZEN YEARS. HE IS CURrently going through Narcotics Anonymous. Mary works for a boss who gets wicked pleasure from making his employees miserable. Richard pastors a church in which a rogue elder is doing his level best to wrestle leaders for control of the congregation.

All three of these people have something wonderful in common: They have access to God's great escape — marriage.

I don't know about you, but I have a tendency to fret. I stew over problems. I bring the anxieties and concerns home, and they hang like a low-lying cloud over my head, covering my demeanor and affecting my spirit.

But here's the wonderful, soul-scouring truth of marriage: It gives us something else to focus on. Fretters know it's hard to stop thinking about any particular concern unless you can focus on something else; marriage gives us that something else.

Take Frank, for example. He and I talked about how drug addiction tends to make people even more self-centered than they normally are. Even recovery can become "all about me" as they look for people to support them and as they focus on getting through the day without resorting to drugs. But holiness must strike sin at its root, and since one of the roots of sin is selfishness, Frank needed to find something to make it *not* about him—perhaps for the first time in his adult life.

That "something" was actually "someone"—his wife. "Every day," I said to him, "you've been waking up asking, 'How can I get those drugs?' or, 'How can I cover my tracks?' and more recently, 'How can I make it through this day?' But now, you have the opportunity to use your marriage as a way to focus on someone else. Wake up every morning and ask God, 'Lord, how can I love my wife today like she's never been or ever will be loved?' You've said yourself that you've made her life miserable for over a decade. Now's your chance to spoil her. Think about her when you're tempted to think about drugs or to dwell on yourself. Do all you can to love her and serve her and affirm her. Lose yourself in adoring her, and experience the joy—perhaps for the first time in your life—of selfless living."

Mary had an inviting opportunity because of her experiences with her tyrannical boss. Like me, Mary is a big-time fretter. As she went to bed each night, she had a hard time fighting back the bitterness and resentment aroused by her boss's venom and malice. If she woke up in the middle of the night, she could forget about going back to sleep; invariably, her mind fixated on her boss's latest fiasco, and she found herself silently fighting him all night long.

"Instead of thinking about your boss's ego," I told Mary, "think about your husband's strengths. Tell him why you respect him. Write notes that express why you admire him. Turn every temptation regarding getting back at your boss into an invitation to love your spouse. Eventually, Satan will get the hint, but even if he doesn't, your husband is going to feel really special! Either way, you win."

Richard's opportunity came as a result of his struggle with the power-hungry elder. For many pastors, the church can become an extension of who they are—a mistress of sorts. Now Richard has the opportunity to place the matter in God's hands while making sure that his heart remains fully invested at home. As a pastor, he needs to respond to this elder's shenanigans—but he shouldn't fret because of this evil man. How not to fret? Every time he feels tempted to think about the rogue elder, he can instead focus on doing something special for his wife. He can love her, just as Christ loves the church. If Richard does this faithfully, this elder may be one of the best things that ever happened to Richard's marriage.

What about your situation? How can God use as a great escape your call to love one person like he or she has never been or ever will be loved? What spiritual travail do you face that you can overcome by turning all the negative thinking and fretting into a positive act of love and affirmation?

One of the great blessings of marriage is that the call to love is so pervasive, so comprehensive, so time-consuming, and so gigantic that it really does provide a great and healthy escape from a world in which evil people dwell. If, like me, you have a difficult time keeping yourself from fretting, stop resisting and start substituting. Use every temptation to fret as a call to pray for, and act lovingly toward, your spouse. This week, revel in God's great escape.

38

Sanctuary

Your love is more delightful than wine....
Your name is like perfume poured out.
Song of Songs 1:2, 3

Nancy Belcher and her husband, Chris, arrived in Italy to run the Venice Marathon. They registered in a town called Mestre which, like many Italian cities, doesn't allow cars in the city center. Nancy told Chris she'd jog to the registration area, pick up their packets, and meet him back outside after he found a place to park.

But after Nancy picked up the race packets and left to look for her husband, she found herself surrounded by six thousand runners and their family members, most of them drinking, laughing, and talking in different languages. Nancy spent a frantic hour looking for Chris; they hadn't planned a meeting place, nor did they yet have a hotel room. They intended to just meet and then check in somewhere, but everything felt so new and so disorienting that Nancy had no clue where to look for Chris—and it was all so crowded!

Finally, Nancy remembered Chris had a cell phone, so with the help of an Italian desk clerk, she called her husband. Initially, Nancy felt reassured to hear the dial tone, but her heart sank when she heard a ringing in her purse—she had Chris's cell phone!

It was now 9:30 p.m., the night before the marathon, and as Nancy noted, "I had no dinner, no car, no hotel, and no husband."[31]

Nancy wandered back into the registration area, milling around aimlessly until finally she heard her husband's familiar whistle. At that moment, it was the most beautiful sound she could imagine:

"I felt so relieved I hugged him and started to cry. My reaction so surprised him that he started to laugh. There we stood, among thousands of partying marathoners in an unfamiliar foreign city, crying and laughing."

I love this story because it's a picture of the sanctuary that marriage can become. In a foreign land, the one familiar face Nancy wanted to see more than any other was that of her husband, Chris. We may walk in a crazy world, but if we're married, we have the privilege, the refuge, the sense of security, the sense of comfort, pictured in Nancy and Chris's embrace.

Of course, we don't have to leave home to appreciate this sanctuary. A man with whom I hadn't had a significant conversation in more than ten years once publicly attacked me. Though the charges later proved silly, it certainly felt sobering to become the focus of such venom. One night during this ordeal my wife snuggled up to me, kissed the back of my neck, and said, "I love you, Gary." Earlier in the day, she had told me how a woman had apologized to her because when they first met, the woman had said, "Oh, *you're* Gary Thomas's wife! I heard him on Focus on the Family." The woman said she was sorry she had defined Lisa by her spouse, but Lisa told her, "You don't have to apologize. I *love* being known as Gary's wife!"

When you're attacked, it does something wonderful to your soul when your spouse glories in your relationship. Lisa knows me better than anyone else. She knows more of my history, more of my temptations, and more of my private devotion than any other human. She has spent more time with me, shared more words with me, and eaten more meals with me than anyone else.

Even so, she loves me. In fact, she even loves being known as my wife!

Her affirmation in the midst of such an ordeal, the reality of being deeply loved by the person who knows me best, provided a wonderful sanctuary where I could find shelter.

A few weeks later, the roles got reversed. A woman who didn't understand Lisa's situation misread her motives and erroneously applied a Bible verse to back up her rather blunt opinion. Lisa cried as we talked on the phone. "Honey," I said, "I know you better than that woman ever will. She doesn't understand your situation, and furthermore, biblically, she's just wrong. You're doing the right thing."

"You really think so?" Lisa asked.

"I *know* so."

There is great leverage when the person who knows you best can encourage you most.

In a good number of these devotions, I've talked about some of the struggles of marriage—how it's worth the pain, how it calls us to sacrifice, commitment, and so forth—but please, let's not forget the great joy and blessing of being known and being loved. Our marriages can become sanctuaries, sheltering us from a world that hates us. We might be lost in a foreign country, attacked in our hometown, challenged in our own Bible study, but what a joy to find refuge in the arms of a loving spouse!

The Bible is honest—evil people exist:

- "The wicked plot against the righteous and gnash their teeth at them" (Psalm 37:12).

- "And pray that we may be delivered from wicked and evil men, for not everyone has faith" (2 Thessalonians 3:2).

- Jesus said, "Blessed are you when [note: not *if*, but *when*] people insult you, persecute you and falsely say all kinds of evil against you because of me" (Matthew 5:11).

There are those who will tear us down, assume we have evil motivations, be inclined to think the worst of us, and even misrepresent us to others. They will gossip, slander, and ridicule. But God has given us a mate, a shelter in the storm, who knows us better than anyone.

When that mate loves us, adores us, and respects us, what it does to our souls is without question one of the most gratifying experiences in all of human existence. It is a powerful, powerful ministry to honor and adore your spouse, to become his or her sanctuary in a world that often seems predisposed to hate, to wound, to hurt, and to tear down.

Because you know your spouse better than anyone else, you have the opportunity to minister to him or her on a much deeper level. When Lisa said she loved me at just the time I needed it most, when she made a point of telling me how delighted she is to be known as my wife, she won my loyalty for life. She already had it, of course. It's what I had promised on the day we got married. But in those words, uttered when I needed them most, she unleashed a new torrent of thanks and affection to accompany that original commitment.

Lisa and I have faced our share of trials and troubles—but I would cross this world on Lisa's behalf. I would face all the demons in hell to defend her. She has been my sanctuary—and I will adore her for all of eternity.

Real People

Light is sweet,
    and it pleases the eyes to see the sun.
However many years a man may live,
    let him enjoy them all.
But let him remember the days of darkness,
    for they will be many.
ECCLESIASTES 11:7–8

I WAS SPEAKING AT A "SACRED MARRIAGE" SEMINAR AT A HOTEL about two hours away from the host church. On Saturday night I spoke on sexual intimacy, and afterward the leaders handed out candles and Hershey's Kisses for the couples' private evening together.

This has happened several times before. Given the situation (at a hotel far from home, away from the kids), the setup (a Saturday night talk on sex), the intimate gifts (a candle, and on one occasion, massage oil and bath salts), the conversation that inevitably follows ("Well, honey, I guess we better go apply the Word!"), everybody all but knows that practically everybody else is going to enjoy sexual intimacy that night. The seminar host even made a point of saying the Sunday morning session wouldn't start until 10:00 a.m., "so you can sleep in" (wink, wink).

While Lisa wasn't with me, I did have the fun of watching Clemson beat up on Florida State in a college football contest — not quite as satisfying as sex, of course, but as I pointed out to some of the attendees, my entertainment lasted a good bit longer than theirs did!

I also had a chance to pray, and I came back the next morning with a word of comfort, as I guessed that at least one and perhaps several couples felt frustrated that, for whatever reason, they didn't enjoy sexual intimacy—and therefore felt even worse about their marriage than they had before. They knew what their friends were doing, and they may have felt cheated about their own circumstances. I stressed that it is unwise to evaluate your marriage based on any given moment. Marriage is a long journey, with many seasons; that reality, plus the fact that we are married to real people, with real physical and emotional problems, can combine to create frustrating moments. In such times, I said, we need to die to our expectations and focus on our obligations—loving them "anyway."

That night I got to apply my own words. Because I had spoken to two groups back to back, I had been gone almost an entire week, and I was *really* missing Lisa—in more ways than one! Unfortunately, her period arrived two hours before I did.

That kind of thing doesn't happen in the movies, or in novels, or in the latest Top 40 song.

But it's real life.

Lisa was so apologetic. Later that evening as I put the kids to bed, she got out of the bathtub and said, "I'm supposed to be doing all this and you're supposed to be resting and—"

I cut her off. "I'm just glad to be home," I said.

I'm married to a real person. In real life, marriage moments don't always turn out the way we wish they would. That's why I think we have to guard against expectations that deny our fallen condition in a fallen world. Sickness, frustration, the frailty and foibles of the human body, eventually find their way into most homes. If we don't expect this, then we make an already difficult situation that much worse, acting as though we're the only couple facing such struggles when, in fact, virtually every couple faces a variety of similar issues. It may not be at the same time we do (that's where comparisons become dishonest), but eventually, all marriages face most of the same hurdles. Eagerly anticipated moments collapse into agonizing disappointments.

That's why I believe we have to exchange our expectations for our obligations. Instead of focusing on what I *wish* would happen, I should concentrate on my duty and call to love. In this fallen world, there are many things we simply can't control. If we place ourselves at the mercy of these things, we become spiritual slaves, easily frustrated and discouraged.

But when I live by my obligations to love and to serve and to remain faithful, I rise above the circumstances of this fallen world. Whatever happens, my duty is clear, and my marriage — my *real* marriage to a *real* person — is served.

Expectations assault a marriage that doesn't live up to perfection; obligations protect a marriage at its weakest moments. Expectations slowly wear down a marriage, while fulfilling obligations steadily builds up that union. Expectations foster fear and disappointment; meeting our obligations births intimacy and love.

In most cases, expectations are the enemy, and obligations are the protector. By which one are you going to live your life?

40

A Difficult Road

"I tell you that anyone who divorces his wife, except for marital unfaithfulness, and marries another woman commits adultery."
The disciples said to him, "If this is the situation between
a husband and wife, it is better not to marry." Jesus replied,
"Not everyone can accept this word,
but only those to whom it has been given. . . .
The one who can accept this should accept it."
MATTHEW 19:9–12

SOME HOW-TO MARRIAGE BOOKS FALL SHORT BY PRESUMING THAT the difficulties of marriage can be overcome. Every marriage, no matter how you look at it, is hard and will be hard.

That's why I like to correct a spouse who says, "I have a difficult marriage." There's no need to personalize it: "*I* have a difficult marriage." At various points, *every* marriage is difficult. The problem isn't necessarily with *your* marriage, it's with marriage in general.

Let's look at the honesty of the ancients who went before us. I'm not necessarily endorsing all of the following comments, but it helps to get a historical perspective on how earlier generations viewed marriage.

When Jesus told his disciples that marriage was for life and that only adultery could break its bonds, they immediately blurted out, "If this is the situation between a husband and wife, it is better not to marry" (Matthew 19:9).

Jesus doesn't refute this! He simply says, "The one who can accept this should accept it."

Chrysostom, a fourth-century church father, argues that when Paul attacks divorce, his real aim is to dissuade people from getting married: "For anyone who hears that, after marriage, he will no longer be his own but will be subject to the will of his wife ... will not even take the yoke upon himself, since once he has done so, he must be a slave as long as it pleases his wife."[32]

Cicero says this: "Is a man free when he is under a woman's orders? She imposes laws, prescribes, commands, forbids whatever seems good to her; and as for refusing when she gives a command, he cannot or dare not. In my opinion he should be called, not a slave but the most wretched of slaves, though he be born of the noblest family."

A writer from the Council of Trent has a word for prospective wives:

> Subject to her husband in everything, she must put up with his moodiness, contrariness, nights of eating too much and drinking too much, jealousy, suspicions, incontinence, adulteries, quarrels, blows. She must follow him, be with him everywhere, obey and serve him like a slave.... He uses up the money they have on dice, card games, drink, dinners, lavish gifts, ruinous contracts, ill-advised lawsuits and other ways, and the wife can apply no remedy.

And Jerome, writing in the fourth century, gives this whimsical warning to prospective husbands:

> Then throughout entire nights [you must endure] the long-winded complaints: "That woman has nicer things to wear outside.... Why were you looking at the woman next door? ... What did you bring back with you from the forum?" No friend may we have, no companion. She suspects that love of the others is hatred for her. Then, too, there is no chance to try a wife out. You take her as she is. If she is hot-tempered, lazy, deformed, conceited, ugly—whatever defect there is, you learn after the wedding.... You have to keep noticing her face all the time and praising her and telling her how pretty she is for fear that, if you look at

another woman, she'll think she's unattractive. If you entrust the entire house to her to be managed, you have to be her servant. If you reserve anything to your own judgment, she doesn't think you trust her. Then she turns to hatred and quarrels; and if you don't look out at once, she'll get some poison ready.

Jacques-Bénigne Bossuet, a French preacher from the late 1600s, made this observation:

> Each [spouse] has moods, prejudices, habits, associations. Whatever be the things they have in common, people's dispositions are always different enough to cause a frequent chafing in so long a life together. They see each other so near at hand, so often, with so many defects on either side, in the most natural situations and ones so unexpected that it is impossible to be prepared. They get tired. The thrill is gone. The other's imperfection is irritating. Human nature makes itself felt more and more.... They love their cross, I am happy to say, but what they are carrying *is* the cross.

Even the patient and pastoral Fénelon warned, "They get tired of each other in this need of being almost always together and acting in unison on every occasion. It requires a great grace and great fidelity to the grace received to bear this yoke patiently.... A person must prepare for it in a spirit of penance when he believes he is called to it by God."

In an ironic way, I hope this honesty encourages you. When you grow discouraged, when you ask, "Am I the only one who struggles like this?" when you wonder why, at times, the requirements of marriage seem so burdensome, take heart in knowing you are not alone. You've chosen a difficult life.

But if marriage is so hard, why stick with it? For starters, except for those called to celibacy, marriage is God's will for us. It's how he designed us to live. But secondly, there can be great glory in tackling an almost impossible challenge. Marriage is based on a grand design created by God, extremely difficult but in some peculiar way extraordinarily satisfying. How else can we explain why two people who describe their marriage as "hell on earth" get divorced and then both get remarried within twenty-four months? Even knowing how painful it can be, they can't wait to jump back in and give it another try, albeit with someone else.

It's not so much that *your* marriage is difficult; the *state* of marriage is difficult. Don't be discouraged. It's the price we pay for a glorious return. Certainly, there's a place for the how-to approach; we *can* learn how to communicate better, how to resolve conflict, and a host of other skills. But we *can't* overcome the reality that it'll never be easy to be married.

I originally wanted to title my book *Sacred Marriage* something else: *The Greatest Challenge in the World*. I know of few other challenges like it; certainly, I can't imagine any that last as long and test you so personally and so deeply. But that, in an odd sort of way, is its very appeal: "The one who can accept this should accept it."

The difficulty of marriage is both its challenge and its glory. It can make us, and it can break us. It may indeed be a difficult road, but it is a holy road that can lead us toward God.

41

The Ministry of Noticing

O Lord, you have searched me
and you know me.
You know when I sit and when I rise;
you perceive my thoughts from afar.
You discern my going out and my lying down;
you are familiar with all my ways.

PSALM 139:1–3

IT STARTED OFF AS YOUR AVERAGE MARRIAGE MORNING. LISA AND I
went out for an early walk, then stopped off at a Starbucks on our way
to the grocery store to get some items for dinner later in the day. As
Lisa walked up the steps, she turned and looked at me to say something. I remember the way the morning sun highlighted her hair, and
I thought, "She is so beautiful to me."

Ten minutes later, I told Lisa what I had been thinking. "This has
been a rather mundane marriage morning—going for a walk, getting
a cup of coffee, stopping at a grocery store—but I just want you to
know, when you paused on the steps I thought to myself, 'I am deliriously in love with that woman.'"

"Buuuuttt—," Lisa said.

"No 'but.' That's it."

"That's it?"

"That's it."

"Oooh, baby, what do you want?"

"I don't want anything! I was just thinking I'm still deliriously in
love with you after almost twenty years of marriage and thought I
should share it with you."

"No, I mean it. You name it, you've got it."

For the voyeuristically curious, I kissed her on the forehead and left the room (not that it's any of your business!), struck by the power of simply *noticing* my wife and telling her about it. It dawned on me that this is what much of God's love is all about. He notices us. He doesn't take us for granted. The rest of the world is usually too busy to pay attention, but God remains passionately interested in and meticulously aware of our situation in life.

There was a time when Israel amounted to nothing but a tiny, insignificant family. But God noticed them: "The LORD did not set his affection on you and choose you because you were more numerous than other peoples, for you were the fewest of all peoples" (Deuteronomy 7:7). Even so, God chose this "fewest of all peoples" to become his "treasured possession" (7:6).

While on earth, Jesus carried on this same ministry. He noticed those whom the Pharisees in their religious blindness had forgotten. He paid attention to the woman at the well, a woman other "respectable" rabbis would have ignored. He welcomed children into his circle instead of shooing them away. He put up with repentant prostitutes and focused his ministry on those who seemingly could offer the least to his work: "Go back and report to John what you hear and see: The blind receive sight, the lame walk, those who have leprosy are cured, the deaf hear, the dead are raised, and the good news is preached to the poor" (Matthew 11:5).

So when Paul tells husbands we're supposed to love our wives like Christ loves the church (Ephesians 5:25), for one thing, he's telling us we're supposed to *notice* them. Everyone else may take them for granted, but not us. Their bosses or employees, their children, maybe even their parents, may be too busy to slow down and offer much by way of gratitude or encouragement, but it's our job to take the time to notice and affirm them.

Wives, you can do this as well. Particularly by the time we reach middle age and our bodies soften while our hair thins (or disappears), and younger men get promoted over us while youthful dreams die

—when we feel invisible to the rest of the world—you can replenish our souls by not taking us for granted, by simply noticing your husbands and telling them what you're thinking.

Some of my most intimate moments with my heavenly Father come when I realize he's watching, he's noticing, he's getting it all down. When I pray, he sees. When I give, he takes notice. When I overcome a temptation that no one else knows about, he encourages me. He knows "when I sit and when I rise," he "perceives my thoughts from afar." He knows when I go out and when I lie down. He is "familiar with all my ways." Where can I flee from his Spirit? Nowhere. Where can I hide from his presence? That place doesn't exist (Psalm 139:1 – 10).

Loving begins with noticing. It is more than that, surely, but it can never be *less* than that. I argue in *Sacred Marriage* that the opposite of love isn't hate; it's apathy. Apathy is a form of blindness, becoming oblivious to another person. If I want to truly love my spouse, I must begin by remaining aware of her, noticing her, and letting her know all the while what I'm thinking.

We live in a self-absorbed world where we are all taken for granted in one form or another. May God grant us the grace to notice our spouses and love them like God loves us.

Notice your spouse this week—and then *tell him* what you're noticing.

One Day at a Time

And God is able to make all grace abound to you,
so that in all things at all times, having all that you need,
you will abound in every good work.
2 CORINTHIANS 9:8

THE SPIRITUAL BRILLIANCE OF MARRIAGE CAN ALSO SEEM LIKE ITS greatest curse. Because God has created a relationship that only death is to break, we have the security of working through issues we might otherwise feel tempted to run from. But that blessing can, during difficult seasons, seem like a curse. Because only death or adultery can break the bonds of marriage, it may sometimes feel like the dark season we're in has no end in sight — night without a coming dawn, winter with no ensuing spring.

And that can make us panic.

It all comes down to how we look at it. When I ran my first marathon, I had a clear goal in mind. Because the usual mistake is to go out too fast, I made an ironclad decision to run the first thirteen miles at a certain pace. When I started to feel the strain, I didn't think, "How can I keep this up for another two hours?" Instead, I told myself, "Just focus on this: can you run the next mile in this amount of time?" Taking it one mile at a time, I ran the race much faster than my goal pace.

If you're in a difficult season in your marriage and you start to think, "How can I take another ten or twenty or, God forbid, thirty years of this?" you're headed for trouble. You're asking God to give you the grace for something that hasn't happened. Instead, break it down to a single unit—a single day: "Just focus on this: can I love my husband [or wife] for this day?" Don't think about ten years down the road, or even ten months! Can you love your spouse *for this one day*?

Some friends who knew I was running the Seattle Marathon asked me, "How did you do that for twenty-six miles?"

My answer? "One mile at a time."

How do you stay married for twenty-six years?

One day at a time.

Break it down. Focus on the here and now. Put the future in God's hands. Some miles will seem easy, and some will feel hard, but you need to focus only on the one you're currently running. Let the others remain in his care.

Can you love your spouse *for this one day*?

43

You Don't Understand: Role Reversals

Do nothing out of selfish ambition or vain conceit,
but in humility consider others better than yourselves.
Each of you should look not only to your own interests,
but also to the interests of others.
Your attitude should be the same as that of Christ Jesus.
PHILIPPIANS 2:3–5

LISA ACCOMPANIED ME ON A TRIP OUT EAST WHEN EVERYTHING started going wrong. Our flight out of Seattle got delayed, we had to stand in line for forty-five minutes to get our rental car, meals had to be put off, and so on. Our heads didn't hit the hotel pillows until after midnight.

"This is *exhausting*," Lisa said. "I can't believe you do this every week!"

"She finally gets it!" I said to myself. "This is great! Now she knows why I can be so tired when I come home."

One evening the next week, back at home, Lisa was gone — and I was trying to get dinner on the table. Our dog followed me around as if she hadn't been fed in thirty days, even though she had already eaten two meals and two snacks. The kids were all busy with homework: Kelsey asked me how to find the length of a diagonal when the sides of a square are eight inches long, Graham wanted to run some ideas by me about a feature article he needed to do for a writing class, and Allison had to complete a timeline for Israel, Egypt, Greece, and

Rome. And I was about to pull out what little hair I have left on the top of my head.

"Was Julius Caesar AD?"

"No, he was BC."

"OK," another kid pushed up to me, "so the sides are eight inches. Now, if I multiply—"

"Just a second, Kelsey, let me just stir this, and I'll look at the problem."

"Dad," Allison cut back in, "when was the fall of Jerusalem?"

"AD 70. You should look it up to be sure, but I'm pretty certain that's right. OK everybody, let's go ahead and eat the salad while the lasagna is settling."

Worse, after I got dinner on the table, the kids still had more homework, so instead of cooking and answering questions, I was now doing dishes and answering questions. And as the clock inched forward, the questions became more desperate: "Daaaad, I think I mixed up the Peloponnesian and the Punic Wars!"

"OK, there were three Punic Wars—"

By the time Lisa walked in the door at 9:30, I was just barely hanging on. Then it dawned on me: While I'm waiting in rental car lines, driving to hotels, and trying to adjust to different time zones, Lisa's at home doing this almost *every night*.

You know what? It's a bear having to travel sometimes. *And* it's a bear trying to cook dinner and help three kids with homework.

Most spouses feel underappreciated. We think our husbands or wives don't understand how difficult we have it, and we're probably right—they usually don't. We're tempted to grow resentful when our hard work is taken for granted. But the truth is, in today's world, *both* spouses usually face a lot of stress. Different stresses, yes, but stress nonetheless. The problem is that, in our narcissism, we assume we have it worse and expect to receive all the empathy, without taking the time to notice the other spouse's challenges. The end result is that both spouses fixate on their own difficulties while remaining blind to the other's challenges, and thus both resent the lack of support they receive from each other.

From a spiritual perspective, this means that pride is the wedge that drives most marriages apart. Looking only to our own situations, we become arrogant, opinionated, and fixated on *our* situations and how our spouses don't appreciate *us*.

Christian marriage invites us to a new way of thinking and acting, a way Paul and the ancients called *humility*. "Each of you should look not only to your own interests," Paul writes, "but also to the interests of others" (Philippians 2:4). This follows an exhortation to consider others "better than yourselves." One commentator suggests how "such a disposition will promote unity, for it binds believers together in mutual interest, respect and appreciation."[33]

Notice this, please: mutual interest, respect, appreciation—all are key virtues for family life, but they're virtues often buried under arrogance, selfishness, and blindness.

Considering our spouses is an *active* charge; it's a decision to spend time actively ruminating on the challenges our spouses must overcome.

"But my spouse *doesn't* have it tougher than I do!" some of you are thinking. Notice Paul's next line: "Your attitude should be the same as that of Christ Jesus" (Philippians 2:5).

Look—if Jesus can take this approach, *we* can take this approach!

Pride pushes us away from each other. It exalts itself, it seeks to win arguments, and it aims to advance self and get noticed. Humility draws us toward each other, it seeks to understand, and it aims to achieve intimacy. Pride is one of the greatest enemies of marriage; humility is one of marriage's greatest friends.

Sadly, while pride comes naturally, humility must be pursued. Unless we consciously practice humility in our marriages, we'll naturally fall into a prideful disposition. To help us counteract this, Paul gives us an effective spiritual exercise: Pause for a moment. Don't look only to your own interests—look to the interests of your spouse. Think about him or her. Consider his or her challenges. Empathize with the stress your spouse is feeling. Do this in such a way that you can see how, in some ways, he or she has it tougher than you. Now, show your empathy. Be genuine in your encouragement and support.

Pride is a wedge; humility is a glue. Which spiritual tool will you wield this week?

44

Worth the Pain

Consider it pure joy, my brothers,
whenever you face trials of many kinds,
because you know that the testing
of your faith develops perseverance.
Perseverance must finish its work so that you may be
mature and complete, not lacking anything.
JAMES 1:2–4

ONE OF THE BIGGEST TEMPTATIONS I FACE ON THE ROAD IS MY ATTI-tude toward worship leaders. I'm ashamed to say I have a running feud with these servants of God. While I do my best to fight my negative attitude, it's still difficult for me not to think, as they are being introduced, "So *there's* the enemy."

Whence cometh this sinful disposition?

So many times, a pastor has told me I'll have thirty minutes to preach, but because there's a second service, I need to make sure I quit speaking at, say, 10:10. I then watch as the worship leader goes from chorus to chorus, and then, just in case he thinks we didn't get the message the first thirteen times we sang an earlier song, goes back to it yet one more time for the grand finale. Suddenly my thirty minutes has shrunk to twenty. On the way to the podium I have to mentally cut out a third of my sermon, frantically trying to manufacture new transitions to cover over the points that now will never get delivered.

Recently, I was told I'd have about thirty-five minutes because, the pastor said, "I told the worship leader I want you to have all the time you need." As the service wore on, I looked at my watch

— already past the point where I was supposed to be up there — and thought, "Well, I can drop the opening; that's just humor, and it's not really that relevant to the point." As the music kept going, I decided I could drop the point about how this truth related to marriage. Another song dragged on, and I thought, "Well, I can also drop the point about how this applies to parenting, and just make it about our relationship with God." Yet another round, and I thought, "I'll have to drop the second passage from Matthew — I hope the PowerPoint guy can make the jump and skip those slides." Unbeknownst to me, the pastor had been trying to signal "cut" to the worship leader, but she felt so "inspired" she never saw it. When I got behind the pulpit, I looked at the clock and realized I had just fourteen minutes before I was supposed to stop.

That day the church got a sermon summary.

Afterward, I could actually laugh about it with the pastor. God seems determined to make me confront my bitterness over this, and until I do, I fully suspect he's going to "inspire" many other worship leaders to commandeer the service and keep my guest sermons short. Some people may chuckle when I call this a temptation, but it is. My attitude is wrong, and it needs to change. That's a painful and soul-wrenching process.

It's easy to romanticize spiritual growth. It sounds so clean and fulfilling — but the process can actually feel exhausting, frustrating, and very painful. To grow in grace, I have to face ugly realities that truly irritate and inconvenience me — like tyrannical worship leaders! But not just *once*; it seems God is determined to make me face the same situation again and again and again, until his work in my heart gets perfected.

Put in the context of marriage, spiritual growth can even be excruciating. I returned home after that same trip where I had delivered my fourteen-minute sermon summary, and my wife and I faced an issue we've discussed three dozen times if we've discussed it once — but still no progress. Once the issue came up, I became depressed, discouraged, and even more exhausted. Especially coming home from a long trip where

God had worked on my attitude toward worship leaders, I wanted to return to a refuge, not a battlefield—but here I was regardless.

It took me two days to break through my funk. Even though the issue never got resolved, I could move past it, following a generous move by Lisa.

But it took two days.

I reveal this because I don't want to imply that the principles put forward in my book *Sacred Marriage* or in *Devotions for a Sacred Marriage* are easy to apply. My wife and I struggle as much as, if not more than, any other couple in living out the truth that is greater than us. Our sinful failings make us just as miserable as they make anyone else. We become just as frustrated, just as exhausted, and just as tired. We think, "Can't we *ever* move past this?"

But these tired moments are the seedbed of growth. I don't like them, but I need them—and so do you. If there were another way, I'm sure God would let us walk it, but there must not be. You will grow so familiar with certain struggles in your marriage that the bad spiritual taste they leave behind can be brought up by memory! It'll help you to remember that such problems aren't a problem just between you and your spouse; they represent the problems of marriage in general. Some issues aren't easily resolved, and some desires may never be fulfilled for the simple reason that *even the best marriage cannot erase the effects of humanity's fall into sin.* It is asking too much to live with another sinful human being without experiencing any tension, any frustration, and any reason to ever practice forgiveness.

It's normal to go through difficult seasons and to occasionally fall into a funk. These are the gritty realities of real marriage. Don't kid yourself. Spiritual growth is not easy; it is about the most difficult exercise known to humankind. But please, don't give up! Seasons of struggle are not the time to evaluate your marriage; they are the time to evaluate *yourself.* The perseverance these seasons produce is worth it.

The catchphrase that helps me press on is this: "I don't like this, but I need it." Repeated often enough, I can even make myself believe it. And sometimes, I can even thank God for its truth — though more often in retrospect than in the moment itself.

Marriage can be difficult; spiritual growth can be exhausting — but they are worth the pain. In the end they produce a far deeper life and a much richer existence than living in a world of superficiality and throwaway relationships.

45

What Do You Do?

Enjoy life with your wife, whom you love....
For this is your lot in life.
ECCLESIASTES 9:9

THE HERO OF *OBLOMOV*, A RUSSIAN NOVEL BY IVAN GONCHAROV, gets asked, "What do you do in life?"

Is there a question we get asked more frequently? Probably not in today's society. Yet this character responds with something refreshingly different: "What? What do I do? Why, I am in love with Olga!"[34]

What a refreshing change of pace for us Westerners! So often, we reply to such a question with a word about our vocations or our hobbies: "I'm an executive at Bank One, and I like to golf and sail on the weekends," or, "I work in marketing for a printing company, and I lead the women's ministry at my church," or even, "I homeschool our three children."

But what, really, is our *biggest* charge? If we're married, isn't loving our spouses at least in the top three? And yet, how often do we mention it or even *think* it? Have you *ever* listed your duty to love your spouse when someone asks you what you do? "What do I do? I focus on loving Bill!" "What do I do? I romance my wife, Melissa."

Maybe it's not helpful to pit vocation against marriage—after all, we do have to earn a living—but isn't something wrong with our sense of priorities, or even our way of thinking, when someone asks us what we do, and loving our spouses doesn't even come to mind?

This may be the core disease of marriage in the West. We don't give enough to it, and we don't derive enough from it. During the week, we're married *after* we work all day, read the newspaper after supper, and watch television all evening. On the weekends, we're married *after* we take the kids to their sporting events; repair what needs fixing; go to church on Sunday; and catch up on laundry, lawn work, and washing the car.

Marriage gets the leftovers—leftover energy, leftover excitement, leftover creativity, and leftover thoughtfulness. We do everything else first, and then, if there's time and we're not exhausted, *then* we'll see if there's something special or loving we can do for our spouses.

I wonder what would happen if we flipped this around, if we started working after we focused on being married; if we fit our play and recreation around our duty to our spouses; if the kids had to occasionally give up something in order for Mom and Dad to get together—instead of the other way around. What would our marriages be like then?

I like Oblomov's response to the question "What do you do in life?"

"What do I do? Why, I am in love with Olga!"

46

Open Marriage

I have chosen the way of truth.
PSALM 119:30

"GARY, DO YOU HAVE ANYTHING YOU WANT TO TELL ME ABOUT?"

"No."

"Nothing about where you went between getting your haircut and picking up Allison at the bus stop?"

"No, not that I can think of."

"I found the evidence. Graham [our son] saw it in your car."

"You know," I said, rising to my own defense, "some wives expect to find other women's phone numbers, or maybe magazines lying around. But an empty Starbucks cup?"

Lisa laughed, but in truth, I do spend more money than I should at Starbucks. We had just bought our own espresso machine, hoping to cut down on the expense, but I was out and about on a winter day, had an extra ten minutes, and could taste the relief even before I bought it.

This episode provided just another reminder that everything I do, I do in front of my spouse.

To have or build secrets is to reject the spirit of marriage. The call to become one, the journey toward intimacy, requires an open marriage of honesty and truth. I talked with a man once whose wife suspected he was viewing pornography. He denied it but admitted to keeping a post office box he had never told his wife about. "I can't think of a single good reason to have a secret post office box," I confessed, "but I can think of several bad ones."

The post office box amounted to a giant sinkhole sucking the intimacy out of his marriage. Not surprisingly, he and his wife got divorced several months later. When you start to build a separate life, you pave the way to the ultimate separation—divorce.

Lisa and I laughed one time as we listened to a talk radio host speak with a woman who felt terrible because her husband had caught her going through his wallet. "What's so bad about that?" Lisa wanted to know. Lisa considers my wallet her personal ATM machine. She likes it because it doesn't require a PIN.

Much to our surprise, the host called the woman's actions despicable. The caller fell completely in line, admitting her husband was appalled, confessing she felt ashamed of herself. She proceeded to ask how they could ever get over this "sordid mistake."

Maybe Lisa and I are just weird, but she can go through my wallet anytime she wants to. She knows my email passwords, and I know hers. She has a key for our business post office box. I don't have a single relationship she doesn't know about, and she doesn't have any I don't know about.

It all comes down to this: Are we going to be married, or not? Are we going to be 60 percent married, 75 percent married, 90 percent married, or are we committed to living life together 100 percent as a unit?

The irony is that most of us truly desire to be fully known. That's what creates a sense of belonging and intimacy and fulfillment. But then we create static in our marriage by lying, covering up, or carrying on secret activities. In doing so, we sabotage the very fulfillment we seek. We may lie out of shame, regret, embarrassment, or selfishness, but whenever we do, we strangle the intimacy that comes from knowing and being fully known.

Make the courageous choice to be fully married. When you lie to your spouse, you reject the very spiritual benefits marriage provides: the chance to repent, the motivation to change, the opportunity to be spiritually transformed, the exciting journey of loving and being loved. As soon as you lose the spiritual benefits of marriage, the structure of marriage will start to feel like a restriction instead of an intimate relationship, and the marriage will start to die. You'll lose sight of the purpose and feel overwhelmed by the seemingly negative limitations, and before long, you'll want out. In relationships, deception is the threshold that leads to destruction.

How about if this week you decide to create a new beginning in your relationship—a new honesty and openness, a commitment to truly walk in the light and to choose to "walk in the truth" (3 John 3)? If you've been keeping secrets, this will feel like a new marriage, an entirely new journey. God didn't design a relationship as intense as marriage to be fulfilling when it's done halfway. Be *fully* married, *completely* open and honest with each other.

"I have chosen the way of truth."

47

The True Image of Love

So God created man in his own image,
in the image of God he created him;
male and female he created them.
GENESIS 1:27

"WHAT DOES SHE SEE IN HIM?"

I'd be surprised if you haven't, at least once in your life, asked this question about a couple you've met. Maybe the genders were reversed: "What does he see in her?" but it's likely you, too, have asked this—or, at the very least, thought it.

I believe the answer is hidden in a divine and prophetic reality. God has made us in such a way that it is natural for us to grow strongly attached to someone—on occasion, to someone many others may have passed over.

Why?

Two realities are going on. First, God has a way of revealing himself to us in surprising places—or, in this case, through surprising people. Anyone who has any history of walking with God can testify how God often seems to keep quiet during the weekend fasting retreat, but while you move the clothes from the washer to the dryer, or while you shampoo your hair in the shower, he speaks. He has made us in his own image, and he has the ability and the will to reveal that image to us as he sees fit.

Keep in mind, Jesus was really and truly the Messiah, the glory of God behind a human veil—but not everyone saw him that way, did they? Some saw him as a common man from a common town; others saw him as a threat. Still others saw him as a devil. Only a select few —indeed, the minority to whom God chose to reveal himself—saw him as God in flesh.

In the same way, God can reveal himself to you through a person who appears to have comparatively little going for him or her—but somehow, when love enters the mix, you can't imagine how everyone isn't breaking down the door to get at this incredible person who occupies all your thoughts and fills your heart until it seems about to burst. Just as some see God more clearly in a forest than in a cathedral, so some experience God more fully living with an introvert than an extrovert, or vice versa.

But I also think there's a prophetic dimension to this reaction. Though our future glory as immortals remains masked, we are, in Christ, on the way to this incredible unveiling. Something about love lets us see a glimmer of this future unmasking, even when others remain blinded to it. C. S. Lewis captures this in a famous quote:

> It is a serious thing to ... remember that the dullest and most uninteresting person you talk to may one day be a creature which, if you saw it now, you would be strongly tempted to worship.... It is in the light of these overwhelming possibilities, it is with the awe and the circumspection proper to them, that we should conduct all our dealings with one another, all friendships, all loves, all play, all politics. There are no *ordinary* people. You have never talked to a mere mortal. Nations, cultures, arts, civilization— these are mortal, and their life is to ours as the life of a gnat. But it is immortals whom we joke with, work with, marry, snub, and exploit.[35]

I think it's safe to say that when we lose this sense of awe regarding our spouses—we're married to future immortals we might be tempted to worship if they were fully unmasked—it's not because God has stopped speaking or stopped revealing his nature to us through them, but because we have stopped listening to him and have stopped seeing with his eyes. The failure of married love heralds the onset of coldness toward God; it is a rejection of his presence, his insight, and his amazing dedication to love even the ungrateful and the wicked (Luke 6:35).

If our love begins to fail, it certainly isn't God's perspective that has changed — no, it's ours! The same glory remains hidden behind the facade of that nagging wife or that silent husband. Our resentment or hatred or bitterness may keep us from seeing the hidden glory within, but it's still there.

The maintenance of love requires a partnership with God — what you might even describe as an ongoing act of revelation. We learn to look at these persons as sacred beings made in the image of God and through whom God wants to reveal himself to us.

If mere emotions rule our eyes, we can forget about consistency. I know a man who was eagerly pursued by a young woman over two decades ago. She felt thrilled when he returned her affection. They got married, and for a while she felt delighted to be with him — but her heart grew cold and callous, and she divorced him.

Then this divorced man met a new woman. The new woman seemed just as thrilled with this man as his first wife had been twenty years before. They married, and she can't even begin to imagine why this man's first wife would choose to be alone instead of spending her days with him. The same man elicited three successive reactions — delight, disgust, and then delight once again. Is he truly three different men, or is he simply being viewed through three different lenses?

Love has been compared to a rose, an emotion, a policy, an organ (the heart), a season (spring), and even a physical act (sexual intimacy). But perhaps, to be more biblical, we should see love as a pair of bifocals — the lenses through which we see someone as others don't see them or have stopped seeing them. Instead of changing spouses, maybe all we really need to do is clean our lenses and ask God to show us what he showed us before.

Jesus was the Messiah, though some saw him as the devil. I've talked to some who have gone to both lengths in the way they view their partners. At one point, they saw these persons as temporal saviors, the "missing piece" that gave their lives joy and meaning and purpose. Now these spouses have become the devil incarnate, making their lives miserable. In truth, these men or women were neither messiah nor devil, but merely the clouded lens through which God desires to reveal *himself.*

Your spouse may delight you as well as exasperate you; she may frustrate you as well as overwhelm you with her love. In any situation, during any season, through every emotion, and in every stage of life, your quest should remain the same: to recognize the God who is in and behind the man or woman you love.

"What does she see in him?" some might ask. "What does he see in her?"

The Christian's answer is as shocking as it is true: "I see God, that's what I see. I see *God.*"

48

A Call to Listen

This is my Son, whom I love. Listen to him!
Mark 9:7

Marriage is a call to listen.

Even when our spouses misbehave or create difficult situations for us, we're to tune in to God's still, small voice and ask, "What is it you want me to learn from this? How are you stretching me at this time? What are you trying to do in my soul?"

Instead of listening, our impatient souls immediately want to provide commentary. Our natural, arrogant selves are eager to speak, to be heard, and to be understood. We can't wait to express our opinion, state our outrage, or make clear our intentions; yet the Bible warns, "When words are many, sin is not absent" (Proverbs 10:19).

You know what this tells me in a practical sense? The pause button on my tongue's remote control should get much more use than the play button.

In one of the most remarkable sermons I've ever heard, my friend Darell Smith spoke of his battle with multiple sclerosis. He talked about how for years he kept asking God, "Why?" But finally he learned to ask a more appropriate question: "What?" "*What* is it, God, that you want me to learn from this? What lessons do I need to practice? What character issue are you eager to transform?"

"Why" questions are interrogations; we're asking for an explanation. "What" questions humbly ask for insight. "Why" questions assume God has to defend himself; "what" questions more correctly put the onus on *us*: how do *we* need to change?

432

A Call to Listen

Marriage is a brilliant school for the art of listening. If you're at all like me, listening will initially feel almost like an unnatural act, requiring supernatural assistance. When I'm angry or feel put out, I don't want to listen to *anyone*, God included; I want to state my case.

But God knew what he was doing when he called us into marriage. Listening is an active discipline, and in our sin we are passive people. Listening requires tremendous motivation and about as much humility as any spiritual obligation we'll ever accept. It also provides the foundation for our spiritual health. Jesus spent a good bit of his time urging people to just listen:

- "Listen and understand" (Matthew 15:10).
- "He who has ears to hear, let him hear" (Mark 4:9).
- "Again Jesus called the crowd to him and said, 'Listen to me, everyone, and understand this' " (Mark 7:14).
- "Consider carefully how you listen" (Luke 8:18).
- "Listen carefully to what I am about to tell you" (Luke 9:44).
- "My sheep listen to my voice" (John 10:27).

Listening is the motor oil for both spiritual growth and marital health. Without it, the friction and the heat will cause the gears of our souls to jam and break, blowing up the engine. Relationships start to break down when both parties keep talking and stop listening. Being together, building intimacy, and growing in oneness *require* listening. When we stop listening, we stop loving.

It all begins with our prayers. If we keep rattling off a list of things we want God to change about our spouses, we're not paying attention to the list of things God wants to use our spouses to change about *us*. My morning prayers have become virtual marching orders. God almost never points out something my wife needs to do for me; ninety-nine times out of a hundred, he reveals to me what I'm to do for her.

Listening, of course, requires a monumental shift in attitude. We should enter each day of marriage as learners, not teachers. God uses the challenges of marriage to teach us about ourselves. He uses our spouses to teach us how the other gender thinks and reacts. He uses marriage to give us perspective, and perhaps even a new outlook. God does not limit his lessons according to the gifting of the persons with whom we live; he is well able to speak through even the worst of sinners.

But when we refuse to listen, we miss all this. You can change the entire spiritual climate in your home merely by choosing to listen. It's amazing what this simple spiritual act can do. Days of despair get transformed into days of discovery; disappointment gives way to discernment.

The best way to change your marriage is to start listening more than you talk. And when you pray, listen to God more than you complain about your spouse. Use your ears, and watch how God uses those floppy appendages to reawaken your heart. I have found that God can use *any* situation in life to teach me something, if only I'll listen for that lesson.

This week, listen—for a change, for a new life, and for a new marriage.

49

The Estate of Marriage

*For this reason a man will leave his father and mother
and be united to his wife, and they will become one flesh.*
GENESIS 2:24

IT ALWAYS AMAZES ME HOW CONTEMPORARY ANCIENT WORKS CAN be. Martin Luther penetrated the twenty-first century when he gazed into the souls of sixteenth-century couples in his essay titled "The Estate of Marriage." Since we live in a day when marriage is coming under increasing attack, we would do well to listen to Luther's words.

Luther begins his essay by reminding us that respect for marriage flows from acknowledging the One who designed marriage — God: "Do not criticize this work, or call that evil which he himself has called good. He knows better than you yourself what is good and to your benefit, as he says in Genesis [2:18], 'it is not good that the man should be alone.' "[36]

Luther urged his listeners to ignore the "pagan" voices decrying marriage:

Young men should be on their guard when they read pagan books and hear the common complaints about marriage, lest they inhale poison. For the estate of marriage does not set well with the devil, because it is God's good will and work. This is why the devil has contrived to have so much shouted and written in the world against the institution of marriage, to frighten men away from this godly life and entangle them in a web of fornication

435

and secret sins.... The world says of marriage, "brief is the joy, lasting the bitterness." Let them say what they please; what God wills and creates is bound to be a laughingstock to them.

In Luther's mind, it is not enough merely to be married; we must appreciate God's purpose in calling us into marriage. God calls us into family life to shape our souls and to create a stable foundation for the next generation:

> To recognize the estate of marriage is something quite different from merely being married. He who is married but does not recognize the estate of marriage cannot continue in wedlock without bitterness, drudgery, and anguish; he will inevitably complain and blaspheme like the pagans and blind, irrational men.... Now the ones who recognize the estate of marriage are those who firmly believe that God himself instituted it, brought husband and wife together, and ordained that they should beget children and care for them. For this they have God's word [Genesis 1:28], and they can be certain that he does not lie. They can therefore also be certain that the estate of marriage and everything that goes with it in the way of conduct, works, and suffering is pleasing to God. Now tell me, how can the heart have greater good, joy, and delight than in God, when one is certain that his estate, conduct, and work is pleasing to God?

This assurance that *God has called us into marriage* will most help us when marriage becomes a struggle. Luther urges us to remember that even the most difficult aspects of wedlock can bring joy when we see them as part of God's plan for us. Certain "blind" people run from the challenges of marriage because

> they fail to see that their life and conduct with their wives is the work of God and pleasing in his sight. Could they but find that then no wife would be so hateful, so ill-tempered, so ill-mannered, so poor, so sick that they would fail to find in her their hearts' delight.... And because they see that it is the good pleasure of

their beloved Lord, they would be able to have peace in grief, joy in the midst of bitterness, happiness in the midst of tribulations, as the martyrs have in suffering.

In Luther's view, because God has created marriage, we, God's children and followers, should embrace *all* aspects of it—even the tough parts—because we know it is his will and his design. But when life's pleasantness becomes more important than the spiritual foundations, we lose the discernment to appreciate marriage:

> We err in that we judge the work of God according to our own feelings, and regard not his will but our own desire. This is why we are unable to recognize his works and persist in making evil that which is good, and regarding as bitter that which is pleasant. Nothing is so bad, not even death itself, but what it becomes sweet and tolerable if only I know and am certain that it is pleasing to God.

Luther sums up the estate of marriage this way:

> I say these things in order that we may learn how honorable a thing it is to live in that estate which God has ordained. In it we find God's word and good pleasure, by which all the works, conduct, and sufferings of that estate become holy, godly, and precious so that Solomon even congratulates such a man and says in Proverbs, "Rejoice in the wife of your youth," and again in Ecclesiastes, "Enjoy life with the wife whom you love all the days of your vain life." Solomon ... is offering godly comfort to those who find much drudgery in married life.

While *Devotions for a Sacred Marriage* isn't a book on the theology of marriage, it's essential for us to possess a basic theological understanding of marriage, and that understanding is this: God designed and created marriage as a lifelong institution between one man and one woman, and he calls most of us into this estate. The fact that he created marriage and called us into marriage makes this estate a holy one, a right one, and a spiritually healthy one. We should humbly surrender to God's will.

Armed with this understanding and insight, even the most difficult of marriages have value. To requote Luther, "Now tell me, how can the heart have greater good, joy, and delight than in God, when one is certain that his estate, conduct, and work is pleasing to God?"

God designed this relationship. God called you into this relationship. Therefore, marriage—with all its joy and all its trials, all its comforts and all its sufferings, all its happiness and all its pain—is good.

50

Passive Persecution

I opened for my lover,
but my lover had left; he was gone....
I looked for him but did not find him.
I called him but he did not answer.
SONG OF SONGS 5:6

AN ENTIRE CATEGORY OF WOUNDING IN MARRIAGE RECEIVES LITTLE notice, though it wreaks great havoc on many relationships. For lack of a better phrase, I call it *passive persecution.*

There is a moment in a marriage when neglect—a passive reality—becomes persecution—an active wound. What is withheld starts hurting, and it becomes a living irritant. Its devastation grows worse when the sore wound gets regularly pummeled by continued neglect.

What makes passive persecution so pernicious is that those who cause the injury almost never realize it, or if they do, they minimize the pain their partners feel. "I'm not doing anything," they protest—but that's precisely the point! It's their "not doing anything" that hurts so much.

When a man can go an entire week without having a single conversation with his wife that goes beyond utilitarian purposes; when he can go two weeks without inquiring about how his wife is really feeling, what went on inside her when her sister accused her of something or a friend stood her up—she suffers an ongoing wound. The first cut came when she recognized the neglect, thinking, "He let me down." The second cut comes when her husband doesn't even realize their emotional intimacy has dipped to about 1.5 on a scale of 1 to 10.

It's only a matter of time until "He let me down" becomes "He doesn't even care that he let me down." Now it's no longer an event that upset her; it's turned into an ongoing assault. It won't be long before disappointment morphs into resentment, resentment evolves into bitterness, and then, more often than not, the husband will eventually run into an explosion of bottled-up emotions suddenly unleashed over the seemingly smallest event: "So I forgot you had a doctor's appointment today and didn't ask you about it; what's the big deal? Does that make me a bad husband?"

Men often feel passive persecution in the bedroom. When a man gets denied, regularly put off, or even just not approached, after a season he starts to hurt, as if something active were being done to him. Every day feels like a wound. The wife may think, "We had sex a week ago; we've been busy. What's the big deal?" But he's thinking, "It's now been seven days," and the silence of the last five nights feels like a slap in the face — yet another malicious assault. The wife thinks nothing is being done, but that *nothing* feels like *something* to her husband. And he begins to shut down.

I don't know how else to describe it, but something takes place in a sexually neglected man's soul. He doesn't just step back physically; he removes part of himself spiritually and emotionally as well. In spiritually acute situations, he may begin to look elsewhere, even if only through his eyes or in his thoughts, which can open the door to any number of evils our fallen world eagerly exploits.

Passive persecution doesn't have a unilateral remedy. Many times, it's born in high expectations, and the spouse who feels persecuted will need to reevaluate his or her disappointment and honestly explore whether the offense he or she is feeling springs more from narcissistic self-focus and demands than from true, honest neglect.

But this is not to say that the offended spouse may not have a case — in most instances, they *do*. Marriage asks so much of us that it's inevitable we will let things slip. When we do, it's our responsibility to ask for forgiveness, sincerely try to empathize with our spouses' feelings of abandonment and hurt, and pledge ourselves to get better at providing active care.

Here's a word picture that may help: let's say you're on a hike with your spouse. It's hot, and you feel like you'd kill for a drink of water. You're so thirsty your body has started to shut down, so that almost all you can think about is something to drink. Your spouse keeps staying just far enough ahead of you that when you cry out, he can't hear your voice. He finally stops at a lookout, allowing you to catch up, and you watch as he consumes the last swallow of Gatorade.

"Give me some of that!" you say, only to hear, "Sorry, that was the last drop; didn't *you* bring any?"

"I'm out, and I'm dying of thirst!"

"Oh well, there's a stream a few more miles up the trail; it shouldn't take us more than another hour or so."

You'd probably be furious at your spouse, and understandably so. In that wilderness, he represented your only source of refreshment. It may not have been his fault that you're so thirsty, but certainly, he could have eased your pain and yet chose not to or, at least, simply neglected to consider you.

What aren't you hearing today? What neglect, what passive persecution, might you be leveling against your spouse at this very moment? There are some things in life *only* a spouse can provide; if you deny these things, it becomes an absolute denial.

Here's a challenge: why not ask your spouse, "Hey, are you thirsty? If so, in what way?" I've talked to enough couples to know there's almost always at least one area in which your spouse feels neglected. The duties of marriage are too many and too diverse for that not to be the case.

Let's allow kindness and even generosity to govern us. The person you're talking to took a tremendous risk. Out of all the billions of people on the face of the earth, he or she chose to spend this life with *you*. When your spouse made this decision, he or she put himself or herself at your mercy, since, as we said before, there are certain things only a spouse can provide. Let's honor that trust with open hands and enthusiastic hearts. You may think you're not doing anything, but remember that "not doing anything" can well be a direct assault on your spouse: "You gave no water to the weary and you withheld food from the hungry" (Job 22:7).

Is that how you want to be remembered? By what you *didn't* do?

51

Kindness Matters

Love is kind.
1 CORINTHIANS 13:4

"WHAT FIVE OR SIX QUALITIES WOULD YOU CHOOSE IN A MATE IF YOU were looking for a wife?" someone once asked me.

After some thought, I rattled off six items.

"You didn't even mention physical appearance," said the man.

"Hmmm," I said. But after thinking about it some more, I realized the omission was no accident.

"Let's say you were married to Charlize Theron," I explained. "For the sake of argument, let's say you've been married for seven years. If you're rushing to get ready for work and she comes out of the shower stark naked, you know what you're going to say? 'Honey, have you seen my brown belt? I can't find my belt and I need to leave in ten minutes.' As crazy as it may sound, you would actually be more excited at the sight of that leather belt than you would be watching your naked wife walk to the closet."

The way we're wired, physical attraction of even the highest nature, over time, quiets down. Sometimes I forget I'm married to a very attractive woman. I see her every day, and so it's easy to take it for granted. But you know what I *don't* take for granted? Every individual act of kindness.

For some reason, I never seem to grow callous toward kindness. In fact, just this morning, as I was trying to get back into my office, my wife saw I was preparing a cup of chai and said, "Here, let me get that for you."

"You sure?"

"Yeah. Go down to your office; I'll bring it to you."

I'm sipping the tea as I write this, getting my midmorning caffeine boost and thinking very pleasant thoughts about my wife.

I say in *Sacred Marriage* that most couples don't fall out of love; they fall out of repentance.[37] It's our selfish, unkind attitudes that poison our affection for each other far more than anything else, and it's our acts of generosity and kindness that keep intimacy alive.

I was speaking spiritually, but now, apparently, there's sociological evidence to back this up. Dr. John Gottman is a professor of psychology at the University of Washington and one of today's foremost authorities on what makes marriages work and what leads to divorce. Listen to his words:

> At the heart of my program is the simple truth that happy marriages are based on a deep friendship. By this I mean a mutual respect for and enjoyment of each other's company. These couples tend to know each other intimately — they are well versed in each other's likes, dislikes, personality quirks, hopes, and dreams. They have an abiding regard for each other and express this fondness not just in the big ways but in little ways day in and day out.[38]

These "little ways" are nothing more than practical expressions of kindness. Listen to how this worked its way out in a couple known by Dr. Gottman:

> Take the case of hardworking Nathaniel, who runs his own import business and works very long hours. In another marriage, his schedule might be a major liability. But he and his wife, Olivia, have found ways to stay connected. They talk frequently on the phone during the day. When she has a doctor's appointment, he remembers to call to see how it went. When he has a meeting with an important client, she'll check in to see how it fared. When they have chicken for dinner, she gives him both drumsticks because she knows he likes them best. When

he makes blueberry pancakes for the kids on Saturday morning, he'll leave the blueberries out of hers because he knows she doesn't like them. Although he's not religious, he accompanies her to church each Sunday because it's important to her. And although she's not crazy about spending a lot of time with their relatives, she has pursued a friendship with Nathaniel's mother and sisters because family matters so much to him.[39]

Romantic feelings come and go, but biblical love is supported by *chosen* thoughtfulness and kindness. Nathaniel doesn't want to go to church, but he goes because it's important to his wife. Olivia doesn't particularly enjoy having a close relationship with her husband's family, but she wants to please her husband, so she makes the effort. In other words, they *choose* to be kind, and that kindness colors their entire relationship.

Dr. Gottman suggests that consistent, small acts of kindness provide a surer foundation than sporadic romantic vacations and extravagant anniversary gifts. Paul gave this same prescription two thousand years ago in much fewer words when he wrote, "Love is kind." We can choose to transform the climate in our homes by adopting these attitudes of godliness — patience, gentleness, selflessness, kindness, love — which the Bible urges us to adopt. Conversely, the things Paul says love is *not* are the very qualities that make home life so miserable: "It does not envy, it does not boast, it is not proud. It is not rude, it is not self-seeking, it is not easily angered, it keeps no record of wrongs" (1 Corinthians 13:4–5).

In other words, a satisfying marital experience has far more to do with character than emotional attraction, romantic feelings, sexual acumen, or physical appeal. As believers filled with God's Holy Spirit, we can choose to be kind. We can choose to be patient. We can choose to be gentle. But when virtue becomes a stranger, any relationship will begin to sour.

I stand by what I wrote several years ago: Most couples don't fall out of love; they fall out of repentance.

52

Oases of Sanity

He is like a tree planted by streams of water,
which yields its fruit in season
and whose leaf does not wither.

PSALM 1:3

THANKS TO THE HOSPITALITY OF THE HAWTHORNE GOSPEL CHURCH
in Hawthorne, New Jersey, Lisa and I got to spend two days in New
York City without the kids. Since we had already visited the city with
our children, we were able to do more "grown-up" things. Lisa wanted
to find some "funky shops"; we thought we should take in a Broadway
or off-Broadway play and eat at some exotic ethnic restaurants.

Even though I've been to New York several times, it's hard to
get used to Times Square, particularly at night. There's a desperate
grab for your attention, and the tacky commercialism hits you from
all directions. At night, eighty-foot video advertisements shine on
buildings, gigantic billboards light up, and 3-D sculptures hawk the
latest cell phones and cars. Then there are the eccentric people, such
as the colorfully dressed religious groups passing out literature, or the
"Naked Cowboy"—a guy who wears barely legal briefs, covered by
his guitar, and charges you to have your picture taken with him (we
politely declined).

We attended two plays, one of which at the time was considered
to be the best and biggest play on Broadway. Everybody we talked to
said, "If you're going to see only one play, you need to see this one."
We saw it—and we felt shocked at its raunchiness. As people filed
out of the theater, raving over the performance, we thought we were

living in a world where everything had been turned upside down. "Are we really *that* out of touch?" we asked each other.

But then, on our way to Central Park, we passed David Wilkerson's Times Square Church. Something almost monumental happened in my soul at the sight of that otherwise nondescript building. I took a huge spiritual breath, as though I'd been holding it for days and only now had permission to let it out. This relatively simple church provided a physical reminder of a different life, a different purpose, a deeper calling—a quiet oasis in a noisy city. We didn't go in (it was a Saturday), but it was uplifting just to be reminded of the reality this church represents.

It struck me that, spiritually, we live in the middle of Times Square. Movies, books, music, advertisements, magazines (even if you don't read them, you see the covers in the grocery stores), and television all carry various messages about sex, marriage, dating, and family life. It's like a daily assault on our spiritual senses. If we don't seek out oases of sanity, we can become buried by the world's conflicting messages.

I pray that *Devotions for a Sacred Marriage* has been one of those oases for you—because we need many. If we don't consciously remind ourselves of the spiritual purpose of marriage, the Christian's duty to be God-centered in marriage, the greater good of marriage, and God's design for marriage, we'll soon get buried by the world's caricatures, advertisements, and lies. We'll begin asking of our marriage what God didn't design it to give, while discounting those aspects of marriage that God does intend but that the world doesn't value.

Though you've reached the end of this year of devotions, I hope it's just one vacation among many you'll take in the future. I hope you continue to find materials that inspire you to remain devoted to each other as an expression of your love for God.

I hope you'll also influence others, reminding them of the goodness of marriage as God designed it—the way that holiness serves a family better than any illicit excitement ever invented by the devil; the way that a proper spiritual perspective can turn even the trials of marriage into sweet opportunities for growth. For not only do we need the Times Square churches to point us back to real life; we can become Times Square churches in our own communities. Each godly marriage can be an oasis for those who have forgotten what marriage is supposed to look like.

With great challenges come great rewards; that's what I'd tell a couple contemplating marriage. You're about to be challenged as you've never been challenged before, but the struggle is worth it. The pain is worth it. Because through it all, you'll experience life as God created it and called you to live it, and there is absolutely no better place to be in this world than the place God has ordained for you.

Acknowledgments

As always with a book of this sort, I need to first thank my wife, Lisa, not only for walking this life with me, but also for being so gracious to open up our lives for the benefit of others and for being so instrumental in the editing process. Several friends reviewed these devotions and made many helpful suggestions, including Todd and Lisa Fetters, Annie Carlson, Brad and Mary Kay Smith, Byron Weathersbee, and Dave and Dina Horne. Thanks are due to Dirk Buursma for his customary good care of the manuscript during the editing process, as well as to the baristas at the Barkley Village Starbucks. Thanks for keeping the chai teas (seven pumps, nonfat, extra hot) coming! I also owe a big debt to John Sloan at Zondervan. One day I merely mentioned the idea of a marriage devotional book and, much to my surprise, discovered a contract offer in the mail a few months later — no agent; no haggling, no hassle, not even a proposal. This has been, without a doubt, the easiest publishing process I've ever been through!

Notes

1. Cited in Cal Fussman, "Al Pacino," *Esquire* (July 2002), 110–12.

2. Terri Orbuch et al., "Marital Quality Over the Life Course," *Social Psychology Quarterly* 59 (June 1996), 162–72.

3. I discuss this more fully in my book *Authentic Faith* (Grand Rapids: Zondervan, 2002), 235–41.

4. Cited in Rick Reilly, "A Paragon Rising above the Madness," *Sports Illustrated* (March 20, 2000), 136.

5. Cited in Carolyn Mahaney, *Feminine Appeal* (Wheaton, Ill.: Crossway, 2003), 7.

6. C. J. Mahaney, *Sex, Romance, and the Glory of God: What Every Husband Needs to Know* (Wheaton, Ill.: Crossway, 2004), 56–57.

7. Cited in *The Little Flowers of St. Francis*, trans. Raphael Brown (New York: Doubleday, 1958), 92–93.

8. J. W. L. Hoad, "Mercy, Merciful," in *The New Bible Dictionary*, ed. J. D. Douglas (Grand Rapids: Eerdmans, 1962), 809.

9. Cited in Mahaney, *Sex, Romance, and the Glory of God*, 42.

10. Reported in Barbara Dafoe Whitehead and David Popenoe, "Who Wants to Find a Soul Mate" (National Marriage Project, June 2001); can be viewed on the Web at http://marriage.rutgers.edu/Publications/ SOOU/TEXTSOOU2001. htm.

11. Clement of Alexandria, cited in John E. L. Oulton and Henry Chadwick, eds., *Alexandrian Christianity: Selected Translations of Clement and Origen* (Philadelphia: Westminster, 1954), 71.

12. Andrew Murray, *Humility*, rev. ed. (Springdale, Pa.: Whitaker House, 1982), 44.

13. Elton and Pauline Trueblood, *The Recovery of Family Life* (New York: Harper & Row, 1953), 56–57.

14. Cited in Dana Mack and David Blankenhorn, eds., *The Book of Marriage* (Grand Rapids: Eerdmans, 2001), 467.

15. Story and quotes taken from Rick Reilly, *Who's Your Caddy?* (New York: Doubleday, 2003), 246 and following.

16. Reilly, *Who's Your Caddy?* 255.

17. Gene Stratton-Porter, *Freckles* (Wheaton, Ill.: Tyndale House, 2000), 1. Note: The actual text is written in accent. I Anglicized it to make it easier to read.

18. Ibid., 17.

19. Paul Evdokimov, *The Sacrament of Love* (Crestwood, N.Y.: St. Vladimir's Seminary Press, 1985), 112.

20. Cited in Mack and Blankenhorn, *The Book of Marriage*, 199.

21. Henry Drummond, *The Greatest Thing in the World* (London: Collins, 1930), 51.

22. Ibid., 57.

23. Ibid.

24. Ibid., 57–58.

25. Ibid., 52.

26. Ibid.

27. Ibid., 54.

28. I cover in greater detail the virtue of detachment in my book *The Glorious Pursuit: Embracing the Virtues of Christ* (Colorado Springs: NavPress, 1998).

29. Pat Conroy, *My Losing Season* (New York: Doubleday, 2002), 143.

30. C. F. Keil, *The First Book of Moses* (Grand Rapids: Eerdmans, 1949), 103.

31. Nancy Belcher, "Venice Marathon: An American Runner in Venice," *Northwest Runner* (February 2004), 27.

32. This quote and the others used in this devotion are taken from an essay compiled by Joseph Kerns, "The Theology of Marriage," in Mack and Blankenhorn, *The Book of Marriage*, 405 and following.

33. Jac Muller, *The Epistles of Paul to the Philippians and to Philemon*, New International Commentary on the New Testament (Grand Rapids: Eerdmans, rep. 1980), 75.

34. Ivan Goncharov, *Oblomov* (New York: Macmillan, 1915).

35. C. S. Lewis, *The Weight of Glory* (Grand Rapids: Eerdmans, 1949), 14–15.

36. This quote and others in this devotion are from Mack and Blankenhorn, *The Book of Marriage*, 368.

37. See Gary Thomas, *Sacred Marriage* (Grand Rapids: Zondervan, 2000), 96.

38. Cited in Mack and Blankenhorn, *The Book of Marriage*, 466.

39. Ibid., 467.

Gary Thomas

Feel free to contact Gary at glt3@aol.com. Though he cannot respond personally to all correspondence, he would love to get your feedback. Please understand, however, that he is neither qualified nor able to provide counsel via email.

For information about Gary's speaking schedule, visit his website (www.garythomas.com). Follow him on Twitter (garyLthomas) or connect with him on Facebook. To inquire about inviting Gary to your church, please e-mail his assistant: laura@garythomas.com

Sacred Marriage

What If God Designed Marriage to Make Us Holy More Than to Make Us Happy?

Gary Thomas

Your marriage is more than a sacred covenant with another person. It is a spiritual discipline designed to help you know God better, trust him more fully, and love him more deeply.

Scores of books have been written that offer guidance for building the marriage of your dreams. But what if God's primary intent for your marriage isn't to make you happy — but holy? And what if your relationship isn't as much about you and your spouse as it is about you and God?

Everything about your marriage is filled with prophetic potential, with the capacity for discovering and revealing Christ's character. The respect you accord your partner; the forgiveness you humbly seek and graciously extend; the ecstasy, awe, and sheer fun of lovemaking; the history you and your spouse build with each other — in these and other facets of your marriage, *Sacred Marriage* uncovers the mystery of God's overarching purpose.

This book may well alter profoundly the contours of your marriage. It will most certainly change you. Because whether it is delightful or difficult, your marriage can become a doorway to a closer walk with God and to a spiritual integrity that, like salt, seasons the world around you with the savor of Christ.

Available in stores and online!

How Raising Children Shapes Our Souls

Sacred Parenting

Gary Thomas

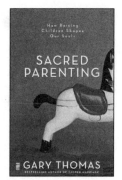

Many books have been written about how to parent a child effectively, how to become a better parent, and how effective parenting produces better kids. But *Sacred Parenting* delves into a different reality: how parenting affects the parent. It explores the spiritual dynamics of parenting, and why caring for children is such an effective discipline in shaping our souls and forming the character of Christ within us. Parents of all children will be encouraged by seeing how others have successfully handled the challenges of parenting and will be inspired by stories that reaffirm the spiritual value of being a parent.

Devotions for Sacred Parenting

A Year of Weekly Devotions for Parents

Gary Thomas

Spend time once a week for an entire year contemplating the soul-transforming journey of parenting.

Devotions for Sacred Parenting continues this journey with fifty-two short devotions, containing all new material. The life-related devotions are creative and fresh, and readers will be inspired, challenged, and encouraged as they explore the spiritual joys and challenges of raising children. Each devotion will point them to opportunities for spiritual growth — and help them become more effective parents at the same time.

Sacred Pathways

Discover Your Soul's Path to God

Gary Thomas, Bestselling Author of Sacred Marriage

"Thou shalt not covet thy neighbor's spiritual walk." After all, it's his, not yours. Better to discover the path God designed *you* to take—a path marked by growth and fulfillment, based on your own unique temperament.

In *Sacred Pathways*, Gary Thomas strips away the frustration of a one-size-fits-all spirituality and guides you toward a path of worship that frees you to be you. If your devotional times have hit a snag, perhaps it's because you're trying to follow someone else's path.

This book unpacks nine distinct spiritual temperaments—their traits, strengths, and pitfalls. In one or more of them, you will see yourself and the ways you most naturally express your relationship with Jesus Christ. Whatever temperament or blend of temperaments best describes you, rest assured it's not by accident. It's by the design of a Creator who knew what he was doing when he made you according to his own unique specifications. *Sacred Pathways* will reveal the route you were made to travel, marked by growth and filled with the riches of a close walk with God.

Available in stores and online!

Holy Available

What If Holiness Is about More Than What We Don't Do?

Gary Thomas, Bestselling author of Sacred Marriage

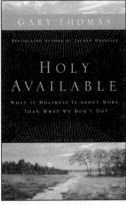

Previously titled
The Beautiful Fight

True Christian faith is a profoundly transformational experience in which every part of our being is marked by God's change and energized by his presence. This transformation takes us far beyond mere sin avoidance to a robust, "full-bodied" holiness in which we make ourselves "holy available" to God every minute of the day. From Starbucks, to the office, to the soccer fields, to the boardroom, believers have the opportunity to carry the presence of Christ wherever they go.

God offers the reader more than mere forgiveness; he wants to radically change and fill them with his presence, so they can experience an entirely different kind of life based not just on what they do or don't do but on who they are.

Yet while many Christians today profess belief, their Christianity has no pulse. Previously titled *The Beautiful Fight*, *Holy Available* is a manifesto of fully alive faith. Gary Thomas issues a compelling call for readers to see with Christ's eyes, feel with Christ's heart, and serve with Christ's hands. We make ourselves available to become "God oases," places of spiritual refuge where God can bring the hurting and lost to enjoy his presence and ministry.

Available in stores and online!

Pure Pleasure

Why Do Christians Feel So Bad about Feeling Good?

Gary Thomas, Bestselling Author of Sacred Marriage

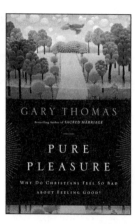

Discover the power of guilt-free pleasure.

Pleasure is a good thing. It's a powerful force that feeds your relationships, helps protect your spiritual integrity, and brings delight to our heavenly Father. Pleasure isn't something Christians should fear, shun, or disparage; it's something we should learn to cultivate in our lives.

Acclaimed spiritual growth author Gary Thomas will guide you into this way of life, which is foundational to a healthy relationship with God, with your loved ones, and with the world. He'll show you that, for the redeemed, pleasure can be a powerful and holy force for good, leading to increased worship, spiritual strength, and renewed relationships.

In this invigorating and liberating book, Gary Thomas will energize, inspire, equip, and challenge you to experience life as God meant it to be: overflowing with pleasure.

Authentic Faith

What If Life Isn't Meant to Be Perfect, but We Are Meant to Trust the One Who Is?

Gary Thomas, Bestselling Author of Sacred Marriage

What if the spiritual disciplines that bring us closer to God are not the ones we control? Bestselling author Gary Thomas reveals the rich benefits that derive from embracing the harder truths of Scripture. With penetrating insight from Scripture and the Christian classics, along with colorful and engaging stories, Thomas's eye-opening look into what it means to be a true disciple of Jesus will encourage you, bolster your faith, and help you rise above shallow attachments to fix your heart on things of eternal worth.

Thomas shows us that authentic faith penetrates the most unlikely places. It is found when we die to ourselves and put others first. It is nurtured when we cultivate contentment instead of spending our energy trying to improve our lot in life. It is strengthened in suffering, persecution, waiting, and even mourning. Instead of holding on to grudges, authentic faith chooses forgiveness. And it lives with another world in mind, recognizing that what we do in this broken world will be judged.

Available in stores and online!